JAPAN AND ASIA

Economic Development and Nation Building

JAPAN AND ASIA

Economic Development and Nation Building

SHINICHI ICHIMURA

Kyoto University, Japan

World Scientific

NEW JERSEY • LONDON • SINGAPORE • BEIJING • SHANGHAI • HONG KONG • TAIPEI • CHENNAI

Published by

World Scientific Publishing Co. Pte. Ltd.

5 Toh Tuck Link, Singapore 596224

USA office: 27 Warren Street, Suite 401-402, Hackensack, NJ 07601

UK office: 57 Shelton Street, Covent Garden, London WC2H 9HE

Library of Congress Cataloging-in-Publication Data

Ichimura, Shinichi, 1925– author.

Japan and Asia : economic development and nation building / Shinichi Ichimura, Kyoto University.

pages cm

Includes bibliographical references and index.

ISBN 978-9814632096

1. Japan--Economic conditions--1945– 2. Asia--Economic conditions--1945– 3. Economic development--Political aspects--Japan. 4. Economic development--Political aspects--Asia. I. Title.

HC462.9.I3294 2015

338.95--dc23

2014042628

British Library Cataloguing-in-Publication Data

A catalogue record for this book is available from the British Library.

In-house Editor: Lum Pui Yee

Typeset by Stallion Press

Email: enquiries@stallionpress.com

Preface

This book is a selected collection of my articles and essays on the *economic development and nation-building* of Japan and Asian countries. It contains most of the important, professional articles that I wrote on that subject from the early 1980s to 2014 and did not re-publish in the monographs. Since, I am planning to edit another volume on *Japan and China*; I have excluded most articles and essays relevant to the problems of China from this volume.

During my long academic career, I have done many kinds of research. Introduction to this book: *My Research on Asian Development* explains how I pursued my research works, and Appendix at the end of the book gives a list of monographs and main published papers. Among those 230 papers, I have selected 18 articles under four sub-headings:

I. The Present and the Future of Japan and Asia,
II. Stages of Economic Development and Nation-Building,
III. Empirical Survey Studies of Southeast Asia,
IV. Political and Cultural Problems of Asian Nations.

If the reader kindly glances through Introduction, Appendix and Table of Contents, he will notice that this book deals with my deepest concern in the research on Asian development. Its central thesis is that economic development can be achieved only with sound nation-building. In other words, sustaining modern economic growth requires to build up a solid modern state, and *vice versa*.

Five chapters in Part I were presented at the Korean Academy of Sciences in 2012 and at the International Demography Convention in Pusan, 2013. In essence, it deals with the lost two decades of the Japanese economy and the declining population. I have presented briefly a modest pessimism for the future of Japan and many Asian countries.

Four chapters in Part II deal with the central thesis of this book: the relations of economic development and nation-building in stages. Economic policies must be adequate for each stage of development. Design of nation-building must be adjusted to each stage of nation-building like centralization to decentralization of fiscal administration or regional development policies.

Seven chapters of Part III are the most substantive survey researches that I have untaken with my colleagues in East Asia and China. The subjects are (1) the socio-economic behaviors of Thai and Indonesian peasants, (2) adaptation and application of new appropriate technologies in manufacturers in Thailand, Indonesia and the Philippines, (3) Japanese style management applied in Singapore, Indonesia, and three districts in China and an international comparison of eight countries in East and Southeast Asia. In my opinions, the political economy of development must pursue such survey methods as empirical studies rather than individual scholars' field observations. This part occupies about half of this book.

The first chapter in Part IV presents my opinions on Asian nationalism, taking Sun Yat-Sen and Sukarno as samples, and the second chapter is my critical review of Samuel Huntington's *The Crash of Civilizations*.

In retrospect, this is the second time that I have published a volume of collected papers. The first was *Political Economy of Japanese and Asian Development*, Springer-Verlag, 1998, a selection of my papers from the 1960s to the early 1980s. The present one publishes the substantive parts of my research works, except for econometric modeling works, after I became Director of Kyoto University Center for Southeast Asian Studies in 1969 until now, through Osaka International University (1988–1995), International Center for the Study of East Asian Development (1995–2005). I hope that I shall be able to offer the reader the third volume: *Japan and China* before too long.

July 16, 2014
Shinichi Ichimura

Contents

Detailed Table of Contents

List of Figures and Tables

Acknowledgments

The author wishes to acknowledge and express his hearty gratitude for the great help rendered by many foreign and Japanese organizations and friends to make these large scale of survey studies possible in Southeast Asia. In *Thailand*, the Japanese Overseas Enterprises Association's Office in Bangkok helped us contact the various offices in the Thai government, and the National Research Council. The Thai government officially issued the permit to secure the interviewees' cooperation for our survey. The interviews were conducted by Prof. Prasert Yamklinfung and Dr. Surichai Wun'gaeo of Chulalongkorn University. The country report was prepared by Prof. P. Yamklinfung. In *Indonesia*, our survey was the first of this kind ever conducted. Without willing cooperation of the Agency for Industrial Research and Development and its capable young staff, the survey could not have been implemented. The findings were summarized in a detailed and comprehensive tableau and two brief reports prepared by Mr. I. Sucipto Umar under the supervision of Dr. R. N. Suhartono. In the *Philippines*, the work was entrusted to Dr. Eduardo Roberto and his staff at Consumers Pulse Inc. at the recommendation of Dr. Filologo Pante, Director of the Philippine Institute of Development Studies, National Economic Development Authorities (NEDA). A concise list of well-organized tables containing the survey findings and a summary of various statements by interviewees and interviewers were given to the author. Chapter 10 is a synthesis of all these tables and reports. In preparing the final report, I greatly benefitted from many constructive comments by Prof. Susumu Watanabe (Tokyo International University now; Technology and Employment Branch, ILO, then).

Thanks go also to the following journals and publishers for permission to reproduce the papers and book chapters listed below.

A. National Academy of Sciences, the Republic of Korea

Ichimura, Shinichi (2011). "The Lessons of the Lost Two Decades of the Japanese economy," in *Stability and Growth of the Korean Economy*, a report of the International conference held on October 2011 in the National Academy of Science.

B. Asian Growth Research Institute (formerly, ICSEAD)

Ichimura, S. (1997). Management Style of Japanese Multinational Corporations in China. *East Asian Economic Perspective*, Vol 8.

Ichimura, S. (2001). "A Postmortem Diagnosis of Asian Financial Crisis." *East Asian Economic Perspective*, Vol 12.

Ichimura, S. (2009). "Decentralization policies in Asian Development." *Viewpoint to East Asia*, Vol 20, No 2.

Ichimura, S. (2009). "Transition of Socialist Countries to Market Economies." *Viewpoint to East Asia*, Vol 20, No 4.

C. The East Asian Economic Association

Ichimura, S. (2011). When Can Asia play a Leading Role in the World? *Asian Economic Journal*, Vol 25, No 1.

D. Institute of Yamaguchi Economy

Ichimura, S. (2009). Who are responsible for the World Financial Crisis in 2008? *The Yamaguchi Economic Monthly*, January 2009.

E. Osaka International University

Ichimura, S. (1989). The Choice of Appropriate Technology and Socio-Economic Factors and Government Policies in Southeast Asia. *The OIU Journal of International Studies*, Vol 1, No 1.

F. Kyoto University, Center for Southeast Asian Studies

Ichimura, S.; Mizuno, Koichi; Tsubouchi, Yoshihiro; Asano, Toshio; Yamklinfung, Prasert; Rabibhadana, Akin; Sakdejayont, Yut; Mubyarto; Singarimbun, Masuri (1974). "The Socio-Economic Behavior of Peasants in Central Java and Central Thailand. *Southeast Asian Studies*, Vol 12, No 3.

Ichimura, S. (1985). "Japanese-style Management in Asia – Introduction." *Southeast Asian Studies*, Vol 22, No 4.

Urabe, Kuniyoshi (1985). "Japanese-style Management in Singapore." *Southeast Asian Studies*, Vol 23, No 1.

Ichimura, S. (1985). "Japanese-style Management in Indonesia." *Southeast Asian Studies*, Vol 23, No 1.

G. The Mito History Association

Ichimura, S. (1997), "Asian Nation-Building Leaders." *The Mito Historic Review*, No 46.

Needless to say, any remaining error or misinterpretation is my responsibility.

Introduction

My Research on Asian Development

1. Economic Theory and Empirical Study of the Japanese Economy

In 1946, I entered the Economics department at the Kyoto University and started my serious study of economics by repeatedly reading Yasuma Takata's *Principles of Economics*.[1] Next year, I attended the *seminar*[2] of Professor Hideo Aoyama[3] and began reading J. R. Hicks's *Value and Capital* very attentively. By the time of graduation in 1949, I had had the chances of attending several professors' *reading seminars* to learn J. M. Keynes's *General Theory* and L. R. Klein's *Keynesian Revolution* (Michio Morishima), some chapters of Leon Walras's *Elements d'Economie Politique Pure ou Theorie de la Richesse Sociale* (Ryoji Shimazu), and parts of Max Weber's *Objectivitat von sozial wissenschaften* (Ryoichi Yamaoka). At the same time, Prof. Aoyama urged me to upgrade my knowledge of mathematics in linear algebra and analysis, so I could read and understand Paul A. Samuelson's *Foundation of Economic Analysis* that was released in 1947. Upon graduation,[4] I entered the graduate school of economics at Kyoto University and began reading professional articles in *Econometrica*

[1]Yasuma Takata (1883–1972) Professor of Economics, Kyoto University, Osaka University and others. He was a great sociologist, economist and poet. As Martin Bronfenbrenner appropriately called, he was a Marshall in Japan.

[2]All students in most Japanese universities must choose only one professor's seminar where they are trained strictly under his guidance. They are allowed, however, to attend any number of *Reading seminar* to read foreign texts in English, French or German.

[3]Hideo Aoyama (1910–1992) Professor of Economics, Kyoto University, Kwansei Gakuin University.

[4]In July 1949, I was appointed as a research associate at economics department, Wakayama University and generously employed during my study in the US.

and other journals. The first article of mine "A Note on the Definitions of Related Goods" was published with J. R. Hicks' appraisal comment in *The Review of Economic Studies*, 1950.

Soon after graduation in March 1949, the occupation authorities held a nation-wide competitive examination for GARIOA[5] Fellowship to study in the US, to which I applied and fortunately passed. In June 1950, we were flown[6] to various universities in the US and began our studies. I was assigned to Columbia University graduate school of economics. As my fellowship was limited to one year, I applied to several universities for fellowships to stay on. Toward the end of 1950, I was granted some generous fellowships from outstanding universities, including MIT, Columbia, Stanford and Chicago. I chose MIT to pursue my PhD.

During the allowed two years,[7] I completed all the requirements for my PhD in economics at MIT and also published the following two articles: (1) "A Note on Consumer's Surplus," in *Econometrica*, July 1953 and (2) "Toward a General Non-linear Dynamic Theory of Economic Fluctuations," in K. K. Kurihara (ed.), *Post-Keynesian Economics*, Rutgers University Press, New Brunswick, 1954. The second one was a central part of my PhD dissertation. Several other parts of my dissertation were published in some other forms in English as are shown in my list of articles in Refs. [5–7, 14, and 15].[8]

Clearly, all my published articles were dealing with economic theory. To me, they were valuable only as the first step of my research in economics because I believed and still believe that economics as a science must progress — from theoretical to empirical economics and to applications (economic policies) — as does physics — from theoretical physics to experimental physics and applications. Besides, my strong motivation to

---

[5]Government Appropriation for Relief in Occupied Area was abbreviated. Part of it was released as a fund for fellowships for students to study in the US. Soon it was taken over by the Fulbright Funds.

[6]The airline planes having carried GI's to Korea took it to the US. Korean war had broken out on June 25, 1950.

[7]GARIOA fellows had to go home after a *maximum* of three years, so that I had only two years left to complete the degree.

[8]The reference numbers refer to those in the *Appendix*. Monograph numbers are indicated as {·} and article numbers are indicated as [·].

alleviate poverty in Japan made me choose economics as my specialist subject. Therefore, when I came back to Wakayama University, I searched for some challenging issues to tackle poverty in Japan.

I quickly noticed the differences between Keynes type of American Effective Demand policies and the Japanese Classical policies to control the excessive consumption and investment. I regarded it due to "a dilemma between unfavorable balance of trade and unemployment." I presented my analysis in Refs. [4] and [13].

In relations to the business cycles in Japan, one type of empirical research that attracted my attention was a study of the time series of economic statistics such as price, wage, industrial production, and national income. The methods used were just casual empiricism or simple diagrams. In Japan then, NBER's *Diffusion Index* was not yet known, though national income accounts were well-known and widely used. The first approach was taken by Miyohei Shinohara,[9] whereas the national income approach *a la* Simon Kuznets was taken by Yuzo Yamada and Kazushi Ohkawa. Along with me, two of my colleagues at Wakayama University (Masao Baba and Ippei Sugiura[10]) used both the simple time-series and national incomes and could easily confirm the existence of "growth cycles" as above-mentioned scholars maintained.

In order to learn more of these time-series, I visited the Department of Statistics and Research at MITI (Ministry of International Trade and Industry) in Tokyo. While working on the data with the staffs, they told me that they were trying to produce the first tentative input–output table of the Japanese economy and asked my opinions on the statistical procedures of producing the interindustrial table. Although my knowledge of compiling IO table was very limited, I fortunately had worked at Wassiley Leontief's Harvard Economic Research Project in the summer of 1952 to produce sectoral and intersectoral capital coefficients from the Industrial Census data. Therefore, I could easily contact Prof. Leontief and his staff. This

[9]M. Shinohara (1919–2012) Professor, Hitotsubashi University; Y. Yamada: (1902–1996) Professor, Hitotsubashi University; K. Ohkawa (1908–1993) Professor, Hitotsubashi University.

[10]I. Sugiura (1925–2009) Professor of Statistics, Wakayama University and Osaka Sangyo University; M. Baba (1923–1985) Professor, Wakayama University and Kyoto University.

immediately led Department Director Shinetsu Nagase officially to request my participation in their IO Project. This chance re-directed my interest from business cycle studies to the compilation of Interindustrial Relations Table of Japanese Economy for 1951 and its applications.[11] The table was completed in 1955 and was made available in Japanese and English. We published many books and papers but they were mostly in Japanese [4, 6–9, 14]. In English, M. Tatemoto[12] and S. Ichimura, "Factor Proportions and Foreign Trade–the Case of Japan," *The Review of Economics and Statistics*, 1959 [23] made our works well known abroad. It was also available in discussion papers such as those in Refs. [24] and [26].

In addition to this national IO table, I undertook a project to produce the first interregional IO table in Japan under the sponsorship of Kansai Economic Federation. It was published in Japanese as Ref. [6] in 1958: *The Japanese Economy and Regional Economy Interregional Input–Output Analysis for Kinki*, Sobunsha, Tokyo. Its inter-regional IO tables were distributed worldwide with English translation and a brief exposition. I made a number of applications of national and interregional IO analyses and offered them to the business and academic circles [7, 9]. This was a pioneering work of interregional IO table. The Japanese government succeeded it and repeats it every five years until now. See Akita in Ref. [68].

2. Macro-econometric Modeling of the Japanese Economy

As soon as we accomplished the compilation of interregional IO table for the Japanese economy and the Kinki Region, I went to the Johns Hopkins University as a visiting lecturer of mathematical economics. While abroad, I was notified that our Institute of Social and Economic Research, Osaka University received a large research grant from the Rockefeller Foundation that was enough to cover the expenses needed to invite a few world-famous economists for several months to Japan. Indeed, it was a great opportunity. It was true that the newly developing Japanese school of mathematical economics was attracting attention abroad. At Morishima's and my pleas,

[11] I wrote on the work in Introduction of Ichimura-Klein, 2010 [68].

[12] M. Tatemoto (1924–1997) my classmate, Professor, Osaka University, Kyoto University and Tezukayama University.

Prof. J. R. Hicks agreed to come with Mrs. Ursula Hicks about a month in the Spring of 1960, and Prof. Klein agreed to come during the summer vacation in 1960 with his family. We immediately prepared a series of seminars around the Hicks, inviting outstanding theorists from other universities.[13] I came back from my visit at Johns Hopkins University early April 1960.

When Prof. Klein arrived, we were ready with our capable, young staff in Faculty of Economics and the Institute of Social and Economic Research[14] to start a big project of constructing an econometric model of the Japanese economy superseding anything in Japan and abroad. Klein had already produced the Klein-Goldberger model for the US (1955), and Klein-Ball model for UK (1959), but SSRC Project for a large US model was not yet under way. At first, we discussed what kinds of model would be appropriate to analyze and diagnose the Japanese economy in the 1960s, and according to Klein's guidance, we started the project. During the hot summer of 1960, we sweated out the necessary statistical data and began estimating the empirical equations for the core of the model (the manufacturing sectors). The details of our research outcome were made available mainly in the form of ISER Discussion Papers, as each part was completed. Estimation of the core part equations were finished in mid-1962, but the supplementary parts dealing with international trade and the monetary sector were not finished until mid-1964. Finally, a whole set of estimated equations was ready to be integrated. Clearly, our work schedule was delayed. Moreover, this last step was by no means easy. The important reasons were the following.

(1) We grossly underestimated the difficulty and the requirement for time and human efforts in collecting statistical data and adjusting them to the requirements for the model.
(2) We grossly underestimated the time required to estimate many equations with alternative specifications. Without personal computers then, one good econometrician could estimate only 2 or 3 equations a day.

---

[13]Morishima took care of the economic theory seminar, so that I did not discuss it here.
[14]They were Susumu Koizumi (Michigan PhD), Kazuo Sato (Yale PhD) besides Masahiro Tatemoto and myself *plus* outstanding younger staffs like Kiyoshi Kuga, Yoichi Shinkai, Mitsuo Saito who all became professors later.

(3) The total number of our estimated equations turned out to be about 230 with the same number of endogenous variables and about 150 exogenous variables. All variables and equations must be consistent in the definitions and statistical bases.
(4) To run a final test of this whole system, we must solve our system of equations for 230 endogenous variables. At Osaka University then, however, neither any computer nor any software was available to get an inverse of matrix as big as 230×230.[15]

During 1965–1966, I was a visiting professor to the University of California, Berkeley and learned that a better IBM computer there can solve the last problem. I concentrated in improving my equations of the monetary sector (See Ref. [26] etc.). Then no good model of the financial sector was available to my knowledge. While teaching, I continued the works of Osaka ISER Project, given a capable research assistant Mr. Chen and consulting with Prof. D. Jorgenson.

For the next academic year 1966–1967, I was invited to the University of Pennsylvania where computer facilities were about the same level as the UC, Berkeley, so that I could continue the same modeling project. I ascertained the consistency of all variables in the definitions and linearized all nonlinear endogenous variables. The inverse of coefficients matrix was obtained and multiplied on the exogenous parts of the system. This calculation was repeated several times to improve the results of our final tests. Many equations had to be re-estimated. The final test improved step by step. Calculation of the dynamic properties of the Osaka ISER model was finally completed in Philadelphia in early 1967. They were reported as Ref. [37] in 1967. A complete report of the entire Osaka ISER Model was, however, made available to outsiders as late as 1977.[16]

---

[15] Since many of our equations were nonlinear in variables, to solve our system, it is essential to linearize the nonlinear variables at some point and obtain the matrix of the coefficients in front of the variables and obtain its inverse matrix of 230×230. Gauss–Saidel or similar methods like TSP became available around 1973.

[16] It is [29]: *An Econometric Analysis of the Japanese Economy*, The Japanese Society for Asian Studies, 1977. I am responsible for the delay, because nobody else had a grasp of the entire model by that time. When I came home in May 1967, there was a request from Kyoto University to be the director of a new research institute. Soon the student riots began disturbing universities in Osaka, Kyoto and Tokyo. I could not concentrate on the academic works.

3. Directing the Center for Southeast Asian Studies, Kyoto University

In November 1968, I moved from Osaka University (Institute of Social and Economic Research: ISER) to Kyoto University (The Center for Southeast Asian Studies: CSEAS) to be the director of that institute in April 1969. The CSEAS was still an infant during that time but was expected to grow as a large research institute. A number of professors at Kyoto University whom I respected told me to develop and contribute significantly to the growth of the Kyoto University. When I had an offer, I had some hesitation. I had just accomplished the Osaka ISER Model and wanted to explore its potential usages, because in the US, the Brookings Model was faltering,[17] and Klein had switched back to a medium size quarterly model.

Nevertheless, thinking over for some time, I made up my mind to completely switch my own research field from the Japanese economy to Asian developing economies.[18] The main reasons were two. First, if I wish to work on North–South Problems as an economist, this offers me a precious chance to design one institute for that purpose almost from the scratch. Second, unless I go now, I cannot implement my best plan.

The CSEAS at Kyoto University had been established in 1965 under the following principles for research approaches, which was mainly laid out by Prof. Shinobu Iwamura[19]:

(1) We combine the area studies of human and social sciences with those of natural ecology.

---

[17] The Brookings Model was not solved as a whole for the same reasons as ours.

[18] After working on Osaka ISER model for seven years, I was greatly attracted by one problem in econometric modeling. That was the inventory investment functions in the short-term forecasting models. I came to recognize that the statistics of inventories in Japan needed a fundamental re-estimation and had started to re-estimate the time series data from by using the computer tapes of government statistical offices. It was painful for me to give up this project. A positive factor supporting my decision was an opinion popular among economists that anti-cyclic policies were no longer as important as before. This opinion, however, turned out to be wrong, because in the 1970s oil shocks, liberalization of exchange rates and US–China rapprochement hit Japan.

[19] The first director was Azuma Okuda, but he soon became President of Kyoto University. The next director was Shinobu Iwamura who was a well-known professor of Mongol socio-economic history. He really guided the CSEAS before I arrived. The third director was Iichi Sagara whom I succeeded.

(2) We emphasize the contemporary studies.
(3) We emphasize the *field surveys* rather than bookish readings.

I supported these principles. When I arrived, it consisted of two "chairs."[20] For the first chair, three staffs were employed, and I was supposed to be a professor for the second chair. The Center had a strong basic support of the majority of Kyoto University faculty members,[21] despite the strong objections of left-wing faculty members' and Marxist students. When the Ford Foundation gave a grant of $350,000 to build up CSEAS at Kyoto University, there was a tremendous uproar against it among them. Both the administration committee members and I did not mind for the opposition on the campus. We were ready to fight to defend academic freedom and firmly believed that this anti-American movement would fade away after several years.[22] We were right.

At the first administration committee meeting of CSEAS that I attended, I requested to give me a chance of visiting some world-famous research institutes on developing countries. With their support, I visited Development Research Institutes in Stockholm, Copenhagen, Moscow, Prague, Heidelberg, London, the Hague, Paris, Ithaca, Cambridge, New York, Washington DC, San Francisco, and Hawaii. I have learnt a great deal from the frank talks with my predecessors and received warm encouragements. Among the lessons and warnings then, I have kept in my mind the following:

(1) A good institute is the one that has good individual researchers.
(2) Library is very expensive.

[20]In most Japanese universities, one *chair* has a specialty and is allotted with one full professor, one associate professor and one or two research associates.

[21]Kyoto University had organized an unofficial center for Southeast Asian studies before 1965. Southeast Asia was chosen because its Institute of Human Sciences was well established for Chinese studies. Election of the first CSEAS director to the President proves a strong support of CSEAS at Kyoto University. A committee consisting of the representatives from all faculties and some relevant institutes until 1970 administered it.

[22]The student revolt was then related to anti-Vietnam war movement in the US and Japan and also to the Cultural Revolution movement in China. In fact, some Japanese students were trained in Mainland China and sent back. Excitement subsided as soon as the Vietnam war and Cultural Revolution were over. Soon after 1978, the Chinese Academy of Social Sciences sent a group of representatives to Japan, and we met them. Then, a representative expressed their regret for disturbing us.

(3) Field surveys are essential.
(4) Researchers must be able to communicate with natives and native scholars preferably in native languages.
(5) Optimum size of a research institute is not much more than 20 mature experts. If more than that, then some sectional division is unavoidable, because daily informal discussions among colleagues are essential to the advancement of research.

By the time of assuming directorship, I have reviewed the research and other records of all the staffs of CSEAS and affiliated project participants from other faculties. When I became the director, I made a few proposals to be discussed.

(1) I agree with the principles laid out by Prof. Iwamura and pursue the same passage.
(2) I would like to strengthen the recruitment of outstanding staff and the training of young researchers. In principle, they should be sent to the doctoral courses at outstanding universities in the US or elsewhere after a few months stay in Southeast Asia.
(3) I would prepare a development design of CSEAS for the first three years as soon as possible.

Though the research grant from the Ford Foundation was generous,[23] it could only be used as seed money. Eventually, we had to obtain grants from other sources for funding the expensive research works abroad. Fund raising was a heavy burden from the very beginning, and I had many informal talks with President Okuda, former directors and Masamichi Inoki, respected professor of political science.

---

[23]After three years, the Ford Foundation recognized that CSEAS was well on the way to establishing its area research with good staffs and government support, so that it gave the second grant of $300,000 for the following three years. But the objection of the revolting students gained support of some faculties and research institutes so that President Okuda had to give in and decided to return the remaining amount of the grant. However, in this formative stage, we obviously needed the funds to train the young researchers in the unexplored field of area research in Southeast Asia. I talked to Kansai Economic Federation and Ford Foundation and had an agreement made that both organizations would share half and half to give CSEAS a joint grant of $200,000, slightly less than the amount we returned. This rescued a pinch of our research fund and could maintain my plan of laying the foundation in three more years.

4. Difficulties in Research Works in Developing Economies

In 1969, I visited several important universities in Thailand, Malaysia, the Philippines and Indonesia to talk over with the Presidents and the deans of departments of economics and also wrote letters about the possibility of carrying out field surveys in cooperation with their staffs.[24] What I saw and learned clearly suggested that it was too premature to practice the full scale of field surveys both on the receiving side and on our side in terms of the number, quality and variety of researchers and the extra time and budget needed for research works. I decided to do the following three preparations on our side.

(1) We strengthen the training program for our staffs.
(2) We recruit outstanding graduate students and train them as specialists on Southeast Asian area research.
(3) We establish a research station in Indonesia and strengthen research on the Oceanic side of Southeast Asia.[25]

As for the research methods for field works, anthropologists usually rely heavily on individual researchers' *careful observations.* A field researcher with good academic background can exercise his knowledge and experiences and grind out an excellent original achievement. Such examples are *Clifford Geertz's Religions in Java* or J. C. Abbegglen's *Japanese Factories.* But young researchers' field notes often turn out to be simply too microscopic and can hardly be broadened or generalized to more important social cases. Even such great works of G. Myrdal's *Asian Drama* seems to have been misguided in its pessimism of Asian societies

[24]Before I became the director, CSEAS had done some field works with its own staff and researchers from other faculties and institutes in Thailand. It established a liaison office in Bangkok, renting a house at a convenient location. Their research works were the careful observations by individual researchers with no coordination.

[25]CSEAS had a plan to establish a research station in Myanmar at first, because of the difficulty of conducting the field works, but due to the government's isolationism, we gave it up. Instead, we took up Indonesia as representing the insular part of SEA. It turned out to be a good choice. We had a government regulation to give each researcher a standard per diem per day, so that the cost of living in inflationary Indonesia was not covered thereby. We rented a house, hired a maid and bought a jeep to transport researchers to the fields, so that we could provide them with some research expense a/c. This required transmitting dollars, evading the government's foreign exchange control.

and nations by a number of anthropologists works based on their field works. In other words, it is important to relate any microscopic, partial studies to the macroscopic, overall total. Economics has paid much attention to this aggregation problem.

5. Agricultural Village Survey in Thailand, Indonesia and Malaysia

As an economist, I suggested my colleagues to use the *Questionnaire Survey Method* in statistics or public opinion surveys. Chapter 12: "The Socio-Economic Behavior of Peasants in Java and Central Thailand" was an outcome of this type of research. There are more advantages in this method than the field survey by an individual researcher alone:

(1) Questions to ask are more carefully prepared for all round issues.
(2) Villagers in different environments can be mutually compared.
(3) Representative or average behavior pattern can be ascertained.
(4) Repeating surveys, the changes in behavior pattern can be traced.

Disadvantages are expenses and lack of carefulness in observation, because a longer stay of an individual researcher in a village will allow him to make more careful and comprehensive understanding of villagers' behaviors, though his own bias may not be avoidable.

We chose two types of villages in Thailand and Indonesia. One was villages in delta plain, whereas the other was those in mountainous or hilly villages. We had expected some differences in their behavior patterns between these two types. In reality, we found some differences, but they were not conspicuous. Much more significant was the difference between Thai farmers and Indonesian farmers. For more details, see Chapter 11.

Another survey in agronomy was conducted in Malaysia and published as Ref. [60]: "Social Development and Agriculture in Asia". Since, however, my participation was less, I did not adopt the article here.

6. Provincial Income a/c and Input–Output Table in Indonesia

What surprised me most, when I arrived in Jakarta in 1969 and visited Mr. A. Madjid at the Central Statistical Office and Dr. Widjojo at

BAPPENAS, was how scanty and poor in quality the available statistical data were.[26] This was not the first time, however, that I learned the poor statistical data in the least developing country (LDC). I knew the conditions in the Philippines and Thailand before. But Indonesia was worse. For instance, National Income was estimated only on the production side from *Industrial Census* which was almost the only worthwhile statistics available since the Dutch days. There was no data for tertiary sector. They simply multiplied the ratio of some other country to the value of manufacturing industries' value added. Expenditure side had no data for consumption. Fixed capital formation was estimated from Industrial Census. Consumption was given as the residual: GDP *minus* fixed capital formation. Hence, it included inventory investment and errors and omissions. Thus, consumption figures were unreliable and in fact fluctuated peculiarly, reflecting the cycles in other variables.[27]

Dr. Widjojo asked me what to do. I replied that the first step would be to train a minimum number of statistics specialists who could understand the National Income a/c and to teach them how to compile NI a/c from basic data; and the second step would be to invite some foreign experts to teach the staffs of the Central Statistics Bureau how to produce, on sampling, the minimum basic statistical data such as Household Consumption Survey and the better quality of production data of primary industries. After a few days, Dr. Widjojo telephoned me and requested to organize a few weeks training course in Japan for selected statisticians and economists from Indonesia. I gladly accepted it and promised to do my best. Thus, my research in Indonesia started with training a group of statisticians and economists in the government.

---

[26]At ECAFE workshop in 1959, I learnt such conditions *in general* from Professors J. Tinbergen, G. Correa, B. Higgins, and M. Gosh. Before I moved to CSEAS, I taught at the Philippine Central Statistical Office how to compile the IO Table from the available statistics in the Philippines at the request of its Director Bantegi.

[27]This disappointed me greatly in revealing the unreliability of Indonesian National Income accounts. I had to conclude that perhaps 10 years might be needed for the Indonesian government to forecast its economic conditions with some modeling works. In fact, modeling of Indonesia was done by a Japanese team stationed at BAPPENAS under inter-governmental agreement around 1976, earlier than my expectation.

I requested Dr. Widjojo also to suggest a research project in which Indonesian and Japanese scholars may be able to cooperate and produce something useful for Indonesian development. His suggestion was to consult with his new successor,[28] Director Harsja Bachtiar of LEKNAS (National Institute of Social and Economic Development). He and I talked over carefully on what project to undertake. We finally decided to conduct an economic survey of South Sumatra Province. Its basic objective was to estimate the Provincial gross product and income and by so doing clarify the economic conditions and problems of the Provincial levels. The first fruit of our efforts in Indonesia is: Ichimura. S. and Thee Kian Wee (eds.), *A Regional Economic Survey of South Sumatra Province: 1970–1971*, LIPI,[29] Jakarta, 1975 [25]. It gives the first rigorously estimated provincial income and laid the foundation for regional studies in Indonesia.

This was a new challenge to me, because I had been a user of statistics but never a producer before. I had compiled the IO table in Japan but it was a secondary stage of statistical works. This time we had to obtain the raw data. I knew that I was not qualified enough to guide the whole project alone. As soon as I came home, therefore, I visited the Bureau of Statistics, Prime Minister's Office and requested its well-known Director Minoru Tachi to recommend one expert after a brief exposition of the project. He immediately recommended Mr. Hiroshi Midzuno very highly by saying: "he is not only the best expert for your purpose but nobody else I can recommend from our bureau. I am 100% confident that he will not fail in achieving the work of your project. He never failed anywhere abroad, including Africa". Although Dr. Thee and I edited the report, really the central figure in the whole project was H. Midzuno. The chapter he contributed is very precious for all of us.[30]

[28]Dr. Widjojo was the first director of LEKNAS before he resumed the post of minister of BAPPENAS. This bureau was as important as the Ministry of Finance, because it controls the development budget which is large in amount and a channel to receive international and foreign aid and loans.

[29]LIPI means Indonesian Institute of Sciences. Thee Kian Wee was a great Chinese Indonesian economist respected worldwide (1939–2014).

[30]Hiroshi Midzuno (1920–1976?) was an honorary member of Japan Statistical Association. Our project started with the lectures by him and me. Listening to his lectures and discussing with him, I learned a great deal myself. For example (1) in designing the field survey for

Soon after completing the field work for this Regional Survey, I organized another project by asking Professor Yukio Kaneko who was an IO expert to work on producing a *Tentative IO Table of the Indonesian Economy* by relying mainly on the Indonesian Industrial Census and using the input coefficients in the Philippines IO table. It was already available with my advices.[31] Though it was a tentative one, the pioneering IO table surprised many foreign economists including Prof. Alan Strout who was visiting the University of Indonesia then and immensely pleased Dr. Widjojo and other Indonesian economists. This work established the reputation of Japanese team for statistical work. This IO table compilation project was taken over by the Institute of Developing Economies, Japanese government.[32] They successfully produced more authentic IO tables, as more reliable data become available in Indonesia. Our works and tables were made available as Discussion Papers of LEKNAS as shown below.[33]

7. Japanese Style Management *versus* Native Middles and Workers

In 1974, something unexpected occurred in Bangkok and Jakarta; that is, anti-Japanese demonstrations by Thai and Indonesian students and workers as well as boycotts of Japanese goods by local consumers. They coincided in timing with Prime Minister Kakuei Tanaka's visit to Bangkok and Jakarta. PM Tanaka had to use a helicopter to enter the city of Jakarta. This shocked the Japanese journalists and intellectuals, left or right, and Japanese businesses. No academic specialists on Southeast Asia had predicted that so much anti-Japanese moves would come out on the streets so soon and violently. Apart from all kinds of controversies on international

data collection, the first question he raised was availability of maps and road conditions and how one could reach villages on rainy days. (2) If no good information was available for sampling, he suggested by special subdivision. (3) To estimate the incomes of vendors, he sampled a few at some spots in the city and so on. (4) He spent really a lot of time in discussing with local staffs about the designs of Question Sheets.

[31] The experiences with this project is briefly described in my essay in Japanese, "Asian Long-Term Economic Statistics Project — my observations and worries," Hitotsubashi ALTS Project News Letters, 1999. See Ref. [187].

[32] A researcher of IDE who produced the first real IO Table in Indonesia was Mihira.

[33] See Ref. [42]. It is an early report of our work in Indonesia in 1972 before [25] in 1975.

and diplomatic relations between Japan and Southeast Asian countries, many study plans were proposed by many scholars among specialists on Asia. Prof. Shinkichi Eto at Tokyo University and I had several meetings on the direction of research to organize jointly with the scholars in Tokyo and Kyoto. We gave our joint project a title: "Studies on Culture Conflicts in Asia" and decided to mobilize many varieties of specialists who usually did not show interest in the studies of Asian problems among political, economic and social scientists, historians and literary commentators. We obtained a big research grant from the Ministry of Education.[34]

We chose leaders in several sub-projects. I was responsible for economic and business studies. After consulting with my colleagues, I decided to spend three years for the research in two steps:

(1) the first year *preliminary interview study* in some selected countries;
(2) the following two years of *in-depth study* of the problems in most troubled countries.

The first step study was rather exploratory than specific on any issues, so that I selected varieties of specialists who have broad concerns with culture conflicts. After some preliminary discussions among us, we traveled together to Bangkok and Jakarta to meet and discuss with Japanese and native businessmen and intellectuals. The outcome of the preliminary discussions was written up by each participant. I have edited their reports according to my own judgment. It is the book: {32} *Japanese Firms in Asia*. Toyokeizai Shinpo Sha, 1980. It was well received because it was informative about the current situation to Japanese businessmen in

[34]Besides this big project, I organized another small project of my own on the critical examination of Textbooks in East Asian Countries. ESSO Standard Oil Co. Funds gave us a grant for this project, so that I could purchase the middle school textbooks of history and society in almost all East Asian countries, including Taiwan, Korea and China. After translating the parts relevant to Japan, we asked experts in each field like Japanese history to examine the contents critically. My ideas were that the influence of anti-Japanese contents of textbooks might have influenced the anti-Japanese movements. The tone of textbooks differed very much from one country to another. Strongly anti-Japanese were: Nationalist (Taiwan) and mainland China and Korea. Others were not so much. Similar study was undertaken at Stanford, comparing texts of Japan, China and Korea.

Southeast Asia. But it did not really tackle with the problems facing Japanese enterprises overseas.

We intensively discussed on what to do next. The following were the conclusions:

(1) This anti-Japanese demonstrations by Asian workers should be taken, in principle, as a challenge to Japanese style management. Japanese style management has emphasized so much the family-like human relations in business companies (stable, life-time employment, seniority principle, etc.) and should be workable with native middle managers and workers. If not, we should ask what kind of adjustments are required.
(2) To discuss these matters with Japanese businessmen, working in Southeast Asia or Southeast Asian intellectuals is not enough. We should solicit the opinions of native managers and businessmen, workers (consumers) and government officials.

Thus, we have concluded to conduct a carefully designed Questionnaire Survey of Japanese Style Management in all Southeast Asian countries (Thailand, Malaysia, Singapore, Indonesia and the Philippines). The questionnaire survey was done both to Japanese Top Managers with one schedule, and to native Middle Managers with another schedule. As soon as we completed these surveys, we extended the same surveys to other East Asian countries and areas (Taiwan, Hong Kong and Korea) as well as to Japan for comparative purposes.[35] Our final findings were published as Ref. {38}: S. Ichimura (ed.), *The Japanese Style Management Rooting in Asia*, Toyokeizai Shinpo Sha, Tokyo, 1988. Immediately after the surveys were finished in each country, the country report was written in English by each scholar in charge of the respective country and was published in *Southeast Asian Studies*. Chapters 12–14 are the reproduction of those articles.[36] The methods of our survey and the Questionnaire Schedules have been followed by other scholars in Japan and abroad for similar studies.

[35]China was very much in our mind, but it was controlled by Maoists then. Only in the 1980s, some joint-ventures were allowed to invest. Only in the 1990s, we could undertake similar studies in China. It is {49} in 1998.

[36]I adopt here only Chapter 13: Introduction (summary), Chapter 14 (Urabe): Singapore; Chapter 15: Indonesia, and Chapter 16: China (summary). Malaysia, Thailand and the Philippines reports are written by others. The interested reader should read the articles

Ten years later, we undertook the same kind of surveys in Mainland China, selecting three areas: around Shanghai, Beijing, and Dealing, in cooperation with Development Research Center of the Chinese government. Its summary report is Chapter 15 of this book, and the full report in Japanese is published as {49}: S. Ichimura (ed.), *The Japanese Style Management in China*, Toyokeizai Shinpo Sha, 1998. Both books have been received very well and widely read.

8. Transfer and Choice of Appropriate Technologies in LDC

Around 1978 when we were almost winding up Japanese Style Management Project, I received a request from International Labor Organization (ILO) (Department of Employment and Development) to consider a project on the problems of *appropriate technologies*. Needless to say, one of key factors for developing LDC is the technology transfer, and ILO's department in charge of employment and development was searching for good approaches to the problem. I was invited to one meeting and expressed my views. My opinions were basically two.

(1) In the discussions on the subject, many confusions exist in the conceptual schemes so that different views are not clearly distinguished; whose views, how they look at the issues, in what stages of development they judge, under what environments they decides, etc.
(2) In the postwar world, we already have many observations of successful transfer of technologies and the failures. By and large, East Asian countries have been successful, whereas other areas like Latin America, South Asia, and Middle East have failed. We should conduct some empirical studies in those areas and try to identify the factors for success and failure.[37]

Chapters 9 and 10 reproduce my reports for the first and the second problems: Chapter 9: The Choice of Appropriate Technology — the

in *Southeast Asian Studies* or the books in Japanese. I kept Kuniyoshi Urabe's article here because it is important and he played the central role in this project. It is regrettable that we lost his talent (1920–1986) too early before our final report was out in 1988.

[37] Head of the department, Dr. A. S. Bhalla and head of technology and employment, Mr. S. Watanabe agreed with my views.

influence of socio-economic factors and government policies; Chapter 10: Institutional Factors and Government Policies for Appropriate Technologies — survey findings in Indonesia, Thailand, and the Philippines.

Both chapters have been available only as working papers of ILO. They are substantial in the contents, because they summarize the knowledge of not only my own but also my colleagues' and experts' around CSEAS.[38] Here, I show only two examples of our approach in this study. One is recognition of the process of adopting a certain technology as appropriate in some LDC. It is shown as Figure 1 in Chapter 9. Another is the importance of the types of society consisting of the certain ethnic groups in each country. The details of exposition of this diagram must be understood by reading Chapter 9 itself later, but it would not be too difficult to see this Figure 1 showing the process of technology transfer and the considerations needed

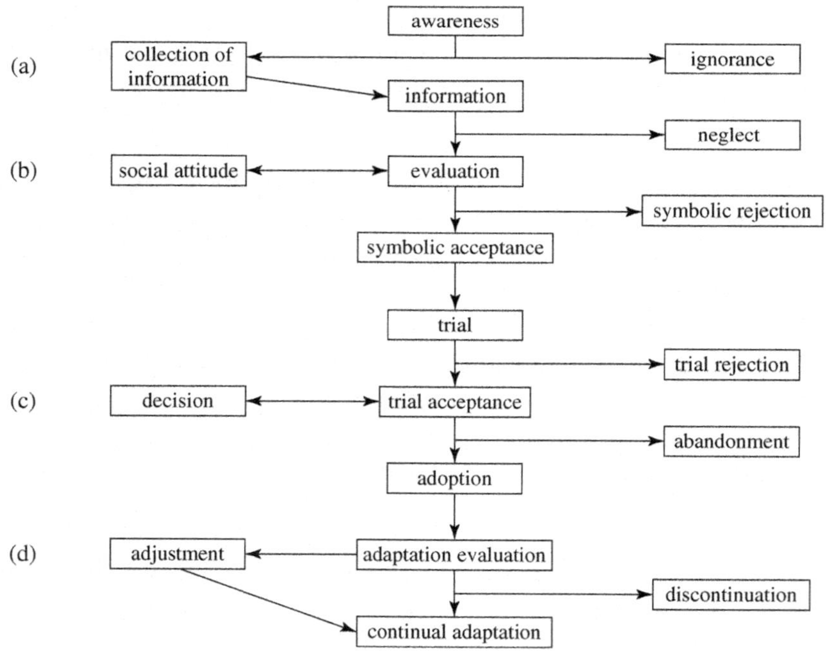

Fig. 1. Flow Chart of Adopting Process of New Technologies.

[38]A summary of the two papers was published: "Institutional Factors and Government Policies for Appropriate Technologies in Southeast Asia" in M. Chatterji (ed.), *Technology Transfer in the Developing Countries*, Macmillan, 1990.

in adopting modern technologies in LDC. Any technology will be adopted by someone who judges that it is appropriate for him or his company. If the government judges that it is not appropriate, it must be as the result of careful examination or trial from some other point of view, which differs from the first user's view.

The second example is the types of social organizations. The reader may remember the argument in G. Myrdal's *Asian Drama* about *tight* society *vs* *soft* society. Emblee defined the Thai villages as "loosely structured society", which corresponds to *soft* society in Myrdal's sense. It is not easy to organize the farmers from soft society as factory workers with modern technologies. Thus, when the social organization is *soft*, appropriate technology may be of smaller scale. Many anthropologists around CSEAS studied SEA villages. Masuo Kuchiba's summary diagram is shown in Figure 2.

Kuchiba observed the behavior patterns of villagers from two points of view: individual-oriented versus group-oriented and achievement-oriented vs harmony-oriented. In Southeast Asia, although particularistic dyadic relations and harmonious relations are highly valued, they do not have the strong group-oriented character of kin as in China or of families and villages in Japan. These characteristics seem to be closely related to the peculiar character of a village community in most Southeast Asian ethnic groups. They permeate into any social organizations, including business and government. The looseness of their social cohesion has important implications for economic development. The following remark by M. Kuchiba[39] may be applicable, with slight modifications, to business or government organizations.

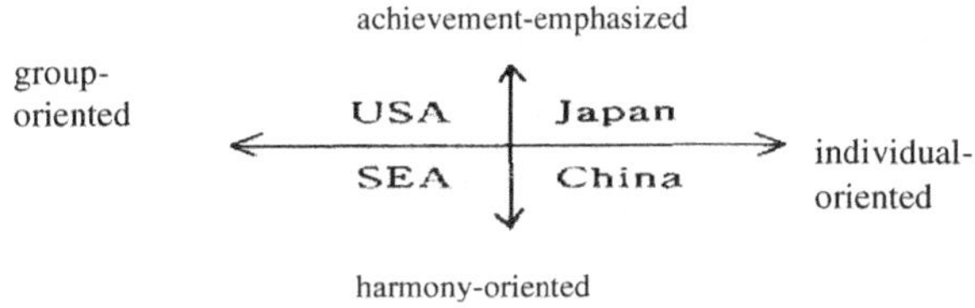

Fig. 2. Types of Social Organization.

[39] M. Kuchiba (1979). "Introduction: Problems and Approaches from Comparative Perspective," in Kuchiba (ed.), *International Comparative Study of Rice-Growing Villages in Asia*, report to the Toyota Foundation.

"The need for a multi-purpose farmers' co-operative is emphasized in Southeast Asia but it is not formed smoothly. In Japan, the self-governing body of a hamlet is often capitalized as a sub-unit of a co-operative organization. In this way, loyalty to the village becomes, at the same time, loyalty to the co-operative organization. Withdrawal from a co-operative organization can easily be interpreted to be a sign of disloyalty to the village and, even though joining is easy, withdrawal is difficult. Sometimes, this strong group orientation becomes a hindrance to implementing a program for forming a broad farming area by consolidation. In Southeast Asia as a contrast, joining a co-operative and withdrawal wherefrom are both a personal matter and simple. The social foundations for membership recruitment, entrenchment, and perpetuation are weak." Our business surveys confirmed these observations.

Our field surveys in Thailand, the Philippines and Indonesia revealed really many previously unknown facts. The most significant one was that the government policies and their implementation played much more important roles on technology in LDC than in advanced countries. The extent to which they are important and the ways in which they influence differed from one country to another. I hope that the reader will find them out by reading these two chapters.

9. Construction of Econometric Models of Asian LINK

Even after moving to CSEAS, I kept writing on the Japanese Economy and its relations with Asian countries as my list of publications shows. At the same time, I had many opportunities as CSEAS director to meet the directors of research institutes in Asian and the Pacific countries. We agreed to organize Association of Development Research Institutes in Asia and the Pacific (ADIPA), and I was offered by the CSEAS to be a secretariat for the Association. I proposed as the first activity of ADIPA to collect the information of all the quantitative studies of our own or other economies and disseminate the information. The outcomes of our efforts are two booklets: *Econometric Models of Asian Countries I*, 1978 {30} and *II*, 1980 {33}. The lists surprised many directors and researchers in the region by revealing that so many quantitative and statistical studies of Asian economies already existed. Earlier, I myself had several occasions to visit Korea and Taiwan to discover that the research department, the Bank of Korea was engaged in constructing a quarterly econometric model of the Korean economy and experimentally tried to use it for forecast, and in Taiwan, a few staffs at the Economic Planning Agency were earnestly building an econometric model of Taiwan economy following the Klein–Goldberger model. In Hong Kong too, Prof. Lin at the Chinese University of Hong Kong just finished an econometric model of Hong Kong Economy. In Thailand, the research department, the Bank of Thailand had built an econometric model of Thailand. In Indonesia, a Japanese team stationed at BAPPENAS[40] had constructed an econometric model on scanty database and was using it for forecast. Thus, I thought that time was almost ripe to try to construct a regional econometric model of East and Southeast Asian economies, similarly to the global model of LINK that L. R. Klein had built for almost all developed countries. By that time the computational problems we faced in the case of Osaka, ISER Model had been solved. Dr. M. Ezaki who was trained under Prof. D. Jorgenson, Harvard University was just back to CSEAS. Several other econometricians like Prof. S. Hirai (Wakayama University) and Prof. H. Niwa (Kwansei Gakuin University) promised to cooperate. Fortunately, Kyoto University was equipped with the best computer in Japan on the campus. I was expecting to retire from Kyoto University in 1988, so that I thought that this Asian LINK model might be a good final product of my career works. It is {38} Ichimura, S. and Mitsuo Ezaki (eds.), *Econometric Models of Asian LINK*, Springer-Verlag, NY-Berlin-Tokyo, 1985. I presented it at the World Congress of the Econometric Society at MIT, Cambridge, in 1986. Its shortcoming was that though a Chinese model by Haruki Niwa was contained in the book, it was not integrated with the other Asian economies. The reason was that the Chinese statistics were based on the Soviet type of Material Product a/c, so

[40]Several years after we constructed a tentative IO Table, IDE produced a proper IO Table of the Indonesian economy. Dr. Saburo Okita (deputy minister of Economic Planning Agency then) suggested Dr. Widjojo (Minister of National Development Agency) that he might consider, as the Japanese ODA was increasing very rapidly then, to allow a Japanese team of economists to stay at BAPPENAS and observe closely with Indonesian officials the development of Indonesian economy. Dr. Widjojo accepted the proposal. Dr. Okita asked me to lead this team. Mr. Sei Kuribayashi from the EPA, Japan produced an econometric model and began offering the forecast of Indonesian economy.

that it was impossible to integrate with the UN a/c data in the rest of Asian countries. UN format national income data in China become available only in 1990.

In 1988, I retired from Kyoto University at the officially designated age of 63 and became the Vice-Chancellor of Osaka International University — a newly established private university — where I continued my research and organized several projects on Asia and Japan.[41] One of them was to collect a set of best econometric models of major countries and regions in the world as a sort of preparation to produce a global model. It was {45}: *Econometric Models of Asia-Pacific Countries*, Springer-Verlag, Berlin-NY-Tokyo, 1993.[42] In Southeast Asia, I continued to lead the Japanese team at BAPPENAS, Indonesia for some years but asked Prof. T. Fukuchi at Institute of Economic Research, Kyoto University to succeed me. My own center of interest moved to China, as the importance of China significantly increased with its development and gradual transformation to market economy.[43]

10. Importance of the Political Economy of Development

Another change in the direction of my own research was my own recognition of the importance of politics and other related sciences in the analysis of developing countries. I recognized this fact in two directions. One is the influence of non-economic factors like the stakes of big businesses

[41] At the same session of World Congress, Prof. Waelbroek presented a world model of the World Bank, but it was a CGE model. The only ordinary macroeconometric model of the world economy was the LINK model at the UN and University of Pennsylvania, led by L. R. Klein. It included a Moriguchi-Ban model of Japan but no Chinese model then. Later L. Lau (Stanford), Klein and I worked on China, and major works are published in {51}: Klein-Ichimura (eds.), *Econometric Modeling of China*, WSPC, 2000.

[42] It was essentially a summary of the best models in two volumes of ADIPA collections. There was no further development out of it. The global model at the UN continued under the leadership of L.R. Klein until recently. But no formal report of the Project was officially published so far. Difficulty with this kind of big models is perhaps that the cost far exceeds the benefit which must be borne by somebody.

[43] Hence, my own research interest shifted from Southeast Asia to China. My research works on China will be collected in the next volume: *Japan and China*, WSPC.

on economic policies. Another is the influence of economic factors like income inequality on the social disorder and political instability. The first was very conspicuous from the very beginning of my undertaking the directorship of CSEAS. For example, foreign economists and domestic scholars alike were talking a lot on corruption when I saw them on my first trip to Southeast Asian capitals.[44] The first impressive work I have read on the subject, however, was Samuel Huntington: *Political Order in Changing Societies*, Yale University Press, 1968. It certainly broadened my vision and knowledge, but most points he raised were previously discussed by Yasuma Takata in his sociological works; such as mobility of social classes.[45] Besides, East Asian experiences were rather different from Latin American experiences which Huntington took the cases to prove his conjectures. Nevertheless, I learnt a great deal from his book and arguments and applied the conceptual scheme to the analysis of domestic fiscal policies in Ref. {43}: Ichimura-Urrtia-Yukawa (eds.), *Political Economy of Fiscal Policy*, UN University Press, Tokyo, 1989, and more generally to "the problems of underdeveloped economies" published in Ref. {70} *Economics Encyclopedia*, 1980.

When, however, J. Morley and I summed up the experiences of East Asian development, we considered it *Driven by Growth*,[46] rather than growth causing instability. But Huntington argument will hold well in some countries in Southeast Asia and China in the future.

The same viewpoint was applied to the earlier stages of economic development and nation-building by extending it to the broader views of Max Weber. The view was presented first in my speech [196] at the Nagoya University to celebrate its 10th anniversary ceremony in 2001 and integrated in my arguments in Chapter 6 of this book.

[44]Indeed, when Dr. Masashi Nishihara came back from the University of Michigan as a fresh PhD in political science and went to Indonesia as a research fellow of CSEAS, I asked him to undertake the study of political corruption in Southeast Asian countries. His first-rate study is published as M. Nishihara, *Political Corruption in Southeast Asia* (J) Sobunsha, Tokyo 1974, and remains a classic on the topic.

[45]I discussed the matters in my book [39] first and then {43} and reprinted in Ref. {48}.

[46]I contributed with J. Morley, "Varieties of Asian Growth and Political Change" [125] to his (ed.) Driven by Growth, The Sharp, NY, 1993. See also Ref. {48}.

11. Regional Gaps As Important As Income Inequality

The Japanese economy before the World War II may be regarded as regionally balanced; Tokyo was a political center, whereas Osaka was an economic center. The postwar growth was undoubtedly biased toward Tokyo.[47] The fundamental reason for this was that the control economy during the war was carried over into the postwar years without sufficiently deregulating government intervention measures.[48] The government had two important guideline plans for its policies: Medium-Term Economic Plans over 4 to 5 years and National Land-Use Plans over 10 to 15 years. Particularly, the latter influenced the regional distribution of economic activities in the private sector, because it gave guidance for government investment in infrastructure. I have been very critical of its basic approaches. All of first three plans took economic and population concentration for granted and never tried to counteract against the trends. Only as late as in 1987, the government's *Forth* Comprehensive Development Plan changed the direction of Land-use plan to *decentralization*, giving it the new title: *Multiple-Poles and Dispersion Type of Land-use Plan*. Chapter 7 is a summary of the arguments of my critical papers on government plans {18}[49] ever since interregional IO works like [6] in 1958. I presented the same opinions at an international conference in China. My wish was to give the Chinese authorities a strong warning against unavoidable trends toward concentration and regional disparity. I am seriously worried about the current inter-regional trends in China.[50]

In Indonesia, my first research project was a regional survey of South Sumatra Province {25} and {29}. Even then, the importance of regional

---

[47] In prewar Japan, the head offices of big newspapers like Asahi, Mainichi and Sankei were in Osaka. The same with big trading companies like Itochu, Nissho, Iwai, Sumitomo, Kanematsu, Gosho, Daimaru, Takashimaya department stores originated in Kyoto. Many of them moved their head offices to Tokyo now. An important point is that corporate income taxes are paid to the government by the head offices, but local governments can collect the additional tax proportional to corporate income tax, so that the tax revenue of Tokyo becomes very big out of proportion with its economic activities.

[48] A great deal of government control measures during the war were removed, but they were not enough and soon.

[49] The book included bitter criticisms on the government's promotion of concentration.

[50] It was held in Jungjing to commemorate the start of Great West Development Plan of the government then.

policies was obvious in such an insular country consisting of varieties of islands, but to discuss the problem in terms of "decentralization" was a *taboo*. For newly born Indonesia, national unification was so acutely required. Now, however, after 40 years later, the central government is moving toward decentralization. As per capita income goes up in LDC, the political requirements for governance change. I have taken up this aspect by organizing a big international conference (2003) at ICSEAD in Kitakyushu, Janna and finally produced in cooperation with Prof. Roy Bahl, [66], Ichimura, S. and R. Bahl (eds.), *Decentralization Policies in Asian Development*, WSPC, 2008.

The second important aspect of regional problems is urbanization. I had several opportunities to study it first in Japan and then in Asia. The first one was in Osaka where I resided over 50 years. Rapid economic growth in the 1960s accompanied tremendous domestic migration. Into Osaka Prefecture, about 200,000 people migrated every year in the peak years. To absorb them, the Prefectural government had to plan building a few new towns around the city of Osaka. At their request, I participated in the Designing Committee. My main task was to predict the future population and the transportation requirements like construction of big streets, highways and suburban railways. Some papers like [36] and [37] were the by-products of my contributions to this committee.[51]

Another precious experience was a study of water supply and demand in Tokyo. The Electric Power Central Research Institute in Tokyo asked me to estimate the future supply and demand for warder in the city area of Tokyo. It revealed the complex system of water supply to Tokyo. My estimates of the water demand in Tokyo and immigration into Osaka prefecture turned out after two decades to be almost right. The main reason for success was that I fitted the nonlinear curves for the water demand and migration trends. See Ref. {33}.[52]

[51]My contributions as such were included in the Local Plan (Chiho Keikaku) of Osaka Prefectural government.

[52]Apart from this work, I prepared, with Prof. Noboru Sakashita, a bibliographic survey [46] of relatively unknown research works on urbanization and its effects on cultural changes up to 1972. He was professor of economics and regional science, Tsukuba University (1933–2003).

In Asia, first I had a chance in China to cooperate with UNCRD[53] during 1986–1988 to undertake a development planning for Wuxi city located between Nanjing and Shanghai. Second, in Indonesia almost a decade later (1998), I organized a research project of ICSEAD on urban problems, mainly environmental issues of the cities of Surabaya, Semarang and Medan and explored the possibility of inter-city cooperation with Kitakyushu City: [185]. Third, similarly in connection with the promotion of inter-city cooperation with Asian cities, we studied surveying the cargo transportation around the Yellow Sea; [189] reported in 2000. Fourth, we looked into the urban transportation problems of Beijing and Shanghai [190]. Unfortunately, the one on Indonesian city are published in Japanese so that they are not included in this book.[54] The others are primarily concerned with China so that they will be published in my next volume: *Japan and China.*

12. Overviews of Japanese and Southeast Asian Economies

Ever since I wrote some papers based on National Income Data and Input–Output Tables, I have often expressed my views on the present conditions and the future prospects of Japanese Economy in Japanese Newspapers and business magazines, especially in the early postwar years during 1953–1970. The main reason was that my views were different from journalistically popular Marxists' pessimism[55] and basically optimistic in regarding the various difficulties in Japan as surmountable by good

[53]In 1986, UN Center for Research in Regional Development, Nagoya, Japan agreed with the Chinese government to organize an experimental project on the development plan of Wuxi city and its suburbs. It was the most rapidly growing urban area in China then. I was asked to join the team to prepare the development plan similar to that for Osaka. The research report was prepared in Chinese and English. See the details in Ref. [113]: *The Report of Basic Development Strategic Plan for Wuxi Area*, Chinese Enterprise Management Ass./Wuxi Enterprise Management Ass. UNCRD, September, 1988.

[54]Its main contents are reported in Ref. [185] and related articles.

[55]In most Japanese universities, more than half of the staffs at economics and business departments were Marxists. Many of them were journalistically popular, such as R. Minobe, H. Arisawa, S. Tsuru, H. Ohuchi and so on. Similarly, ideological bias was very significant in history and political science. This affected many natural scientists until the end of Cold War. After 1990, of course, intellectual circumstances changed in Japan as well as the West.

economic policies. Such views were summed up in my booklet {13}; *The Japanese Economy in the World*, Chuko-Shinsho in 1965.

From abroad, an Australian Journal, *Quadrant*, first requested me to explain why Japan was growing so fast. I contributed: "Challenge of the Rising Sun", in 1970 {40}.[56] This paper listed 10 factors to explain the Japanese rapid growth in the 1960s, but at the same time gave a warning that rapid growth would not be sustained if those factors were to change. About the same time, the Japanese relations with Asian countries became increasingly unstable. To discuss those matters, I contributed [48] to "Japan's Stake in Asia" to Taylor, A. Ballinger, *Perspectives on the US–Japan Economic Relations*, 1974. Then, I had several opportunities to speak at some universities like Seoul National University in Korea and National Taiwan University in Taiwan around 1974 on "Japan: the Rising Sun or the Sinking Ship — the energy and food problems" [52]. In 1979, the famous Encyclopedia Britannica published its Japanese edition and asked me to contribute an article "Japanese Economy" [61]. Since then, I contributed a number of articles to *Newsweek* 1980, annual versions of *Encyclopedia Britannica*, *Business Weeks* on Japan or Southeast Asia throughout the 1980s.

Needless to say, my efforts as the director were bearing the fruits in the early 1970s, despite the student rioting at Kyoto and Tokyo universities. A list of articles at the end of this book will show my works with CSEAS staffs. There are many other papers and monographs of the projects not in the list because I did not participate. Their contents are self-explanatory by the titles of the reports. Depicting some works, I wish to explain the direction of our area research. First: *Thinking of Southeast Asia* (J), Sobunsha, 1974 {20}. The book as a whole presented the guiding ideas of our research on Southeast Asia. On the basis of the Three Guiding Principles of research mentioned above, some concrete examples were presented. (1) Yoneo Ishii, historian, explained the three basic streams of Southeast Asian cultures: Malay-Polynesian, Indian and Chinese cultures before modern Western culture flew in. (2) Takeshi Kyuma, soil scientist, explained what natural conditions like soil or topology in Southeast Asia have influenced the

---

[56]It is Chapter 2 in Ref. {43}: *Political Economy of Japanese and Asian Development*, Springer-Verlag, 1998.

agriculture. (3) I as an economist and director, explained that we follow the established modern scientific methods but with full sympathy with their young nationalism for development and nation-building. Second, *Southeast Asia: Nature, Society and Development*, University of Hawaii Press, 1977: [21], summarized our studies of the natural ecology, societal characteristics and economic development. One distinct characteristic of our studies is that it includes the professional studies of natural ecology as an essential base of our understanding the peoples' living in Southeast Asia. Thus, our study emphasizes ecology. Third, it is my article: "Interdisciplinary Research and Area Studies" in *the Journal of Southeast Asian Studies*, 1975 [54]. It is a methodological paper on different ways of synthesizing the multi-disciplinary studies in various sciences to clarify our area research.

13. Studies on Financial Crises and Problems in Asia

The immediately postwar Japanese financial markets experienced two crises. The first was the press-down of hyper-inflation by Dodge plan immediately after the WWII. The second was the end of fixed exchange rate system in 1972 due to de-linking of US dollars from gold. Apart from postwar hyper-inflation, the Japanese commodities prices were fundamentally stable, so that the monetary sector did not disturb the national economy in any serious way. However, the real-estate prices, especially land price, were exceptions. They have kept rising. The rate of inflation in land price in many districts was significantly higher than the standard rate of bank loans. This made land an object of the safest investment and the surest collateral for loans.[57]

My early econometric research on the financial issues and policies was mainly concerned with the issues before liberalization of exchange rate in 1972. Our Osaka ISER Model of the Japanese economy with detailed equations for the financial variables was completed in 1967 [39].[58] It included the various simulations of monetary policies among others, but then the exchange rate was fixed globally and in Japan.

---

[57] It made most banks lending policy easy, because banks could give loans only ascertaining the borrowers' ownership of land without examining other factors.

[58] The complete model and its simulation results were published in this paper in 1967, but the whole report was made available {56} in 1977, {68} in 2010 and {69} in 2011.

Soon in the early 1970s, the oil crises hit the whole world. Its financial impact caused the cumulated debt problems first in Latin American countries. Japan was, however, not free wherefrom. My analysis of oil crises [93] was contributed to Saburo Ohkita (ed.), *North South Problems* (J), Chuokoron-sha, 1983. I analyzed its financial impact on Asian economies in my article [98] published in *Pacific Economic Papers*, ANU in 1984.

Earlier, however, my concern was on development finance and overseas investment. I studied the issues mainly in Southeast Asia and developing economies in general. Examples are Refs. [81], [82], and others. Some dealt with Japanese investment in Europe [121], [123] and others.

As for the Japanese banking system and the monetary policy, I contributed a general survey [126] to a volume which comparatively surveyed the monetary policies in various countries: Frattiani M. & Salvadore (ed.), *Handbook of Monetary Policy in the World*, West Press, NY. 1992. Soon after then, however, in 1997, Asian Financial Crisis unexpectedly hit some East Asian countries such as Thailand, South Korea and Indonesia. Unlike some economists or international organizations, it did not surprise me, because I had been seriously worried about heavy government debts in many East and Southeast Asian countires.[59] My studies and opinions were repeated at the Korean Academy of Sciences in 2011 as [266] shows. They are reproduced here as Chapters 2 and 3. Earlier, similar financial troubles occurred with the Plaza Accord between the US, Germany and Japan, that really started the long-term recession in Japan and continued to the 2008 Goldman Saks–Lehman Brothers Crises discussed in this volume.

14. Transformation of Socialist to Market Economies

CSEAS did not cover China as its research area, but it is essential to any Asian problem so I always tried to keep my eyes on the important works about Chinese political economy. For instance, I translated with my former students: T. Liu, A. Eckstein and W. Galenson, *Economic Trends of Communist China*, 1979 as {31}. This was the most authoritative study of the Chinese economy before Deng moved China.

[59]When I expressed my worry at an International conference in Singapore in 1984, most economists told that Asian economies would muddle through. Even as late as 1996 many, not all, economists misjudged. See Ref. [97].

Soon after the Deng reform started, I visited Beijing and Shanghai myself and renewed my friendship with old classmates at Kyoto University and their colleagues at the Chinese academies and universities. There were some economists in Japan too who seriously worked on the Chinese economy with scanty information available under the Communist regime such as Shigeru Ishikawa at Hitotsubashi University, Haruki Niwa at Kwansei Gakuin University, and several others. When, however, I myself dared to pioneer a study of East Asian economies as an integrated system of Asian LINK even in the early 1980s: {37}. I put aside the trading relations with China, because its national accounting system of statistics was of Soviet type so that integration with other Asian data was impossible.

The Deng's *reform and open* was quickly in full swing, however, and various experiments of transition to market economy began. In 1985, the United Nations Centre for Regional Development, in Nagoya, Japan asked me to help their project to prepare an urban development plan for Wu Xi city, west of Shanghai — the most rapidly growing urban area in China then. This gave me a chance of applying my own experiences for Osaka Prefecture to a similar city in China. Our report contained many experiences of ours in Japan and was published only in Chinese and English in 1989.[60] (See Ref. [113] in UNCRD report.)[61] At some meetings in Wu Xi, I met a number of Chinese experts in regional planning from Beijing and could share many common issues confronting us over the difficulties in regional planning in China and Japan. As the result, we agreed to help them prepare the very first Interregional Input–Output Table for the entire Chinese economy. My experiences in Japan were used as a text for their training. The Central Statistical Office in Beijing played an essential role to complete this pioneering work. The Interregional IO table and its applications was published in English as Ref. {54} and translated into Chinese by Prof. Li Shanton as Ref. {63} in 2005. It influenced to produce some subsequent interregional IO tables. I was invited to two international conferences to present our successes and failures in Japanese regional planning like [189] and [191].

[60]Maybe for this reason, its precious experiences are little known in Japan.

[61]Then I was freer to choose China as a research area at Osaka International University.

As the Deng reform preceded, the transformation of Chinese Socialist economy gradually moved further. Dr. Seiji Naya, chief economist of ADB (originally from the University of Hawaii) drew my attention to the Asian economists' interest in this topic by requesting me to organize a workshop with Asian economists at my University in 1994. Its proceedings (J) was edited and made available as Ref. {64}. Though transition to market economy took place in China and Vietnam step by step, the trend ignited by Gorvachef–Yeltsin in the Soviet Union and Central–Eastern Europe moved much faster and more radically.

The intellectual and academic impact of the breakdown of Soviet Union and its Communist Party immediately caused the political transition of many Socialist States in Europe to market economies and democratic political systems one after another. The ideological impact was no less shocking in Japan than in Europe. The fall of Berlin wall not only symbolized the end of Cold War but also started a new pilgrimage of ideological conversion. Some leftish magazines disappeared or their editors were dismissed. The self-claimed Marxian Socialists disappeared at most universities in Europe and Japan. The Japanese Socialist party changed its name, yet almost disappeared, though Communist party still remains occupying a few percents of parliamentary seats in Japan. This change in politics certainly changed the intellectual arguments among journalists, economists, and political scientists on the domestic and international problems. In 1995, when I moved from OIU to the director of International Center for the Study of East Asian Development (ICSEAD), I was very strongly attracted to a comparative investigation of the two transitions in Asia and Europe. I knew, however, that I had to wait at least about 10 years for enough observations in both areas, especially in Europe. Then we convened two workshops on the same subject, inviting experts in Europe, Vietnam, China, and Japan to Kitakyushu in 2000 and again to Budapest, Hungary in 2001.[62] After the meetings, we tried to improve the debates by correspondence particularly to supply the authors with the information on both areas to improve our mutual understanding. The final outcome is {67},

[62]To organize the workshops and edit the volume, I was greatly helped by two experts, Prof. Tsuneaki Sato (Yokohama Municipal University, 1925–2014) and William James (Asian Development Bank, former research director, ICSEAD, 1950–2010).

Ichimura-Sato-James (ed.), *Transition from Socialist to Market Economies*, 2009, Palgrave-McMillan. The reader will be surprised by finding so many differences in transitional processes and consequences between East and West.[63]

15. Decentralization Policies in Asian Development

Development economics presumes that a new nation-state can be built only by national unification and economic take-off. Hence, non-democratic dictatorial government often is taken as permissible at the early stage of development like an infantry industry argument. As per capita income goes up, however, the people begin to demand more appropriate administration in accordance to the needs of local conditions. For instance, when I visited Indonesia in 1969, even to talk about the possibility of decentralized administration was a taboo. Now, Indonesian per capita GDP surpassed $2,000, and its central government in Jakarta is promoting some decentralization policies.

Moreover, in the advanced economies like Japan as well, the decentralization policies have been hotly debated in recent decades. Popular Prime Minister Koizumi (2001–2006) was very clever in attracting the peoples' attention with the well-known slogan: "from Center to Local" (decentralization) and "from government to Private" (privatization). Globally in the 1990s liberalization = privatization was very popular with Reagan–Thatcher teams in the West, and at the same time decentralization began to be popularly accepted in a number of developing and developed countries. Knowing of the trends, when Mayor Sueyoshi proposed a series of international conferences on Asian development, I immediately proposed a theme of "Decentralization Policies in Asian Development" after the conferences on *Transition from Socialist to Market Economies*, as we discussed in previous section. Despite the mayor's immediate support, organizing this conference was not easy, because not many experts were available in Japan on decentralization policies in Asia. Two steps were necessary, therefore, to organize this conference: the first preparatory workshop of small scale to choose the main themes and the appropriate

[63]My review article sums up the main points of our book in Japanese: as [207] in *Viewpoint to East Asia*, 2010.

experts; and the second ordinary conference among experts on the adopted themes. For the first one, I invited Mr. Yoshimura (Vice-President of World Bank in Tokyo) and Dr. Lee Jang-hee (Tokyo Office Representative of ADB) and a few young Asian economists who are seriously concerned with the decentralization problems in their own countries. It has become very clear at this preliminary workshop that the World Bank seems to have the most information on this problem in most developing countries and contacts with resource persons, and that little is known abroad about decentralization problems in Japan so that serious interests exist among foreign experts. It was important information that Professor Roy Bahl at the Georgia State University is the expert familiar with the issues in many countries including the ones in India. As for the themes to take up, three groups of issues have been summarized:

(1) Decentralization of political administration and public finance.[64]
(2) Decentralization and local public finance.
(3) Demographic concentration in big cities and urbanization problems.

We tried to list up many detailed issues under the three themes.

Upon recommendation of the participants in the workshop and the other experts we consulted with, we carefully selected the participants and held the conference in November 2003. It was regrettable that for China and Korea, we could not get as many participants as we first planned. After the conference, Prof. R. Bahl and I tried to make our reports as comprehensive and up-to-date as possible by asking a few additional contributors to write on the decentralization policies in their own countries. Prof. Rao's contribution on India was obtained that way. Perhaps even now, the book will be a good starting point to learn about the decentralization policies in Asian countries.

16. Political and Cultural Problems for Asian Development

Needless to argue, economic development necessitates the changes in social organizations and political relations within and among various social groups

[64]The main points of our book {66}: *Decentralization Policies in Asian Development* (2008) WSPC is summarized by my review article as [206] in Japanese: *Viewpoint to East Asia* in 2009.

such as tribes, races, countries, nations, the States or empires. Hence, studies of Asian development can hardly remain within the narrow realm of economics, sociology, politics or some kind of combination of those. No wonder, postwar studies of Asian development began with *Asian Drama* (1968) by Gunnar Myrdal's group, and political scientist Samuel Huntington's (1996) *Crashes of Civilizations* predicted a challenge to the established world order by a crash of Western Christian civilizations and Islam–Chinese civilizations in coalition.[65] Our anthropological, agronomical and socio-economic studies by my colleagues at CSEAS were more detailed and further than their group's single-handed individual observations. As many articles in this book showed, we relied on carefully designed survey findings and group observations by specialists at specific areas. Our conclusions do not necessarily support theirs.[66]

Moreover, bigger scale of economic and political cooperation like Asian Union has been taken up at many international conferences. I was asked also to present my views. See Refs. [146], [155], and [176]. My views have been rather cautious than optimistic on the possibility of organizing East Asian Regional Community as many papers show. Despite the desirability and many people's wishful thinking, there are several important reasons for the difficulty. First, the degree of contact between oceanic countrymen and continental countrymen is still very limited in comparison within the continental countrymen themselves like Western European countrymen. Second, the language barriers are much greater in Asia than in Europe. They have a common letter (alphabet), whereas we have so many different letters.[67] Third, languages in Europe belong to one of three families: Latin, Germanic or Slavic, whereas those in Asia are of so many varieties that mutual understanding is far more difficult. Fourth, Europe consists predominantly of Christian nations, whether they are orthodox, catholic

---

[65] Similar observation was made earlier by Arnold Toynbee in his book, *Civilizations on Trial*, 1948. He pointed out that peaceful coexistence between Western and Muslim civilizations is almost impossible. My book review of Toynbee's book was published in Quarterly *Kwan*, Autumn 2013 in Japanese.

[66] Studies of regional cooperation within or across the national borders in Asian countries were undertaken to investigate such as Kedah Project in Malaysia or the Mekong Project by ESCAP. My colleagues participated in them. They are not published here.

[67] Chinese letters are used only for Japanese, no longer Vietnamese and Korean.

or protestant. Samuel Huntington lump them together as Judah–Christian. But all other civilizations in the world originated somewhere in Asia and still there: Indian, Chinese, Islam and Japanese. In terms of religions, Indian civilization consists of Hinduism and Buddhism: China of Taoism, Confucianism, Chinese Buddhism, and Communism; Islamic nations of Mohammedanism and various sects, and Japan of Shinto and Japanese Buddhism.[68] This makes it more complex for Asian nations to share the common ideals to achieve. The formation of Asian Union, if it is ever to be established, would be politically far more difficult to realize than European Union.

Nevertheless, Asian leaders who achieved independence within a limited number of years after the World War II succeeded in combining the traditional religious beliefs and the requirements of modern democracy.[69] Certainly, Japan demonstrated the same kind of passage of modernization with traditional cultures maintained.[70]

[68] S. Huntington's great work missed the proper place of Buddhism in Asian civilization. This is serious in two ways. First, there exist Buddhist countries like Myanmar, Sri Lanka, Thailand, Bhutan, and Nepal, Campucia, Lao, and Vietnam. Second, its influence permeates deeply into China and Japan. See Ref. [186].

[69] My reference [174] compares Sun Yat-Sen in China and Sukarno in Indonesia.

[70] The best reference to the initial stage of modernization in the case of Japan to my knowledge is Norman, E. Herbert (1940). *Japan's Emergence as a Modern State: political and economic problems of the Meiji period.* International Secretariat, Institute of Pacific Relations.

Part I

The Present and the Future of Japan and Asia

Chapter 1

When Can Asia Play a Leading Role in the World?*

1. The West *versus* the East

Before the Industrial Revolution, no serious difference in the historic process existed between the East and the West. But the political economy of world affairs has completely changed since. The fundamental reason was that the West succeeded in obtaining significantly faster and better means of transportation: Steam engines. This technological advantage, combined with the adventurous political ambition, resulted in the West subjugating the East. In the 20th century, however, Asian responses to the Western challenge began. Now, no colonies exist in the world. Nevertheless, the world is still led primarily by Western powers: namely, in world politics, G-5 (permanent members of the UN Security Council — US, UK, France, Russia, China); and in economic and financial matters, G-7 (US, UK, France, Japan, Germany, Italy, and Canada). In Culture, Science and Technology as well, these countries are leading the contemporary world, as proven by the fact that so many bright students still go to the West to learn. However, not all Asian nations are far behind in many cultural and scientific spheres, but clearly no one can say that Asia is playing a leading role in those areas. Then, when can Asia play a leading role in polity, economy, culture, science and technology? Or how should we think about this problem from an Asian perspective? Certainly this is beyond economics. Allow me to dare to express my personal views on this broad problem. Since the central stage

*This was published in *the Asian Economic Journal*, 2011. The author was the first editor of *the AEJ* for 1984–2000 and the President of the East Asian Economic Association, 1990–1996. This is his luncheon speech given at the EAEA Convention 12 on October 3rd, 2010. The subject theme was suggested by President Yoo Jang-Hee (2008–2012).

of the world is the Eurasian continent and North America, let us begin by observing the major events and ideological trends, after World War II.

2. Dream and Disillusion of Socialism

Joseph A. Schumpeter, well-known author of *Capitalism, Socialism and Democracy (1942)*, wrote his last article: "A March to Socialism" in his dying bed, and Mrs J.A. Schumpeter read it at the AEA convention before he died in 1950. It was included only in the second and final edition of the book in 1953. It reflected a fashionable way of thinking, not only among Marxists or Communists, but also many economists and intellectuals in the world, immediately after the War. A warning by von Hayek in *The Road to Serfdom*, 1944, was regarded as reactionary and unpopular in the 1950s. After postwar reconstruction was over, however, stagflation hit the Western economies. Keynesians who could prescribe good policies so far and in the 1930s could not offer any good policies or reform ideas against excessive government intervention or regulations. New policies and reform plans came from conservative "liberals" like Friedrich von Hayek and Milton Friedman. Those policies were implemented by President Ronald Reagan in the US and Prime Minister Margaret Thatcher in the UK. Admittedly, they greatly improved the efficiency of the West-European and North-American economies. This success recovered the trust in the Free Private Enterprise System.

3. Transition from Socialist to Market Economies

On the other hand, the performance of the planned economies in the Soviet Union and its satellite countries were just miserable after postwar recovery. The lack of liberty under dictatorship finally caused the break-down of the Soviet empire by Gorbachev and Yeltsin. The transformation of Central and Eastern European countries to market economies quickly followed. This opened a road for the European Union and led to the establishment of an orderly region in the western corner of the Eurasian Continent.

4. China and India Crossing the Rubicon

Even before Europe, Chinese leader Deng Xiaoping declared "Reform and Opening" in 1979, after the two blunders by Mao: the Great Leap Forward and the Cultural Revolution. Thereafter, transition to a market economy in China has proceeded more successfully than in the former Socialist countries of Europe, as our book describes. (See: Ichimura, Sato and James, 2009.) Its success in economic performance has been very impressive and by the end of 2010, China's GDP will exceed that of Japan.

Recently, India also joined this march. She has been politically democratic, but economically socialistic and now it is transforming itself into a market economy. Its development in recent years has been remarkable, 8–9% per year. With these two Asian giants joining in the march to capitalistic development with Japan, Korea, Taiwan and ASEAN plus Oceania, some may think that Asia will soon play a more leading role in the New World Order. However, my personal view is that it would be unlikely in this century for several important reasons.

5. Modernization of Asian Nations

Almost all the Asian countries have histories, but have not yet developed into modern states. To transform an old state into a modern state, as Max Weber argued, at least four factors are essential: (1) a modern military system; (2) a bureaucracy; (3) a business enterprise system, particularly joint-stock companies; and (4) a nationalistic spirit to unite the nation. However, it is not easy to satisfy these conditions, with the last condition being the hardest, especially in multi-ethnic countries.

The famous Indian planner, Dr. P. C. Mahalanobis in response to my question to him in Osaka, in the late 1950s: What the greatest difficulty was after independence? "National unification" was his reply. Most Asian countries are multi-ethnic and have multiple religions. This implies that nationalism must be strong enough to unite such heterogeneous people, so it must be enhanced. Thus, British India had to be divided into several states: India, Pakistan, Sri Lanka, Bangladesh and Myanmar. Large states face great challenges maintaining unity as new modern states. Countries like China, Pakistan and Indonesia face such problems. It implies that they are likely to be domestic-oriented, rather than trying outwardly to make contributions to international cooperation.

6. Expansionism After Revolution or Independence

Enhanced nationalism after revolution or independence is likely to lead to expansionism. This was a warning by C. Brinton in *The Anatomy of Revolution* (1938) and in C. Gustavson's *A Preface to History* (1955).

China may be facing this problem at this stage. We have seen many historic precedents such as Napoleon or Stalinism.

7. Economic Development May Cause Political Instability

In addition, even with a successfully growing domestic economy, new nation-states may face political instability, because as S. Huntington pointed out in his *Political Order in Changing Societies* (1968), development causes income inequality which leads to social mobility and requires more political participation. If the social system is not adjusted to the new socio-political environment, political instability will be a consequence. Governance of authoritarian central governments may be endangered. This was based on his studies on Latin American countries.

Furthermore, economic development itself poses two barriers to overcome in the stages of development: One is the $2,000 hurdle to shift from an agrarian to an industrial society and the other is the $10,000 hurdle to establish the industrial-complex. Another problem with economic development is how to deal with regional discrepancies. The larger the size of the country, the more serious will be the regional disparities. As a result, decentralization policies become necessary against the power elite in the central government. (See Ichimura and Bahl, *Decentralization Policies in Asian Development*, 2008.) Indonesia is a typical example. After the Suharto regime was gone, the Indonesian government wisely changed its regional development policy toward decentralization.

At any rate, a simple linear extrapolation of the recent trend into the future is a misjudgment often committed by many economists. On Japan, futurologist Herman Kahn said in 1971, "the 21st Century may be the Japanese Century" to please Prime Minister Sato, and Ezra Vogel wrote the bestseller, *Japan as Number One* in 1979. They were, of course, superficial. Soon Japan suffered from the lost two decades.

8. Importance of Statesmen

Most Asian developing countries must overcome these difficulties one by one. It is not just a simple process of economic policy-making. Often it requires wise and powerful statesmen's leadership, as the reform in the Soviet Union by Gorbachev and Yeltsin, because most policies imply serious conflicts of stakes. China's reform was possible only by the leadership of Deng Xiaoping, so the roles of great leaders are essential for any country in Asia. The great Japanese sociologist Takata Yasuma (1939) once said: "economy is subjugated to polity". Unless great statesmen reappear in a number of Asian countries and succeed in bringing up the development stages of almost all Asian countries above $10,000 per capita, Asia cannot play any important role in the new world order. Already some successful Asian countries have had such great statesmen like Lee Kwan Yew or Mohamad Mahathir. Nevertheless, one should not repeat the mistake of Herman Kahn by saying something along the lines of "the 21st Century is China's Century or India's Century or Asia's Century". Economic development is merely one condition for leading countries.

Economic co-prosperity alone cannot create any regional integration like European Union. It is not enough. On this point I have learned a lesson about European Union from our President Yoo Jang-Hee's book, *Real Success and Financial Fall* (1999). We Asian nations too have fought each other, but in history the war experiences among European nations were much more serious: particularly between Germany and France. Nevertheless, it was indeed these two nations who really laid the foundation of European Union under two great leaders, François Mitterrand and Helmut Schmidt, and achieved mutual reconciliation and cooperation in the western corner of Eurasian continent.

Yoo Jang-Hee's book reminded me of another book I read when I was in college: *On East Asian Nations* (Toa Minzoku Ron), written by Takata Yasuma in 1939. He argued, against the then popular view, "Economic development or co-prosperity cannot be the solid base for Asian cooperation; what is essential is the establishment of the community in East Asia, preferably including India. Asian nations must feel each other as closely as family relations, the same villagers or people on the same boat". I should think that he would say now, unless East Asians succeed in establishing the East Asian Community as much as European nations did before they formed EU, Asian solidarity is utopian rather than idealistic. Community-building in Asia has a long way to go. It will take a few generations with mutual efforts and overcoming many troubles which it will encounter.

Economy is subjugated by Polity. But Polity also needs the support of the Economy, Culture, Science and Technology. Otherwise it is not sustainable. Unless we achieve much more progress in every front of all these areas of civilization, we cannot dream of playing a leading role in the world. Step by step, we should make progress. It does not seem far beyond our horizon. Asian tradition in culture is very rich and unique. Historically, Asian religions seldom fought each other. Confucianism, Buddhism and Shintoism have co-existed in Japan; in China too, Taoism, Confucianism and Buddhism have co-existed for centuries. This is true in many other Asian countries. It is a different perspective of religions from those of the "clashes of civilizations" in S. Huntington's 1996 work by the same title. The influence of Marxism in Asia will fade away sooner or later. Then Asia may begin moving forward to building up the Asian Community and Asian civilizations.

References

[1] Brinton, C. (1938), *The Anatomy of Revolution*, W. W Norton and Co., New York.
[2] Gustavson, C. (1955). *A Preface to History*, McGraw Hill, New York.
[3] Hayek, F. A. (1944). *The Road to Serfdom*, University of Chicago Press, Chicago.
[4] Huntington, S. P. (1968). *Political Order in Changing Societies*, Yale University Press, New Haven.
[5] Huntington, S. P. (1996). *The Clash of Civilizations and the Remaking of World Order*, Simon and Schuster, New York.
[6] Ichimura, S., S. Tsuneaki, and E. J. William (eds.) (2009). *Transition from Socialist to Market Economies*, Palgrave MacMillan, UK.
[7] Ichimura, S. and R. Bahl (eds.) (2008). *Decentralization Policies in Asian Development*, WSPC, Singapore.
[8] Kahn, H. (1971). *The Emerging Japanese Superstate: Challenge and Response*, Prentice Hall, Upper Saddle River.
[9] Schumpeter, J. A. (1950). *Capitalism, Socialism and Democracy*, 2nd edition, Harper and Brothers, New York.
[10] Takata, Y. (1939). *Toa Minzoku Ron* (*On East Asian Nations*), Iwanami, Tokyo.
[11] Vogel, E. (1979). *Japan as Number One: Lessons for America*, Harvard University Press, Cambridge, MA.
[12] Yoo, J.-H. (1999). *Real Success and Financial Fall: A Reassessment of Korean Dynamism*, Ewha Womans University Press, Seoul.

Chapter 2

The Lessons of the Lost Two Decades of the Japanese Economy*

Abstract

During the recent three decades, 1980–2010, the Japanese economy has experienced a period of rapid growth followed by two stagnant decades with serious financial distress and continuous deflation. In this process, Japan established a strong base for manufacturing industries in the world but could not handle the external shocks — the Plaza Accord, the rise of China, the Asian financial crisis and the 2008 financial crisis — and adjust its economy to the dramatic changes in the energy/resources and financial markets.

This chapter sums up the representative views of Japanese economists on these problems and then presents the author's own opinions. A sharp and continuous decline of economic growth was caused not only by external events but also aggravated by the mismanagement of private and public agencies, particularly in the financial sector. The author relies on a number of outstanding works by Japanese and foreign economists like Mitsuo Saito (1927–2010), *The Japanese Economy*, WSPC, 2000; three volumes edited by Fumio Hayashi, *Positive Analysis and Design of Economic Institutions* (J). Keiso Shobo, 2007, besides my own studies: *Political Economy of Japanese and Asian Development*, Springer-Verlag, 1998 and its revised Japanese edition Sobun-sha, 2003 and other essays. One important work is Tadao Kagono, *The Spirit of Management* (J), Japan Productivity Center Pub. Co., 2010 which pointed out that the Japanese government made a mistake in reforming the Corporation law, at the suggestion of the US government, to change the behavior patterns of Japanese entrepreneurs toward less risk-taking when more outward-looking behaviors are required in this uncertain world nowadays, and lost the precious traditional spirit of Japanese-style management. All other important references are given at the end of this chapter with a statistical appendix.

Keywords: External shocks, Plaza Accord, Asian financial crisis, Bankruptcy of Lehman Brothers, Inefficiency of banks and financial sector, Declining rate of capital formation, Technological innovations, Declining fertility rate, Insufficient funds to small and medium-sized enterprises.

---

*This was presented at the National Academy of Sciences and published in *Stability and Growth of the Korean Economy* in the new world order, RO Korea, 2011.

1. A Steady Decline of Economic Growth: 1970–2010

Table 1 summarizes the performance of Japanese economy from 1945 to the present. Postwar recovery and rapid growth continued up to 1972. Then the oil and Nixon shocks (revaluation of Yen and rapprochement with China) hit Japan. Its growth rate suddenly dropped to half 5.2% and continued down to as low as 1% now. In the 1980s, however, Japan still kept a satisfactory rate of growth as a developed economy around $15,000 per capita GDP. Then came the *Plaza Accord* in September 1985 which forced Japan to revalue the yen and ignited the so-called *bubble economy* bursting during 1991–1992.

Another challenge in the 1980s was the success of Deng Xiao-ping's reform and opening-up policies in China. The Asian financial crisis occurred in Thailand in 1997 and later spread to other countries. In 2008, came the Lehman Brothers crisis which soon spread all over the world. Thus, the steady decline of Japanese growth has been partly caused by a series of external shocks and crises originating abroad. One could still ask: if the government policies would have been appropriate, could Japan avoid the

Table 1. Periodization of Postwar Japanese Economy and Growth Rates.

No.	Sub-periods of postwar years	GDP/ population	¥/$ rate	Growth rate (%)
1	1945–1952: the Occupation Period	$380	¥360	5.0
2	1952–1960: the Reconstruction Period	$760	¥360	9.2
3	1960–1970: the Rapid Growth Period	$966	¥360	10.4
4	1970–1980: the Shock Period	$4789	¥217	5.2
5	1980–1990: Internationalization Period	$14,387	¥141	3.8
6	1990–2000: the Reform Period	$32,496	¥110	1.1
7	2000–2010: the Globalization Period	$53,581	¥85	0.65

Notes: 1. GDP per capita in $ is calculated by deflating the nominal Japanese GDP in terms of current exchange rates given in IMF *International Financial Statistics* as the mean over a decade, except for $380 is for 1948 and $760 is for 1956. Hence, they reflect the revaluation of ¥/$ rates.
2. The growth rates of real GDP are calculated as an annual average in each period from real GDPs in Japanese Yen.
Sources: S. Ichimura [4] and Appendix to this chapter.

long-term recession under such circumstances? The answer was that three domestic factors still brought down the Japanese growth.

(1) Rapid revaluation of Japanese ¥ *vis-à-vis* US$ from ¥360 to ¥77 and European currencies nearly five times or more. No other hard currency experienced such a rapid revaluation.
(2) Deflation accompanied the slow growth after the *burst of bubble* in the mid-1990s for almost 20 years.
(3) *Fertility rate* has declined rapidly and *life expectancy* became the longest in the world, making the ratio of active labor force to population the lowest in the world. Recently, the total population began to fall.

2. Changes in Growth Factors for the Lost Two Decades

For the rapidly growing period, 1945–1972, my paper: "The Challenge of the Rising Sun", in *Quadrant* (1970)[1] identified 10 factors for growth that are shown in Table 2.[2]

Table 2. Changes in Growth Factors in Pre- and Post-bubble 1990.

No	Favorable factors for rapid growth	↑↓
1	High rate of capital accumulation	↘
2	High propensity to save	→
3	Industrious, well-educated labor	↘
4	Rapid increase in agricultural productivity	↘
5	Borrowed and improved technology	↘
6	Appropriate choice of industrial composition	→
7	Capable bureaucrats cooperates with private business	→
8	Group loyalty of Japanese employees	↘
9	Banks' positive roles and close cooperation with private companies	↘
10	Political stability	↘

[1] It is reproduced as Chapter 2 in Ichimura [4].

[2] ↘ implies that the factor declined and → implies that the factor remained unchanged. Some new factors emerged as important to determine the growth path in the lost two decades. They are discussed in Section 3.

They worked in a virtuous circle before but gradually disappeared in the 1970s and later on. During the lost two decades, the same factors could no longer work as well as before. The political economy of the domestic and the international circumstances greatly changed and caused a sharp and steady decline of Japanese growth rates. The arrows in the last column of Table 2 show their direction of changes.

How the roles of these factors have changed after 1990 has been studied by many academic and government economists in Japan and abroad.[3] Some emphasized the shortage of effective demand (demand-siders), whereas others pointed out the changes in the supply side of the Japanese economy (supply-siders). We will briefly sketch the main arguments in the order of Table 2, while adding some new growth-deterrent factors that characterize the period of lost two decades and offer our tentative conclusions at the end. Table 3 sums up the changes in the conditions of growth factors and refers to the various studies on which I have based my conclusions. More specific discussions on the Asian financial crisis in 1997–1998 and on the recent world financial crisis after 2008 will be given in Chapters 3 and 4.

(1) *Low Rate of Investment*: From 1960 to 1990, the share of total capital formation in GDP was around 30%. During the lost two decades, it

Table 3. 10 Growth Factors During the Lost Two Decades.

No.	Factors	Sources
1	The low rate of capital accumulation	Horioka [3]; OECD
2	The propensity to save did not change	Horioka [3]
3	Low fertility, aging population, and shorter working hours	Saito [18]
4	Weakening of primary industries	
5	Technological innovations slow down	[2] and [11]
6	Insufficient adjustment of industrial composition to meet Chinese and Korean challenge	[2] and [3]
7	Insufficient reform of bureaucratic system and deregulation	
8	Failure in reforming private enterprises	Kagono [7]
9	Poor policies of monetary and fiscal authorities	[1], [10–15]
10	Political instability	[1] vol. I, vol. III [4]

[3]Hayashi [1] gives references to many articles in Japan and abroad.

dropped to slightly above 20%. Sometimes, the investment growth rate became *negative*. This is a cause and an effect of long recessions during the lost two decades and most conspicuous of all the factors characterizing this period. There are many reasons why this occurred.

Some of the external events have been mentioned. Certainly, the increasing uncertainty in the world political economy like the fall of Berlin Wall in September 1989 is important, but an important fact is that Japan seems to have suffered more seriously than other major countries. In the following, we will try to give some reasons.

(2) *Personal Savings*: The propensity to save remained almost unchanged before and after 1990 so that private consumption did not work to press down the growth of GDP. Its growth rate was slightly higher than GDP's.

(3) *Declining Population and Labor Supply*: The most dramatic change in recent Japan took place in the conditions of labor supply. Fundamentally, as Figure 1 shows, the fertility rate has kept dropping after 1970, and now it is 1.34 (slightly up from the bottom). Saito (2000) calculated by simulating his macroeconometric model to attribute the growth rate of GDP during 1960–1973 (9.46%) to the growth rate of population (3.76%) and the growth rate of technical progress (5.56). A decline of population and technical progress naturally explains the radical drop in GDP growth rate — an important proposition of supply-siders.[4]

(4) *Low Productivity of Primary Industries*: Agriculture, fishery, and forestry suffered from the shortage of young workers. In recent years, one can see that the precious cultivable land all over the country

[4]As for the supply side, the quality of labor is important. The nominal level of education in school years or college admission did not change much, but its quality seems to have deteriorated. About 20 years ago, the Ministry of Education lowered the standard of textbooks for mathematics, natural sciences, and other subjects at the primary schools. Although this was corrected some years ago after severe criticisms from university educators and professionals, it is believed that the effects remain for many years to come. *Training on the job* has deteriorated against good tradition of the Japanese enterprises. Moreover, in 1988, the Labor Standards Act was revised to shorten the standard labor hours per week, which reduced the performed labor hours nation-wide (from 44 to 40 hours in 1988–1993). All these elements worked in effect to reduce the TFP.

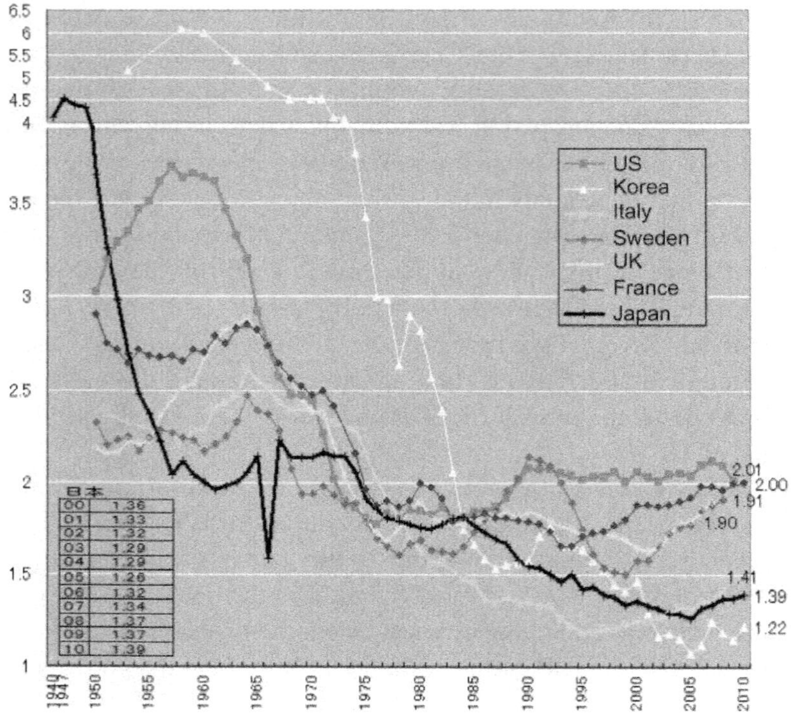

Fig. 1. The Fertility Rates of Japan and Other Countries.

Sources: Ministry of Welfare and Labor, *Special Report on Statistics of Population Dynamics*, 2001; *Statistics of Population Dynamics*, all years; Institute of Population Problems, *Sources of Population Statistics*, 2010; Korea National Statistics Office.
Note: Line colors: purple, USA; light yellow, Korea; dark yellow, Italy; blue, Sweden; light blue, UK; black, France (2.00 in 2010); bold black, Japan.

remains uncultivated simply because of the shortage of farmers. Sons and daughters of farmers went to the urban factories and did not come back. This is not only due to the income differentials between secondary–tertiary industries and the primary industry but also the too restrictive and out-of-date regulations on the use and sale of farming land and forest and protection of fishing rights.

(5) *Insufficient Technological Innovations*: No doubt, the speed of Japanese technological progress has slowed down, broadly speaking, as Japan's technology catches up with the Western technology. Various

studies of total factor productivity (TFP) in Japan show that during the recent two decades, its growth rate has declined but not as much as the first research of Hayashi–Prescott suspected. According to METI report (2002), the statistical data of Science and Technological Patents applied and obtained by Japanese experts in the US and Europe does not seem to show any significant decline, though the data in METI report are not up to date. Since the recent rate of capital accumulation is less than before, and the R&D expenditure is not increasing as much as before, it may be natural that technical progress slows down.

In addition, the 1988 revision of Labor Standards Act mentioned in No. 3 above and no significant deregulation of employment — at the time of Koizumi Cabinet, some deregulation was done — at private enterprises have caused the slower pace of TFP increase. Yet, the slower growth of effective demand could not absorb the supply of aggregate output, causing deflation throughout the lost two decades.[5]

(6) *Adjustment of Industrial Composition*: As the Japanese economy grew up, readjustment of the composition of manufacturing industries became increasingly difficult. Big ships cannot change the direction quickly. Japanese style management based on lifetime employment made it difficult to readjust the composition of employees. A study of Ken *et al.* (2002) showed that labor mobility among corporations in different industries was the hardest factor preventing the exit and entry of new firms from suiting the changing demands. Another factor was a misuse of subsidies allowing inefficient enterprises to survive. Some old enterprises losing the international comparative advantage did not dare to undertake new ventures nor go abroad.

(7) *Insufficient Bureaucracy Reforms and Privatization*: "Reforming the bureaucratic system" was a popular slogan in Japanese politics particularly after the *burst of bubble*, contrasting the appraisal of the cooperation between bureaucrats and businesses in the 1960s and the 1970s. The primary reason was the publicized failure of the powerful ministries like Ministry of Finance (MOF) in managing influential

[5]Some chapters of Vol. I of [1] deals with this issue and the resultant change of industrial composition by dynamic models and SVAR (structural vector autoregression) models. Vol. III of [1] deals similarly with the financial sector.

government banks like Long-Term Credit Bank, etc. Deregulation of the MOF control of the banks and other financial institutions was belatedly undertaken but did not improve the efficiency of the private banks and other financial institutions overnight. The only success case of privatizing public enterprises was the National Railroad Company divided into six JR (Japan Railway) regional companies. The reform of Postal Public Enterprise was undertaken by the Koizumi Cabinet, but it remains to be seen whether it can follow the JR success or not. The core resistance comes from labor unions in bureaucracy and sectionalism among the ministries.

(8) *Wrong Reforms of Japanese Style Management*: Inefficient aspects of Japanese style management have been depicted and often argued as something to improve in the globalizing world economy, as Japanese enterprises must go abroad too. T. Kagono (2010) argues, however, that the reforms having adopted the American standards straightforwardly to the Japanese corporations killed the strength of Japanese style management and made the Japanese top managers more hesitant to undertake the risky investment.

This is one of the reasons for having discouraged Japanese investment during the lost 1990s and later. In particular

(i) share-holders' lawsuit made easy;
(ii) bad timing to introduce quarterly settlement of accounts;
(iii) too detailed specification of governance in the corporation law;
(iv) hasty introduction of current price evaluation of assets and liabilities;
(v) hasty introduction of American style internal control system into the Japanese corporation's law, where they are managed with basically internal promotion and spot decisions.

These bad reforms made Japanese managers much more adverse to risk-taking than before.

(9) *Inappropriate Functioning of Banks and Other Financial Companies*: The Japanese banking system was efficient in the early postwar period up to the time of Plaza Accord in 1985, which agreed among G5 governments to rescue the twin imbalance of the US economy by increasing money supply and devaluating other major

currencies against dollars. This ignited the *bubble economy* promoted by speculation in real-estate finance in many countries, particularly Japan. Until then, the Japanese banks simply responded to the ever-increasing demand for loanable funds with deliberately lowered rate of interest. The banks were content by taking land as certain mortgage or curatorial whose prices ever kept rising. But after the burst of bubble economy, everything changed. Banks and other financial institutions were suddenly thrown into the uncertain and risky markets in the early 1990s with little knowledge nor experiences of deflation. This made them very "defensive" or hesitant to do anything bold. *Credit crunch* or just buying the government bonds became customary in financial investment.

At the same time, hasty liberalization of capital markets, especially the short-term capital market in some developing counties like Thailand or Korea, created the greedy financial speculation in some Asian countries which led to Asian financial crisis during 1997–1998 and also affected the Japanese financial sector. Symbolic was the bankruptcy of Yamaichi Securities Co., one of the major four security companies in Japan in November 1997. Data show a dramatic shrinkage of Japanese bank loans. This must have caused the radical decrease in private investment mentioned as No. 1 factor for the lost two decades.

Furthermore, the sub-prime loans problem occurred, and the Lehman Brothers holdings with more than 500 billion dollars assets filed bankruptcy in September 2008 — the worldwide financial crisis. This shattered the Japanese financial system and made them extremely hesitant in supporting the Japanese domestic and overseas investment. Some studies by Hayashi (2007) showed that the credit crunch was particularly serious to the small and medium size enterprises, much more important in Japan than abroad. This is discussed in more detail in Chapter 4.

(10) *Mismanagement of Fiscal Expenditure and Taxation*: High-ranking officials of the Ministry of Finance used to take pride in maintaining the sound fiscal policy stance and were very cautious to issue the government bonds throughout postwar years. Their mismanagement of some large government banks in the bubble years, however, made

> them lose their authority to resist the political pressure and resulted in giving the bureau of banking which controls the banking sector to the Prime Minister's Office and even changing the name of the historic Okura-sho (Ministry of Public Finance or Exchequer) to American Zaimu-sho (Ministry of Fiscal Administration). The Ministry of Finance in charge of fiscal spending and taxation simply followed the political pressure of populist government parties, one after another, as Table 4 shows, to spend as much as the parties requested with little consideration of fiscal efficiency. Political instability in the lost two decades may be contrasted against political stability in the immediately postwar Japan. Due to the failure in managing the public finance during the bubble years, the Liberal Democratic Party (LDP) lost the support of the general public, which made Japanese politics very unstable. This created uncertainty in the perspectives of entrepreneurs and made them hesitant to undertake any bold investment.

The lost 1990s began simultaneously with two dramatic events in the world: the breakdown of the Soviet Union and the *burst of bubble*. The latter is connected with the Plaza Accord in September, 1985. Then came the Asian financial crisis in 1997, and more recently the Lehman Brothers financial crisis during 2008–2009. If the Japanese government had not been suffering from the heavy fiscal debt, it would have been easy to overcome the recessions with deflation by the standard Keynesian policy with sufficient care for efficiency of fiscal policy. But the weak cabinets one after another, except for Koizumi Cabinet, could not reduce the fiscal deficit. Political instability and weak government was really behind the ineffective economic policies. Table 4 gives a brief picture of political instability in Japan in the 1990s and 2000–2010.

Even under these unfortunate experiences, there are different opinions by some great economists who maintain the more positive Keynesian type of demand-sider policies would have rescued the Japanese economy from plunging into the two decades of recessions and deflation and fiscal deficit all together. That is Klein–Adams–Kumasaka (2007) and S. Shishido *et al.* (2010). Their diagnoses are based on their respective macroeconometric models. Their works are awaiting the close examination of experts. A crucial point of implementation is that such policies must be maintained by the

Table 4. Japanese Governments and Main Events in the World.

Year/	Cabinet	Monetary policies	Fiscal policies	Political events
1990	/2 Kaifu	/3 off.d.r. raised /8 off.d.r. raised	/4 budget not depend on gov. bonds /6 public investment plan	
1991	/11 Miyazawa	/7 off.d.r. lowered /11 off.d.r. lowered /12 off.d.r. lowered	/9 emergency economic policy	/1 Gulf War
1992		/4 off.d.r. lowered /7 off.d.r. lowered	/2 comprehensive economic policy	
1993	/8 Hosokawa	/9 off.d.r. lowered	/9 emergency policy for \ revalued	/11 Maastricht Treaty for EU effected
1994	/4 Hata /7Murayama			/3 New Election L /12 Shinshin Party born
1995		/4 off.d.r. lowered /9 off.d.r. lowered	/5 budget for dissolution, bad house-loan	/2 (Hanshin Earthquake)
1996	/1 Hasimoto		/4 consumption tax raised	/9 Democratic Party born
1997		/11 big bank crisis	/5 budget reform law /12 *ibid.* suspended	/7 Asian financial Crisis /12 Shinshin Party dissolution
1998	/7 Obuchi			
1999		/2 zero interest policy		/1 Euro born
2000	/4 Mori	/8 zero interest policy stops	/4 nursing system	
2001	/4 Koizumi	/3 quant.easing pol.	/1 enterprise management reform	
2002			/12 privatization of 4 highway public corporations /4 Tax reduction; 3/4 Postal Public Corp. Established	
2003				/4 (Liberal Party + Democratic Party)
2004				
2005/				
2006	/6 Abe			
2007	/8 Fukuda			
2008	/9 Aso	quant.easing pol.		US financial crisis
2009	/9Hatoyama	quant.easing pol.		
2010	/6 Kan	quant.easing pol.		
2011	/8 Noda	quant.easing pol.		/3 (Tohoku earthq.)
2012	/12 Abe (2nd			

Note: off. d.r. = official discount rate of BOJ.
quant. easing pol. = quantitative easing policy.

strongly supported governments. Otherwise, the so-called "stop and go" policies can never bear fruits even if the policies are theoretically correct. It is true that the Japanese fiscal debt in terms of total government debt to nominal GDP ratio is the highest in the world, but its annual debt burden is not as high as in the US and much lower than the UK. Thus, this kind of policy can still be experimented under the strongly supported government.

References

[1] Hayashi, F. (ed.) (2007 J). *Positive Analysis and Design of Economic Institutions*, Vols. I, II, III, Keiso Shobo.
[2] Hayashi, F. and E. C. Prescott (2002). "The 1990s in Japan," *Review of Economic Dynamics.*
[3] Horioka, C. Y. (2007). *The Reasons for Stagnant Consumption (J)*, Chap. 1 in Hayashi, F. [11], Vol. I.
[4] Ichimura, S. (1998). *Political Economy of Japanese and Asian Development*, Springer-Verlag. Berlin-NY-Tokyo.
[5] Ichimura, S. (2003). *A Postmortem Diagnosis of Asian Financial Crisis (J)*, Chap. 16 in Ichimura, S. [3].
[6] Ichimura, S. (2003). *Political Economy of Japanese and Asian Development (J)*, Sobunsha, Tokyo.
[7] Ichimura, S. *et al.* (2009). *Transition from Socialist to Market Economies*, Palgrave-McMillan, London.
[8] Ichimura, S. (2009). "Who are responsible for World Financial Crisis?" *The Yaguchi Bank Monthly Report*, /jan.
[9] Ichimura, S. and L. R. Klein (ed.) (2010). *Macroeconometric Modeling of Japan*, WSPC, Singapore.
[10] Kagono, T. (2010). *The Spirit of Management* (*J*), JPC Press, Tokyo.
[11] Ken, K. *et al.* (2002). Why did the growth of TFP stagnate during the 90s? (*J*) in Hayashi, F. [1], Vol. I.
[12] Klein, L. R., F. G. Adams, Y. Kumasaka, and A. Shinozaki (2007). *Accelerating Japan's Economic Growth: Resolving Japan's Growth Controversy*, Routledge, NY.
[13] Lowenstein, R. (2000). *When Genius Failed*, McLante Jackson, NY.
[14] METI (2002). Report on R&D in Japanese Industries (*J*), METI.
[15] Miwa, Y. (2011/1). "A Study of Financing Behavior of Japanese Firms with Firm-Level Data from *Corporate Enterprise Quarterly Statistics* 1994–2009: Introduction and Summary," CARF-F-241.

[16] Miwa, Y. (2011/7). "Are Japanese Firms Becoming More Independent of Their Banks? Evidence from the Firm-Level Data of the Corporate Enterprise Quarterly Statistics, 1994–2009," CARF-F-251.

[17] Miyagawa, T. *et al* (2007) Japanese Productivity and Business Cycles, in Hayashi, F. [11], Vol. I.

[18] Saito, M. (2000). *The Japanese Economy*, Singapore, WSPC, Singapore.

[19] Shishido, S. *et al.* (2010). Policy Alternatives for Japan toward 2020, in [6].

[20] Ueda, K. (2010/10). "Japan's Deflation and the Bank of Japan's Experience with non-traditional Monetary Policy," CARF-F235.

[21] Ueda, K. (2010/11). "Japan's Bubble, America's Bubble and China's Bubble," CARF-F-236/.

Notes: 1. (*J*) means that the publication is in Japanese; 2. CARF is working paper series of University of Tokyo; 3. METI is Ministry of Economy, Trade and Industry.

Appendix: Main Indices of Japanese Economy: 1980–2010

	Growth rate Cabinet %	Real GDP Office billion \	Nominal GDP Cabinet billion \	Exports customs MOF million \	Imports customs MOF million \	Exp.pr. I ¥base BOJ 05 = 100	Imp. Pr. I ¥base BOJ 05 = 100
1980	(3.97)	287,367	248,376	30,058,827	31,477,107	164.7	171.9
1981	(3.15)	298,687	264,642	34,361,528	32,244,575	172.1	181
1982	(3.54)	308,057	276,163	34,068,189	31,762,189	173.4	190.9
1983	(4.77)	318,922	288,773	36,128,954	30,601,496	164.7	173.3
1984	(6.26)	334,111	308,238	41,184,358	32,661,254	168.2	172.2
1985	(1.92)	355,096	330,397	40,731,162	29,079,739	157.1	155.4
1986	(6.08)	361,807	342,266	34,576,395	20,174,729	136.3	97.4
1987	(6.41)	383,873	362,297	33,067,902	22,466,258	130.1	97
1988	(4.58)	408,446	387,686	34,930,866	24,834,121	129.8	93.5
1989	(6.20)	427,115	415,885	38,882,994	30,404,170	137.2	103.6
1990	(2.34)	453,604	451,683	41,874,991	34,171,137	135.3	108.9
1991	(0.71)	464,210	473,608	42,696,582	30,970,420	128.8	97.3
1992	(−0.49)	467,519	483,256	43,052,879	29,225,046	124	93.2
1993	(1.50)	465,277	482,608	39,613,246	26,449,918	114	81.6
1994	(2.29)	472,249	489,379	40,750,346	28,988,814	111	80.3
1995	(2.88)	483,023	497,740	42,069,433	32,952,957	111.4	80.4
1996	(−0.02)	496,935	509,096	46,040,586	39,671,660	115.5	90.2
1997	(−1.49)	496,836	513,613	51,411,190	39,961,469	117.2	92.4

(*Continued*)

(*Continued*)

	Growth rate Cabinet %	Real GDP Office billion \	Nominal GDP Cabinet billion \	Exports customs MOF million \	Imports customs MOF million \	Exp.pr. I ¥base BOJ 05 = 100	Imp. Pr. I ¥base BOJ 05 = 100
1998	(0.74)	489,460	503,324	49,449,349	35,393,751	116.1	86.3
1999	(2.56)	493,049	499,544	48,547,649	36,451,616	105.3	82.2
2000	(−0.80)	505,622	504,119	52,045,240	42,449,369	102.5	85.6
2001	(1.20)	501,618	493,645	48,592,792	41,509,071	105.3	86.5
2002	(2.11)	507,015	489,875	52,727,106	43,067,102	102	85.7
2003	(1.80)	517,713	493,748	56,060,293	44,855,182	98.5	84.2
2004	(2.29)	527,980	498,491	61,719,417	50,385,782	98.5	90.3
2005	(2.30)	540,025	503,187	68,290,157	60,511,292	100.8	104.5
2006	(−1.79)	562,302	510,938	77,460,587	68,447,345	104	115.7
2007	(−3.78)	552,474	515,644	85,113,382	74,958,075	103.8	124.9
2008	(−1.81)	541,017	494,183	71,145,592	71,910,444	96.1	125.4
2009	(1.37)	531,204	476,412	59,012,561	53,780,653	88.7	101.5
2010	(−2.20)	538.500	475.800			88.8	107.1

Note: The figures in 2010 are from different sources due to the change of base year then.

CPI M.T Aff 2005 = 100	**WPI** BOJ 2005 = 100	Monthly average Inter-bank exchange rate BOJ ¥/$	Tokyo Exch. Nikkei monthly average Nikkei ¥	Tokyo Exch. index Sec. I Tokyo Exch. 1968 · 1/4 = 100	Year
78.1	117.7	217.25	6999.0	485.61	1980
81.3	117.9	227.52	7599.1	564.22	1981
83.3	118.2	249.64	7531.1	556.98	1982
84.9	117.4	236.33	9323	694.64	1983
86.8	117.7	244.19	11,061	858.99	1984
88.4	115.7	221.09	12,935	1030.0	1985
88.4	109.6	159.83	18,032	1488.8	1986
88.9	107.7	138.33	24,195	2014.4	1987
89.5	107.1	128.27	28,865	2248.8	1988
92.1	109.9	142.82	34,968	2611.6	1989
95.0	111.3	141.29	26,872	1989.6	1990
97.7	111.8	133.18	23,350	1769.5	1991
99.2	110.6	124.8	17,189	1302.4	1992

(*Continued*)

(*Continued*)

CPI M.T Aff 2005 = 100	**WPI** BOJ 2005 = 100	Monthly average Inter-bank exchange rate BOJ ¥/$	Tokyo Exch. Nikkei monthly average Nikkei ¥	Tokyo Exch. index Sec. I Tokyo Exch. 1968 · 1/4 = 100	Year
100.5	108.7	107.84	19,641	1590.2	1993
100.9	107.2	99.39	19,509	1555.3	1994
100.6	106.1	96.45	18,029	1427.0	1995
101.0	104.5	112.65	20,518	1553.7	1996
103.1	105.5	122.7	17,923	1362.1	1997
103.3	103.3	128.02	14,848	1148.5	1998
102.8	102.5	111.54	18,041	1522.6	1999
102.1	101.9	110.52	15,597	1442.5	2000
101.1	99.4	125.13	11,439	1133.9	2001
100.5	97.7	121.9	9581.9	932.3	2002
100.3	97.2	113.03	9944.4	980.8	2003
100.3	98.8	107.49	11,315	1139.5	2004
100.0	100.5	113.26	13,565	1392.1	2005
100.2	102.5	116.94	16,415	1644.4	2006
100.6	104.9	114.2	15,968	1555.7	2007
101.7	108.2	100.46	10,802	1057.4	2008
100.0	102.6	92.8	9974.3	904.27	2009

Chapter 3

A Postmortem Diagnosis of Asian Financial Crisis*

1. A Series of Financial Crises

There have been a number of financial crises in the world ever since the post-World War II reconstruction was over in the 1970s. The main ones are as follows:

(1) The two oil crises in the 1970s and the subsequent financial crises mainly in Latin American countries.
(2) 1979 debt crisis in Poland.
(3) The mid-1980s crises for Savings and Loans Associations in the US.
(4) 1994 Mexican financial crisis.
(5) The early 1990s burst of the bubble economy in Japan.
(6) 1997 financial crisis in East Asian countries.
(7) 1998 financial crisis in Russia.
(8) 1998 financial crisis in Brazil.
(9) 1998 bankruptcy of Long Term Credit Management (LTCM) in New York.

In light of not only observations in East Asia but also the experiences of countries all over the world, a re-examination of the financial crises must be made.

*References of Chapters 2 and 3 are the same as those in Chapter 1. This chapter is a modified version of Chapter 16 in Ichimura (2003) which is not included in English version: Ichimura (1998).

Table 1. Diagnosis Tableau of Financial Crises.

Symptoms to observe	J	K	T	Ph	HK	Th	M	S	In	C	US
1. Real estate price inflation	*X*	*X*	∇	*X*	*X*	*X*	∇	∇	∇	∇	∇
2. Stock prices inflation	*X*	*X*	∇	*X*	*X*	*X*	∇	∇	∇	∇	∇
3. Flexible exchange rate	*O*	∇	∇	∇	*X*	*X*	∇	∇	∇	*X*	*O*
4. Appropriate exchange rate	*O*	∇	∇	∇	*X*	*X*	∇	∇	∇	*X*	*O*
5. Foreign debt	*O*	*X*	*O*	∇	*O*	*X*	*X*	∇	*X*	∇	*X*
6. Short-term debt	*O*	*X*	*O*	∇	*O*	*X*	∇	*O*	*X*	*O*	∇
7. Monitoring foreign debt	*O*	*X*	*O*	∇	*X*	*X*	∇	*O*	*X*	∇	∇
8. Capital transaction control	*X*	*X*	∇	∇	*X*	*X*	∇	*O*	*X*	*O*	*X*
9. Excessive gov. guarantee	*O*	*X*	*O*	*O*	*O*	*X*	∇	*O*	*X*	*O*	*O*
10. Ample foreign exch. reserve	*O*	*X*	*O*	∇	*O*	*X*	∇	*O*	*X*	*O*	*O*
11. Conservative bank manage.	*X*	*X*	∇	∇	*O*	*X*	∇	*O*	*X*	∇	∇
12. Good corporate governance	∇	*X*	∇	∇	*X*	*X*	∇	*O*	*X*	∇	∇
13. Corruption (politicians, bureaucrats, & business)	∇	*X*	∇	*X*	*X*	*X*	∇	*O*	*X*	∇	∇
14. Sound fiscal management	*X*	∇	∇	∇	*X*	*O*	∇	*O*	∇	∇	*O*
15 Sound monetary policy	∇	∇	*O*	∇	*O*	*X*	∇	∇	∇	∇	*O*
16. Overall evaluation	−2	10	−7	2	3	13	1	−9	9	−2	−4

2. Diagnosis Tableau of East Asian Financial Crises

In order to carefully observe and comparatively examine the various experiences of financial crises in different countries, the tableau, Table 1 may be useful.

Overall evaluation is mechanically made by giving -1 to ∇, $+1$ to X, and 0 to O. I gave the scores in Table 1 by my own judgment around the time of crises in each country, mostly in the late 1990s. The higher the score is, the more likely the financial crisis is to occur in the country. Interpretation of this table requires some explanation.

Most symptoms on the list would be understandable, but some items like capital transaction control may not be straightforward in its implication for financial crisis. In advanced economies like the US and Japan there is no control of capital transaction. In Taiwan, Singapore, or China, however, control of capital transaction is very strict. This has helped them avoid the financial crises, so that the scores must be given more carefully. Nevertheless, my given scores based on these symptoms seem overall to demonstrate which countries were more likely to encounter the financial crises.

Clearly, Thailand faces the largest danger of financial crisis, and then follows Korea and Indonesia. In fact, financial crises did not occur in all the countries or areas in East Asia in the late 1990s. There are significant differences in the degree of exposure to financial crisis among the East Asian countries and areas. Thailand, Korea and Indonesia encountered the most serious crises for the good reasons.

3. The External Debt Situations in Korea, Indonesia and Thailand

The most important in Table 2a is the external debt situations of the critical three countries in East Asia. Table 2a shows the situations. This was then the most reliable up-to-date information available to outsiders.

Table 2a. External Debt of Korea, Indonesia and Thailand (Units: billion $, %).

	Korea			Indonesia			Thailand		
External debt	1997	1998	1999	1997	1998	1999	1997	1998	1999
— long-term	159.2	148.7	1364*	136.2	150.9	—	93.7	86.2	75.6
— public	95.7	118.0	98.3*	100.3	121.7	—	56.5	59.4	61.9
— private	—	—	—	55.9	66.9	—	22.3	28.1	23.6
— short-term	—	—	—	44.5	54.7	—	34.1	31.3	25.5
(GDP)	63.6	30.7	38.1*	32.9	20.1	—	34.8	23.5	13.7
External debt/GDP	476.5	320.7	414.5	215.7	94.2	141.7	150.6	112.2	126.3
— long-term	33.41	46.36	32.91	63.12	160.24	—	62.23	76.77	59.83
— public	20.08	36.79	23.72	46.51	129.22	—	37.49	52.93	49.01
— private	—	—	—	25.90	71.10	—	14.82	25.05	18.67
— short-term	—	—	—	20.61	58.12	—	22.67	27.88	20.19
	13.35	9.57	9.19	15.23	21.36	—	23.13	20.96	10.83

Notes: 1. GDP in 1999 is calculated by assuming our projected growth rates: Korea (8.5%), Indonesia (0.0%), and Thailand (4.0%) for their own real income in terms of its own currency unit. 2. Figures with * are preliminary. 3. The External Debt of Korea on the basis of World Bank (WB) and Asian Development Bank (ADB) may be extrapolated by the rate of change in Ministry of Finance and Economy (MOFE). It is the one in Table 2b.
Sources: Korea (MOFE, http//epic.kdi.re.kr); Indonesia (ADB, WB); Thailand (ADB, http//www.bot.r.th); ADB: key indicators; GDP: ICSEAD (2000); WB: Global Development Finance.

Table 2b. External Debt (Units: billion $, %).

	WB base			MOFE base		
	1997	1998	1999	1997	1998	1999
External debt	137.0	139.1	127.6	159.2	148.7	136.4
— long-term	72.1	94.1	—	95.7	118.0	98.3
— public	33.9	58.0	—	—	—	—
— private	38.3	36.1	—	—	—	—
—short-term	53.8	28.1	34.9	63.6	30.7	38.1
(GDP)	476.5	320.7	414.5	476.5	320.7	414.5
External debt/GDP	28.75	43.37	30.8	73.79	46.36	32.91
— long term	15.14	29.33	—	44.36	36.79	23.72
— public	7.10	18.07	—	—	—	—
— private	8.03	11.26	—	—	—	—
— short-term	11.29	8.770	8.43	13.35	9.57	9.19

4. Lessons from the Financial Crises

Thus, we are able to draw some lessons from the financial crises in East Asia and other countries. Main lessons are as follows:

(1) Pay attention to the competition and complementarity between China and other East Asian economies.
(2) Do not forget the business cycles in the East Asian economies.
(3) Over-valuation of its currency *vis a vis* main trade partners' currencies is dangerous.
(4) Watch the debt service ratio. If it does not go below 30% for many years, such growth rates are not sustainable.
(5) Sudden surge in the inflow of short-term capital funds is a red signal.
(6) The extraordinary increase of real estate values is a symptom of financial crisis.
(7) The hyper-inflationary increase of stock prices due to speculation is a symptom of financial crisis. Similarly, the steady decline of stock prices is also a symptom of financial crisis.
(8) Financial crisis will hit most seriously the greedy, mismanaged banks and enterprises with poor corporate governance, particularly in assets and liabilities management.

(9) Financial crises are usually related to the corruption connecting politicians, bureaucrats and executives. Conversely, if corruption remains moderate, serious financial crises are unlikely to take place.
(10) Excessive guarantees of the government and the central banks without adequate backup of foreign exchange reserve often aggravate the crises and create the country risks.
(11) The so-called "Washington Consensus" was not necessarily the best diagnosis of the critical conditions in most East Asian economies. Their analytical capability and policy suggestions have limitations.[1]
(12) The objections of the US government and the international financial institutions to the increase of the capital funds have turned out to be inadequate. This requires the further consideration as follows:

    1. What is most urgently needed and very important in all the countries is the reform of regulations and institutions to require the strict monitoring of all the important financial transactions of the banks and financial corporations.
    2. Such re-regulations or de-regulations and reorganization of financial institutions and activities are needed not only domestically but also internationally.

5. Reform of International Financial Organizations

Half a century has passed since the Bretton Woods system was established. As we discussed at the beginning, many financial crises have occurred in the world. Every time, the International Monetary Fund (IMF) and the World Bank moved to overcome those crises. Their policy prescriptions were based on the "Washington Consensus", which were not necessarily adequate in all the cases or unfairly implemented in many cases. For instance,

(1) The IMF experts did not understand the underlying problems of East Asian economies. For instance, just before 1997 crisis, they said that Indonesia was an ideal borrower.

---

[1]Criticisms on "Washington Consensus" were repeated later when Central European countries faced the financial crises in transition from socialist to market economies. See Ichimura *et al* (2009).

(2) The policies implemented in Thailand and Korea were based on the "Washington Consensus" and could have been free from grievous faults, but those in Indonesia were quite inadequate in demanding the cut of subsidies to kerosene oil and food as well as stopping the loans to many small enterprises. Such policies forced the bankruptcy of many enterprises in the country where no bankruptcy law existed. After all, those policies had to be greatly remedied later.

(3) On the other hand, Malaysia could overcome the crisis with neither any help nor advice from the IMF.

(4) The rescue plan for Russia was determined with no regard to the "Washington Consensus". It was simply a political decision. Who are responsible for such a decision may be questioned.

(5) The US government was against the monitoring of international financial transactions by "hedge funds" and other credit funds, but after the bankruptcy of LTCM,[2] it seems to have changed its position.

(6) Clearly, some international regulations are needed, particularly from the viewpoint of small economies, to monitor and regulate the large amount of capital transaction into and out of the less developed countries (LDC).

In other words, problematic is the monopolistic position of the World Bank and the IMF combined in dealing with the financial crises in any place of the world. As the World Bank is supplemented by the Asian Development Bank and other regional development banks, so does the IMF need to be supplemented by the regional monetary funds. Now, three specific problems are important with them.

1. Both the World Bank and the IMF have insufficient funds to cope with the serious financial crises in the contemporary world. This has been recognized by the authorities of the Bank and the Fund, but it was the US government and the US Congress that have been consistently against the increase of capital in both organizations. In handling, the East Asian financial crises the amount of loans extended to the suffering countries from the IMF did not exceed

[2]This important event is relatively unknown abroad due to the control of information by New York Federal Reserve Bank (NY FRB). However, this is very closely related to the World Financial Crisis in 2008.

one quarter of the total loans to almost all the countries. The main supplier of the loans was the Japanese Overseas Cooperation Bank. The US government pledged a certain amount but never implemented it.

2. The Funds officials visit but stay in the region at best for a few years. It would be impossible for those from Washington DC to learn the socio-economic conditions in so many developing countries in Asia in a few years. Hence, the Funds must be supplemented by a regional monetary fund like ADB for WB.

(7) The Japanese government proposed soon after the financial crisis in Thailand in 1997 to establish an Asian Monetary Fund, but it was the US government that flatly refused even to consider it. Later on, however, when a similar idea was proposed as an informal Miyazawa initiative, all the governments concerned including the US supported it. Again later, the US government as well as Chinese and other Asian countries supported the mutual agreement to accommodate the necessary funds among Asian economies at the time of crises.

What is needed now is the reform of the international financial institutions and to devise the adequate regulations and institutions to handle the globalized international economy. The establishment of EU and Euro has given an impact to reorganize the world economy. It is moving toward the Tripartite world; namely, the American continent, the European hemisphere, and the Asian world. How to manage them is one of the great tasks of the world organizations. The first step will be to establish some regional financial organization capable of handling the kind of financial crises we just had in the past decade.

Chapter 4

Who are Responsible for the World Financial Crisis in 2008?

1. Wrong US Policies[1]

Now (mid-2008) the world economy seems to be at an entrance to the "Great Depression". If any serious mistakes are made in economic policies, the "Great Depression" like the one in the 1930s may come again. Many excellent studies on the "Great Depression" are available to learn from history. More recently the Japanese economy has just experienced the miserable recessions mainly due to the burst of the bubble economy in the early 1990s. Therefore, if we have learnt the lessons from the experiences and adopt the appropriate policies, we should be able to overcome the recessions in a year and half to two years. Similar to the US and Europe, many outstanding economists and financial experts are there too. Yet they are repeating the same kinds of blunders over and over again. Why couldn't they anticipate the serious recessions to aggravate so much and take appropriate policy measures? One could not be too optimistic about the future if we had to extrapolate this past stupid repetition of mistakes. One could ask; who are really responsible for this World Financial Crisis in 2008?

Postponing the detailed discussions, I state my frank conclusions first. Exposition follows later. The heaviest responsibility lies on the three bodies:

(1) The US government's "super-optimism" on the US economy,
(2) Credit Rating Agents fraudulently rating securities and derivatives,
(3) Investment banks' speculation with extreme leverage ratios.

---

[1]This is a revised version of my essay in Japanese published in the *Yamaguchi Bank Monthly*, January 2009 but it was written in mid-2008 and privately circulated to bankers and politicians earlier.

2. Why was the World Financial Crisis not Anticipated?

Was it so difficult to anticipate the 2008 World Financial Crisis? Of course not. Inflation of real estate prices has been continuing since a few years before. The same was true in Europe. Particularly in big cities like London, Paris, etc., it was very conspicuous. Many economists as well as journalists had already observed the burst of bubble in Japan in the early 1990s and Asian Financial Crisis in Thailand in 1997. So many experts warned against the burst of bubble economy. However, no government in any country took any stern action against it. Why? The circumstances are just the same as the one in Japan in the late 1980s. Everyone knows that it cannot go on, but while one believes that nothing will happen a few more months, suddenly the end comes.

Inflation in real estate price stimulates the demand for and investment in housing and thereby prolongs prosperity. The US government at war needed a continuation of booms so that it stimulated housing investment by tax reduction for housing loans. These tax exemption policies stimulated housing investment and maintained prosperity longer and kept the US growth rate higher than usual for the time being.

3. Tricks of Sub-Prime Loans

The financial crisis this time was ignited by the sub-prime loans. It looks like a kind of low interest-rate loan for housing. Actually the low interest charge is only for the beginning few years. After the initial period, the interest rate becomes normal and repayment of principal begins. If inflation of real estate goes on, one could get the house only with the low payment at the beginning and sell the house before the higher payment starts. But if inflation stops and house prices come down, then many buyers cannot continue to repay the higher monthly payments and the loans become unpaid. Many banks faced an enormous amount of unpaid loans with low value mortgages and bankrupted. Mr. Greenspan, an outstanding former chairman of the Federal Reserve Bank (FRB), admitted at the Congress hearing on this issue that the practice of this kind of loans extended widely without any prudent examination or checking, was a serious mistake and failure of the FRB. This really resembles with the cases of Japanese commercial banks at the time of bubble years.

4. Fraudulent Rating of Credit Rating Agencies

The World Financial Crisis this time is much more serious than the burst of the bubble economy in Japan in the early 1990s. If the US government had not given the government loans to private banks, insurance companies, and security companies at all, then almost all the famous financial companies in the US — as some say, except for Wells Fargo Bank — would have bankrupted. In the case of Japan, many banks and security companies would have bankrupted too, but the main ones like Mitsubishi, Sumitomo, and Nomura would have survived. European banks would have faced the situations closer to the US. Perhaps, however, the situations might have been more serious than in the US.

There are some significant differences between Japanese financial institutions and US–European institutions. The first difference is that almost no "derivatives" are dealt within Japan. The second is that the banks' "leverage ratio" is far lower in Japan than in the US or Europe.

The most problematic is "derivatives". A few decades ago dealing with the real estate by securitization began. Then the object of investment was clear. One of initiators was Professor Edwin Mills, now at Northwestern University. Then began dealing with a combination of some securities. Such securities were devised as a new security and put on the market. Then again a combination of such combined securities was marketed as "derivatives". By combining some securities, it was argued, one could reduce the risks involved. It was believed that risks would be further reduced by combining the combined securities so that they carried even higher rating than the original components, according to the rating given by credit-rating agencies. But nobody knows what they have bought or sold. Even professionals were actually cheated by the dealings of "derivatives". Then the so-called credit-rating agencies like Moody or Standard & Poor's have appeared. They gave their ranks to each kind of security like AAA or AA, etc. Customers trusted their ranking and bought the securities and derivatives. But during the crisis, almost all securities including AAA dropped the values. Responsibility of grading companies is extremely important, but they take no responsibility. In other words, their rating has turned out to be utterly unreliable. They never specifically announced or publicized the reasons for their ranking. The most fundamental reason of the crisis this time lies in this point.

To perceive this danger would not have been too difficult, because we have already known the case of Long Term Credit Management (LTCM) taking place earlier for almost the same reason. In Japan, a famous mathematician and essayist Masashi Fujiwara pointed out the Genius' erroneous calculation in his famous book: *Nobility of Nations* earlier.

5. Why did the Financial Crisis Spread to Europe?

Further discussions on some other reasons for financial crisis in the US will be omitted here. But another important aspect is that it spread quickly to Europe and caused more serious crises in some countries like Iceland. The reason is that even major banks in UK, France, Germany and Switzerland relied heavily on the borrowing for their loans. This is the same as in the case of Lehman Brothers. It is demonstrated by their leverage ratio (total loans to own capital ratio). The ratios of European banks were almost twice as high as American banks, as the Table 1 from *Fortune* magazine shows.

European banks relied on the borrowed funds about half for loans, whereas American banks did the same about 30% or less. Hence, the damage from the fall of derivatives value was much more serious to European banks than American banks. The reasons why European banks invested so much in the "derivatives" in the US was their high rates of return that was made possible by the continued prosperity of the US economy. It was mainly due to the short-term success of the US government's stimulating cyclic policies. Given the triple dilemma of the low rate of saving, fiscal deficit, and trade imbalance, however, it is inconceivable for the US economy to maintain the 4% growth rate any longer.

6. Failures in American Economic Policies and their Future

Business cycles are unavoidable in the US economy. It was wrong on the part of the US government to have ignored such historic facts with unrealistic

Table 1. Leverage Ratios: (Each Bank's Loans)/(Own Capital).

Barclays Bank	61.1	Bank of America	11.1
Deutsche Bank	53.1	Goldman Sacks	26.1
ING group	49.1	Lehman Brothers	31.1
UBS	47.1		

super-optimism. Some journalistic columnists blame the "market fundamentalism", but it is not right. There is no theory or fundamental preaching in economics to say that market solves the vicissitudes of business cycles by market mechanism. What were wrong were the economic policies of the government and the FRB. More concretely the excessive stimulus given to housing investment and loans plus the lack of supervision of those policies on the part of the government authorities and the FRB. On this score, the responsible advisers in the Bush administration were too simplistic. In the middle part of September 2008 there was a general meeting of the Mont Perlin Society in Tokyo, in which I had a chance to raise this question to the chairman of the Committee of Economic Advisers, Dr. Edward P. Lazear. I asked him, "As I believe, there is an excessive financing leading to the speculative investment in housing loans in the US. Don't you think that some restrictive regulations are needed on financing such speculative investments?" He flatly answered, "No, I don't agree with you". After the session, I had some further talks with him, but he had no recognition of the danger to show up in the US then. It is very clear, however, that he must have changed his opinions by now if he supports the later views of Secretary of Finance and the chairman of FRB. Changes in the American policies were at least too late by a year and half or two years. They changed the policies only after the bankruptcy of Lehman Brothers and the consequent fall of stock prices. But too late were the policy changes in Europe and Japan as well. In October 2008 the President of the US called for an international conference with 20 major nations' government representatives and put on the table 16 proposals and an action plan, including the reform of the International Monetary Fund (IMF) to increase its funds. Most of the proposals are appropriate but belatedly proposed. How much of them and how soon they will be implemented is crucial. If not implemented soon, the world may face more serious recessions like the "Great Depression" in the 1930s again.

Chapter 5

Policies for Aging Population with Declining Fertility Rate*

1. Policies for Aging Society with Declining Fertility Rate

1.1. *Committee for Aging and Few Children*

Japanese population is rapidly aging. As the consequences, various social problems attract people's attention in many areas in the country. To cope with such situations, the central and local governments have organized their own "Committees for Aging and Few Children" and tried to prepare the policies to overcome the problems. This paper outlines some basic ideas proposed at a committee I chaired in Kitakyushu city, Japan. These proposals may be applicable not only at different districts in Japan but also abroad. I must add, however, that such committees to tackle with demographic problems will soon face also the other equally important social problems such as juvenile delinquency, breakdown of family-home, family discords, domestic violence, etc. Hence, the policies to cope with the aging population with declining fertility must be carefully designed not to cause the deterioration in the other problems. Besides, the demographic trends are prevalent almost all over the world so that we must be prepared for tackling very tough problems to fight against such global trends. Clearly, we are dealing with the most fundamental issues of family-households and communities in our age.

---

*This chapter consists of two parts. The first section is taken from Ichimura [4] and my contribution to Ichimura and Shimizutani [6]. The second section is my comments on the three articles presented at the IUSSP International Convention in Pusan in 2013 quoted as [1], [2] and [3] in References. All three dealed with the fertility decline in Korea. The papers will be available at the Pusan Population Institute.

On the global population problems, many research projects are internationally organized. One of such research outcomes in Japan is [5].

1.2. *Community Center to Cope with Declining Fertility Rate*

What is most directly affecting the demographic trend in Japan is the low marriage percentage of childbearing age women. The average number of children among married couples is 2.2 as of year 2013, though the ideal number is regarded as 2.6. The actual reproduction rate of women is slightly above 1.4 as of year 2013. This implies that only as low as 63% of childbearing age women are actually married and bearing children. In Japan, the babies are hardly born by the unmarried women.

This is interpreted that the social customs of the old Japanese society have not been functioning in arranging the meeting opportunities for young couples nor the new social customs have emerged yet.

Moreover, married couples have a small number of children. This may be caused by the pessimistic prospect of their own living in Japan or the Japanese economy as such. Since the 1990s, rather pessimistic future prospects have prevailed in daily newspapers or TVs. Such perspectives have become prevalent in all aspects of social life in the recent years. Unless such pessimism is taken over by optimism after the current stagnation is over, the young married couples will not have more than two children. There does not seem to be any good reason to be pessimistic for Japan in the 21st century.

In the city called Kitakyushu in Japan, the mayor has been trying under such circumstances to overcome the pessimistic views and initiate a very successful community building by establishing a "Community Center" in each school district. The Municipal Office has offered the counseling services to the families in the city at three levels:

1. "Social Welfare Center" at each school district.
2. "Social Welfare Office" in each county.
3. "Bureau of Social Welfare" in the city office.

They have been offering the various services, including the ones of nursing facilities, library and other facilities for children and so on. The so-called "three layers of social welfare" became known as "Kitakyushu Formulas". Many volunteers participated in the program and made this undertaking succeed particularly for the old persons. The City expanded its functions and facilities to the issues of fewer children next year. Then,

Table 1. Polices for Declining Fertility and the Aging Societies.

Problem (1)	Weakening in the wishes to marry
Acting agents	1. School teachers. 2. Social education. 3. Mass media. 4. Public organizations.
Ideas of policies	1. To give the chances of learning the love, happiness and importance of marriage, family and bringing up children. 2. To educate the human relations among individuals, families, and in the communities and the nation. 3. To let the youth think of the entire life including the old age.
Policies	1. Increases the chances of learning such ideas. 2. Prepare good texts and manuals. 3. Give the youth the chances to contact babies and children.
Note:	Key is to recognize the importance of family bondage.
Problem (2)	**Increase in unmarried youth and decrease in late marriage**
Acting agents	1. Hotels, enterprises, and non-profit organizations. 2. High schools and universities. 3. Social organizations.
Policy ideas	Increase the opportunities for young couples to meet.
Policies	1. Participation of young boys and girls in various events. 2. Events as businesses.
Problem (3)	**Infertility**
Acting agents	1. Hospitals and clinics. 2. Welfare organizations. 3. Municipal offices.
Policy ideas	1. Disseminate the medical information. 2. Subsidize the medical care.
Policies	1. Early medical care. 2. Subsidies for medical expenses.
Problem (4)	**Small number of children born and brought up**
Acting agents	1. Municipal welfare centers. 2. Volunteer organizations. 3. Schools. 4. Public organizations.

(*Continued*)

Table 1. (*Continued*)

Problem (4)	Small number of children born and brought up
Policy ideas	1. The same as (1). 2. Reduce the burden to bring up children. 3. Increase the chances of enjoying the child-care. 4. Housing for bigger families. 5. Counseling for child-raising families.
Policies	1. Establish counseling centers for child-bearing and nursing. 2. Foster the good counselors. 3. Good manuals and its revision. 4. Improve the facilities to make child-nursing easier. 5. Improve the facilities for the handy-capped. 6. Better facilities for pregnant and postpartum mothers.
Note:	Overcome selfishness and have sense of security.
Problem (5)	Social care for the old
Acting agents	1. Municipal welfare centers. 2. Enterprise associations. 3. Volunteer organizations.
Policy ideas	1. Improve social network and facilities for the old and its practical use. 2. More efforts of enterprises to improve the better working conditions for women with children. 3. Improvement of the holidays for child-bearing and fostering.
Policies	1. Improve municipal welfare centers and disseminate their service information. 2. Enterprises and unions must regard the cooperative living of couples as their new social obligations.
Note:	Importance of enterprises' decisions.
Problem (6)	Social reform
Agents	1. Central and local governments. 2. Enterprises. 3. Venture businesses.
Policy ideas	1. Recognize the seriousness for economic prosperity and nation. 2. Undertake the necessary reform in institutions and legal systems.
Policies	1. Wage and salary systems must be revised to favor more children. 2. Fellowships and grants more favorable to the families with more children. 3. Generous immigration policies.

the "Committee for Few Children and Aging Population" I chaired was responsible for proposing the policies for the purpose. Table 1 summarizes the committee's concrete proposals.

1.3. *A Summary Table of Problems and Policy Proposals*

I omit the exposition of this summary table, trusting that to most readers it is almost self-explanatory. Only a few remarks are in order, because some points of my view are different from many economists' views. If the majority of women work in the same way as men do, then a decline of fertility rate is almost a necessity unless serious adjustments are made in working conditions and remuneration systems.

2. Comments on the Policy Requirements for Aging Population with Declining Fertility Rate

2.1. *Similarity of Korea and Japan in Demographic Trends*

Three papers are assigned me to discuss; namely, Lee and Mason (2013), Chang (2013), Jones and Cho (2013). All of them are excellent in tracing not only historically the economic and demographic development of the Korean nation but also discussing their future implications. In both aspects, I am surprised to find the Korean situation almost the same as the Japanese and more or less similar to what many other advanced economies have experienced. Any author, however, has not seriously taken up the latter global similarity, otherwise, I agree with their analyses and perspectives during several decades in this century, as I touched briefly the Korean situation in my own paper on the Japan's lost twenty years presented at the Korean Academy of Sciences in 2011 (see Ichimura, 2011).

2.2. *My Pessimistic Perspectives*

If, however, we forecast our perspectives further beyond 2040 and try to see the probability of success for the socio-economic policies of present Korean and Japanese governments, I am much more pessimistic than the authors are. For that matter, my pessimism is just the same for China too, but not for the Association of Southeast Asian Nations (ASEAN) countries. Pessimism comes from my sad experiences as the chairperson of the "Committee for Preparing the Policies for Low Fertility and Aging".[1] The committee members had many chances to interview men and women of different age groups in the business companies and government offices. One surprise was to have learnt from almost all unmarried men and women that they regretted very much not having married when they were younger. They all admitted their dreaming about partners until too late. In the private sector, most business corporations disappointed us by non-cooperative attitude to provide women employees with better conditions favorable for increasing the fertility rate. Final disappointment was that the City Council did not approve to implement any of our recommended policies within a few years time (see [4]).

2.3. *Modern Civilization Disease is Incurable*

What is the trouble with so many nations now? Russians, European whites, American whites, Japanese, Chinese, and Koreans and so on are decreasing the populations. Exception is almost none. Almost all civilized nations suffer from the same problem, Is it all right? No! Without technical progress, without innovations of all kinds, the increasing total population cannot be sustained forever. Now technically advancing nations are decreasing in the proportion of human population. Technically advancing modern civilization is killing itself. In this sense, it is indeed "modern civilization disease".

2.3.1. *Optimality of population and its growth*

Some will remember that J. R. Hicks once wrote in his "*Social Framework*" in 1947, "women have their proper work to do at home" *a la* Marshall Victorian philosophy. The labor participation ratio in England then was not much higher than 30%. Now that much more than 50% of childbearing ages of women work in the conditions equal to those for men, we are observing the consequences. Economics never distinguished between men and women in treating labor, except for demography. Management sciences seldom discussed the same issues until very recently. Even demography

---

[1] My experiences in Kitakyushu city are described in the first Part. ICSEAD is an abbreviation of International Center for the Study of East Asian Development. It is a compact research institute established in the city of Kitakyushu.

does not handle appropriately the economic and social roles of women, so that it did not discuss how to maintain the sound age and sex proportions and reproduce its optimum number. Similar to the environmental issues, economics and management science must take up as research subjects, sustainable or optimum growth of population in connection with economic growth.

2.3.2. *Distinction of men and women in employment*

Under the present circumstances, men and women as employees must be clearly distinguished. The relations between employment and wage conditions at business corporations must be discussed differently for men and women, particularly for women of childbearing age. Only elementary attempts have just begun like baby-care holidays.

2.3.3. *Taxation system*

It must be reconsidered to maintain the more favorable conditions to bear babies while working. Public services like nurseries must be more amply supplied, should be cheap and so on. The fiscal burden to support the childbearing families must be born by those with no children. The authors seem to have under-estimated the burden of bringing up the fertility rate.

2.3.4. *Migration problems*

A new problem in connection with increasing fertility rate is how to welcome migrants from abroad. This brings in the issues of integrating different ethnic groups within a nation. Chang (2013), Lee and Mason (2013) discussed the issues appropriately. This has been going on historically to some extent, but not very extensively. Sometimes, it has caused the serious tragedies. The cases in Balkan are well known. There may be a limit to the absorptive capacity of a nation. Economists must learn the conditions necessary to absorb them in law and order.

References

[1] Lee, R. and A. Mason (2013). Population and economic growth in the Republic of Korea, in [7].

[2] Chang, K. S. (2013). South Korea's transition from developmental to post-developmental regime of demographic changes: a perspective recount, in [7].

[3] Jones, G. and L.-J. Cho (2013). South Korea's remarkable half century of demographic and human capital growth: what of the future?, in [7].

[4] Ichimura, S. (2011). The lessons of the lost two decades of Japan to Korea. In *Stability and Growth of the Korean Economy in the New World Order*. The National Academy of Sciences of the ROK.

[5] Ogawa, N. and S. Ichimura (2002). Policies to meet the challenge of an aging society with declining fertility: Japan and other Asian countries. *EAEP*, 13, LJ Cho (ed.), ICSEAD.

[6] Ichimura, H. and S. Shimizutani (2012). Retirement process in Japan: new evidence from the Japanese study on aging and retirement (JSTAR). In *Aging in Asia: Findings from New and Emerging Data Initiatives*, in J. P. Smith and M. Majmundar (eds.). National Research Council of the National Academies, Washington DC: The National Academies Press, pp. 173–204.

[7] Cho, Lee Jay (ed.) (2015). *Demographic and Socioeconomic Change in the Republic of Korea*, the Pusan Population Institute, Pusan.

Part II

The Stages of Economic Development and Nation Building

Chapter 6

Economic Development and Nation Building in Stages*

1. Four Stages of Economic Development

This chapter offers a conceptual and analytical framework for understanding the process of economic development and nation building. Most new nations emerging in the 20th century have come through the four stages of development; namely,

1. Least Developed	Below $300	3. Developing	up to $10,000
2. Underdeveloped	Up to $2,000	4. Developed	Above $10,000

In order to step up from one stage to the next, any country must overcome some barriers each time; namely, the barriers to take-off around $300 per capita gross domestic product (GDP), the barriers to industrialize around $2,000 and the barriers to modernize around $10,000. Historically those jumps were by no means easy, because each country has had to overcome not only the economic difficulties but also reform its political, institutional and spiritual conditions. It is nothing but a process of nation building. Economic development is indeed inseparable from nation building.

Some great economists[1] have discussed about various aspects of this process. For instance, Walter W. Rostow took up the saving ratio to increase by about 5% or Ragner Nurkse[2] took capital formation as a key variable to break through the barriers to take-off. Joseph A. Schumpeter emphasized the

*Beginning parts of this chapter were presented at the Singapore Economic Review Conference in 2009. The rest is newly written for this 2013 version.

[1]Ichimura, S (1998). *Political Economy of Japanese and Asian Development*. Berlin and Tokyo: Springer.

[2]Rostow, WW (1960). The Stages of Economic Growth — Non-Communist Manifesto. UK: Cambridge University Press; Nurkse, R (1953). *Problems of Capital Formation in Underdeveloped Countries*. New York: Oxford University Press.

role of entrepreneurship and innovations to overcome the barriers to industrialize,[3] but Simon Kuznets drew more attention to technological progress or technology transfer in the narrow sense. There are also a few varieties of so-called "Big-Push Theory". They include the ones emphasizing the role of not only new technology like steam engines but also the creation of new business institutions like joint-stock companies or even political change. In view of the historical records of different countries, these ideas all contain some elements of truth. Simon Kuznets presented a moderate and balanced view on the conditions for modernization in his *Modern Economic Growth*.[4] Earlier, Max Weber gave a more profound view on the broad sociological factors required for modernization in his *Wirtschaft und Gesellschaft*. Learning from those books and my own observations of Japanese and Asian development and modernization, I try here to summarize the process of modern economic development and nation building in stages.

Now, 68 years after the World War II and 20-odd years after the end of Cold War, many countries remain in the stage of the least developed economies. Some countries and areas, however, have remarkably developed and become the middle-income countries or even as well off as the advanced economies. What caused such big differences? Were the causes primarily external like resource endowments given to the countries or internal like the capacities of the people or the societies? By observing and analyzing the development experiences in various countries in four stages, we try here to identify the ways to move up the ladder of economic development and nation building.

Most East Asian countries have achieved rapid economic growth. Among the Association of Southeast Asian Nations (ASEAN) countries, however, Myanmar did not even take-off until very recently. Vietnam, Indonesia and the Philippines have failed in going beyond the barriers of $2,000 until recently, whereas China is already beyond $2,000 for over a decade. The newly industrialized economies (NIEs): South Korea, Taiwan, Hong Kong and Singapore have successfully gone beyond $10,000. The following sections describe how they have overcome these barriers.

---

[3]Schumpeter, JA (1911; 1961). *The Theory of Economic Development: an inquiry into profits, capital, credit, interest and the business cycle* (translated from the original 1911 German book by Redvers Opie). New York: Oxford University Press.

[4]Simon, K (1966). *Modern Economic Growth*. New Haven: Yale University Press, pp. 6–8.

Table 1. From Independence to Economic Development.

States	Year	End of fighting	Year	Switch to economic growth
Hong Kong	1945	End of World War II	1949	Shanghai Businesses came
Thailand	1945	End of World War II	1960	Industrialization Plan
Indonesia	1945	Independent from Holland	1965	Suharto New Order
Philippines	1946	Independence from US	1986	Successful Aquino Govern.
S. Korea	1948	Independ. from Japan	1972	Park Government Reform
Taiwan	1949	Nationalist Party enters	1954	Village Reconstruction Commi.
China	1949	Communist Revolution	1979	Den Xiao Ping Open Reform
Vietnam	1949	Independent from France	1986	Doi Moi Reform
Japan	1952	End of Occupation	1960	Income Doubling Plan
Malaysia	1957	Independent from UK	1966	End of Domestic Fighting
Singapore	1965	Independ. from Malaysia	1965	Lee Kwan Yue Govern.

2. Barriers to Take-off

In any country, a historic turning point when rapid economic growth began, can be identified. Usually it is the time that the political leaders could make a crucial decision to put aside the domestic struggles among political groups and concentrate on economic development. Table 1 shows such memorable years in modern East Asian history.

For example, Deng Xiaoping's great order of "Reform and Open" in China around 1978 was such a decision. In Vietnam, it was the adoption of Doi Moi (Reform). In Indonesia, it was the Suharto regime's decision after 1965 *coup d'état*. In South Korea, President Park determined to develop the economy with law and order even under the military dictatorial government. In Malaysia or Sri Lanka in earlier periods, however, civil wars continued after independence so that economic development became secondary. Thus, to take-off and start economic development the very first pre-requisite is this:

"*Condition* 1: *switch from polity to economy*".

Next, the least developed countries are often multi-ethnic. So that the political leaders of new nations face the difficulty in obtaining the national consensus on non-economic issues like religious creeds or political goals in addition to the burden of rescuing people from poverty. Various ethnic or other social groups should not insist on their beliefs of social, religious or political goals to lose the national unification. Nevertheless, if they could not make any compromises, then there will be no choice but disintegrating into several separate countries. British India was divided into so many independent countries. Looking back, that choice was very wise. Sometimes leaders must have the courage to determine or change the territory of a country, because national unification is an absolute requirement for a nation to remain a nation-state. Otherwise, economic development is inconceivable. They need the courage and wisdom to choose such a sense of historic timing of stopping civil wars and switch to economic development. The great Chinese leader Deng had that wisdom. Many Soviet leaders before Gorbachov did not, so that national unification of former Soviet Union was completely lost. It is the sense of balance between the requirements for economic development and the necessity of national unification. Thus,

"*Condition* 2: *national unification must be maintained*".

Thirdly, in the contemporary world, the amount of information for a national economy to take-off is enormous. Hence, any country must open the doors to the outside world and obtain the scientific, social, cultural and other information through TV, internet, newspapers and journals, visits to foreign countries and so on. Thus,

"*Condition* 3: *open doors to the World*".

Otherwise, the flow of precious information from abroad would be limited, so that no matter what the government does to compensate the loss of information, the game will be lost eventually. The Soviet Union amply demonstrated it. True, in some cases, it may result in the brain drain. However, one should not be afraid of it. The net effect of brain drain will be plus eventually.

Fourthly, everybody wants to be better off. The worst aspect of Socialism was that it restricted the human freedom to choose and work by controlling price and wage and rationing land use and production. A typical failure in Socialist Myanmar was controlling rice price too low, resulting in the shortage of rice. Thus,

"*Condition* 4: *emancipated human want to become better-off*".

Freedom of economic behavior, however, must be restrained by moral self-control and legal regulations.

Fifthly, the most crucial to take-off is to increase production. Production must be undertaken positively by innovative enterprises and farmers. However limited such opportunities may be in the least developed countries, incentives of all kinds must be given to those willing to take initiatives and risk to produce more and better goods and services.

"*Condition* 5: *give incentives to vigorous entrepreneurs*".

Sixthly, the extreme inequality of income often observed in the least developed countries must be overcome as soon as possible. The Gini ratio is often over 50%. This deprives the opportunities to foster the middle-income class and leads to social instability. Thus,

"*Condition* 6: *avoid extreme income inequality*".

The middle-income class is the base to supply talents in all the fields. The clue to materialize this objective is for the government to maintain fairness in tax-collection and its redistribution policies. Often corruption takes the forms of large subsidies or income transfers or even straight bribing given to politically linked businesses or families. Fundamentally, this is the moral responsibility of high-ranking political leaders.

Seventhly, important policies should be made after proper consultation with experts and their advices.[5]

"*Condition* 7: *keep the government and bureaucratic policies publicly transparent*".

These are the necessary conditions to take-off. How should the government proceed in taking off? Since it is impossible to develop many

[5]As the leader of Japanese economists' team about 20 years until 1988 and even later as an adviser to Japanese International Cooperation Agency (JICA) on Official Development Aid (ODA) policies. I kept telling the Indonesian authorities that they should reduce the debt service ratio below 30% as soon as possible. However, they never took my advice seriously, because the International Monetary Fund (IMF) and the World Bank kept telling the government then that Indonesia was an ideal borrower. If my view and their views had been openly known, the government would have been criticized before the 1997 crisis. Lack of transparency is often a source of corruption or misjudgment.

industries at the same time, it must select one or two key industries and develop them first. Often agriculture and textile industry are chosen, but in some countries tourism or other service industries may be important.

3. Barriers to Industrialize

In the discussion of industrialization, China and the rest of East Asia must be distinguished, because China is a big economy. Although the Chinese economy as a whole is in the beginning step of Stage 2, the coastal provinces and major municipalities are in the beginning step of Stage 3. The rest of the economy, especially the agrarian regions, is in Stage 2 or even in Stage 1. Regionally China may be following the domestic "flying geese pattern" of growth. Hence, China may be regarded as facing the barriers to take-off and industrialize at the same time.

The barriers to industrialize in the case of a middle size economy with population around 20 to 100 millions seem to be the following.

"*Condition* 1: *government must promote industrial policies in selecting and supporting some leading industries and policies for income redistribution*".

"*Condition* 2: *appropriate technologies are transferred from the advanced economies, and the middle level engineers are domestically supplied*".

"*Condition* 3: *trade and foreign direct investment are liberalized with an adequate flow of financial capital from abroad*".

"*Condition* 4: *free and fair competition in the market is guaranteed, and sound business rules and morals are maintained*".

"*Condition* 5: *legal system appropriate for modern transactions is enacted, and impartial jurisdiction is established*".

"*Condition* 6: *the community of business executives and its non-corrupted cooperation with bureaucrats and academic circles are established*".

"*Condition* 7: *equal opportunities to fundamental education are open to everybody, and chances for employment and further training are fair to everyone*".

The importance of these conditions needs no explanation. In addition, however, at this stage there is one essential consideration for government

Table 2. Socio-political Linkage Equations in Development and Nation Building.

Peoples' Dissatisfaction =	(Material Want)/(Consumption Level)
Social Grievance =	(People's Dissatisfaction)/(Income Equality)
Political Discontent =	(Social Grievance)/(Mobility of Social Classes)
Political Instability =	(Political Discontent)/(Political Participation)
Political Crisis =	(Political Instability)/(Strength of Political Creeds)

policies. That is to have social and political stability maintained, so that the business communities can concentrate on their own industrial development with little worries about non-economic matters.

"*Condition* 8: *social order and political stability are maintained, despite the changing social relations due to the economic growth*".

The formula of Table 2 holds at this and the following stages. This is a synthesis of some assertions of Samuel Huntington and other political scientists on political disorder of changing societies in developing countries. The exposition is omitted here.[6]

4. Barriers to Modernize

As the stage of economic development approaches to the level of $10,000, the countries must prepare themselves according to the social, political and cultural as well as economic conditions as the modern, advanced countries. Since the countries and compatriots must associate themselves with the members of the other advanced countries, they must behave more or less according to the global standard rules. The conditions to consider follow.

"*Condition* 1: *freedom of speech, information exchange and publication as well as business contract*".

"*Condition* 2: *liberalization of private property and capital ownership as well as opening of stock exchange*".

[6]The formula relating economic development to socio-political instability was originally proposed by Karl, D (1961). Social mobilization and political development. In *The American Political Science Review*. Samuel Huntington applied it with some modifications to his studies of Latin American countries, Samuel, H (1968). *Political Order in Changing Societies*, Yale University Press. See Huntington and CH Moore (eds.), *Authoritarian Government in Modern Society*. New York: Basic Books. See Ichimura, S, *op. cit.*

"*Condition* 3: *liberalization of banking system and foreign exchange*".
"*Condition* 4: *perfect liberalization of academic and scientific research and international communication*".
"*Condition* 5: *absorption of requests from special interest groups and democratization of policy-making*".
"*Condition* 6: *gradual political democratization toward admission of factions in a single party, multiple party system, and election of political leaders*".
"*Condition* 7: *strengthening the autonomous status of minorities or admitting the independence in their own districts*".

Further exposition will be postponed to the following sections dealing with the stages of nation building to avoid repetition. Only the case of China needs some notes as a special case.

5. The Future of China as a Nation-State

China is special in its size and history. At least two additional factors must be kept in mind to diagnose its development. One is its aspect as a transitional economy; another is its multi-ethnic heterogeneity. As a transitional economy, it faces the following matters.

1. Reform and transformation of State-Owned enterprises (SOE).
2. Dissolution of deficits of SOEs and central and local governments.
3. Reform of social security system to reduce heavy debt.
4. Inefficiency and corruption of one party political system.

As for the SOEs, the Central Committee of Communist Party of China and the central government have taken a number of measures to privatize them, and admitted many foreign or joint enterprises in various forms. Now such non-SOE companies produce far more than a quarter of GDP. The other three matters are still waiting for better solution. Mishandling these matters may disrupt even its national unification, because they are deeply related to the fundamentals of Socialist China and its historic past.

No doubt, the foundation of the People's Republic of China (PRC) was laid down by Mao Ze-Dong to establish China as Socialist China, but now in the whole world no solid Socialist States exist. Realistic observers would tell that China has already transformed itself from the principles of original

Communist systematically. How far she goes or how she goes remains to be seen. Certainly, there may still be many Chinese politicians, officials and military officers who believe in the great ideals of Communism, but very few Chinese graduate students, intellectuals or social scientists in China and abroad would believe in the ideology.

Many sinologists might say that the traditional Chinese teachings are not contradictory with more democratic political system, as Mencius taught, "the wishes of people are the Heaven's voice". Great cultural heritage like Confucianism, Taoism and Buddhism in China will assert their teachings sooner or later and are bound to influence the future course of Chinese nation building.

Moreover, the Chinese government has not faced seriously the problems of ethnic minorities, despite the international criticisms. Soviet Union's complete failure in integrating the other ethnic republics with the Russian republic may give precious lessons to China. The minority problems in China are more complicated and serious than in former Soviet Union, so that the Chinese government is bound to fail in handling non-Han minorities. Since, however, this is beyond the scope of this paper, we do not take it up here.

The last difficult problem with China is her international relations with neighbors like Japan and ASEAN members, particularly the territorial issues. This is certainly related to the nation building of China, but we do not deal with them in this paper.[7]

6. National Independence and Unification: Stage I

The development of most Asian developing economies started simultaneously with their independence from the former colonial status. Hence, economic development is inseparable from nation building. Number one problem of a new nation-state is how to unite the people. Professor Mahalanobis, well known as the economist who prepared the first Indian Five Year Plan pointed out that the most important and difficult problem for independent India was national unification.[8]

---

[7]Clearly, China and Japan are the key countries to form the East Asian Economic Community. As for the lessons to learn from France and Germany in forming EU, see Chapter 1 or Ichimura, S (2011). *Asian Economic Journal*.

[8]In his speech at Kansai Economic Federation in Osaka in 1957.

An easy way to achieve national unification is to close the country to foreign countries and control the domestic adversaries by force. This "Closed Unification" was adopted by Japanese Shogun, Korean and Chinese emperors in the 16th century, the Bolshevik right, Chinese and Vietnam Communist governments after the revolutions, the Sukarno regime for a while after independence and Myanmar military until very recently. On the other hand, a more enlightened way is to open spontaneously the national economy to foreign countries. This required the leaders and the majority of government officials not to fear the temporary imbalance of trade but rather appreciate a closer association with the outside world. East Asian nations chose this road eventually. Thus,

> "*Stage I of nation building is to achieve national unification and maintain it for some time to solidify the foundation of a nation-state*".

National unification is impossible without two essential factors. One is an ideal to inspire the leaders and the elite to devote their efforts and even sacrifice themselves for the sake of public objectives. Nationalism provided such an ideal in Asia, motivated by the antagonism against centuries of Western colonialism and the romantic ideals to build their own independent nation-states.[9] Another factor is the establishment of a modern government system. This second aspect in Stage I was more difficult for most Asian countries to materialize mainly due to the shortage of capable personnel. Any new government must at minimum recruit police officers, soldiers and civil servants to keep law and order, collect tax as well as manage the civilian administration. Such governance mechanism essential to any nation-state needs a sufficient number of educated persons who are able rationally to think and calculate the consequences of certain actions. Those civil servants must work as a system to form a government. In summary, nationalistic idealism and the dedicated elite personnel are essential.

Unless the devotion of elite groups is very strong, the foundation of a new nation-state remains shaky. Soon the government may lose its control

---

[9] From the writings and the recorded talks of many leaders in Asian independence movement, I have detected that Asian nationalism had some common factors. For instance, Sun Yet-Sen's "Three Principles of the people: nationalism, people's rights, people's living", and Sukarno's "Pancha Sila: nationalism, humanism, guided democracy, social justice, creed to God". See Chapter 17 of this book.

of people, and civil wars may start. Almost all Asian countries achieved national unification at least once, but soon some faced the civil wars or hot wars. China, Vietnam, Campuchia, Nepal, Pakistan, Korea were the examples. Some more may face the same difficulties again.

New nation-states without successful economic development may not be able to maintain their domestic stability and manage their governments. Gunnar Myrdal pointed out pessimism in his "*Asian Drama*" that emancipation from colonialism did not lead to economic development. Economic development requires not sheer capital accumulation but, as we have already discussed, some reforms of socio-political conditions. Many of them are similar to the barriers to modernize, but others are the conditions related to nation building in Stage II.

7. Creation of Modern National Economy: Stage II

To found a modern nation-state and achieve its economic development implies not just to establish but create a modern national economy, because it requires introducing many new social, political and institutional changes into the old regimes. The kind of changes required are in the wide range of

(1) new advanced military and industrial technologies.
(2) modern government administration.
(3) better business management and so on.

Except for Japan, no country in East Asia in the late 19th century was ready for undertaking the task of creating such a modern national economy in a few decades.[10]

At the end of World War II, the educated personnel for government administration were available only in the former British and Japanese colonies. In the ASEAN business world, many merchants of Chinese origin were available, and quite a few migrated out of China after the war. However, in technical, business and administrative fields the shortage of educated personnel was very serious in most East Asian countries. For example, in Indonesia at the time of independence the personnel with higher education were only slightly more than one hundred.[11]

[10]Literacy rate for men and women was higher in early Meiji Japan than in Europe then.
[11]Harsja B. PhD dissertation, Harvard University.

Under these conditions, the process of creating modern national economy must proceed gradually. Priority must be carefully chosen. The following is more or less a standard order of importance according to the experiences in most Asian countries.

7.1. *Creation of Modern Army and the Central Government*

The most essential factor for a modern nation-state is legitimately to obtain the monopoly of compulsory power (Max Weber). Fundamentally, the government can grasp this power by controlling the police and the military forces. Usually whoever controls the military force become the political leaders. In fact, the first political leaders of most new nation-states in East Asia, except for two old empires and two unique kingdoms: Japan, Thailand, Malaysia, and Brunei, were the military leaders or generals who led and won the independence wars.[12] China, North Korea, South Korea, Taiwan, Indonesia, Laos, Campuchia, Vietnam and Myanmar were all such cases. The military in modern nation-states or modern army is different from the warrior forces in the medieval or feudal times, but we do not enter this discussion.[13]

7.2. *Establishment of Bureaucracy*

The second essential step in creating a modern nation-state is to establish bureaucracy. It is the bone frame and nerve system of any modern nation-state and has the following important characteristics.

1. Functional specialization and over-all organization of government offices.

---

[12]Hong Kong remained as a colony. Singapore attained its independence from Malaysia by agreement and has been governed by Socialist Action Party.

[13]Warriors were loyal only to the specific local clan or their families. The modern army was trained to be loyal to the nation-state, whoever becomes the political leader or the king. In newly created nation-states where the military group is the only organization with governing capability and system, often there may be no alternative to the military leader becoming or self-appointing the president or the prime minister. Sometimes the military may support non-military figure as the political leader. Since the military is essential for keeping law and order, whom the military supports is very important in new nation-states. These are often the real problems behind the so-called succession problems.

2. Personnel management of employment, promotion and salary by rules.
3. Establishment of systems for administrative ways and measures.
4. Communication and recording by documents and other means.

Until very recently, government offices were not adequately organized to deal with daily works in most Southeast Asian countries. Division of labor among many sections of bureaucratic offices was not defined, and the allocation of persons and resources were not well organized in order to deal with and finish the administrative works as a system of offices. The situations have gradually improved as the number of capable staffs increase and the experiences have taught them how to do work more efficiently. However, at the same time the daily works have become increasingly complex.

7.3. *Enacting Written Laws and Establishing the Rule of the Laws*

The third step is to establish the norms of the system to keep the consistency of administration. This can be partly maintained by the sense of responsibility of bureaucrats but more certainly by the established rules of work, which every one must observe. They must be legally enacted as applicable to the whole society. Such legal systems must be supported by lawyers, judges and prosecutors as well as the public understanding and observance of the laws. These are essential to keep the law and order in the modern society. This is rather a high standard of requirements missing in some developing countries. For that reason, normal economic activities of reputable enterprises encounter the unexpected hindrances.

Particularly in connection with economic development, the Commercial law and the Corporation law are important. They rule not only the activities of private enterprises but also the relations between the government and the markets. In older States or societies, the governments were organized mainly based on community type of villages and towns where residents mutually trust each other like families or neighbors, and the industrial bases were primarily agriculture with limited artisan activities. The merchants' activities were often kept outside the community. In Japan the first political leader who intervened into commercial activities was Oda Nobunaga in the 16th century, and he protected the safety of the market for merchants. Only in modern times even in Western countries, merchants found the "Modern State" as the best protector of law and order and expansion of economic transactions. The government first authorized the markets as giving bilaterally the benefit of economic activities to the merchants and the State and then promoted such markets further as being more beneficial to the "Modern State".

In this undertaking, the role of bureaucrats is important in managing the markets. Their fair administration produces the rational behavior of executives' management, whereas easy going, shortsighted or corrupted administration produces inefficiency and misallocation of resources. In many underdeveloped countries, such misconducts are often observed. For these reasons, the enactment of the Commercial Law and the Corporation Law and their proper execution are essential to sustain the steady development.

7.4. *Book-Keeping the Calculation of Capital and Profit*

In the "modern national economy", households and entrepreneurs behave differently. The latter's profit maximization achieves the rational behaviors in economic transactions and realizes efficiency in optimal use of scarce resources. Various managerial devices like double entry book-keeping help it.

The rational calculation for profit maximization in the market must be clearly distinguished from the parasitic profit maximization by cheating or using political and personal connections. They are as old as the "Old Testament" days and still more prevalent in many developing countries than most developed countries. The mafia businesses after the collapse of the Soviet Union are exactly like those.

Max Weber regarded this rationality in calculation by double entry book-keeping as crucially important for founding Capitalism.[14] He evaluated it highly along with other types of rationality like "value rationality, profit rationality, and objective rationality".

In connection with profit maximization, one note may be necessary to insert; i.e., Japanese lifetime employment with seniority wage system.

---

[14]The Japanese merchants in the Edo period developed a double-entry book-keeping system, equivalent to the Western modern accounting. The Nakai family developed it.

Although this system is often welcome in many Southeast Asian countries, the companies find it hard to keep the system and remain successful in conducting the businesses, because it sometimes contradicts the rational capital calculation. Most companies seem to be modifying the old practice.

7.5. *Organizing Modern Joint-Stock Companies — Big Businesses*

The last step for any modern nation-state to complete creating modern national economy is to succeed in incorporating large companies and thereby undertaking some large-scale ventures. Three difficulties must be overcome. 1. How to mobilize huge capital and labor? 2. How to manage them? 3. How to share the risk? To avoid 100% foreign company or predominantly foreign joint venture, developing countries have no choice but to domestically raise a huge amount of capital by shares — joint-stock company is a device for that purpose. The number of employees also expands. Finding workers may not be hard but training them is. For this purpose and effectively to use huge capital, the corporations must be organized and governed similarly to government bureaucracy.

Organizing a big joint-stock company solved not only the first two difficulties but also the sharing of risk involved, because each share of the company could be divided into small amounts. It is said that overseas Chinese had difficulties in organizing big companies, whereas Japanese business leaders with the warriors' experiences of running "Han" (local clan) readily accepted the joint-stock companies in the 19th century.

8. Democratization of Political Economy: Stage III

Even if some conditions mentioned above are not satisfied, however, a modern national economy will be created with some weak aspects here and there. The markets will function with gradual modification, and the governments will adjust the organizations and policies to the needs. In the extreme case of failure like the Soviet Union, the national economy collapses. Occasionally, however, the national economy suffers from the long depression, as the developed economies experienced in the 1930s. In order to avoid such failures and maintain the successful working of the created modern national economy, what is needed are some wise relations between the private sector and the government sector as well as the good international relations in communications and policy adjustment. I have named it "democratization of the political economy". Domestically it is the Government's regulations of markets and consumers' and businesses' participation in policy-making. Internationally, the exchange of information, policy adjustment and negotiations are becoming more and more important in the globalized world. Often the negotiation is mixed with the national interests of the countries concerned. Here, I refrain from going into the details of such international aspects but concentrate on the domestic aspects of policy-making and its implementation. As economic development progresses, procedure becomes increasingly complicated and important. Closer cooperation among researchers of different disciplines is required. In these political issues not only the contents of policies but also the process to reach the conclusions is important.

Figure 1 tries to describe the political implications of economic policies from the viewpoint of democratization of the society. For this purpose, the vertical axis measures the degree of participation in decision-making on the part of common citizens and enterprises. The lowest is the case of dictatorial system, whereas the highest is the society permitting free election. The horizontal axis measures, however, two aspects of economic activities. One is the degree of competition in the markets: monopoly *versus* free completion. Another (shown in parentheses) is the degree of freedom of association and speech: or government's control, permission. This way the origin shows the most dictatorial, controlled political and economic system, and the upper-right corner indicates the multi-party polity, free

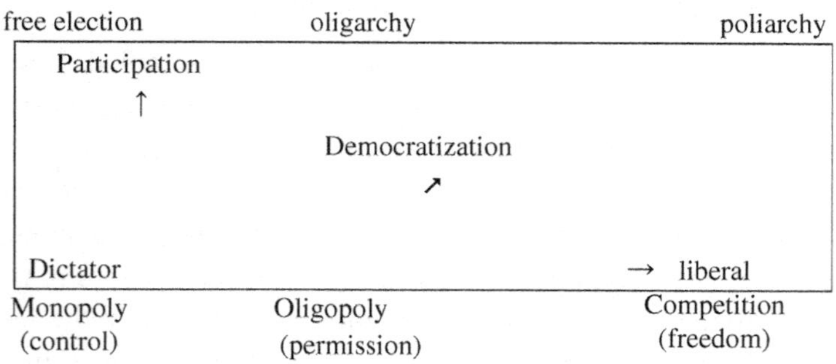

Fig. 1. Political Implications of Policy-making.

market economy and the most deregulated competitive society with free entry. The degree of democratization increases, as an arrow points, the characteristics of the social system moves upward and rightward.

Another viewpoint to characterize the political process of policy-making is centralized *versus* decentralized governments. Feudal societies in Western Europe or Japan or federalism in modern times had decentralized governments or fiscal systems, whereas in most modern countries the central government has the most authoritative power in policy-making and fiscal budget allocation. The Japanese feudalism was unique in the sense that it was a centralized feudal system. We do not go into this aspect here. It will become increasingly important as economic development reaches ever-higher levels.

The passage to freedom in political and economic activities is not common to all the countries even at the same level of economic development. The historic process has not been as simple as one could hope for. The broad characterization of East Asian countries in the conditions of political and economic freedom in the 1990s is shown as Fig. 2, according to my bold judgmental opinions. If the reader agrees with me more or less, then the following remarks may not be too far from the truth. Measuring the performance of economic development in terms of per capita GDP, it is clear that there is rough contrast in the degree of political and economic freedom and economic development between high-income countries like Japan, Hong Kong, Singapore and such low-income countries as Indonesia, Myanmar, and North Korea. However, the relations are not clear-cut. Among the countries like South Korea and Taiwan at the similar income

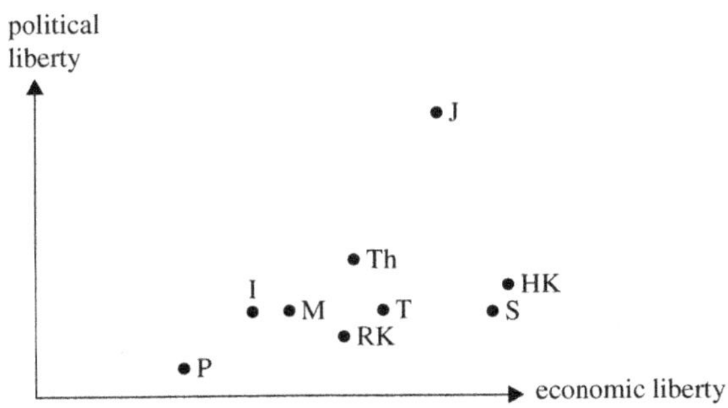

Fig. 2. Political Liberty and Economic Freedom.

levels, South Korean economy is very oligopolistic but Taiwan economy is not. What determines the degree of economic freedom in each country requires further studies of industrial organizations of those countries. Such studies are very scarce even now. Furthermore, the degree of political liberty in Asia needs a more careful investigation. It does not seem to make a simple correspondence to per capita GDP in each country.

9. Special Interest Groups and Policy Decisions

As economic development advances, industrial composition becomes complex. The stakes of various social groups become diversified and harder to coordinate. In order to analyze the roles of special interest groups in policy coordination, we define five groups: (GB) = Government bureaucrats; (PP) = Political parties; (AE) = Academicians or experts; (SIG) = Special interest groups; (PM) = Prime and other ministers.

How they work together to produce some policies are generally the following. First, SIG demands certain type of policies, or PP and GB notice the need of some policies. Then, PP, GB and AE work together in the government offices, PP committees, and parliament committees to produce some budget requests or new regulations. After preparing the tentative drafts for policies, PP and PM try to pass the related laws in the parliament. The typical ways of reaching some policies are A, B, and C.

A brief exposition of the process of policy-making and the influence of SIG in Japan are provided here (Table 3), with supplementary Table 4

1. (A) when the circumstances change but administrative guidance or new interpretation of the existing regulations cannot handle the cases; the officials in charge usually start preparing the new regulations.
2. Usually they consult or adjust with the officials in related sections.

Table 3. The Process from Policy Proposal to Implementation.

Proposal		Discussion		Agreement		Implementation
A: GB	—	PP, AE, SIG	—	GB · PP · SIG	—	PM
B: PP	—	AE, GB, SIG	—	GB · PP · SIG	—	PM
C: SIG	—	PP, AE, GB	—	GB · PP · SIG	—	PM

Table 4. The Process of Policy-making in Japan.

[Drafting proposals] →	[Decision in each ministry] →	[Cabinet Decision] →	[Implementation]
(Coordination inside ministry)	(Inter-ministerial coordination)	(Cabinet Committees)	
GB ...... [Information, Proposals, Debates, Reconsideration]			
PP ...... (Parliament, Committees)			
SIG ... (Discussions, Coordination)			

3. They contact the AE, specialists of SIG and PP either at the official committees or informally with some individuals in those organizations before finalizing the draft.
4. Many committees at each ministry or Prime Minister's Office are the places for such policy discussions with representatives of SIG, PP or AE specialists or thought experimentation for bureaucrats.
5. In the important cases, PP carefully drafts the proposals after examining closely the involved stakes. Table 4 shows this process.
6. In some other cases, the initial proposals may come from parliament members (B) or some special interest groups (C); the following process may differ accordingly.

These Japanese ways of policy preparation and implementation are very participatory and democratic.[15] However, it often takes too much time and is excessively compromising.

Policy-making in other Asian countries is simpler and is more easily influenced by SIG or some politicians. Thus, it must have invited more corruptions. Particularly important is an adequate balance of the influences of GB and SIG in Japan. The balance of these two groups in East Asian countries in the 1990s may be like Fig. 3 according to my own observations and consultation with friends in Asia and Japan.

One should not necessarily interpret the influence of SIG and GB as undesirable. What matters is the balance between the self-interests of

[15] An important problem of the regional imbalance in development and income level is not taken up here. To resolve those gaps, regional policies and decentralization of political administration and public finance are important. See Chapters 8 and 9 of this book.

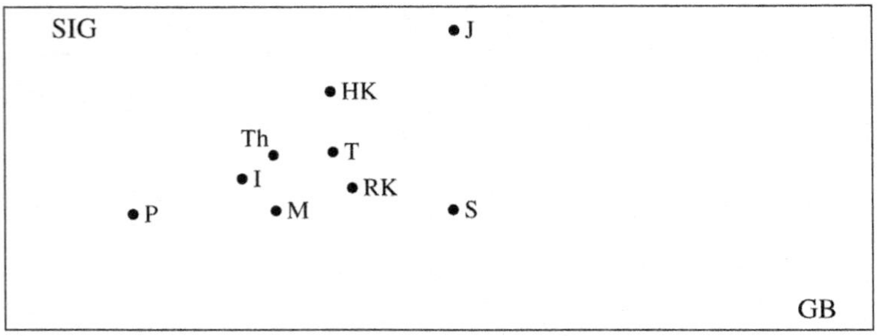

Fig. 3. The Degree of Influence of SIG and GB in East Asian Countries.

those private groups and the public interests of the nation as a whole — a requirement of political democracy. Furthermore, what is desirable from the viewpoint of nation building is not only the balance between private interests and national interests but also the long-term steady growth of national well-being.

Chapter 7

Regional Development Policy*

—Its Success and Failure in Japan—

1. Introduction

In order to reconstruct and develop the devastated economy after the World War II, the Japanese government has carefully designed its overall policies in the following six areas.

(1) Macro demand management policies, (2) Industrial policy, (3) Distribution policy, (4) Regional development policy, (5) Manpower and education policy and (6) Research and development policy.

However, the Japanese postwar policies were unique in relying far less on the market and designed the various policy measures to cover the wide areas related to economic issues. All of these policies have been officially reported and documented very well in the so-called "white papers".[1] This chapter takes up only "Regional Development Policy" and discusses its success and failure throughout the postwar years.

*This was presented at the International Conference on Great Development of Western Region in Jungjing, China, 2000.

[1]The most famous one is *Economic White Paper*. Others are also well-known: *Foreign Trade White Paper*, *Science and Technology White Paper*, *Education White Paper*, and so on. Similarly official documents are available on regional plans in each National Land Comprehensive Development Plan. We will take them up here. Many books and articles are also published in Japan and abroad. See National Land Agency (1999 J). Ever since I seriously argued with W. Isard at Leontief's Harvard Economic Research Project, regional development policies have been my serious concern. His book [4] is the first authoritative work in the field.

2. History of Regional Development Policy in Japan

"Regional development policy" is, in other words, the use of national land in different regions; namely, where to locate industrial plants and population, mainly by choosing the regional allocation of public investment, subsidies, transfer payments and loans. Its importance is obvious, because land is the scarcest factor and its efficient use is number one problem for the long-run development. Pursuit of economic efficiency or profit in the short run alone by private enterprises and public entities almost necessarily leads to excessive concentration of industrial activities in major cities, particularly the capital city Tokyo. In order to avoid it, the Japanese government has had plans for land use from the very beginning of postwar reconstruction as well as before the war. They are well known as "National Land Comprehensive Development Plans"[2] required by National Comprehensive Development Law enacted as early as in 1950.[3]

So far five national plans of the same kind have been prepared in 1962, 1969, 1977, 1988, and most recently in 1998. They have designed and guided the regional distribution of industrial activities and population. Table 1 sums them up and demonstrates how the government has dealt with regional allocation of land use at successive stages of development for the past half century.[4] In fact, the government had regional development plans long before 1962 and started its regional development design for guiding regional distribution of industries and people's migration immediately after the war.

In order to explain the regional development plans in Japan, two preparations are necessary; the first is a brief sketch of Japanese economic geography, and the second is the periodization of the stages of postwar Japanese economic development. The first column of Table 1 shows six periods dividing the postwar years to be explained below.

---

[2]It is a translation of (Zen Koku Sogo Kaihatsu Keikaku).

[3]There are two ways of implementing government policies. One is based on legal laws or regulations; another is administrative guidance (gyosei shido). The latter was discretionary to the administrative advices of the officials in the ministries of the central government. But important policies requiring preferential treatment of some companies or regions can be implemented only if they are legally permitted.

[4]As for the history of Japanese regional development plans, there are a few excellent handbooks. The old but good one is published by National Land Planning Association (1981J) and the latest one is published by the Ministry of Construction (1999J).

Table 1. Economic Plan and Regional Development Plans.

	Economic plans	Regional dev. plans	Regional policy
1945–1952	• Reconstruction plan interim report (12/47) • Three year self-reliance plan (1/51)	• Basic guidelines for national land use (9/45) † Land development law (50) † Hokkaido development plan (10/51)	1. food production increase 2. reconstruction of devastated land, infrastructure, and housing 3. resource development 4. inflation control
1953–1960	• On economic self-reliance (12/53) • Economic self-reliance five year plan (12/55) • New long-term economic plan (12/57)	(1) National comprehensive development plan (9/54) † Tokyo metro plan (7/58) † Tohoku development plan (8/58) † Kyushu development plan (11/59)	1. construction of infrastructure for industrial development 2. calamity prevention 3. correction of regional income gaps 4. relocation of plants to correct regional concentration
1960–1970	• National income-doubling plan (12/60) • Medium-term economic plan (1/66) • Economic & social develop. plan (3/67)	† Shikoku development plan (10/60) (2a) National comprehensive dev. plan (10/62) † Promotion of new industrial city law (62) † Hokuriku development plan & Chugoku development plan (2/64) † Kinki metro plan (5/65) † Chubu metro plan (6/68) (2b) New national compreh. dev. plan (5/69)	1. prevention of too rapid urbanization 2. development of new industrial centers 3. reduction of regional differentials in income and industrial location 4. preparation of Tokaido megalopolis industrial and urban zones 5. overcoming pollution problems
1970–1980	• New economic & social development plan (5/70) • Economic & soc. fundamen. plan (2/73)	† Biwa lake development plan (12/72) † Promotion of industrial relocation law (72) † Okinawa development plan (6/74)	1. reorientation of nationwide land use 2. reduction of regional gaps in environmental conditions

(*Continued*)

Table 1. (*Continued*)

	Economic plans	Regional dev. plans	Regional policy
	• Economic plan for late 1970s (5/76) • New economic & social comprehensive develop. seven year plan (9/79)	• National land use plan (5/76) (3) Third national comprehensive development plan (11/77)	3. construction of transportation and communication network 4. harmonious existence of nature and humans
1980–1990	• Prospect & guidelines for the 1980s (8/83) • Five year plan for economic management (5/88)	(4) Fourth national comprehensive development plan (6/87)	1. decentralization of metro Tokyo's functions 2. development and specialization of Tokyo and local centers 3. multicolor use of land
1995–2015	—	(5) Grand design of national land use in the 21st century	—

Notes: (1)–(5): Nation-wide land-use plans; † regional plans; ‡ land use legislation.

2.1. *Economic Geography of Japan*

Figure 1 shows the map of Japan and major cities. A chain of Japanese islands extends in the shape of bow from 24° to 46° North Latitude. The regional discrepancies in topography, economic conditions, industrialization and urbanization have been very significant among the various parts of Japanese archipelago. This has become particularly noticeable in the process of Japanese modernization after the "Meiji Reform". Pre-modern Japan was a feudal society where many local clans governed each territory in its own way, although Shogun coordinated the nation-wide administration and its external relations of Japan.

Japanese economic development centered around four major growth poles or growth centers: Tokyo, Nagoya, Osaka and Fukuoka–Kitakyushu. In order for any urban city to be a growth pole to drive the development around it and attract people into the area, it must satisfy the following four conditions: (1) industrial activities, (2) cultural and academic attraction,

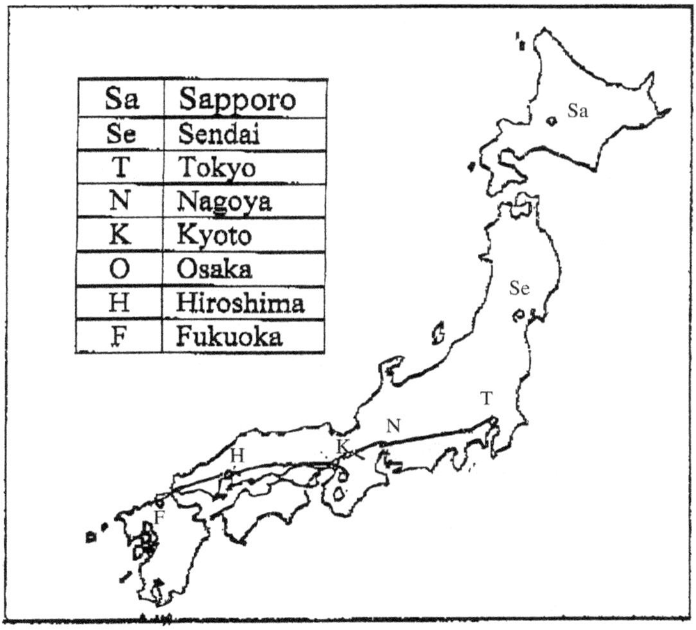

Fig. 1. Map of Japan and Major Cities.

(3) port facilities, and (4) ample water.[5] In Japan there are only four urban areas that satisfy these four conditions. The above-mentioned four cities are the ones: Metropolitan Tokyo–Yokohama area, Nagoya area, Kyoto–Osaka–Kobe area, and Northern Kyushu area. Other cities and areas are secondary. It happens that all of these four areas are located along the Tokaido–Sanyo Shinkansen railroad line, as is shown in Fig. 2.

This figure shows the characteristics of regional development of Japanese economy at the present time. It is common to divide the Japanese archipelago into seven sub regions. It is shown in the upper part of the Fig. 2. In order to understand the economic geography of a national economy,

[5]In addition to these four factors, one may wish to add some other factors to be growth center such as availability of capital, land and labor, access to foreign economies, location of central and local governments. The attraction of Northern Kyushu is cheaper availability of land and labor, while concentration in Tokyo is caused by the excessive concentration of power in the central government so far.

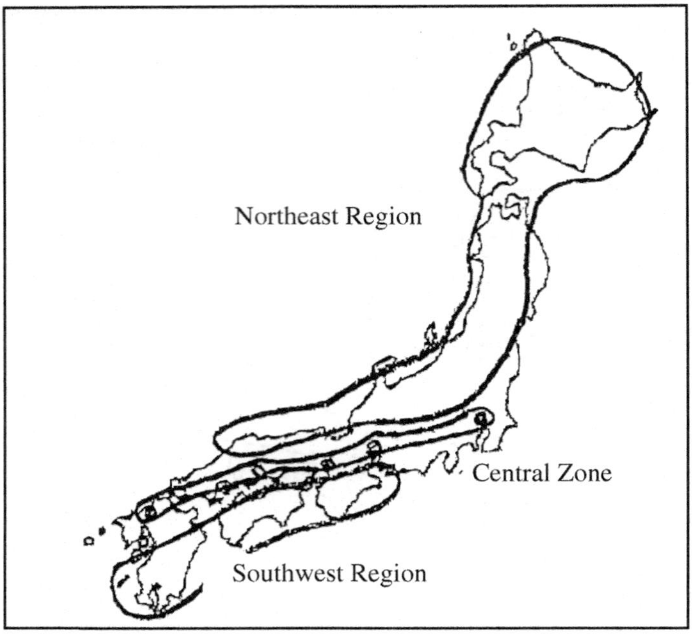

Fig. 2. The Regional Structure of Japanese Islands.
— Tokaido–Sanyo Megalopolis —

the bone structure of the economy must be grasped. That is the regional linkage of the distributed areas by transportation and communication lines such as rivers, railroads, highways, telephone lines and airlines. In Japan its spine is what is usually called the Tokaido Megalopolis or Tokaido–Sanyo Megalopolis which links Tokyo, Osaka, Kobe, and Hiroshima to Kitakyushu–Fukuoka, as is shown in the lower part of Fig. 2. Nearly two-third of Japanese population live along this megalopolis and about two third of industrial establishments are located there. The areas away from the spinal axis are less developed areas. Figure 2 indicates them as the Northeast area and the Southwest area. The differential in per capita income between the lowest Kagoshima Prefecture and the highest Tokyo Prefecture has been about one to three. The more serious was the difference in employment opportunities. As a result a large number of young people have migrated from remote country sides to the urban areas along the Tokaido Megalopolis.

2.2. *Stages in Postwar Japanese Economic Development*

Periodization of postwar years may be briefly sketched: namely,

1. Occupation Period (1945–1952)
2. Reconstruction Period (1952–1960)
3. Rapid Growth Period (1960–1970)
4. Shocks Period (1970–1980)
5. Internationalization Period (1980–1990)
6. Deep Recession Period (1990–2000) and
7. On trial period (2000–2010 beyond).

Table 2 is a summary of this periodization.[6] Five regional development plans were prepared more or less corresponding to these periods. The fourth column in Tables 1 and 2 show the distinctive characteristics in the basic ideas of regional development policies. Table 1 shows more in details about the actual names of economic plans and regional development plans all over the country.

3. Features of Japanese Regional Development Policy

Some features of the regional development plans, as they are announced by Japanese central and local governments may be summarized.

Table 2. Periodization of Economic Plans and Regional Development Plans.

Period	Characteristics	Economic policy	Regional policy	Period
1945–1952	occupation	3 D's	resource exploration	1945–1955
1952–1960	reconstruction	recovery	building industrial base	1955–1960
1960–1970	rapid growth	income doubling	eliminate regional gap	1960–1972
1970–1980	shocks	oil crisis	reorient land use	1972–1977
1980–1990	globalization	liberalization	stable industry complex	1977–1987
1990–2000	deep recession	finance-fiscal crises	multi-polar relocation	1987–2000
2001–2015	Japan on trial	back to steady growth	multiple axis and centers	2001–

Notes: National Land Comprehensive Development Plan was prepared in 1962, 1969, 1977 and 1988.

[6] See Ichimura (1998 E).

3.1. *Reconstruction and Development*

The beginning stage of regional development plan was, needless to say, to reconstruct the devastated economic conditions. Those regional plans started not as the national plans but the prefecture or local government plans earlier. Table 1 summarizes the details of regional plans in various districts and prefectures which the central and local governments prepared and implemented the regional development policies. The importance of provincial plans is clearly demonstrated by many local plans listed in Table 1. Indeed, the first National Comprehensive Land Development Plan was prepared by synthesizing the earlier provincial development plans, particularly in less developed regions such as Hokkaido.

3.2. *Development and Regional Discrepancy*

As reconstruction and development of the Japanese economy began, the regional gaps widened between the urban and rural areas. Thus, the second and the following stages of regional development policy emphasized to reduce the regional gaps as well as to promote further development of the whole national economy. As the result, many regional plans have been prepared not only by the central government but also by the prefecture governments under the guidance of the Ministry of Construction or the National Land Agency. They have been the national and regional guideposts in allocating the enormous amount of public investment in land reclamation, constructing highways or developing special industrial zones. The chosen localities have received great benefits, so that the choice has been politically very sensitive. Hence, such regional development plans have always been closely related to and coordinated with the general national economic plans. Table 1 shows the parallel preparation of national economic plans and regional development plans more or less along the same lines.

3.3. *One Pole Concentration in Metro Tokyo*

In connection with the regional development plans, as Table 2 shows, some experts divided the post-war years into several periods. They clarify the problems in the third to the last periods. In each period the government tried to achieve development efficiently while mitigating the concentration of industries particularly around established urban centers like Tokyo, Nagoya, and Osaka. Nevertheless, Japan could not avoid concentration of industrial and other economic activities particularly around Tokyo. The reason was that the orientation of government policies was "development first, regional balance second". In fact the earlier plans emphasized efficiency by concentration. It was only in the Fourth National Comprehensive Land Development Plan in 1988 that the government explicitly mentioned "multi-polar dispersed use of national land". It did not seem, however, that the fourth plan succeeded because it was not supported by appropriate laws to promote decentralization or dispersion of industrial and political administration.[7]

3.4. *Pros and Cons of Japanese Regional Development Policies*

Thus, on the whole we cannot regard the Japanese regional development policies as a straight-forward success, because in the latest Comprehensive Plan in 1988 the authorities themselves had to advocate a completely reversed direction of regional policies; namely, "multi-polar dispersed use of land". Those should have been the policies to be advocated from the very beginning, as this author maintained in his articles since 1965.[8] The wrong regional policies were behind the inflation of real estate prices in the 1980s, which caused the so-called "bubble economy" in Japanese big cities in the early 1990s. Look at the urban land price index of six major cities: 1970 (10.1), 1975 (18.9), 1980 (24.5). 1985 (33.6), 1990 (100), 1991 (103.0), 1992 (87.0) and 1997 (44.7). This is an unsuccessful aspect of Japanese development policies, which is now too obvious but was neither told then nor popular in the early 1970s. The same mistakes seem to have been repeated, however, in many cities in East Asia. Nevertheless, there were some interesting ideas as guiding principles of regional development policies applicable to many other countries in all the past Japanese regional plans.

---

[7]The law of Decentralization was only recently passed by Parliament in 2000.

[8]See the articles of mine published in popular monthlies like *Chuo-Koron* and included in my book (Ichimura, 1970 J). "From Metropolis to Megalopolis", "Urbanized Society will Decline", "Disperse the Functions of Tokyo" and "Beautiful and Efficient Use of Land". They are translated into Chinese and published (Ichimura, 1995 C). They were written primarily as criticisms on the second New National Comprehensive Land Development Plan in 1969. My contention was that if the policies of that plan were pursued, the concentration into Tokyo would become extreme. Undoubtedly this has happened.

4. The Basic Ideas of Regional Development Plans

The national regional plans have been basically the guideposts in allocating the enormous amount of government public investment in land reclamation, public investment like constructing highways or developing special industrial zones. Some basic ideas in these national regional development plans at different stages are very precious ones and will be explained as follows.

1. The first stage of regional development plan was, needless to say, to reconstruct the devastated economic conditions in post-war Japan. It emphasized to develop the areas with rich natural mining resources like coal, copper, or gold.
2. The second stage was to promote the rapid growth of Japanese economy, even though it might lead to the excessive urbanization. The Second NCLDP (National Comprehensive Land Development Plan) emphasized the construction and improvement of transportation and communication networks and developing the "New Industrial Cities" at various sites in Japan. It soon became very clear, however, that the regional gaps were widening further between large cities and rural areas and have posed serious problems for human habitation.
3. Thus, the Third NCLDP took it up much more seriously to reduce the regional gaps and tried to establish many "Settled Habitat Zones (Teiju Ken)" at various districts in Japan and decentralize the economic activities and budget allocation. The government always claimed to achieve development efficiency while mitigating the concentration of industries around established urban centers like Tokyo, Nagoya, and Osaka. The trends of concentration of industrial and other economic activities particularly around Tokyo, however, never declined. The reason was that promotion of development was more emphasized than mitigation of centralization. The orientation of government policies was development first, regional balance second or third. In fact the earlier plans emphasized efficiency by concentration.
4. In the Fourth National Comprehensive Development Plan in 1988, however, the government authorities themselves finally had to advocate a completely reversed direction of regional policies; namely, "dispersed

and multi-polar location of growth centers"[9] and "promoting their mutual networking"[10] in Japan. These should have been the policies from the very beginning, as this author maintained his articles since 1965. It does not seem, however, that even the fourth plan succeeded because it was not supported strongly enough by laws to promote decentralization or dispersion of industrial and political administration yet.[11]

5. The "bubble economy" in the late 1980s proved the most serious failure of Japanese regional development policies. It is now too obvious, but it was neither told nor popular by most influential government and journalistic economists in the early 1970s.

5. The Grand Design of National Land Use in the 21st Century

In 1998, reflecting on unsatisfactory regional imbalance and deterioration of environmental conditions in major cities, the Japanese government changed the direction of regional development plan and prepared a new type of regional development plan, i.e., "the Grand Design of National Land Use in the 21st Century" in 1998. It has tried to overcome the defects of the past regional development plans, some of which have been pointed out above. Its basic approaches are briefly explained first and commented next.

(1) It looks at the Japanese archipelago from the viewpoints of four axis's of national land, as is shown in Fig. 3.
(2) It inherits the basic idea of the Fourth NCLDP in recognizing the needs of multiple growth centers in Japan and decentralized decision-making in allocation of public investment in infrastructure construction. It inherited the idea of "Settled Habitat" in the Third Plan and redefined it with the new name of "New Local Habitat Zones" and identified more localities all over the country. It paid adequate attention to preserving the natural environment and beauty in developing the various regions.
(3) In this connection, the Plan emphasized correctly the importance of seeking the "participation and cooperation (Sanka Renkei)" of

[9]This is a translation of Takyoku bunsan Gata Kokudo Keisei.
[10]This is a translation of Renkei Kankei Kyoka.
[11]A number of laws and regulations were laid down and they are still effective to implement the policies now.

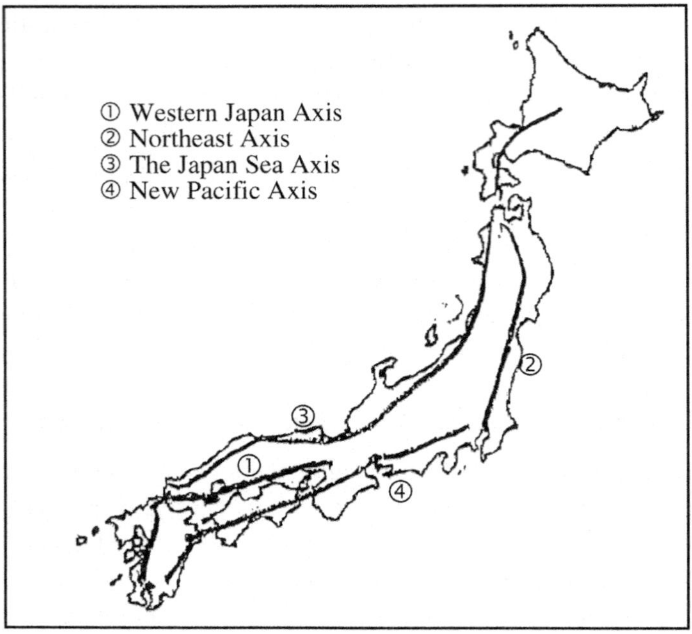

Fig. 3. Image of Four Axes of Japanese Land.

common citizens and local authorities in the process of planning and its implementation. It emphasized the importance of not-for-profit organization (NPO) and non-governmental organization (NGO) groups in promoting the decentralized development in many areas in Japan.

(4) It also paid much more attention than before to the importance of international relations even in local cities — the so-called "local to local relations".

(5) It also emphasized the importance of economizing the budget in public investment, selecting the projects with strict priority and improving the accountability of public investment activities.

All these new directions were proposed with the recognition of the changing trends in the Japanese society and the world perspectives. It pointed out such well-known trends:

1. Globalization and international competition
2. Few children and aging of population

3. Information technology society
4. Diversified values among citizens and inclination to seek for spiritual values and natural beauty
5. Increasing roles of women in the society
6. Need for revitalization of remote rural areas and overcoming the inefficiency and waste of overcrowding in big cities
7. Loss of love for home provinces among urban citizens.

This new NCLDP has been followed by many supplementary laws and regulations. Among others, important are the law of supporting the brain, location law and also others which specify the localities in order to give priorities.[12] If these conclusions and recommendations had been followed since the 1970s, the failures of Japanese regional development policies could have been avoided. This is a precious and expensive lesson to learn.

References

[1] Ichimura, S (1998 E). *Political Economy of Japanese and Asian Development.* Berlin–Tokyo–New York: Springer-Verlag.

[2] Ichimura, S (1995 C). *Japanese Economic Development and External Relations.* Beijing, China: Beijing University Press.

[3] Ichimura, S (1970 J) *Economic Power on Trial.* Tokyo: Nihon Keizai Shinbun.

[4] Isard, W *et al* (1958 E) *Methods of Interregional and Regional Analysis.* UK: Ashgate.

[5] Ministry of Construction (1999 J). *Handbook of Regional Planning.* Gyosei, Tokyo.

[6] National Land Agency (1999 J). *Grand Design of National Land Use in the 21st Century.* Jiji Tsushin-sha, Tokyo.

[7] National Land Planning Association (1981 J). *Handbook of Regional Planning.* Asakura Shoten, Tokyo.

(Note: Letter after published year means J: Japanese; E: English, and C: Chinese).

[12] As for the specific designation of localities under some laws and regulations, see Ministry of Construction (1999 J), pp. 393–396.

Chapter 8

Development Policies in Stages

Pathos and Logos of Development[1]

1. Introduction

This chapter presents a summary and reflection of the development policy experiences in Japan and other Asian countries during the post World War II period and thereby offers a frame of reference for designing the development policies in the other countries including transitional economies. The Japanese economy grew in terms of per capita gross national product (GNP) from US$300 in 1948 to $12,750 in 1987 and nearly $30,000 in 1992. The rate of converting from Yen to US$ is the official exchange rate prevailing around 1990. This implies that the average growth rate of Japanese economy over the past 45 years is about 11%. The Japanese economy achieved it while transforming the war-time controlled economy to predominantly free private enterprise economy now. Thus, she has demonstrated a successful performance of economic and political development as an Asian nation from the poverty-stricken pre-modern State to the modern, post-industrial society only in several decades. Perhaps this demonstration is the greatest contribution of Japan to other Asian economies. In addition, it is not just a demonstration of growth performance but offers a jewel box of policy instruments as well. Such

[1]This paper — *Structural Reform in India*, was presented at the conference on Structural Reform in India in New Delhi (1996) co-sponsored by *CEG* (The Center for Economic Growth), *ICRIER* (The Indian Council for Research on International Economic Relations), *and AID*.

Table 1. Sub-periods of Post-war Japanese Development.

Years	Sub-period	Characteristics	Income level
1945–1952	Occupation period	3D* policies, liberal unions	$500
1952–1960	Reconstruction period	Recovery	$1,000
1960–1970	Rapid growth period	Income doubling plan	$3,500
1970–1980	Shocks period	Oil shocks, Nixon shocks	$10,000
1980–1990	Internationalization period	Free trade	$20,000
1990–2000	Political economy period	Global, regional free trade	$30,000

Notes: *means de-militarization, de-monopolization and democratization: occupation policies.

an authoritative study known as the "Hla Myint report", undertaken by an Asian Development Bank (ADB) study group just before 1970, predicted only a modest 5.5% growth rate for East and Southeast Asian countries in the 1970s (ADB, 1971). Their actual performance turned out to be 7.4%, faster than any other region in the world, whether industrialized or underdeveloped, including even the oil-rich Middle East. Despite the successful performance of Japanese and Asian economies on the whole, many failures were unavoidable in some aspects. With better policies, therefore, they could have achieved far better than really in the past. Table 1 shows that the post-war Japanese economy has come through some characteristic periods.

The post-war performance of Asian economies surprised everyone in the world. A World Bank report called it "Asian Miracle". But Asia was once known as the place of Oriental despotism and widespread, irreducible poverty. Even as late as 1968, "*Asian Drama*" was written as a tragedy of stagnation by Dr. Gunnar Myrdal, a world authority on Asia. It did not take long, however, for pessimism to gradually yield to optimism, as most Asian underdeveloped countries began to follow suit to the fast growth of Japan.

2. Factors for Japanese and Asian Rapid Growth

First of all, the main factors to explain the successful development of Japanese and Asian economies have to be summarized in order to explain what policies have been adopted.

2.1. *Ten Factors for Japanese Economic Growth*

The reasons for rapid Japanese economic growth were the following.[2]

1. High rate of capital accumulation.
2. High rate of saving.
3. Industrious and well-educated labor force.
4. High rate of growth of agricultural production.
5. Quick learning and improving of foreign high technology.
6. Excellent management and labor relations.
7. Very adequate fiscal and monetary policies.
8. Excellent guidepost of government industrial policy.
9. Banking sector's excellent counseling for private enterprises.
10. Political stability.

Most factors would require no explanation. These factors explain the mechanism or logos of Japanese rapid growth.

2.2. *Ten Factors for Asian Economic Development*

The factors responsible for the economic development of Asian economies are very similar to those for Japan. In another context I discussed them and mentioned the following ten factors.[3]

1. The high rate of capital accumulation.
2. The high rate of saving.
3. The successful transfer of technology appropriate for Asian agriculture and manufacturing industries in each stage of development.
4. Good quality of labor force and declining rate of fertility.
5. Export-oriented development strategies in the open economies.
6. The locomotive roles of the United States and Japan.
7. Relatively sound fiscal and monetary policies.

[2]The interested reader may be referred to my old paper: (1970). The challenge of rising sun. *Quadrant*.

[3]Ichimura, S (1988). The pattern and the process of Asian economic development. In *Challenge of Asian Developing Countries*, S Ichimura (ed.). Tokyo: Asian Productivity Organization. Both papers in footnote 2 and here are reprinted in Ichimura, S (1998). *Political Economy of Japanese and Asian Development*. Berlin and Tokyo: Springer-Verlag.

8. Tolerable distribution of income.
9. Steady build-up of bureaucracy and private enterprises in every stage of development.
10. Infrequent occurrence of social unrest and political instability.

The relative importance of these factors differs from one country to another and from one stage of development to another. In the early stage the contribution of mobilizing surplus labor or disguised unemployment is very significant. But it will be exhausted quickly unless the economy successfully reallocates the various other resources and investment from abroad to more efficient industries. The success of "Green Revolution" in most Asian countries was brought about not just by mobilizing the surplus labor in the rural areas but also by introducing new technology and new inputs like chemical fertilizers even in paddy villages in Java. Such pessimistic views like Paul Krugman's or Kunio Yoshihara's "*Ersatz Capitalism*"[4] do not seem to be supported by evidence in East and Southeast Asian performance so far.

In the case of other Asian economies, the human elements of no. 4 among the ten factors above were especially noteworthy in comparison with the underdeveloped countries in the rest of the world. The economic policies of respective governments have much to be desired. We shall briefly discuss them here and then add some remarks on the common features of Japanese and Asian development in two respects: (a) acceleration and deceleration of growth rate and (b) income distribution in Asian countries.

3. Seven Aspects of Policies for Economic Development

In order to realize fully these factors, the Japanese government carefully designed its over-all economic policies in seven aspects listed in Table 2. Japan is unique in covering widely these seven aspects of development policies and reporting the details of them in the official documents.

First, "Macro Demand Management Policies" are nothing but the standard policies in American texts. They are designed to control the business cycles in the market economy. The so-called Keynesian policies to

---

[4]Krugman, P (1994). The myth of East Asia's miracle. *Foreign Affairs*, Nov/Dec, pp. 2–16; Yoshihara, K (1988). *The Rise of Ersatz Capitalism in Southeast Asia*. Oxford: Oxford University Press.

Table 2. Seven Policy Aspects and Government Offices in Charge.

Policy levels or aspects	Government offices in charge
1. Macro demand management policies	Ministry of Finance & Bank of Japan
2. Industrial policy	Ministry of International Trade and Industry
3. Distribution policy	Ministry of Finance & Ministry of Welfare *et al.*
4. Regional development policy	National Land Agency & Ministry of Construction
5. Man power and education policy	Ministry of Education & Ministry of Labor
6. Research and development policy	Science and Technology Agency
7. Regulation; institution reforms	Prime Minister's Office; special committees

control the aggregate demand and money demand and supply are the main instruments so that no further elaboration is needed here.

The authorities must carefully analyze the market conditions not only in each country but also in the world. Every year Japanese government publishes two White Papers: "*Economic White Paper*" and "*World Economy White Paper*" for this purpose and offer their careful analyses of the domestic and global economic conditions. These documents usually give the guideposts of government's analyses and policy orientation to the business community. In addition, the Japanese government publishes from time to time the medium-term economic plans. These plans are simply the indicative plans to give the prediction of likely course of Japanese economy in five to seven years to come, and offer the guide-lines for macro fiscal and monetary policies to the government agencies and private enterprises. They are widely circulated and read by government officials, businessmen, bankers and university students. Often the typical questions for the entrance examinations of government ministries and best enterprises are taken from these White Papers. There are plenty of discussions on macro economic policies in Japan so that they will not be taken up here.

The success of Japanese policies is clearly shown by the achievement of high growth rate with little inflation. Serious recessions in the recent years are exceptional failure of fiscal and monetary policies at the time of two oil shocks and liberalization of the financial sector in Japan.

Second, Industrial Policy is very unique to post-war Japanese economic policy and has attracted much attention even from American economists and foreign governments. It may be regarded as the "Supply Side Policy" that was practiced successfully in Japan, long before the debate in the United States and somewhat unsuccessful introduction under the Reagan administration. The essence of Japanese Industrial Policy is to help the private sector develop new industries as the Japanese economy move up the world market and many private enterprises restructure their production activities as the consumers' demand and the composition of exports shift. The macro management of aggregate demand alone cannot create quickly enough the corresponding supply of necessary products in the domestic economy. Industrial Policy had two clear purposes. First, it was designed to develop the export industries critically important in each stage of development. Second, it tried helping the declining industries restructure themselves as well as the medium and small enterprises improve their technologies and management. As the result, the medium and small enterprises survived to maintain the high level of employment in the ever changing industrial world. The tools and measures of industrial policy have changed over time. It must be emphasized that somewhat substantial support to some selected industries such as ship-building industries in early stage or electronics industry in later stage were undertaken under the special laws which permitted the government do preferential treatment to these industries. However, support to some relatively less important industries and coordination or reconciliation of industries' stakes were often undertaken through "administrative guidance" by the Ministry of International Trade and Industry (MITI). One cannot claim that the government's industrial policies have been successful in all the cases, but in many cases they seem to have guided the future course of Japanese industrial restructuring well and particularly in making the declining industries die less painfully and the small and medium companies adjust their production lines soon enough to survive and move up the market with better technologies. There are many valuable works on this subject so that I need not repeat their works but simply point out the importance of these policies[5] in Japan.

[5]Among many works, important are: Hiroya, U (1987) *Industrial Policy in Japan* (in Japanese) and Ryutaro, K (ed.) (1984). *Japanese Industrial Policy*. Tokyo: University of Tokyo Press. A brief exposition is given by my working papers: "Japanese industrial restructuring policies," 1980, 1981 and "Moving up the market," 1982, quoted in Appendix. Both are reprinted in my *Political Economy of Japanese and Asian Development*, *op. cit.*

Table 3. Tableau of Industrialization Stages and its Structural Shifts.

	Domestic production	Export	Import	Government support	Capital	Exchange rate
Agriculture	U →	L↑	H↑	—	—	—
Resources	—	—	—	L↑	—	—
Light industry	L↑	L↑ U↑	H↑	L↑ U↑	L↓	—
Heavy industry	H↑	U↑ H↑	L↑ I↑	H↑	L↑	H↑
Information industry	I↑	I↑	—	I↑	I↑	I↑

Notes: U: Underdeveloped stage, L: Light industry stage, H: Heavy-chemical industry stage, I: Information industry stage.

In this connection the most important problem is how to select a few key industries to promote in each stage of development. Table 3 clarifies the necessity of the problems and its related aspects of policy-making in each stage of development. In the under-development stage, domestic production is limited to agricultural production and some limited light industries and in some countries the exploration of natural resources. In an early stage of industrialization, the exports consist of light industry' products but imports the products of heavy industries. The capital will be imported and the exchange rate had better remain weaker. In some cases the exchange rates are deliberately kept too strong even in this stage due to the need of repaying the debt of imported capital for industrialization. In later stage of development, however, the balance of payments begins to be favorable or it becomes easier to import with favorable conditions. Government subsidies and other forms of support must be given to the new industries to be developed. In the country like Japan whose scale of economy was large enough, it was possible to follow the American pattern to develop one set of industries of every kind, taking the US manufacturing sector as a model. But as her industrialization becomes more competitive and challenged from below, she has faced the problem of selecting old industries to give up as well as new industries to promote. The former is more difficult than the latter. In the case of a national economy of smaller scale, selection must be sharper. Specialization is an economic necessity.

Third, the Japanese government has paid very careful attention to the "egalitarian distribution of people's welfare". As Table 18 shows, a simple comparison of income distribution in major countries proves how egalitarian the Japanese economy has been throughout the post-war years. Indeed, the Gini ratios show an improvement even in the early stage of post-war reconstruction period against the famous "Kuznets' thesis". Policies to prevent the distribution of income and wealth from deterioration or improve the income distribution may be called "Distribution Policy". The most fundamental step to this effect was, as is well-known, the "Land Reform" in the early stage of post-war years. The same was done in Korea, Taiwan and mainland China.

In addition, Japanese taxation levies a very heavy inheritance tax and very progressive income tax. The former has made the distribution of wealth very egalitarian, whereas the latter redistributes the personal incomes more equally. In Japan tax evasion is not so prevalent. A well-known expression "Ku–Ro–Yon" (Nine–Six–Four) may prove it. It means that the wages and salaries are caught 90% for taxation, the corporate profits of medium and small enterprises 60%, and the farmers' incomes 40%. Some serious empirical studies supported that this popular guess figures were more or less correct. It seems clear that tax evasion in most Asian countries[6] is at least as bad as these figures show.

This tax evasion had the effect of improving, good or bad, the distribution of incomes among different professional groups, because those evading the taxes are relatively poorer section of the citizens. "Distribution Policy" has several other aspects, besides working on the incomes of households and corporations. There are many other policies in Japan that work to improve income and wealth distribution such as transfer payments to unfortunate families, carefully designed welfare system; particularly the generous public medical care system, which reduces the medical expenses of the aged above 70 to 10% of the cost. Subsidies and support to the small and medium companies are practiced as Industrial Policy. Other supplementary policies and similar supports provided to the relatively poor regions like Hokkaido and Okinawa in Regional Development Plan certainly have the distribution effects to be discussed next.

Fourth, "Regional Development Policy" is mainly concerned with the use of national land: where to locate industries and which districts must be developed by public investments. Table 4 demonstrates how the

[6]Konishi, S. (1992). Estimate of tax evasion in Thailand and Indonesia. *Presented at the Seoul Convention of the East Asian Economic Association*, August.

Table 4. Economic Plans, Regional Development Plans, and Regional Policy.

	Economic plan	Development plan	Regional policy
1945–1952	* Reconstruction plan Interim report (47.12) * Three years self-reliance plan (51.1)	* Basic guidelines for national land use (45.9) * Land development law (50) + Hokkaido development plan (51.10)	1. Food production increase 2. Reconstruction of devastated land, infrastructure and housing 3. Resource development 4. Inflation control
1953–1960	* On economic self-reliance five year plan (53.12) * Economic self-reliance plan (55.12) * New long-term economic plan (57.12)	* Preparation for national comprehensive development plan (54.9) * Tokyo metro-plan (58.7) + Tohoku development plan (58.8) + Kyushu development plan (59.11)	1. Construction of infrastructure for industrial development 2. Calamity prevention 3. Correction of regional income differentials 4. Appropriate relocation of plants to resolve regional differentials in concentration and scarceness
1960–1970	* National income doubling plan (60.10) * Medium-term economic plan (65.1) * Economic & social development plan (67.3) * New national comprehensive development. plan (69.5)	+ Shikoku development plan (60.12) * National comprehensive development plan (62.10) * Promotion of new industrial city law + Hokuriku & chugoku development plans (64.2) + Kinki metro-plan (65.5) + Chubu metro-plan (68.6)	1. Preparation of Tokaido Megalopolis: prevention of too rapid urbanization 2. Development of new industrial centers 3. Reducing regional gaps in income and industrial activities 4. Megalopolis industrial and urban zones 5. Overcoming pollution

(*Continued*)

Table 4. (*Continued*)

	Economic plan	Development plan	Regional policy
1970–1980	* New economic & social development plan (70.5) * Economic & social plan (74.6) * Economic plan for late 1970s (76.5) * New economic & social comprehensive development seven year plan (79.9)	+ Biwa lake development plan (72.12) * Promotion of industrial relocation law (72) + Okinawa development fundamental plan (73.2) * Third national comprehensive development plan (77.11)	1. Reorientation of nation-wide land use 2. Reduction of regional gaps in environmental conditions 3. Construction of transportation and communication network 4. Human habitation harmonious with nature
1980–1990	* Prospect & guideline for the 1980s (83.8) * Five year plan for economic management (88.5)	* Forth national comprehensive development plan (87.6)	1. Decentralization of functions performed by Metro-Tokyo 2. Develop and specialize other local centers 3. Multi-polar use of land

Notes: * represents nation-wide plans; + represents regional plans.

government has dealt with the problem. Land is the scarcest factor in Japan, so that efficiency in land-use is number one problem in regional development. Efficiency requirement by necessity leads to concentration and urbanization. From the very beginning of post-war years as well as in the pre-war days, the government has had the national plans for land-use, but have never been very successful. So many regional development plans listed in Table 4 tried to guide the location of industrial activities and direct the enormous migration for the past four decades but in vain. The regional development policies for guiding the location of industries and habitation of people have been reported mainly in four "National Comprehensive Development Plans" in 1962, 1972, 1977 and 1988, although the government had many other regional development plans long before 1960 and thereafter.

Many regional plans were prepared by the prefectural governments under the guidance of the Ministry of Construction or later the National Land Agency. They were national guide-posts in allocating the enormous amount of public investments in reclamation land and constructing many highways or special industrial zones. The chosen localities receive great benefits so that the choice is politically very sensitive. Table 4 gives a list of the many regional development plans prepared in each district. The first regional development plan was prepared to synthesize the preceding provincial plans particularly in under-developed areas like Hokkaido.

In relations to these regional plans as Table 5 shows on its right-hand side, the post-war period is sometimes sub-divided into the following six periods. They correspond to the ones presented in Table 1. The title of each sub-period suggests what issues were targeted in each National Comprehensive Development Plan. It began in the third period. Any regional and preferential treatment of expending public investment must be based on some special laws; otherwise, any regionally differential treatment would have been very limited in Japan. As Table 3 shows, the government has tried hard to mitigate the concentration of industrial activities in certain areas, particularly around the established centers like Tokyo, Nagoya or Osaka; especially Tokyo. That is the reason why the Fourth National Total Development Plan at last admitted the idea of "Multi-Polar Dispersed Use of National Land". Nevertheless, nobody believes that this Fourth Plan materializes itself, unless it is substantiated by the political decisions in the form of some laws to decentralize or disperse all the activities in Tokyo by even moving the Capital.

Table 5. Growth Stages and Regional Development Plan Periods.

Growth sub-periods			Regional development plan sub-periods		
1	1945–1952	Occupation period	1	1945–1955	Resource development
2	1952–1960	Reconstruction period	2	1955–1960	Industrial base construction
3	1960–1970	Rapid growth period	3	1960–1972	Eliminate region gaps
4	1970–1980	Shocks period	4	1972–1977	Reorient land-use
5	1980–1990	Globalization period	5	1977–1987	Establish stable habitation
—	—	—	6	1987–	Relocate with multi-polar

Fifth, "Man Power and Education Policy" is concerned with the improvement of human factors. Long before the supply side economics was brought up in the United States as if it were something new, Japanese economists and policy-makers were in full recognition of the needs and importance of the policies affecting the supply side of national product. They recognized the importance of not only Industrial Policy discussed above but also the policies related to education, science and technology. Many official documents report on these policies and the related analyses of the demand for and the supply of labor in various qualities. The best documents are the "*White Paper On Labor* (Rodo Hakusho)" and the "*White Paper on Education* (Kyoiku Hakusho)". The basic information on education is collected by the Fundamental Survey of Education (Kyoiku Kihon Chosa). This survey not only covers the various matters in school education as such but also the demand side for education like the industrial composition of employed graduates from high schools, colleges and various departments of universities. There was also the corresponding Fundamental Survey of Labor (Rodoryoku Kihon Chosa) for similar purposes. The Japanese government and private enterprises made the efforts to match the supply of various types of labor and human resources to the demand of the economy or the society at various stages of development. This is neither new nor special, because the emphasis on education and training on and off the job was non-controversial ever since the very beginning of modernization in the Meiji Era.

The improvement of labor quality has two aspects: first, education and second, morale of the representative or average citizen. Improvement of education in pre-war and post-war Japan can be seen in the Table 6. The percentage of junior high school graduates proceeding to high schools is almost 95% in 1989, and those to universities and junior colleges are 36.3%. It is comparable with the US figure of 42% of the same age group enrolled in the colleges and universities. Since the US figures of students include part-time students, they may be interpreted about the same. This was achieved around 1975 long before Japanese per capita GNP caught up with that of the US. Historically the Japanese government spent a very high portion of its expenditure for education right after the Meiji Restoration. Primary schools increased from 12,597 in 1873 to 24,303 in 1875; middle schools from 20 to 116; colleges from 26 to 110 in the same two years. As Table 7

Table 6. The Number of Students (million; thousand).

	Population	Primary	Middle	Girls	Normal	College	High school	University
1873	35.1	1,326	1.8	—	—	4.1	—	—
1880	36.6	2,349	5.6	—	5.2	5.1	—	—
1890	39.9	3,096	11.6	3.1	5.3	10.3	4.4	1.3
1990	43.8	4,684	78.3	12.0	15.6	14.9	5.7	3.2
1910	49.1	6,862	122.3	56.2	25.4	33.0	6.3	7.2
1920	55.9	8,633	177.2	151.3	26.6	49.0	8.8	21.9
1930	64.4	10,112	345.7	369.0	43.9	90.0	20.6	69.6
1940	71.9	12,335	432.3	555.6	41.4	141.5	20.3	82.0
1945	72.1	12,818	639.8	875.8	56.3	213.0	21.7	98.8
1947	78.1	10,639	271.0	358.1	61.2	231.4	30.6	129.7
	—	—	Junior high	High school	Engineering college	Junior College	University	Others
1950	83.2	11,191	5,332	1,935	—	15.1	224.9	503.4
1960	93.4	12,590	5,899	3,239	—	83.4	626.4	1275.4
1970	103.7	9,493	4,716	4,231	44.3	263.2	1406.5	1403.5
1980	117.1	11,826	5,094	4,621	46.3	371.1	1835.3	1249.1
1989	122.6	9,606	5,619	5,645	52.0	461.8	2066.9	1280.5

Notes: 1. The original name for engineering colleges is Koto Senmon Gakko, which was started in 1965. The number here includes only those at the level of colleges; the last two years students and also those in national schools for training engineering teachers. 2. Others include various vocational schools.

Table 7. Public Expenditure for Education as % to National Income.

Year	Japan	US	UK	France	Germany	USSR
1961	4.6	6.9	4.5	3.0	5.1	7.1
1970	4.7	7.2	7.0	4.7	4.7	8.6
1975	6.5	7.6	8.2	5.0	6.4	9.0
1980	7.2	7.2	7.5	5.4	6.3	8.7
1983	7.1	7.3	6.0	6.4	8.2	—
1994	8.2	3.2	—	17.0	4.1	—

Table 8. Public Schools *versus* Private Schools: 1989 (1,000).

	School	Private (%)	Students	Private (%)	Teachers	Private (%)
Total	65,613	27.6	26,770	24.3	1,354	20.5
Kindergarten	15,080	58.3	2,037	77.4	100	75.0
Primary school	24,853	0.7	9,606	0.7	445	0.7
Middle school	11,264	5.4	5,619	3.5	286	3.2
High school	5,510	23.7	5,645	28.4	284	22.7
Engineering junior college	62	6.5	52	5.7	4	4.4
Junior college	584	83.9	462	90.1	20	82.5
University	499	72.9	2,067	7,206	121	50.8
Graduate school	—	—	85	31.8	52	30.6
Other schools	7,760	82.3	1,197	92.7	42	76.1

shows, the present level of government education expenditure is about the same as those in most Western countries.

This does not mean that the expenditure spent in Japan is about the same as the US per capita, because the private schools are much more predominant at least at higher education in Japan than in Europe or even the United States. Table 8 shows the division between the private schools and the public (national and local governments') schools. The figures in % columns show the proportions occupied by private schools in all levels of educational institutions in Japan. Clearly, except for the primary and junior high schools that are compulsory in Japan, the private schools are predominant. This does not mean that all the expenses of the private schools are completely supported from the private sources. Approximately half of the expenses for teachers in private universities are subsidized by the governments, so that a fair amount of public expenditure for education goes to private educational institutions. Nevertheless, it is true that a predominant portion of the expenditure for education has been borne by the private sector.

The domination of private schools particularly at higher education seems to have had pros and cons. An advantage was that education could respond more quickly to the demand side, but a disadvantage was that the inexpensive fields of education are developed beyond the social needs. Examples of the former are the engineering departments, whereas examples of the latter are the development of too many easy-going liberal

Table 9. Specialty Composition of University Departments and Graduate Schools (%).

	Undergraduates		MA courses		Doctoral courses	
	1978	1988	1978	1988	1978	1988
1. Humanities	13.3	14.7	15.3	10.5	15.8	13.0
2. Social sciences	41.2	39.1	12.6	9.5	13.8	9.8
3. Science	3.1	3.3	10.0	10.3	15.8	10.9
4. Engineering	19.7	19.8	42.6	45.1	15.2	14.1
5. Agronomy	3.4	3.4	7.7	8.4	6.3	5.7
6. Medical science	3.8	3.9	—	0.2	26.8	40.2
7. Pharmacy	2.0	2.0	3.0	3.7	2.2	2.1
8. Home economics	1.8	1.9	—	—	—	—
9. Pedagogy	7.5	7.5	4.0	8.0	3.3	2.4
10. Others	4.2	4.4	4.8	4.4	0.8	1.0

arts colleges. On the whole the advantages seem to have dominated the disadvantages by responding efficiently to the social needs and offered various kinds and levels of education to the education fervor among the Japanese families and ever-growing industries.

As Table 9 seems to show, the response to the social needs seem to be more clearly observable at the graduate school levels. But the inflexibility of department composition of universities seem to show the different degrees of correspondence to the social requirements as Table 10 shows. A more careful study is possible from the data of the Fundamental Survey of Education to see if graduates are employed in their proper specialties.

The improvement of labor quality has been achieved by on and off the job training within private enterprises and government offices. Japanese style management is based on life-time or stable employment, so that training and job-rotation are inseparable from the employment and management style. This requires the solid establishment of enterprises themselves and excellent management. The degree of practice in Japan is: 86.0% for stable employment and 51.6% for job-rotation. The quality of labor shows up also in the morale of workers in the jobs. This can be seen in the number of hours lost in one year, the rate of accidents, labor disputes, absenteeism and generally the social crime rate. In these aspects Japan shows significantly lower rates than other advanced countries.

Table 10. The Rate of Employment for Graduates (%).

	Undergraduates		Junior Colleges	
	1978	1988	1978	1988
Total	71.9	77.8	71.0	82.0
1. Humanities	57.1	74.5	68.7	82.7
2. Social sciences	77.4	86.1	71.4	80.4
3. Liberal arts	—	—	64.6	81.7
4. Sciences	63.3	69.2	—	—
5. Engineering	82.4	81.0	77.4	80.9
6. Agronomy	69.4	78.0	72.0	66.9
7. Medical & health	44.1	42.5	84.2	82.5
8. Medicines	2.7	1.1	—	—
9. Dentists	66.1	48.2	—	—
10. Pharmacy	64.0	72.1	—	—
11. Other medical streams	76.4	83.7	—	—
12. Sea men	89.1	52.0	—	—
13. Home economics	60.5	82.0	68.1	83.5
14. Pedagogy	73.5	68.9	78.3	85.2
15. Arts	49.4	64.1	49.0	61.3
16. Others	63.0	79.2	83.8	92.2

Table 11. Technological Balance of Payments.

	Bank of Japan (million $, %)			Bureau of Statistics (billion ¥, %)					
	Receipts	Payments	Ratio	Receipts	Payments	Ratio	Receipts	Payments	Ratio
1966	17	192	0.09	—	—	—	—	—	—
1971	60	488	0.12	27.2	134.5	0.20	(11.1)	(15.6)	(0.71)
1980	376	1439	0.26	159.6	239.5	0.66	(74.3)	(27.7)	(2.68)
1987	1385	4177	0.33	215.6	283.2	0.76	(44.8)	(56.2)	(0.79)

Notes: The figures in parentheses in Bureau of Statistics data are those of new contracts.

Sixth, "Research and Development Policy" is the last but important aspect of development policies. It is said that Japan borrowed Western technology and improved it. The "Technological Balance of Payments" demonstrates it. Japan has two sources of data: Bank of Japan and Bureau of Statistics. Tables 11 and 12 sum them up and show that Japan is still far behind the US, but already ahead of most European countries.

Table 12. Technological Balance of Payments of Major Countries: 75–92.

		Japan	US	UK	Germany	France	Italy
1975	Receipts	233	4,008	589	264	394	90
	Payments	592	473	578	679	472	480
	Ratio	0.39	8.47	1.02	0.39	0.83	0.19
1980	Receipts	644	6,617	779	430	688	233
	Payments	966	762	672	1,025	823	662
	Ratio	0.67	8.68	1.16	0.42	0.83	0.35
1985	Receipts	982	16,669	848	614	894	144
	Payments	1,229	6,215	692	1,206	1,064	546
	Ratio	0.80	2.68	1.22	0.51	0.84	0.26
1987	Receipts	1,490	22,281	980	1,081	1,348	301
	Payments	1,958	8,877	908	2,443	1,732	788
	Ratio	0.76	2.51	1.08	0.44	0.78	0.38
1992	Receipts	2,982	19,922	2,846	7,109	2,012	1,324
	Payments	3,268	4,987	2,374	10,125	2,791	2,404
	Ratio	0.91	3.99	1.20	0.70	0.72	0.55

Note: Figures in 1992 are taken from OECD, Data Base for Industrial Outlook, which is different from the ones in earlier years, so that they are not comparable.

The expenditure for R & D has increased very much in Japan as well as in many advanced countries, but that in Japan jumped in the 1970s and the 1980s in comparison with other countries as Table 13 shows. One may observe that from 1966 to 1987, GNP of Japan increased 8.9 times, whereas R & D expenditure increased 18.4 times — the annual rate of increase is 14.8%, of which the government funds increased 11.5 times. From 1970 to 1988, the number of researchers increased 2.6 times; the annual rate is 5.5%. With this remarkable increase in R & D expenditure and the number of researchers, one should certainly expect, the high returns resulting in the increase in technological innovations. It is showing up in the increase in the patents obtained in Japan and abroad. From 1966 to 1987, the patents applied in Japan increased from 62,962 to 311,006; 5 times. The patents granted were 3.1 times more.

Japanese policies for development have been coordinated at these six levels. The first macro-policies were primarily the responsibility of Economic Planning Agency, the Ministry of Finance and the Bank of Japan. The second industrial policies are mainly undertaken by the Ministries of International Trade & Industry (manufacturing industries), and agriculture,

Table 13. R & D Expenditure in Selected Countries (billion, $).

		Japan	US	USSR	Germany	France	UK
1975	Expenditure	15.5	—	—	—	—	—
	%/National income	2.1	—	—	—	—	—
	%/Public fund	27.5	—	—	—	—	—
1980	Expenditure	27.8	62.6	—	—	—	—
	%/National income	2.4	2.6	—	—	—	—
	%/Public fund	25.8	47.1	—	—	—	—
1985	Expenditure	48.2	107.4	—	—	—	—
	%/National income	3.2	3.0	—	—	—	—
	%/Public fund	19.4	47.7	—	—	—	—
1987	Expenditure	62.3	118.7	43.1*	31.6	20.5	12.9*
	%/National income	3.3	3.3	5.0	3.1	2.5	2.7
	%/Public fund	19.9	48.2	48.3	37.7	43.7	38.5
1993	Expenditure	13,709	17,875	—	6,293	4,025	2,822
	% /GNP	2.91	2.53	—	2.51	2.43	2.12
	%/Public fund	21.6	42.3	—	—	45.6	35.4

Notes: 1. Those with *; USSR and UK figures are for 1986. 2. The figures for Korea are: in 1986, 1,523 billion which is 2.3% of national income and its 19.0% comes from the government funds. 3. Figures for 1993 are trillion Yen so that they are not comparable with others.

fishery and forestry (for primary industries) by the Ministry of Agriculture, Fishery and Forestry. The third "Distribution Policy" is a mixture of various fiscal and other government policies. In Japan there was no ministry quite responsible for consumers; only a bureau in Economic Planning Agency is responsible to monitor the living conditions of the nation and issues the While Paper on nation's living conditions every year. From time to time it issued an excellent report like "Economic Growth and Income Distribution, 1987" and reported the changes in the distribution of income and wealth and other related issues. In addition, social welfare policies were taken care of by the Ministry of Welfare. The social welfare in Japan reached by now a very high standard, particularly in medical care and unemployment insurance. This last policy must have contributed to the recent stability in labor relations and extinguished social unrest in Japan in recent years. The Ministries of Construction, Transportation and Communication are responsible for "Regional Development Policies". In order to coordinate their respective policies better, a new agency called

National Land Agency was created in 1980. The "Man Power and Education Policy" has been the responsibility of the Ministries of Labor and Education. Their excellent reports have already been quoted above. The sixth "Research and Development Policy" has been primarily handled by the Science and Technology Agency but MITI has been also extensively involved in connection with its Industrial Policy. MITI has a special Institute of Industrial Technology which employs more than one thousand scientists and engineers for developing industrial technologies. All the policies and their evaluation are well documented by the ministries in charge usually in the form of some White Papers. They are well organized as a whole.

4. Investment in Human Capital and Liberalization Policy

These six aspects of Japanese policies are very important as a whole. Among them two policies are absolutely essential to economic development: first, policies for education, second, liberalization of foreign trade and capital movement. There are some differences among Asian less developed countries (LDCs). The reasons for the differences seem to be attributable to these two aspects. First, the human and social aspects of Asian countries may be seen in the Table 14.

As these figures and more recent data show, the education investment in human capital is very impressive in most Asian countries. No doubt all Asia–Pacific countries have emphasized education and thereby improved the quality of workers, engineers, salaried persons, executives, government officials and intellectuals. The result is that the majority of workers in these countries have now secondary education, and there are enough middle managers and engineers to facilitate the transfer of higher technologies. In particular, Korea is outstanding. Among ASEAN-4, Indonesia is significantly behind, and Malaysia is behind others, particularly in higher education. In most East and Southeast Asian countries the spread of secondary education is so wide that most factories have no difficulty in employing workers with secondary education. As the result, the transfer of technology and training for new technologies can be done with little difficulty, and an introduction of such recent devices as QC circles is possible with no difficulty in Asian NIEs. By way of comparison, in South Asia only Sri Lanka and Burma have made such an extraordinary

Table 14. Indices of Social Development in Asian Countries (%).

	Literacy		Newspapers		Primary education		Secondary		Higher	
	70	85	70	85	65	85	65	82	65	85
I. *Asia*										
Japan	99	99	520	569c	100	102	82	96	13	12
Asia NIEs										
Singapore	72	86	200	279	105	115	45	71	10	12
Hong Kong	77	88	498	560	103	105	29	69	5	13
Taiwan	85	92	—	—	98	100	59	80	8	18
S. Korea	88	96c	136	192c	101	96	35	94	6	32
ASEAN-4										
Malaysia	58	73	75	173	90	99	28	53	2	6
Thailand	79	91	20	52	78	97	14	30	2	20
Philippines	83	86	14	37	113	106	41	65	19	38
Indonesia	57	74	—	14	72	118	12	39	1	7
Giant Economies										
China	43	69c	—	19	89	124	24	39	0	2
India	33	43	16	19	74	92	27	35	5	9
South Asia										
Pakistan	21	29	—	18	40	47	12	17	2	5
Sri Lanka	78	87	49	106	93	103	35	63	2	5
Myanmar	66c	81	9	14	71	102	15	24	1	4
Nepal	13	25	2	7	20	79	5	25	1	5
Bangladesh	23	33	—	8	—	100	—	43	—	3
Socialist Economies										
Vietnam	—	84k	—	8	—	100	—	43	—	3
Kampuchea	—	—	—	—	77	—	9	—	1	—
Laos	44c	84	—	—	40	97	2	18	—	—
N. Korea	—	—	—	—	—	—	—	—	—	—
II. *Latin American Countries*										
Argentina	—	—	—	—	101	108	28	70	14	36
Brazil	—	—	—	—	108	104	16	35	2	11
Chile	—	—	—	—	124	109	34	69	6	16
Colombia	—	—	—	—	84	117	17	50	3	13

Note: Figures for newspaper subscription are per thousand; c: 1980; k: 1979.

educational effort and thereby achieved such high literacy rate. The health of workers also has improved substantially. It is known now that while calorie intake differs among the different groups of economies, the majority of workers in every country get more than the required minimum daily amount of calories now so that they can work as hard as they are willing to.

Another important feature of the improvement in the quality of labor is the demographic transition showing a decline of fertility rate. It has progressed in most Asian countries, however, with the big gaps among the groups reflecting the policy differences. The correlation between the level of per capita GNP and the fertility rate is very high, except for China, where a population policy has been very aggressive.

Thus, in summary, three domestic directions and three external conditions seem to be crucial for achieving economic development.

On the domestic economic policies:

1. Fundamentally to open the national economy to the outside world and adopt the liberal policies for trade, foreign direct investment and international finance.
2. Government policies are basically oriented to growth, especially export-oriented growth.
3. The foreign exchange rate is maintained below the purchasing parity level for exportable price-elastic products, so that exports are promoted, imports restrained and capital inflow encouraged.

On the international environments:

1. The trading partners' markets are open for their imports under the conditions of free competition.
2. The supply, offer or transfer of capital equipment, technology, management know-how, and capital funds are freely and generously made to developing countries.
3. The law and order needed for free and fair trade and transactions are not disturbed by political or military conflicts.

Since the external conditions are more or less common to all the countries, what are more important for development are the domestic policies of respective countries. My own personal evaluation in each Asian

Table 15. Characteristics of Economic Policies in Asian Countries.

	Trade			Capital, loan			Exchange rate	
	Ex-pro	Imp-lib	permit	JV	Loan	permit	Undervalue	flexible
Japan	A	B	A	A	A	A	A	A
NIEs Singapore	A	A	A	A	A	A	B	B
Hong Kong	A	A	A	A	A	A	A	B
Taiwan	A	B	B	B	A	B	B	B
S. Korea	A	B	B	B	A	B	B	B
ASEAN-4 Malaysia	B	B	B	B	A	B	B	B
Thailand	B	B	B	B	A	B	B	B
Philippines	B	B	C	C	C	C	C	C
Indonesia	B	B	C	C	B	C	B	B+
Giant Economy China	B	C	C−	C−	C−	C−	C	C
India	B	C	C−	C−	C−	C−	C	C
S. Asia Sri Lanka	C	C	C−	C−	C−	C−	C	C
Pakistan	C	C	C−	C−	C−	C−	C	C
Myanmar	C	C	C−	C−	C−	C−	C	C
Nepal	C	C	C−	C−	C−	C−	C	C
Bangladesh	C	C	C−	C−	C−	C−	C	C

Notes: A = satisfactory, B = slightly restrictive, C = very restrictive, C− = extremely restrictive.

country around 1987 on these scores is shown in Table 15 above. After 1987 significant steps have been taken toward liberalization for trade and foreign direct investment. No doubt some Asian countries liberalized the restrictions and regulations of permit for trade, direct investment and loans more than other countries. Needless to say, the more restrictive the policies of one country have been, the less successful the performance of economic development of that country has been. Crucial policy decision in an early stage of development seems to make foreign direct investment open against some special interest business groups. Some Asian countries need a reconsideration of their policies on these matters.

5. Acceleration and Deceleration of Growth Rate in Development

A noticeable feature of Asian growth is its acceleration in growth rate since the 1960s. In the 1950s, even East Asian countries by no means gave the impression to such famous economists as Rosenstein Rodin that they would achieve such an impressive growth as we observed above. This is not only due to the high rate of capital accumulation and the high rate of saving, but also as can be seen from Table 12, the increase in these rates as per capita incomes of the countries go up. In programming the future development, an important consideration is how high the expected rate of growth in GDP should be set. In this connection, we carefully analyze the trends of growth rate in development with the data in Table 16.

Table 16. Capital Accumulation and Savings in Selected Asia–Pacific Economies: 1965–1986.

	GNP/ Population	Rate of capital accumulation				Saving ratio			
	1986	1965–1972	1973–1978	1979–1983	1986	1965–1972	1973–1978	1979–1983	1986
ASIA									
Japan	12,840	31.9	35.9	32.0	28.0	30.8	33.6	36.8	32.6
Singapore	7,410	36.7	34.9	40.4	40.0	23.6	32.8	35.6	40.0
Hong Kong	—	—	—	—	—	—	—	—	—
Taiwan	4,000	26.2	30.6	32.4	—	23.1	29.3	37.0	—
S. Korea	2,370	24.1	29.0	30.0	29.0	14.9	24.9	23.7	35.0
Malaysia	1,830	19.6	25.7	33.4	25.0	20.8	27.3	26.3	32.0
Thailand	810	23.8	25.4	25.3	21.0	21.3	23.6	20.5	25.0
Philippines	560	20.9	28.6	29.6	13.0	1,701	23.9	23.3	19.0
Indonesia	490	12.6	20.6	23.0	26.0	6.9	18.8	20.1	21.0
China	300	—	—	33.6	39.0	—	—	33.2	36.0
India	—	—	—	—	—	—	—	—	—
Latin American Economies									
Venezuela	2,920	29.1	35.4	26.2	20.0	29.8	36.1	29.3	21.0
Argentina	2,350	20.4	24.6	20.5	9.0	20.3	26.2	17.9	11.0
Mexico	1,860	21.3	23.4	26.1	21.0	19.2	20.2	24.2	16.0
Brazil	1,810	25.6	28.1	22.5	21.0	24.0	24.0	20.5	20.0
Chile	1,320	15.3	15.3	17.2	15.0	13.0	11.9	7.0	18.0
Ecuador	1,160	18.6	26.4	24.2	20.0	11.3	20.4	20.5	20.0
Colombia	1,139	19.0	18.8	20.0	18.0	15.4	19.1	17.2	20.0
Peru	1,090	16.7	16.0	17.0	20.0	15.2	11.4	13.5	18.0

Notes: Figures for Taiwan are in 1970 instead of 1965, and those of Singapore are in 1982 instead of 1983.
Source: World Development Report, 1985, 1986, 1988 and National Statistical Years.

A steady increase in the rate of capital accumulation is a characteristic of Japanese history for the past one hundred years. Nevertheless, the pre-war Japanese rate of capital accumulation did not exceed 15% of GNP, whereas in post-war years, the ratio has jumped from 14.6% in 1953 to as high as 32% in 1965, then leveled off at 28–30% in the early 1980s. The ratios of Asian NIEs' and ASEAN-4's capital formation to GNP has increased from somewhat below 20% in the 1960s to nearly 30% or even higher in the early 1980s.

The saving rates in our sample countries have been very high. The saving ratio went up quickly from about 16% in the late 1960s to over 20% of GNP in the early 1980s. In Taiwan and Singapore it has been even above the Japanese gross saving ratio of about 30%. Government's special policies in the two countries have played an important role. In Singapore forced saving through a device called the "Central Provident Fund" is responsible, whereas in Taiwan its government's saving is particularly high. Apart from these, however, the household saving rates are also very significant in most of our samples. Such steady increases in the rates of capital accumulation and saving with rising per capita income over the past three decades are the most fundamental characteristics of the Asia–Pacific economies. It is the fundamental cause of acceleration of growth rate in Asian countries. One should not take this fact as something which automatically accompanies economic growth in any country. For instance, in the case of Latin American countries these ratios did not increase with the rise in per capita income. In some countries the saving ratios have stabilized at around 20%, and in some countries they are coming down; whereas among the Asia–Pacific countries of our samples, only the Philippines shows a saving behavior similar to that of Latin America.

Except for Singapore and Taiwan, household saving rates for our sample reach a ceiling slightly below 30% regardless of per capita income level. Significant though this is for the relative success of the growth strategies for all these countries, the effect of the disparities in per capita income level among our four types of economies is clearly reflected in the resource gap each has characteristically experienced and consequently in the extent to which each has had to borrow from abroad to sustain its rate of capital accumulation and growth in the recent past.

Even if the rate of capital accumulation is high, rapid growth may not result unless capital is efficiently utilized. The so-called incremental capital–output ratio (ICOR) — the amount of additional capital required to increase an additional unit of gross domestic product (GDP) — is an overall index of efficiency in the use of capital. ICOR is important, because the ratio of capital formation to GDP divided by ICOR determines the growth rate of GDP. Usually as per capita income goes up, the ICOR increases. Table 17 shows that this is true for all our Asia–Pacific countries. The increases have been relatively mild owing to their successful learning of modern technology. Especially, Taiwan has kept an impressively low ratio. The Indonesian ICOR, though relatively low, must be considered relatively high for the country with its low per capita income. South Korea has a per capita income slightly lower than Taiwan's. Nevertheless she has an ICOR slightly higher, mainly because it has adopted deliberate policies to emphasize heavy-chemical industries. Malaysia and Singapore have high ICORs corresponding to their high and rising per capita incomes. The Philippines with an income level similar to Thailand has an ICOR as high as Japan's.

Despite the variations in the rates of capital accumulation: the ratios of capital formation to GDP and the values of ICOR, there seem to be a general trend in most Asian economies including Japan, the former tends first to increase and then decrease, as per capita GDP goes up. The latter seems to show a trend to increase as per capita GDP goes up, but the degree of increase seems to differ significantly from one economy to another. This implies, then, that if the demand for GDP matches more or less to the increasing level of capacity of the national economy, the rate of growth in productive capacity expressed in real GDP in each national economy has a trend of acceleration at an early stage and deceleration in later stages. Simple formulas will be the following:

$$dY/Y = (I/Y) \div I/dY, \quad \text{or}$$

$$(\text{Growth rate of } Y) = (\text{Rate of capital accumulation}) \div (\text{ICOR}),$$

where the rate of capital accumulation has the reversed U shape as a function of per capita GDP, fundamentally reflecting the similar shape in the savings

Table 17. International Comparison of Incremental Capital Output Ratio: 1965–1983.

	1965–1973			1974–1983		
	Growth rate	Investment/ GDP	ICOR	Growth rate	Investment/ GDP	ICOR
ASIA						
Japan	9.8	30.0	3.1	4.3	22.7	5.2
Singapore	13.0	36.7	2.8	8.2	37.6	4.6
Hong Kong	—	—	—	—	—	—
Taiwan	10.1	26.2	2.6	8.5	31.5	3.7
S. Korea	10.0	24.1	2.4	7.3	29.5	4.0
Malaysia	6.7	19.6	2.9	7.5	29.1	4.0
Thailand	7.8	23.8	3.1	6.9	25.4	3.7
Philippines	5.4	20.9	3.9	5.4	29.1	5.4
Indonesia	8.1	12.6	1.6	7.0	21.8	3.1
China	—	—	—	—	—	—
India	3.9	18.3	4.7	4.0	23.2	5.8
Pakistan	5.4	16.3	3.0	5.6	15.9	2.8
Sri Lanka	4.2	16.1	3.8	5.2	23.1	4.4
Myanmar	—	—	—	5.5	15.8	2.8
Nepal	—	—	—	3.7	13.8	3.7
Bangladesh	—	—	—	5.2	9.4	1.8
Socialist Econ.						
Vietnam, Kampuchea, Lao, N. Korea				—	—	—
Latin America						
Argentina	4.3	20.4	4.7	0.4	22.6	56.4
Brazil	9.8	25.8	2.6	4.8	25.3	5.3
Chile	3.4	15.3	4.5	2.9	16.3	5.6
Colombia	6.4	19.0	3.0	3.9	19.4	5.0
Mexico	7.9	21.3	2.7	5.6	24.7	4.4
Peru	3.5	16.7	4.8	1.8	17.5	9.7
Venezuela	5.1	29.1	5.7	2.5	25.8	10.3

Sources: World Development Report, 1985 and 1986; National Statistical Year Books and Asian Development Bank, Key Indicators of Developing Member Countries of ADB.

function as depending on per capita income; ICOR is an increasing function of per capita GDP. Since the growth rate of GDP minus the rate of increase in population is the growth rate of per capita GDP, this equation can be reduced to a simple non-linear differential or difference equation for per capita GDP, ignoring the difference between GNP and GDP for the time being. If the functional shapes of I/Y and ICOR as a function of per capita

GDP are not too complicated, one can derive the passage of Y over time by solving the equation. But without going through such calculation, it can be seen that the growth rate of GDP will go up if I/Y increases while ICOR remains unchanged or increases only slightly. This seems to have been the case for most Asian developing countries.

Fortunately most countries had the very high saving ratios so that they could grow fast without relying on foreign loans as much as Latin American countries. But if ICOR goes up as was the case in the Philippines or most South Asian countries, the acceleration of growth rate cannot take place. As per capita income goes up further, I/Y begins to taper off and ICOR starts going up, so that the growth rate slows down. This has been the case of Japan and some newly industrializing economies in recent years.

From these observations one may get the impression that even in the Asia–Pacific countries capital may be excessively utilized, and the ideal value should have been something like Taiwan's. But India has an extremely high ICOR despite its low income level, implying its inefficient use of capital. ICOR values in Latin America also are particularly high. Even if we consider the conditions of debt-ridden recession, still their ICORs are too high, because even under the hypothetical growth rate for 1974–1983 remaining the same as that for 1965–1973, the ICORs for Argentina, Peru and Venezuela are 5.3, 5.0 and 5.1 respectively. With the exception perhaps of the Philippines, it is clear that the usage of capital has been much more efficient in the Asia–Pacific region than in South Asia or Latin America.

As for technological innovation in Asia during the period under investigation, the most remarkable is the Green Revolution, which introduced high-yielding varieties of cereals, including rice, the most important crop in the Asia–Pacific region. New technology offered new opportunities to increase productivity in Asian agriculture, where the use of land was already very intensive and the potential for extensive expansion of production was very limited. This seems to have made it possible to increase agricultural production without too much capital requirements, although an introduction of high-yielding varieties of rice required additional investments in fertilizer and irrigation. Unless the "Green Revolution" made it possible to increase not only production but also had allowed to absorb the enormous surplus labor in the rural areas in Asia, the distribution of income and social stability would have been much worse in all agrarian areas in Asia.

6. Economic Growth without Serious Political Disruption

Japanese development was achieved not without political disruption, as we argued in earlier sections, but considering the speed of growth, the degree of political stability maintained is impressive. Alfred Marshall warned that too rapid growth might lead to social unrest. Simon Kuznets mentioned that economic growth had to be thought as a process of social disruption as well as improvement of social welfare. Since the growth of Japanese economy has been so rapid, it is no surprise for Japan to have experienced the kinds of political turbulence discussed in earlier sections. What is surprising is that she could manage to go through the hardships with only that much political disruption. The reasons why serious political instability did not result from Japanese rapid growth may be explained by the following formula adopted from Karl Deutsch's and Samuel Huntington's formula which are somewhat more complex.[7]

Economic Discontent	= Material Want/Consumption
Social Discontent	= Economic Discontent/Income Distribution
Social Frustration	= Social Discontent/Social Mobility
Political Instability	= Social Frustration/Political Participation

Economic discontent of the representative Japanese household did not increase, very much thanks to the fact that most Japanese households kept their material want modest, and that rapid economic growth increased per capita consumption more than most families expected. Of course many families were still dissatisfied, but their discontent did not spread and reach the degree of social frustration, because income distribution in Japan remained very egalitarian. The Gini ratios throughout the post-war years indicate that they did not only deteriorate much after the war but soon improved. Nevertheless, some degree of social discontent remained significantly in urban areas primarily due to the poor living conditions. This

[7]Karl, D (1961). Social mobilization and political development. *American Political Science Review*, September; Huntington, SP (1968). *Political Order in Changing Societies*. New Haven: Yale University Press; Myron, W and SP Huntington (ed.) (1987). *Understanding Political Development*. Boston: Little Brown & Co. See Ichimura, S and J Morley (1992). Economic growth and political change in East Asia. Introduction in *Driven by Economic Growth*, Morley, J (eds.). New York: ME Sharpe.

is proven by the fact that the opposition parties obtained more support in the urban areas than in the country sides.

In other Asian countries except for Taiwan income inequality is much more serious, as Table 18 shows. There seem to be good reasons to believe that these figures probably grossly underestimate the inequality of income in most countries in Asia as well as in other parts of the world. Distribution of income such as those shown here may be regarded as an index expressing the sharing of welfare among the various social groups to be derived from the growth of national income. Comparison with the degree of inequality of Japan's income distribution is perhaps an improper comparison, since Japan's is extraordinarily low even by world standards. If one compares the income distribution in the Asian countries other than Japan with other developing countries, one finds those in our sample to be unusually equitable. Table 18 gives the percentage of income of the richest 10% and 20% of the population, and the poorest 20%, based on household expenditure surveys of various countries. The study years are different from one country to another, but they do give a rough impression that the income share of the richest 10% in Asia is in the 30% range, whereas that in Latin America is between 40 and 50%. The income share of the poorest 20% in Asia–Pacific countries ranges from 3.5 to 6.6%, whereas in Latin America except for Argentina it varies from 1.9 to 2.9%. If we define an index of inequality as the average income of the richest 10% divided by the average income of the poorest 20%, the indexes derived are those shown in the last column of Table 18. Argentina seems to be exceptional among the Latin American countries for its relative equality. The Philippines and Malaysia seem to be exceptional among the Asia–Pacific countries for their relative inequality. It is also true that inequality in the Philippines and Indonesia may be underestimated. It is not reasonable to suppose, therefore, that income distribution poses no problems in the region. Nevertheless, even with these qualifications, one cannot escape the conclusion that in general the income distribution in the societies of our sample is much more egalitarian than that in the societies of Latin America. As for the relationship between economic growth and income inequality, the inverted U-shaped relation of Simon Kuznets is well known; income distribution tends to worsen in the early stages of industrialization until a turning point is reached at some level of per capita income. By comparing

Table 18. Income Inequality of Selected Asian and Latin American Countries.

		Lowest 20%	High 20%	Highest 10%	Degree of inequality	
	Year	A	B	c	b/a	2c/b
I. *Asia–Pacific Industrial, market*						
Japan	1979	8.7	37.5	22.4	(4.3)	5.4
Asian NIEs						
Singapore	1975	5.4	48.9	28.7	(9.1)	10.1
Taiwan	1979	8.6	37.5	22.0	(4.4)	5.1
South Korea	1976	5.7	45.3	27.5	(7.9)	9.6
Hong Kong	1980	5.4	47.0	31.3	(8.7)	11.6
Developing Economy						
Malaysia	1973	3.5	56.1	39.8	(16.0)	22.7
Thailand	1976	5.6	49.8	34.1	(8.9)	12.2
—	1981	5.4	51.5	—	(9.5)	—
—	1986	4.6	55.6	—	(12.1)	—
Philippines	1971	5.2	52.5	37.0	(10.1)	14.2
—	1985	5.2	52.5	37.0	(10.1)	14.2
Indonesia	1976	6.6	49.4	34.0	(7.5)	10.3
Giant Economy						
China*	2005	1.8	47.9	32.0	(26.6)	35.6
India	1976	7.0	49.4	33.6	(7.1)	9.6
India*	2005	3.8	42.4	28.3	(11.2)	14.9
II. *South Asia*						
Sri Lanka	1981	5.8	49.8	34.7	(8.6)	12.0
Bangladesh	1982	6.6	45.3	29.5	(6.9)	8.9
III. *Latin America*						
Argentina	1970	4.4	51.4	34.6	(11.7)	15.8
Brazil	1972	2.0	66.6	50.9	(33.3)	50.9
Mexico	1977	2.9	57.7	40.6	(19.9)	28.0
Peru	1972	1.9	61.0	42.9	(32.1)	45.2

Source: World Development Report, 1985, 1986 and 1988; National Statistical Yearbooks, Thai Development Research Institute (TDRI) 1989. Quarterly Newsletter; *China and India figures were taken from WB (2012). *World Development Indicators*.

the income inequality indexes of Asian countries with fertility rate, share of employment in agriculture, the improvement of the level of education and other economic indices, one seems to obtain the following correlation there.

(1) The famous Kuznets hypothesis seems to hold for most countries, but not for Japan and Taiwan. Japan may have already passed a critical point. Taiwan had a special circumstance where the land ownership is in the hands of Taiwanese farmers, and they could obtain a significant share of industrialization from the rising prices of land and rent. This contrasts with the Philippine and Thai conditions of land ownership.
(2) Income distribution tends to worsen with higher fertility rate.
(3) Countries at the similar per capita income levels with higher shares of employment in agriculture tend to have worse income distribution.
(4) Improvement of the level of education has the positive correlation with the improvement of per capita income and income distribution.

This relative inequality was mitigated when the economies developed primarily by successful agriculture and labor-intensive manufacturing industries in the Asian economies, which included a wide range of small and medium size farmers, proprietors and enterprises. Taiwan and Japan are the typical cases. In other countries where large corporations or State enterprises are conspicuously dominant, income inequality will increase social frustration which has no outlet to be released. Serious social unrest has to be expected under such circumstances.

Such social discontent was mitigated by the high degree of social mobility in post-war Japanese society. Very few Japanese would doubt that graduates from good universities had equal opportunities in the best private businesses and government bureaucracy. The percentage going to higher education in Japan is almost as high as that in the US but higher than those of all European countries. Needless to say, some social frustration especially among the urban workers and sometimes dissatisfied farmers have been reduced by the political participation in various forms like strikes, demonstrations or occasional success of obtaining power in local election by the opposition parties. But the free and fair voting seems to have permitted most frustrated citizens to participate in politics in many ways. This sense of participation mitigated the political discontent and kept Japanese and some other Asian domestic politics within reasonable stability.[8]

7. The Stakes of Interest Groups in Policy-making

As we have argued, policy-making always requires the coordination of the stakes of all those concerned. This policy-making process must be carefully observed.[9]

---

[8]The interested reader may refer to my paper: (1990). The role of Japan in Asia and contributions of her private enterprises. IIR working paper no. 4. Japan: Osaka International University, January. It shows on the basis of surveys that the Japanese style management is practiced in bigger corporations more widely than small and medium size enterprises, and the difference is significant.

[9]This part is based on my article: (1989). "A conceptual framework for the political economy of policy-making," In *The Political Economy of Fiscal Policy*, Ichimura, S, M Urrutia and S Yukawa (eds.). Tokyo: United Nations University.

Chapter 9

Decentralization Policies in Asian Development

1. Development Requires Decentralization and Privatization

In 2003, International Center for the Study of East Asian Development (ICSEAD) and Kitakyushu City co-sponsored the first international conference on Asian Development. The theme was Decentralization Policies in Asian Development. The outcome was examined, revised, and we further solicited some additional articles. The final fruit published was *Decentralization Policies in Asian Development* by Ichimura S. and R. Bahl, World Scientific Publishing Company, 2008 [11].[1] It dealt with the current political and fiscal decentralization policies in Japan, China, India, and Southeast Asian countries; the hot subject being debated in all the countries.

In the initial stage of economic development and nation-building, national unification and economic take-off are essential and require, by necessity, concentration of power and resources. Hence, the political system of new nation-states is likely to be authoritarian and tends to be centralized. As economic development progresses, however, the majority of common citizens and private companies demand the government to offer more and better public services, employment, and business opportunities. In particular, the experiences in most countries show that development widens the regional gaps in the nation-state, and residents and business centers far from the capital often request the government offices to come closer to their localities and offer better services; namely, decentralization of political and fiscal decision-making. On learning about such demands in the private sectors, the government officials and politicians began seeking ways and means of decentralizing the decision-making in administrative and fiscal

[1]This review article was published in *Viewpoint to East Asia*, 20(2), 2009. I wish to thank Prof. Sadayuki Takii, Seinan Gakuin University for his editorial assistance.

policies. For instance, in Indonesia where even talking about decentralized administration, like federalism, was a taboo in the 1970s or even the 1980s, the government itself is now geared toward decentralized administration and fiscal policies.

Most East Asian countries have achieved its independence after World War II and by now has reached the level of middle-income countries with around $2,000 per capita Gross Domestic Product (GDP). They are already facing the widely-spread demand for decentralization among households and business groups. Such demands have remained, however, unsatisfied, and national economies demonstrate the sufferings of excessive centralization and urbanization, especially around the capital city. Each chapter of the book will tell stories on some country in Asia.

Japan is no exception. Popularity of Prime Minister Junichiro Koizumi (2001–2006) was mainly due to his adoption of this issue as a central political theme of his Liberal Democratic Party. The extremely popular slogan in his election campaign was "from Center to Local", and "from Government to Private". The slogans were widely accepted and have become popular in Japanese politics ever since. It was following the contemporary trends of the Reagan–Thatcher type of deregulation and privatization after the end of the Cold War. Clearly, the people's concern with decentralization was unusually enhanced. They began to openly voice and prevalently demand for quick and closer public services, and no intervention to the private businesses. The Ichimura-Bahl book under review [11] contains three chapters on Japan as shown below and describe vividly the current circumstances in Japan.

China and Vietnam are, however, different from the other countries. They are Socialist countries. The third Socialist country, Myanmar, is not taken up in the book.[2] The decentralization policies in those three countries must be discussed from different points of view, particularly with regard to land ownership and State-Owned Enterprises (SOE). Hence, their decentralization policies must include not only those of political administration, but also privatization of SOEs. Such transitional policies

[2]As of 2014, Myanmar has changed its basic policies and is moving boldly towards market economy and welcoming the Foreign Direct Investment, except from China. Its future course may be as market-oriented as Vietnam.

were in fact undertaken in the Asian Socialist states long before Gorbachev became the secretary of the Communist Party in Soviet Union in 1985. In China, Deng Xiao-Ping initiated the policies in Shanghai in 1979. In Vietnam, it was started in 1986 by privatization policies called *Doi Moi* (reform) with the impact of Chinese reform. Thus, Asian Socialist countries have embraced mixed economies similar to other countries in Asia. Privatization and decentralization deal with separate issues. We have treated them in another book titled *Transition from Socialist to Market Economies: Comparison of European and Asian Experiences* by Ichimura Shinichi, Tsuneaki Sato and William James (eds.), Palgrave-Macmillan, 2009. As far as decentralization issue is concerned (Chapters 4 and 9) in our book under review show no significant difference from the rest of Asia.

In Japan, the government reform policies for decentralization and privatization seem to move in parallel. The arguments on political decentralization started even before World War II. A postwar official move by the government was to set up a Committee on Local Administration in the government in 1981, which simply revived the prewar arguments with no commitments. The Committee revived the serious discussions in 1989–1992 and made a proposal to submit a new law to the Congress which admits the integration of prefectures in Japan. In 2004, this law was passed by the parliament, and the sheer argument of "Doshu-Sei" (the state system) became legally possible to materialize. On the other hand, a little earlier, the Nakasone Cabinet (1982–1987) succeeded in privatization of National Railroad (NR) and opened ways to privatize the Nippon Telegraph and Telephone Corporation (NTT), National Telephone and Telegram Public Corporation, and recently Koizumi Cabinet's privatization of Postal Service Public Corporation in 2007. National Railway was regionally sub-divided into several private companies, and others like postal services were sub-divided on activity bases.[3]

[3] Surprisingly the academic works on the problems of decentralization and privatization are so few in Japan that while I was the directors of research institutes at Kyoto University, Osaka International University, and ICSEAD, I wished to take up the theme for projects, but was unsuccessful. The main reason was that my own knowledge and acquaintances were not adequate enough to organize such international teams.

2. The First Asian Development Conference

In early 2002, Mayor Koichi Sueyoshi asked me if an international conference on Asian development in Kitakyushu will be meaningful and welcomed. I agreed to participate, particularly if the theme was "decentralization". Mayor immediately accepted because decentralization issues were hot topics for local and also central governments then.

How to approach the issues was, however, not very clear to me yet, because I have not personally known many experts in the field, especially from abroad. Following a standard method in conducting the first field survey at underdeveloped areas, I adopted a two steps approach and decided first to hold a preliminary workshop of small scale before holding an international conference for real purposes. For the preparation I consulted Vice-President Yukio Yoshimura (World Bank in Tokyo), Dr. Jang-soo Lee (Asian Development Bank, Tokyo representative) and few economists in East Asian countries about the specialists to invite to the preliminary workshop and a list of other main issues.

The workshop served the purposes very well in providing us with some important information:

1. It is the World Bank research department that has a group of experts on decentralization issues and is the best contact network in the world.
2. The greatest authority in this field is Professor Roy Bahl, at Georgia State University, who already has many accomplishments and best contacts with experts.
3. Experts in this field are so busy that to invite the best experts simultaneously would be hard.

Based on preliminary discussions, we chose the following topics.

1. Political decentralization and fiscal decentralization,
2. Decentralization and local government's public finance,
3. Urban concentration and related issues.

We decided to hold the main conference in November and tried to assign each expert an issue from the three topics.

As we were afraid of, some experts could not come to the November conference due to conflicts in dates. Nevertheless, 22 experts accepted and presented the articles and earnestly discussed with the pre-assigned discussants. Prof. R. Bahl gave a keynote address summarizing the main problems of decentralization policies and a perspective of the present state of research. In addition, responding to the high interest in "*the present stage of Japanese decentralization policies*" among foreign experts, we organized a panel discussion meeting attended by the following participants:

- Tatsuo Hatta: coordinator, (Professor, University of Tokyo)
- Taku Kajiwara: (Chair, National Governors Association)
- Koichi Sueyoshi: (Mayor, Kitakyushu City)
- Keiji Araki: (Secretary General, Decentralization Reform Promotion Association)

The panel discussions greatly attracted the attention of foreign and Japanese participants. Its details are reported in the mimeographed report in Japanese. Its English version, however, did not contain an in-depth report. Instead, we asked Prof. Toshihiro Ihori (University of Tokyo) to contribute a new article on Japanese decentralization policies. The book under review is not just a selection of the articles submitted to the Conference, but includes such articles that we requested the new authors to contribute to fill the gap between our original design and what we achieved through the actual conference. In addition we asked all the authors to rewrite their papers on the changes that took place during the recent five years. Here is *the Table of Contents* of our final version.

Appendix: Conference on Asian Development and Decentralization

1. Program of ADC, 2003
2. Comments on Seminar A: Fiscal Decentralization
   (Chuo University) Hiroko Kudo
3. Report of Seminar B: Local Public Finance
   (Hitotsubashi University) Motohiro Sato
4. Report of Seminar C: Urbanization
   (Kitakyushu University) Hidehiko Tanimura

On decentralization policies so many debates go on in journalism, but not much in academic journals. We hope this book will stimulate serious discussions on the subject. This book does not sufficiently deal with problems as urbanization, industrial location, environments, regional gaps, or fiscal decentralization to local public finance. Particularly insufficient are the studies on those issues in China and Korea because the specialists we first invited could not accept the invitation and come to Japan. We deeply regret that we could not absorb the outstanding works of those countries. We look forward to the next opportunities to examine the difficult and serious issues in them. There may be some more problems that still remain unexplored. The following summary of arguments mainly relies on the summary by R. Bahl in his Introduction.

3. Plus and Minus of Decentralization

Decentralization policies in Asia have been mostly in the direction of strengthening the local governments, as in other developing countries in the other areas. Former Socialist countries' transitional policies always have decentralization as one item. In industrialized countries policies differ from one country to another. Canada is reconsidering decentralization, whereas Spain and Japan are moving to strengthen them.

3.1. *Plus of Decentralization = Benefits*

The greatest benefit of strengthening the self-reliance and tax-collection right of local governments is to make them closer to the people. That is why efficiency-conscious economists support such policies.[4] If the heads of local governments or the members of local congresses are elected, or government officials are employed locally, the local government administration may be expected to become more adequate for local residents. At least more accountability of governing side will be requited for residents, and the quality of the services will be better than the ones entirely offered by the central government. As a result, the residents will be more positive in paying the taxes. The key to this effect will be that local election is fairly conducted on the right information, and government officials are employed with no personal favors. However, these conditions are not necessarily satisfied everywhere.

The second benefit is that it often increases the revenue of local governments. If the local officials familiar with the local conditions are in charge of collecting the taxes, the revenue will tend to increase. This will decrease the subsidies from the central government, and eventually both local and central governments will benefit. This presupposes the comparative advantage of local government in grasping the real conditions of real estate in the localities. However, very few Asian countries seem to have succeeded in materializing it.

3.2. *Minus of Decentralization = Cost Accountability*

Decentralization definitely has a *minus* effect, at least to the central government. That is why they are the greatest resistant. The first *minus* point is that the central government looses its advantage to influence upon the macro economy by policies to change tax rates, fiscal expenditure, or government loans, depending on the current economic conditions. The central governments of developing countries are always under the domestic and foreign pressure, including International Monetary Fund (IMF) or World Bank, to control its government deficit and the easy loans of the Central Bank. If sub-national governments too are given strong authorities, they may not be able to be self-restraint. For instance, some articles in this

[4]As for *plus* and *minus* of fiscal decentralization, see Oates (1972), Bahl and Linn (1992), Bahl and Wallace (2005), Litvack, Ahmad, and Bird (1998), Bird and Vaillancourt (1998), Tanzi (1995), and Dillinger and Webb (1999).

book demonstrated that the cumulated debt of local governments in India (Rao, Chapter 5 in [11]) and Japan (Ihori, Chapter 3 in [11]) reached as much as 10% and 40% of GDP respectively by the end of the 1990s.

In the Philippines, the growing share of national tax collection earmarked for local governments compromised budgetary position of the central government (Diokno, Chapter 7 in [11]). Even if the transfers from central to sub-national governments are not bound to a certain fixed proportion to national tax revenue, reduction of such transfers is difficult, as a fixed proportion of personnel payments, transfer incomes for the poor, or the ties of powerful ministries tiled with some provincial governments.

A second cost of decentralization to the central government is that it could lose some control over infrastructure development in cases where sub-national governments have discretionary spending power. The net result of fiscal decentralization will be a shift of resources from central governments that have higher rates of capital spending to provincial and local governments who spend at a greater rate on consumption goods and services. Fiscal decentralization, therefore, could lead to a lower overall rate of spending on infrastructure, and national growth could be slower. Fiscal decentralization also may lead to a shift in the composition of public capital investments. This is because national priorities for capital investment differ from the ones in sub-national governments. The national government's interest is investments in infrastructure that benefit regions and nation; such as, large scale irrigation projects, national (interstate) roads, and electric power. Provincial and local governments will focus more on capital investments with benefits in their areas.

Some countries are moving away from conditional grants. Indonesia replaced its "Inpres", i.e., a large number of grants for specific purposes ranging from re-greening to the construction of public markets, with a general purpose grant allocated by formula (Fengler and Hofman, Chapter 10 in [11]). Japan is moving away from conditional subsides to local taxes (Saito and Yunoue, Chapter 11 in [11]).

A third cost of decentralization is that it does not necessarily reduce the regional gaps. Rather concentrating on the revenues is more likely to contribute to narrowing the gaps. Decentralizing into smaller areas with taxable sources tend to enlarge the differences in tax revenues. Rather the ways in which the central government collects all the taxes and redistributes will be easier to narrow the revenue gaps among the sub-regions. It certainly has potential, but nobody knows if it is really done. Redistribution policies for equality greatly differ from one country to another. Greatly appraised independence may cause decentralization, which tends to result in larger revenues to industrialized areas or big cities and widen the regional gaps. To cope with this situation, it is necessary to prepare an overall program to reduce the regional gaps within the area. A practical example is shown in the republic of South Africa, where 90% of its fiscal revenue comes from the big cities and an equalization program is available (Reschovsky, 2003).

The last point is whether the provincial/local governments can manage their public finance or not. If they cannot, the central government must repeat the same work, doubling the cost and trouble. Some maintain that the central government collects the main taxes, leaving the rest to local offices. In practice, taxes that are hard to collect are often left to the local governments. Some maintain that the more locally collected taxes are, the more corrupted the taxation officials are.[5] Many supporters of decentralization do not agree with this view of local officials' low capability, but maintain that many devices can be made like tax-rates being locally determined but collected by the central government. (McLure, 1997). As for administration services, it is a general view that local government officials can learn quickly, once it is decentralized.

3.3. *The Practice*

The real move of decentralization policies in most countries has been very slow. According to IMF Statistics of Government Finance, the share of local governments' expenditure in total government expenditure has remained around 13–14% for the past 30 years.[6] Its stability surprises us. The same can be observed in the Organization for Economic Co-operation and Development (OECD) countries.

Table 1 traces the practice of local and central governments' revenues and expenditures (Bahl and Linn, 1992). The average numbers for each

---

[5]Empirical work on the relationship between decentralization and corruption is inconclusive. Fisman and Gatti (2002), for example, find that corruption is lower in more decentralized countries; Treisman (2000) finds corruption to be higher in federal than in unitary countries.
[6]This is a flawed measure of fiscal decentralization because it does not indicate if the sub-national government has any significant influence over how the money will be spent.

Table 1. Fiscal Decentralization Indicators.

	1970s		1980s		1990s		
	LDC	OECD	LDC	OECD	LDC	OECD	SOC.C
Local tax/total tax	10.44 (43)	18.71 (22)	7.70 (35)	18.75 (22)	9.27 (28)	19.13 (20)	16.59 (14)
Local gov. expenditure/ total expenditure	13.01 (48)	33.78 (22)	13.24 (43)	32.27 (23)	13.78 (54)	32.41 (23)	26.12 (23)

Note: Sample size in ( ).
Source: IMF, Government Finance Statistics Yearbook.

group in Table 1 clearly supports the stability mentioned above. However, the individual countries' figures differ from each other and are not necessarily stable.[7] Bahl and Wallace (2005) say that the reasons can be explained by the general observations that the share is higher in countries with higher per capita GDP, larger population and low corruption rate.

4. Policy Instruments for Decentralization

Many fiscal policy instruments have been used in implementing decentralization. Three of the most important and controversial are sub-national government taxes, intergovernmental transfers, and the requirement of a hard budget constraint.

4.1. *Sub-national Government Taxes*

The sub-national taxes as effective policy instruments must be large enough to occupy a significant portion of the provincial/local government's expenditure and heavy enough to most taxpayers. Only under such circumstances, the sub-national governments realize their own responsibility for self-government and budget control. And only then it becomes obvious that the demand for more services implies more tax payments, and it reduces the pressure for more services. In almost all advanced economies there is no limit for sub-national governments to introduce new taxes. In the US and Canada, every state has almost perfect discretion to introduce new state tax of any kind, unless it involves inter-state transactions. In Denmark and

[7] Local Tax is defined in the following arguments only as taxes whose rates can be determined by local governments.

Sweden about half of local government expenditure is covered by local taxes. (Owens and Norregaard, 1991). In Switzerland, it is more than half. Japan is behind those countries in this respect, but in the recent years she seems to have switched to the same direction (Ikawa, Chapter 2 in [11]).

Resistance is especially strong on the part of central governments in Less Developed Country (LDC). Table 1 shows that the share of local tax in LDC is about 10%, and that of OECD countries is about 20%. It almost doubles in LDC, so that provincial/local governments depend heavily on the transfers from the central government. The central government is not willing to give its authority to collect taxes to sub-national governments. In Pakistan, for instance, sub-national governments are allowed to impose tax only on agricultural income, labor services and trading of real estate. Their tax collection occupies only 1% of GDP (Bahl, Wallace, and Cyan, 2008). In the Philippines, the sub-national government's tax revenue occupies as high as 1/3 of its annual revenue, because it is admitted, in the same way as in Japan, to charge on corporate incomes, but the tax rates cannot be determined by themselves, similar to Japan. As a result, the revenue is far less than the expenditures for each sub-national government to cover (Manasan report, Chapter 14 in [1]). In Cambodia, Vietnam and China, sub-national government's revenue is less than 5% of its total revenue.

4.2. *Inter-governmental Transfers*

No policy instrument of fiscal decentralization is more discussed, or more often reformed, than intergovernmental transfers' reform. On the one hand, transfers are preferred to local taxation in most developing and transition countries because they recognize the superior tax administration capabilities of the central government and also allow a greater measure of central control. On the other hand, transfers are an object of criticism precisely because of the central control; because in some countries they discourage local revenue mobilization; are not adequately equalizing; and are not transparent. Reform in most countries has concentrated on finding a middle ground between central control and the goals of decentralization.

An error often committed is to confuse the measurement of total pool of the revenues to transfer with the method of allocating it to the state governments. The former is called *vertical balance* between the central government and state governments, whereas the latter is known

Table 2. Alternative Form of Intergovernmental Grant Programs.

Method of allocating the divisible pool among eligible units	Method of determining total divisible pool		
	Specified share of national or state tax	Ad hoc form	Reimbursement of admitted expenditures
Origin of tax collection	A	Na	Na
Formula	B	F	Na
Total or partial reimbursement of costs	C	G	K
Ad hoc	D	H	Na

as *horizontal balance* among state governments. Decentralization policies are concerned with both balances (Bahl and Linn, 1992). Table 2 shows the classification of formula for the transfers.

Table 2 shows the classification of formula for the transfer. The right-hand side three columns show the three formulas to pool the funds for the central government to allocate to state governments, whereas the left-hand column shows the four methods to allocate it.

The cells in the table 4×3 show the possible types of formula for transfer. Typical three types in Asia are: (1) Non-conditional Transfer, (2) Conditional transfer, (3) ad hoc transfer.

(1) is the most suitable for self-reliance of sub-national governments to be achieved by decentralization policies. If a certain pre-determined *percentage* of national taxes is allocated to this (column 1 in Table 2), sub-national governments can rely upon it for their expenditures, even though the absolute amount may fluctuate. Many Asian countries adopt this formulas, though the percentage differs; the Philippines (40%), India (30%), Indonesia (25%), Pakistan (41%).

In allocating among sub-national governments, China adopts formula A, which favors rich provinces. Formula B is followed in Japan, Taiwan, and the Philippines. Their effect entirely depends on the contents of formula. Rather the objectives to achieve determined the formula. Some Asian examples are shown:

- In the Philippines, the distribution formula for the Internal Revenue Allotment (IRA) grant is based on population size, land area and equal shares. It is transparent, but has no explicit element that rewards local revenue mobilization. The equal shares allocation, which favors smaller governments, reflects on equalization concern. Diokno (Chapter 7 in [11]) argues that the increased vertical share of the IRA grant has dampened local government revenue mobilization.

- Pakistan distributes its National Finance Commission awards based on population size. This is transparent, and is a compromise solution that has been accepted by the four provinces. This formula recognizes expenditure needs in a broad way, but does not recognize taxable capacity, nor does it provide an incentive for the four provinces to increase tax effort (Bahl, Wallace, and Cyan, 2008).
- Thailand uses a formula based on population size, land area, equal shares and revenues raised. The inclusion of revenues raised (inverse) effectively penalizes increased tax effort. The equal shares element in the formula arguably adds an equalization component.
- In India, the grant component of Finance Commission transfers is distributed according to a formula that includes population, land area, the inverse of income level, and measures of both expenditure needs and tax efforts (Rao, 2008). While the system is equalizing, the weight attached to tax effort probably is not large enough to stimulate increased revenue mobilization.

Many have argued that a proper equalization grant would recognize both expenditure needs and fiscal capacity. Japan's local allocation tax grant attempts to do this, by distributing grants according to the difference between "standard expenditure" and "standard revenues". Taiwan more or less follows the same system as Japan. A similar approach is followed in Vietnam, which prefers a strong equalization effect (Hofman and Guerra, 2005). Indonesia distributes grants with a formula that include measures of both revenue capacity and expenditure needs. None of these programs, however, provide an incentive for increases in revenue mobilization by sub-national governments. The systems in Japan and Vietnam would appear to provide a disincentive.

Are intergovernmental transfers in Asia equalizing? If the criteria are whether transfers reduce per capita expenditure disparities, Hofman and Guerra (2005) conclude that there is some degree of equalization in the systems in China, Philippines, Thailand, and Indonesia, and a stronger equalization in Vietnam. Bahl, Wallace, and Cyan (2008) find a slight degree of equalization in Pakistan, using the same criteria. Rao (2008) concludes that India's finance commission transfers have reduced the disparity between higher and lower income states. Saito and Yunoue (2008) find evidence of equalization in the Japanese transfer system. Tokyo, for example, receives a near zero amount from the local allocation tax transfer.

Now some discussions on Conditional Transfer and ad hoc transfer are in order, but since they are beyond the scope of this book, we skip them and briefly take up three important issues in decentralization policies; namely, policy designs must be comprehensive, sequencing the policy implementation, and political implications of decentralization.

5. Policy Design Must Be Comprehensive

For decentralization policies to succeed, a comprehensive blue print must state the objectives, strategies, and its process of implementation. It must assure that the people and groups concerned with the new institutions are maintainable and can handle any difficult issues. The policies involve the fundamental aspects of governance of the nation-state. It goes well beyond public finance and implies the changes in election system, regional culture, and tradition. It is nothing but a political reform. The Vietnam and China articles explain this very well. Indonesians called decentralization appropriately a "big bang".

6. Sequencing of Decentralization Policies

Decentralization policies cannot be implemented all at once. The road map to proceed or sequencing of policies before implementation is equally important. If implementation is slow, the energy for reform will be lost. Table 3 (Bahl and Martinez-Vazquez, 2006) gives an excellent sample of the road map of implementation and says that two principles are important: the Rule of the Law and Transparency.

7. Politics of Fiscal Decentralization

Of course, decentralization is not the problem of sheer administration or public finance, but will be a great reform of national political system.

Table 3. Sequencing Decentralization Policies.

Step 1:	Stir up a national debate on the issues of decentralization policy
Step 2:	Design policies and develop a White Paper.
Step 3:	Pass the Decentralization Law.
Step 4:	Develop all the Implementation Regulations.
Step 5:	Implement the program of decentralization policies.
Step 6:	Monitor, evaluate and retrofit the practice.

Source: Bahl and Martinez-Vazquez, 2006.

Such a political reform requires the strong support of the general public and the powerful support of political authorities, especially in the Socialist countries like China and Vietnam. The two chapters on China (Zuo, Chapter 4 in [11]) and Vietnam (Hung, Chapter 9 in [11]) covered these topics thoroughly.

Exactly on such political problems of Socialist countries, I edited another book: *Transition from Socialist to Market Economies* (2009), Palgrave-McMillan, London [12]. Japan is certainly not a Socialist economy, but faces many similiar political problems. Reforms are easier said than done.

The trends in the world on public finance and political administration has changed, however, towards decentralization in the recent decades. There is no doubt, therefore, that the arguments in this book will occupy the important domestic discussions in most countries, whether developed or developing, all over the world for many decades to come. Finally attached is a list of important books and articles on the subject that our book dealt with. The list includes some works that are not quoted in the text of this chapter but relevant to the issues discussed in the original review article.

References

[1] Alm, J., R. Bahl and R. Aten (2001). "Can Indonesia decentralize successfully? Plans, problems and prospects," *Bulletin of Indonesian Economic Studies*, 37(1), 83–102.

[2] Bahl, R. (2008). "Opportunities and risks of fiscal decentralization: A developing country perspective," in G. Ingram and Y.-H. Hong (ed.), *Fiscal decentralization and land policies*, Cambridge, Mass: Lincoln Institute of Land Policy.

[3] Bahl, R. and J. F. Linn (1992). *Urban Public Finance in Developing Countries*. New York: Oxford University Press.

[4] Bahl, R. and J. Martinez-Vazquez (2006). Sequencing fiscal decentralization. World Bank Policy Research Working Paper 3914, Public Sector Governance Group. Washington, DC: World Bank.

[5] Bahl, R., S. Wallace and M. Cyan (2008). Pakistan: Provincial Government Taxation. ISP Working Paper. Atlanta: International Studies Program, Georgia State University.

[6] Bahl, R. and S. Wallace (2005). "Public financing in developing and transition countries," *Public Budgeting and Finance*, Silver Anniversary Issue, pp. 83–98.

[7] Bird, R. M. and F. Vaillancourt (eds.) (1998). *Fiscal Decentralization in Developing Countries*. Cambridge: Cambridge University Press.

[8] Dillinger, W. and S. B. Webb (1999). Decentralization and fiscal management in Colombia. Policy Research Working Paper 2122, Latin American and Caribbean Division. Washington, DC: World Bank.

[9] Fisman, R. and R. Gatti (2002). "Decentralization and corruption: Evidence across countries," *Journal of Public Economics*, 83, 325–345.

[10] Hofman, B. and S. C. Guerra (2005). "Fiscal disparities in East Asia: How large and do they matter?" in P. Smoke and R. White (ed.), *East Asia Decentralizes*, Washington DC: World Bank.

[11] Ichimura, S. and Roy Bahl (ed.) (2008). *Decentralization Policies in Asian Development*. Singapore: WSPC.

[12] Ichimura, S., T. Sato and W. James (ed.). (2009). *Transition from Socialist to Market Economies*. London: Palgrave-McMillan.

[13] Inter-American Development Bank (1997). *Latin America After a Decade of Reforms*. Washington, DC: Inter-American Development Bank.

[14] Letelier, L. (2005). "Explaining Fiscal Decentralization," *Public Finance Review*, 33(2), 155–183.

[15] Litvack, J., J. Ahmad and R. Bird (1998). *Rethinking Decentralization*. Washington, DC: World Bank.

[16] Martinez-Vazquez, J., A. Timofeev and J. Boex (2006). *Reforming Regional–Local Finance in Russia*. Washington, DC: World Bank Institute.

[17] McLure, C. E. (1997). "Topics in the theory of revenue assignment: Gaps, traps and nuances," in M. Blejer and T. Ter-Minassian (ed.), *Macroeconomic Dimensions of Public Finance*, London: Routledge.

[18] Oates, W. E (1972). *Fiscal Federalism*. New York: Harcourt Brace Jovanovich.

[19] Owens, J. and J. Norregaard (1991). "The role of lower levels of government: The experience of selected OECD countries" in J. Owens and G. Panella (ed.), *Local Government: An International Perspective*, pp. 3–54, Amsterdam: North Holland.

[20] Prud'homme, R. (1995). "The dangers of decentralization," *World Bank Research Observer*, 10(2), 210–226.

[21] Reschovsky, A. (2003). "Intergovernmental transfers: The equitable share," in R. Bahl and P. Smoke (ed), *Re-structuring Local Government Finance in Developing countries: Lessons from South Africa*, pp. 173–236, Cheltenham, UK: Edward Elgar Publishing .

[22] Rodden, J., G. Eskeland and J. Litvack (eds.) (2003). *Fiscal Decentralization and the Challenge of Hard Budget Constraints*. Cambridge: The MIT Press.

[23] Sethi, G. (ed.) (2004). *Fiscal Decentralization to Rural Governments in India*. Washington, DC: World Bank.

[24] Spahn, P. (1997). Decentralized government and macroeconomic control. Infrastructure Notes FM-12. Washington, DC: World Bank.

[25] Taliercio, R. (2005). "Sub-national own-source revenue: Getting policy and administration right" in *East Asia Decentralizes: Making Local Government Work*, Washington, DC: World Bank.

[26] Tanzi, V. (1995). "Fiscal federalism and decentralization: a review of some efficiency and macroeconomic aspects," in M. Bruno and B. Pleskovic (eds.), *Annual World Bank Conference on Development Economics*, pp. 295–316. Washington, DC: World Bank.

[27] Ter-Minassian, T. (ed.) (1997). *Fiscal Federalism in Theory and Practice*. Washington, DC: International Monetary Fund.

[28] Treisman, D. (2000). *Decentralization and the Quality of Government*. Washington, DC: International Monetary Fund.

[29] Usui, N. (2007). Critical Issues of Fiscal Decentralization. ERD Technical Note No. 21. Manila: Asian Development Bank.

[30] White, R. and P. Smoke (2005). "East Asia Decentralizes" in P. Smoke and R. White (ed.), *East Asia Decentralizes*, Washington, DC: World Bank.

Part III

Empirical Survey Studies of Southeast Asia

Chapter 10

The Choice of Appropriate Technologies I — The Influence of Socio-Economic Factors and Government Policies

1. Introduction

This chapter offers a conceptual framework for the questionnaire survey of native businessmen to find out how they choose the so-called *appropriate technology*. The main relevant issues are (1) how socio-economic or institutional factors have affected their decisions and (2) how the government has tried successfully or unsuccessfully to make the choice of technology more appropriate for the national economy.[1] Based on this chapter, the questionnaire surveys were conducted in Thailand, Indonesia, and the Philippines in cooperation with the local scholars, and the following empirical survey findings were obtained. They were made available in the two working papers of International Labor Organization (WP 66 in 1980 and WP 110 in 1983 of World Employment Programme; WEP 2-22).[2]

2. The Purpose of the Study

No technology is adopted unless it is considered appropriate by someone. Different technologies may be appropriate or inappropriate depending on who views them and from what point of view. They may be (a) individual entrepreneurs, (b) vested interest groups, (c) provincial governments responsible for areas of a country, (d) the central government agency in charge of the national economy, (e) some international agency for some

[1]The author wishes to thank Mr. Susumu Watanabe, Technology and Employment Branch, Employment and Development Department, ILO (now, Professor of Economics, Tokyo International University, Japan) for his constructive comments and suggestions.
[2]The first paper was once published in *the OIJ Journal of International Studies*, December 1988 and Chapter 10 now, and the second is Chapter 11 of this book.

region in the world, or (f) some organization for world economy as a whole. The choice of technology is usually made by (a), (b), (c), or (d). The choice (e) can also be relevant in the context of regional groupings such as ASEAN and the ANDEAN Pact. In the future, it may become increasingly necessary to consider the appropriateness of technology from the global point of view, notably in connection with the shortage of natural resources and farming land.[3] In the context of development economics, however, the basic criterion to judge the appropriateness of a technology is the long-term development of a national economy. The central government of a nation is primarily responsible for the preparation of a development plan including the implementation of appropriate technology. The standard objective of development is to maximize the steady growth of national output with the optimal use of labor, capital, and natural resources. Long-term economic development can be achieved, however, only when it does not conflict with social and political development of the nation. Any technological innovation in a developing economy, therefore, must be carefully evaluated with respect not only to its micro-economic profitability but also to its long-term effects on the economy and the nation state as a whole.

After having clarified the basic concept of "appropriate technologies" in rather abstract terms, the present study will try

(1) to find out what leading policy-makers and influential intellectuals in Southeast Asia have in mind as "appropriate technologies" in the context of their own countries;
(2) to check how closely their ideas of "appropriate technologies" are related to development objectives of employment creation and poverty alleviation;

[3]In order for two-thirds of the world population in less developed countries to be able to enjoy a higher standard of living, it is not good enough for each nation to adopt a set of appropriate technologies only from its own point of view. It seems necessary and highly desirable to see the implication of enormously expanded demand for energy and food to the future technology in the world. It is also important to realize that many industrial technologies, if they are used all over the world, often have undesirable effects on the world climate or the ocean, which may seriously disrupt the life of humankind. CO_2 produced by burning coal is a case in point. All nations including less developed countries, OPEC and industrial countries, therefore, must cooperate to develop and diffuse technologies appropriate for the maximization of global production and conservation of the environment. For the world future, there is no doubt that the technology that saves natural resources and land is very desirable beyond any immediate economic considerations.

(3) to ascertain what institutional and cultural factors in this region have been making it difficult to propagate such technologies as more suitable for such development goals; and finally
(4) to overcome the major obstacles to the diffusion of technological knowledge and information, or to the indigenous generation of appropriate technologies.

The ultimate objective of the study is to contribute to the discovery of ways and means of overcoming various barriers to the generation and diffusion of such technologies. Many scholars have already pointed out that *appropriate technology* in a developing country should suit well not only the development objective of full employment of productive factors (notably labor) in the economy but also the country's social, political, and cultural conditions. (See, for example Bhalla, 1979.) The appropriateness of a technology must be judged taking account of a wide range of factors such as endowments of resources in the society, environmental conditions, equality of income and living conditions among the community members, as well as individuals' capacity to absorb education and training. It is hard simultaneously to satisfy these conditions of appropriateness, while the standard objectives of development mentioned above may be too general as criteria to judge whether a certain technology should be introduced or not. Thus, it is desirable and necessary to define more sharply the particular objective or goal in relation to which the specific technology is considered appropriate.

The basic human needs approach may, for example, define the objective more narrowly with respect to some specific social groups like low-income groups, small enterprises, or some regions rather than the nation as a whole. Appropriateness in this case is judged mainly according to the welfare of the selected groups or regions. The same approach sometimes requires the participation of a wider range of population in production and distribution of output. The decentralized and popular decision-making in technological innovation may be considered appropriate in many ways but it can be practically used only where there are many capable community leaders throughout the country. Such a *grass-root* approach to development also requires a reasonably long-term horizon, and it may be hardly compatible with development plans of most developing countries, which have very limited time horizons.

It has also been well publicized that adoption of modern technology may tend to change or even destroy certain aspects of the traditional way of life, while many regions in developing countries have old practices which are difficult to break (Sachs, 1975). Choosing *appropriate technologies* alone may not mitigate or resolve the tension and conflicts between economic development and socio-cultural tradition. The problems are related to wider aspects of socio-economic life. Old institutions may hinder the implementation of government policies encouraging adopting an economically appropriate technology. We need to identify such institutional factors in concrete terms, since we may have to change them. At the same time, we need to keep in mind the mutual effects of government policies. For example, a hasty introduction of minimum wage and other labor legislations, or various fiscal and monetary incentives for investment have distorted the relative prices of labor and capital, which caused the use of inappropriate technologies.

The concrete features of *appropriate technologies* obviously change from one stage of economic development to another.[4] All governments in Southeast Asia publish the development plans nearly every five years. The changes in industrial plans contained therein and in regulations on foreign investment reflect shifts in their ideas of *appropriate technologies.* By studying the documents and obtaining first hand information from leading policy-makers in these countries, we may be able to gain an important insight into some critical issues of development planning and technology policy.

Choice of technologies is possible, of course, only when a menu of available technologies is known. This menu should include old technologies, even those that have become obsolete in the industrialized countries, as well as contemporary and new technologies. They should include traditional technologies in various areas within the country, other developing countries, or even developed countries. In the agricultural sector, food processing, textile and other cottage industries in developing countries, local traditional crafts and technologies exist and can relatively ease the local needs by modifying them.[5] The productivity of rice farming in Japan, for example,

[4]On this subject, See Chenery and Syrquin, 1975; Weitz, 1971; Griffin, 1974; Johnston, 1970; International Development Research Center, 1976.

[5]On the generation of appropriate technologies in LDC, see Herrera (1979).

increased in this way during the late 19th and early 20th centuries. In the developing world, however, there seem to be all kinds of socio-cultural and political factors that make available information imperfect and hinder diffusion of knowledge and information. Under these circumstances, one can hardly expect creation of *intermediate* local technologies through a combination of modern technologies with indigenous techniques.

3. The Process and Pattern of Technological Innovation: Choice, Diffusion, and Generation

"Nature does not jump" is a basic principle of technological innovations in developing countries. If traditional technologies are skillfully integrated with modern and improved technologies in a continuous manner so that the transfer of technology does not cause any disruptive disturbances to the harmonious life of traditional society, then one could regard such technology transfer as successfully achieved. Then, little intervention by government policies would be necessary. Learning by doing becomes practical in such cases. However, modern technologies often quickly take over old technologies, and people's living and working conditions are seriously affected. This process destroyed many of the village industries. There are, on the other hand, many success stories of continuous shift from conventional to modern technologies.[6] One example in Southeast Asia is the Thai silk industry. It created a unique silk cloth by keeping traditional silk yarns and weaving technique but adopting modern designs to suit the export market. As sales increased, Thai workers learnt new technologies gradually, and not only the design but also the spinning and weaving techniques improved. The successful combination of modern technologies with traditional ones seems to be rather difficult in contemporary less developed countries for some reasons.

First, not all the stock of technologies accumulated over time in many developed countries is available because many of them have been already forgotten or become difficult to rediscover. Second, the latest technologies to produce close substitutes for conventional consumption goods are so advanced that the artisanship of traditional masters is of little use in learning these technologies. Such a large gap between modern and conventional

---

[6]For some concrete cases and significance, see Watanabe (1980, p. 170).

technologies necessitates establishment of a new system of education and training for young engineers, but it takes time. Students must be sent abroad for training, or foreign teachers must be invited. All these effects must precede the acquisition of technologies and technological innovations in any developing country. Hence, one should not expect that many least developed countries (LDCs) could accomplish the generation and adoption of appropriate technologies within a short time.

Third, latecomers often remained latecomers, good or bad, for economic and non-economic reasons. Many institutional or cultural factors are the barriers to break down in order to prepare the ground for modernization. This usually requires a combination of courage, devices, and ingenuity of *entrepreneurship* plus the social support or cooperation.

Finally, although some global action may be needed for implementing the introduction of appropriate technologies in the developing economies, such international cooperation cannot be free from certain biases and adverse effects. For example, financial aids and investment funds flow predominantly to richer developing countries and little to the LDCs. According to the World Bank (Table 1), in 1970, about 87% of external financing resources went to middle-income countries, and the so-called newly industrializing countries, such as Argentina, Brazil, Mexico, South Korea, and Taiwan, received more than 90% of the private loans offered to the non-OPEC developing countries. This illustrates a limitation of the present pattern of external financing of development efforts. Some measures are needed to channel more financial resources to the poorest

Table 1. Allocation of External Finance by Country Groups in 1970 (billion $).

	Low income countries	Middle income countries	All developing countries
1. Net factor income	0.0	5	6
2. Official grants	5	9	15
3. Medium and long-term loans at market	4	45	49
4. Direct investment	−1	−5	−6
5. Private transfer	0.0	2	3
6. Total	8	56	64

Source: IBRD, *World Development Report*, 1979, p. 7.

countries. However, these financial resources have to go along with technical assistance; otherwise, development will not materialize.

In providing such assistance, however, special care must be taken not to kill local people's initiatives and spirit of self-help and thereby prevent development of their ingenuity. They are essential to absorb foreign technologies and integrate them with conventional local ones. The ultimate goal of technology policy in developing countries must be the generation of indigenous technologies, which are economically appropriate and socially acceptable. For a consideration of ways to achieve this goal, one needs a clear idea about the process of search, adoption, adaptation, and generation of desirable technologies. It is shown in Figure 1 and described as follows.[7] Each stage of this process will be discussed here with reference to the problems in Southeast Asian countries.

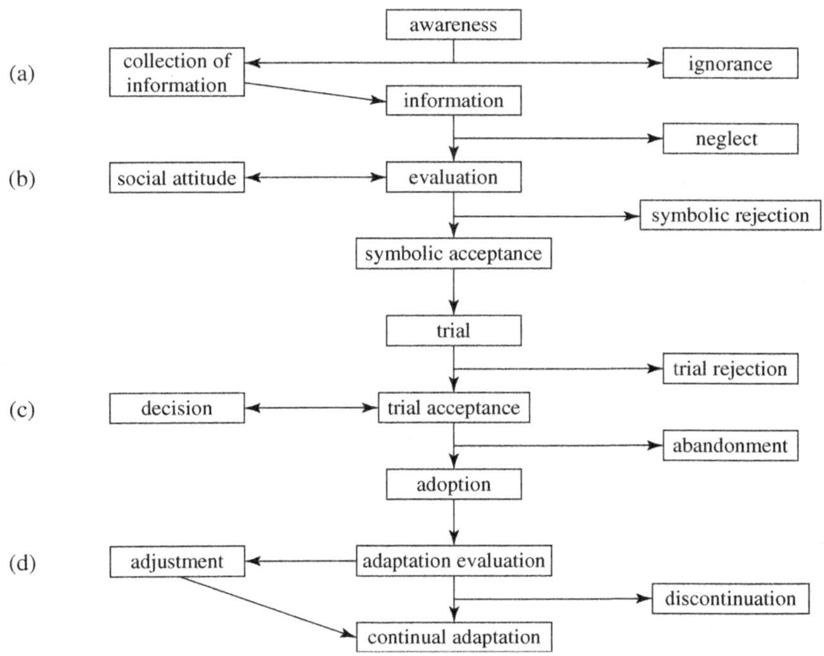

Fig. 1. Flow Chart of Adopting Process of New Technologies.

[7]This schema is a modification of the argument in Klonglan and Coward (1970).

(a) *Collection of information*

The first step of technological innovation in any society is the awareness of a technological gap between its own technologies and more advanced ones available elsewhere. In many developing countries, very few technicians or engineers are capable enough to recognize such a technological gap, most of them being ignorant of the significance of technological innovation to economic development. Under such circumstances, it is necessary, before anything else, to educate some leading figures regarding the importance of the problem and motivate them to take action in obtaining information on more desirable technologies.

Only those who know about problems of technology and can evaluate, more or less, information on various types of technologies, can collect information. Because of the shortage of such capable technical personnel in developing countries, often the real value of accessible information is not appreciated, and precious information is neglected.

This shortage is very noticeable in Southeast Asian countries. In recent years, they have come to realize the importance of technological education. The establishment of outstanding engineering institutes at graduate level like the Asian Institute of Technology in Thailand by international cooperation is symbolic of recognition of this problem in the region. Information is usually not free: it requires effort and cost. Success depends on the number and quality of communication channels: books, scholars, experts, patents, etc. Access to sources of supply is often very limited at either the supply or receiving end for various reasons. Government policies, cooperative efforts by private business companies or global action by international organizations can reduce the obstacle to some extent (Bhalla, 1979). However, information would be more readily used when the user obtains it by his own effort. All other organizations' efforts are supplementary. "You may take a horse to the water but you cannot make him drink".

One important question here is related to the means of communication, particularly language. As Table 2 shows, almost any developing country in Asia was a colony. The familiarity with the former sovereign country's language has largely determined Asian countries' sources of information and channels. It is said that South Korea and Taiwan have had the advantage of having access to technologies and managerial knowhow of

Table 2. Socio-Cultural Characteristics of East and Southeast Asian Countries.

	Country A	Religion B	Ethnic C	Ideology D	Society E	Colonial F	Trade G
1	Japan	S, B	Japanese	FE	Tight	—	US, Cn
2	China	?, T, B, o	Han, min	Sc → FE	Tight	—	Jp, US
3	N. Korea	?,	Korean	Sc	Tight	Japan	Cn
4	S. Korea	C, Ch, B	Korean	FE	Tight	Japan	Jp, US, Cn
5	Taiwan	C, B, T	Han, min	FE	Tight	Japan	C, Jp, US
6	Hong Kong	T, B, Ch	S-Chin, o	FE	Tight	UK	Cn, Jp, US
7	Philippines	Ch, T	Tagalog, o	FE	Soft	US	Jp, US, Cn
8	Vietnam	?, B, Ch, T	Vietnam.	Sc → FE	Tight	France	Jp, US, Cn
9	Laos	B	Laos	Sc → FE	Soft	France	Th
10	Cambodia	B	Cambodian	Sc → FE	Soft	France	Th
11	Thailand	B	Thai, min	FE	Soft	—	Jp, US, Cn
12	Burma	B, o	Bur., min	FE	Soft	UK	Cn, Jp
13	Malaysia	I, T, H, B	Mal. Min	Sc → FE	Soft, tight	UK	Jp, US, Cn
14	Singapore	T, H, I, Ch	S-Ch, Mal, o	FE	Tight	UK	Jp, Cn
15	Indonesia	I, Ch, H, o	Jav, min	FE	Soft	Netherland	Jp, Cn

Notes: ? = Communism, B = Buddhism, C = Confucianism, Ch = Christian, Cn = China, H = Hinduism, I = Islam, S = Shinto, T = Taoism, o = other religion; FE = free private enterprise, Sc = Socialism; min = minorities, N. Korea = North Korea, S. Korea = South Korea, S-Chin = Southern Chinese, S-Ch = S-Chin.

Japanese small and medium enterprises through direct association with them, whereas information from the United States has been more suitable for larger corporations.

(b) *Social attitude*

Information about new or foreign technologies must be evaluated in the light of the needs of existing industries or industries to be established. Such evaluation is not necessarily done purely based on economic calculations. More often, the social attitude towards technological innovation is decisive. It may be unbelievable but it is true that in the 19th century, some Japanese were prejudiced against railroads and refused to have railway stations located in the capitals of their feudal clans. 17th century Japan, Korea, and China chose to close the doors to Western powers because they were afraid of being contaminated by Christianity or conquered by colonialism. Burma at some stage seems to have shown a similar national decision.

Social attitudes in Asian countries towards foreign technologies are now strongly influenced by their historical background, religions, and social organizations, as Table 2 summarizes, those factors in East Asian countries, for the purpose of comparison. Entrepreneurial characteristics and the social attitude towards innovation vary considerably from one society to another in Southeast Asia. Nevertheless, there are two common factors, which are important, namely, nationalism and the role of overseas Chinese.

(i) *Nationalism*: All countries in the region excepting Thailand started their nation building after the WWII. National pride or nationalism is their utmost and vital concern. Often it comes before considerations about national economic development. The Asian version of nationalism normally involves a strong sentiment against colonialism and urges the conscious efforts for establishing a historical and cultural identity as a nation. This holds even with the Western way of business. It is not unusual that anti-colonialism leads to chauvinistic radicalism, which simply repels anything Western, particularly anything related apparently to *capitalism*. This prejudice sometimes extends to modern technologies, whether they are economically appropriate for the national economy or not. In such cases, Western technologies are symbolically rejected. Sometimes, prejudice is based on utter ignorance and misunderstanding of modern technology or superstitious something which common sense cannot figure out. An episode of *Shim-pu-ren* (holy wind group) objecting to the use of electricity in the 19th century Japan was one of those cases.

Even if the social attitude is not so extreme, it is very common that conventional customs cannot easily be modified to accept modern technologies, since they have been established through the historical process of choosing the best and safest customs and techniques among those available under traditional conditions. They often contain the wisdom of ancestors, so that resistance to hasty adoption of recently developed technologies is sometimes justified. Thai farmers' hesitation to accept high-yielding varieties of rice of the IRRI type in the Chao Praya basin is a case in point. As later scientific investigations revealed, this new type of rice is not more productive than the conventional one unless more fertilizers are used, which most farmers cannot afford, and blight and insects easily damage the rice. What is more important, however, is symbolic acceptance rather than rejection. Many developing countries need some symbols for national identity. For this reason, monumental projects like excessively large steel mills or petrochemical plants are often preferred to more modest, economically appropriate projects. Giant enterprises like *Pertamina* (National Oil Corporation) in Indonesia play a role of providing the nation not only with economic resources to support the government but also with national pride to symbolize the global scale of the new nation's wealth, although they simply succeeded the colonial power's properties. Such a consideration tends to cause bias in the choice of industries and technologies towards more capital-intensive and regionally concentrated directions. Under these circumstances, it is difficult to adopt technologies that are appropriate from the viewpoint of national economy.

(ii) *Overseas Chinese*: The economic role of overseas Chinese in Southeast Asia is very significant, although the degree of importance and its nature differs from one country to another. One notable fact is that large, modern factories are predominantly joint ventures with the participation of overseas Chinese. In recent years, the Governments of Malaysia and Indonesia adopted the policies of *bumi-putra* which give preferential treatment to indigenous ethnic people over people of Chinese origin. In Thailand, government policies are oriented toward integration of different ethnic groups, including Chinese Thais. In Indonesia, there are some provincial areas where some indigenous ethnic groups control economic activities; for example, Bataks in North Sumatra, Aceh in Aceh Province, Minangkabau in West Sumatra, etc. In the Philippines, a few large family concerns with Spanish background used to dominate industrial and financial activities. With the exception of such cases, it is still true that overseas Chinese, estimated at about 15 to 20 million, including those in Singapore, continue to dominate at least the commercial businesses in Southeast Asia.

The horizon of their economic calculation tends to be short and they are inclined to plunge into commercial rather than industrial ventures, since this is the way to make money more quickly. At the same time, there is some evidence that this business attitude of overseas Chinese may also stem from their cultural background such as Confucianism and Taoism. Singapore, where overseas Chinese form a majority group, has reached as high a standard of living as US$3,000 per capita but does not show any sign of developing truly manufacturing industries as yet. Those who have become partners in Japanese joint ventures clearly prefer to remain in charge of sales and do not show much interest in manufacturing. Most partners insist on receiving high dividends rather than accumulating internal funds of corporations (Ichimura, 1980). They do not like opening their companies' shares to the public, not extending their confidence beyond their kin's or acquaintances from the same province in China. Here again, their careful attitude towards risk-taking is remarkable. They diversify their investments, not putting all their eggs into one basket.

With such a behavior pattern, overseas Chinese tend to be followers rather than leaders of industrial innovation. This is bound to influence the general pattern of industrial and technological development in Southeast Asia where they dominate in the business world. The allocation of capital and human resources tends to be biased towards trade and commerce, and more basic manufacturing industries that require roundabout production will be neglected. There are, however, some signs of change in their attitude in this respect. They are becoming increasingly integrated with the native population (Hibino, 1975, 1977).

At the same time, intellectuals and governments in Southeast Asia are getting quite enthusiastic about R&D efforts. Most countries have recently established some technological institutes. For instance, the Asian Institute of Technology in Thailand is producing internationally recognized engineers and attracting excellent graduate students from many Asian countries. This certainly encourages the choice and development of technologies more appropriate for respective countries. However, it will take some time for these people to start making their contributions.

(c) *Decision making*: A small number of leaders, either in government offices or in the private sector, must make a decision to accept new technology as a trial and then adopt it. This decision making requires the so-called entrepreneurial spirit. How the societal attitude toward entrepreneurship is important. Unless economic *deliberateness* in Alfred Marshall's terminology or "rationality of calculation" in Max Weber's terminology prevails in the society, entrepreneurs are unlikely to appear and undertake rational economic action or make risky decisions in the uncertain conditions. Still less likely are they to venture into a trial of new, unknown technologies. Regarding these matters among indigenous ethnic groups, one must look into the ethical codes of Southeast Asian religions or spiritual traditions and their relations to entrepreneurship. Other ethical codes on economic behavior are also important for economic development; for instance, industriousness, thrift, and benevolence among workers and consumers. They have directly or indirectly exert as great influence on the choice of technology as entrepreneurship does.

Apart from Catholicism in the Philippines, two Southeast Asian religions are not well known, namely, Theravada Buddhism in Thailand and Islam in Indonesia. Both have their unique local characteristics.

(i) *Theravada Buddhism in Thailand*: It is almost like Christianity in Europe in the medieval age. It permeates through people's life and national politics. At the same time, it is a solid base of nationalism along with the royal family and their pride as the only nation in Southeast Asia that has never been colonized. Its strong identification with the nation, combined with a strong feeling of anti-colonialism, tends to make this religion go along with some kind of "statism", if not socialism. Similarly, in Cambodia and Burma, it has been very common to talk about Buddhist socialism or Dharma socialism. Marxism, on the material side, and Buddhism, on the spiritual side, was a belief of many Cambodians (Ishii, 1973, 1978; Mizuno, 1975). However, this demonstrates that socialism against capitalism and Buddhism against Westernization can be combined so readily in the minds of many Southeast Asian Buddhists. As a result, the rational calculation, which is a core of capitalistic spirits, and entrepreneurship as a basis of free private enterprise are something hard for Theravada Buddhists to understand. Their attitude toward innovation appears less than enthusiastic, According to a study conducted by a Kyoto University group on the cultural values cherished by Thai farmers (Ichimura *et al.*, 1974, pp. 322–343), industriousness and thrift are both highly respected. However, this does not seem to be motivated by ambition to accumulate wealth. Most Thais seem to accept their social positions as given. They interpret a Thai proverb "know oneself" or "know one's position" to mean that their social status must be accepted rigidly. It almost resembles the Hindu belief that everybody belongs to a certain caste and can be reborn in a higher caste only by obeying the law of the caste. The teachings of Theravada Buddhism do not expect the believers to undertake anything positive or creative for spiritual relief. Some argue that something like Protestant reform may be needed (Prasert Yamklinfung, 1974). Until such reform is done, Thai leaders will tend to await benevolent neighbors, realizing that foreign entrepreneurs come to Thailand for their own benefit. If foreign corporations do not invest enough, Thai officials will inquire why investment is not made and may change their policies. The indigenous Thais are, however, unlikely to start their own businesses and undertake the adventurous investments themselves. It is true that they emphasize the value of benevolence and sympathy with the poor, but such teachings do not seem to motivate the Thai intellectuals toward business enterprises nor capital accumulation.

At the same time, however, it must be noted that indigenous Thais have been more innovative in the rural sector, where a number of important intermediate technologies have been developed; e.g., combining traditional local technologies with small pumping motors and cultivating machines. The government has been playing a significant role in promoting agricultural technological innovations but Thai individual farmers have not necessarily responded easily to government recommendations. This is at least partly because the government's programmers, e.g., those of experimental farms, do not always pay sufficient attention to their real problems and conditions.

According to the aforementioned survey by the Kyoto University group, there seems to be a significant difference in the response to government recommendations between Thai farmers and Indonesian farmers. Table 3 shows this difference with reference to new high-yielding varieties of rice.

Table 3. Reasons for Adopting Recommended Varieties.

Village	Reasons												Total
	A		B		C		D		E		F		
Pathum Thani	1	(4)	17	(35)	24	(49)	3	(6)			4	(10)	49
Ayutthaya	2	(8)	8	(32)	10	(40)	1	(4)	2	(8)	2	(8)	25
Saraburi	1	(100)											1
Klaten	4	(22)	11	(61)	6	(33)			7	(39)	1	(6)	18
Demak	6	(38)	7	(54)	8	(61)	2	(16)	1	(8)	2	(15)	13
Gading	5	(20)	6	(24)	16	(64)	2	(8)			3	(12)	25

Notes

1: A = worth trying any new variety; B = recommended by the government or village head; C = seeing the success of neighbors; D = seeing the success in surrounding villages; E = seeing the success at village's seed plot; F = others.

2: Multiple answers were permitted. Figures in ( ) are % in total sample.

Source: Ichimura *et al.* (1974).

Clearly, Indonesian farmers more faithfully follow recommendations by the government than Thai farmers do. Another remarkable fact is that the Thai villagers are less inquisitive than Indonesian villagers are at the first moment of introduction of new high-yielding varieties of rice. The inquisitive persons in column A served as pioneers in introducing the recommended varieties, whereas other villagers followed. Nevertheless, the adoption and adaptation of the IRRI variety took place earlier in Thailand, mainly due to the efforts on the part of the Thai Government Ministry of Agriculture.[8]

(ii) *Islam in Indonesia*: Islam as a religion is even more anti-modernistic than Theravada Buddhism (Geertz, 1978; Mori, 1978). However, its historical functions were not anti-economic. It advocated egalitarianism and promoted urbanization and commercial activities. Trade was regarded as a way of proving one's creed and piety. Thus, Islam gives support to adventurous trading. In the same kind of spirit, innovation in manufacturing can be undertaken but there is no clear indication in Indonesia that these Islamic ideas have promoted technological innovations, or that Muslims in Java are more actively engaged in commerce than those in other creeds. In Sumatra, Muslims are more puritanical. They tend to be synergetic. In particular, Islam in Java is mixed with its predecessors, namely, Hinduism and Buddhism. The influence of Islam on economic activities is also mixed with those of nationalism and other institutional factors, so that it is difficult to discern one from the other. This mixed religion with other cultural factors goes further in Indonesia than in other Southeast Asian countries. It may be called a religion–socio-political mix in modern times Indonesia. It is a central institutional factor underlying the difficulties in Indonesia's nation building. Indonesian modern times from the last quarter of the 19th century to the present may be divided into three phases (Geertz, 1978; Benda, 1958).

(1) The period up to the early 1920s, when a "spiritual balance of power" existed among various groups: like Indio-Javanese syncretism, would-be Islamic orthodoxy of the merchant class, some of the better-off farmers, and most of heterogeneous outer islanders. This balance was workable under the aegis of the Dutch administration.

[8]This reminds the author of Tobata's theory of Japan's agricultural development, which stresses the role of the government as an innovator (Keizo Tsuchiya, 1979).

(2) The period from the early 1920s to 1965, which may be characterized by the politicization[9] and the use of all sorts of voluntary organizations — labor, farm, youth, women, school, charitable — clustering around the political parties. Despite great efforts by the Government, all attempts to establish some kind of new social order in Indonesia had failed by 1965 and the situation exploded the coup and the massacres.
(3) The period from 1965 to the present, which is characterized by (a) army domination in the government and weakening of the party system and (b) "restructuring" of religio-cultural life both in organization and in content.

Throughout these three phases, there has always been some kind of tension between the two processes of nation building: the organization of the civil government with bureaucracy and the establishment of cultural identity as a nation. The former was the political aspect, whereas the latter was the cultural aspect of the same nation.

In a pluralistic society like Indonesia, national unification is particularly difficult in both aspects. The government's policies have been guided by the need to resolve the various stakes among different groups. Policies pertaining to the choice of technologies cannot be free from such political considerations. Often, the stakes of some social groups guide the government's policy in granting concessions to foreign joint-ventures or organizing national projects because the stability of the government depends critically on the balance among these groups. Recently, the government has emphasized to developing employment-creating small enterprises as well as income distribution and regional balance. All these are largely due to the necessity to reduce socio-political tension that had been pointed out by religious leaders and economists. The leaders are often associated with Islamic churches and parties.

Apart from such religio-political influence on policy making in Indonesia, the effect of Islamic belief on economic behavior is also noticeable. A survey of socio-economic behavior of peasants in central Java

[9]They formed four ideological groups in post-independence Indonesian politics: i.e., radical nationalist (PNI), reformist Moslem (Masujumi), traditional Moslem (NU), and radical populist (PKI). It was this system of Indonesian politics that Sukarno tried to synthesize with Pantjasila NASAKOM: i.e., guided democracy expressive politics.

and Thailand quoted above clarified the characteristics of Indonesians in contrast to those of Thai farmers. When asked how to get rich, for example, Thai farmers mentioned something like "working hard" and "not doing anything luxurious", whereas Indonesian farmers replies more typically refer to "working hard" and "luck". Thais are rather pragmatic and Javanese are rather fatalistic. Indonesians tend to regard "hard-working" itself as something valuable for which God will bestow happiness on them.

Thus, one of the important but delicate differences in cultural premises in Java and Thailand, which must have to do with religious differences, is concerned with the notion of "luck". To Thais, "luck" is a consequence of their effort: to Indonesians "luck" is the judgment of God. One may say that Thais can be more easily motivated to act economically, whereas Indonesians need stronger non-economic motivation to achieve some economic goals, including adoption of technologies more appropriate for the purpose of national economic development.

(d) *Adjustment implementation*: Once a decision is made to adopt a new technology, the next step is to put it into practice. This must be done by private enterprise or any other kind of government organization that is equipped with some capital and personnel. Implementation of a new technology also requires some modification or adjustment of the original to the local conditions. This is particularly the case where foreign technologies are imported from industrialized countries, as they are often unsuitable to the conditions and needs of importing, developing countries. The need for capital is well known but the role to be played by personnel and social organizations is not always understood. For any technological innovation, the active agents who discover, adopt, and imitate the new technology are essential. Those who initiate the process must be strongly motivated. Their motive may be for (a) an individual, (b) an enterprise, (c) an industry, (d) the society, or (e) the nation. Individuals sometimes identify themselves with the entities like (b)–(e) and try to act for the sake of them. To some extent, one can argue that the problem of "inappropriate technologies" arises from the gap between individual entrepreneurs' and interest groups' choice, on the one hand, and the optimal choice from the social and national point of view, on the other. If, therefore, innovating individuals and interest groups are more public-minded, the implementation of appropriate technologies will be easier. How an innovator identifies himself with the need for a group or community rather than his personal desire depends on his perception of his role in the society. Egoistic individuals can hardly perceive any role above their family level. Strong motivation seems to come from a good balance of individual motives and his sense of duty to public interests from (b) to (e). How to establish or inscribe such public-mindedness into the minds of leading individuals or civil servants, in the midst of political corruption (Nishihara, 1976), is indeed a fundamental problem of nation building. This problem is very closely related to that of social organizations to be discussed in the next section.

In this connection, it seems crucial for a nation to have some social class that produces public-minded leaders. The Samurai class produced many influential businessmen as well as politicians and generals in Meiji Japan (Ichimura, 1974). Most of the Southeast Asian countries have had no warrior class in their history, nor any other class, which has been as public-minded as the Japanese Samurai.

As regards the diffusion of a chosen technology, it is understood that the more entrepreneurial members there are in one society, the more rapid it will be. The more rapidly modern technology is absorbed and integrated with the traditional sectors of the society, the better the chance will be to generate indigenous appropriate, technologies. Ever since Tarde's classic works on imitation and Ryan-Gross' on the diffusion of hybrid seed corn, it has been recognized that technology diffusion follows an S-shaped pattern (Tarde, 1903; Posner, 1961; Vernon, 1966; Akamatsu, 1965; Kojima, 1972). Initially, only a few adopt the new technology. Having seen their success, more adopt it and the rate of adoption accelerates. Finally, as potential adopters begin to be exhausted, the rate of diffusion declines.

Figure 2A shows a pattern of S-shaped diffusion, and Figure 2B gives the underlying distribution of entrepreneurial ability. If the distribution is more concentrated around the mean, the sharply rising portion of the S-shaped curve will be sharper; namely, the diffusion will start slowly but, once it starts spreading, it will do so within a very short span of time. A country like Japan seems to have shown this pattern of diffusion in many cases. If, however, the distribution is more dispersed, the rising part of the S-curve will be more gradual and the catch-up pattern will be slow and moderate. The slow process of technology diffusion in Southeast Asia must have something to do, at least partly, with this distribution of

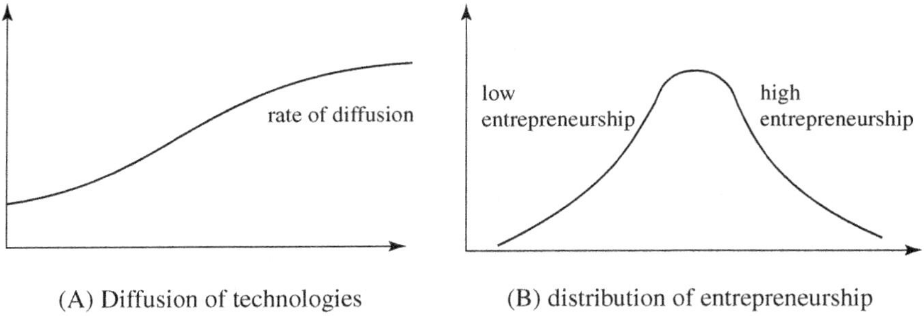

Fig. 2. The Patterns of Diffusion of Technologies and Distribution of Entrepreneurship. (A) Diffusion of Technologies, (B) Distribution of Entrepreneurship.

Table 4. Attitude Toward a New Variety Recommended by the Government.

	Respondents	Reasons mentioned by respondents				
Village	Total	A	B	C	D	E
Pathum Thani	47	37 (76)	—	6 (14)	—	5 (10)
Ayuthaya	33	17 (52)	—	12 (36)	3 (9)	1 (3)
Saraburi	41	17 (27)	—	28 (68)	2 (5)	—
Klaten	30	11 (37)	10 (33)	12 (40)	—	—
Demak	33	8 (24)	2 (6)	20 (61)	4 (12)	4 (12)
Gading	50	6 (20)	16 (53)	6 (20)	3 (10)	—

Notes
1: Reasons are: A = I would plant it before anybody else. B = I would try to plant it after the test at village's seed plots. C = I would plant it if somebody else succeeds. D = I would not be interested in it. E = others.
2: Multiple answers are permitted.
3: Figures in parentheses are percentage of total respondents.
Sources: The same as Table 3.

entrepreneurial capacity in the population. The relationship between the two may be examined empirically either directly through a survey or indirectly by an econometric estimation.

The findings of the Kyoto University group's survey can illustrate the first approach. Table 3 quoted earlier clearly indicates certain patterns of entrepreneurship distribution in different villages. The same survey also included a question on the interviewee's response to government recommendations, which is summarized in Table 4.

Table 5. Time-lag from Acquisition to Adoption (Year).

Village	Information	Adoption	Time lag
Pathum Thani	3.66	3.04	0.63
Ayuthaya	8.76	7.24	1.52
Saraburi	—	—	—
Klaten	2.28	1.61	0.67
Demak	2.38	1.15	1.23
Gading	9.12	8.24	0.88

Note: Responses in Saraburi were few.
Source: The same as Table 3.

Based on the information given in the two tables, one could conjecture that the speed of diffusion of high-yielding varieties of rice might be of the order of Gading–Klaten–Demak in Indonesia and Pathum Thani–Ayuthaya–Saraburi in Thailand.

This conjecture has been tested and confirmed by a third question: how many years before the interview did the respondents obtain information on recommended varieties and actually adopt them (Table 5)? The time lag actually turned out longer in Gading than in Klaten but Gading is a new settlement and may be an exceptional case.

As regards the second approach, a number of quantitative studies on industrial innovations, mostly in developed countries, have appeared in recent years. The analytical framework offered by E. Mansfield (1968 and 1969) may have some applicability even to developing countries. He defines $\lambda_l(t)$ as the proportion of only at time t but not before then. This $\lambda_l(t)$ plotted in the same way as diagram A above would look similar. Mansfield offered a hypothesis that $\lambda_l(t)$ is a function of the fraction of firms that already adopted $\lambda_l(t-1)$: the profitability of the innovation, π the cost of the innovation, C: and other unspecified factors lumped together, D. Thus, by estimating an equation like:

$$\lambda_l(t) = F\{\lambda_l(t-1), \pi_i, C_i, D_i\},$$

he tested a number of hypotheses over different periods, industries and even some innovations. An interesting point is that, from the shape of relation between $\lambda_l(t)$ and $\lambda_l(t-1)$ over the diffusion period, one can infer the pattern of distribution of entrepreneurship in that industry. An international comparison may give an insight into the latent talents of entrepreneurs in different LDCs. By applying variance or factor analyses, some hypotheses may be tested concerning similarities and dissimilarities among countries.

Partial modification or adjustment in the process of implementing new imported technologies in most LDCs is the first step in generating indigenous technologies that are truly appropriate for the national economy. Some problems in this domain will be discussed in the last section.

4. Social Organization, Bureaucracy, and Market

Decision-makers are in the context of the society they belong to, so that the social organization influences the process of decision making and implementation of policies. The organizational structure of various social groups in Southeast Asia is rather mixed. The so-called "loosely structured" society (J.F. Embree, 1950; Eyers, 1969) or "soft" society (G. Myrdal) seems to characterize the bilinear societies of the Siamese, Laotians, Cambodians, Malays, and Javanese. Although the bilinear societies are not necessarily "soft", kinship tends to be weak considerably after a couple of generations, the succession of family properties being extremely fragmented. These societies contrast sharply with the "tight" societies of Chinese, Japanese, Vietnamese, as well as Bataks and Menankabaus in Sumatra. The following schema may illustrate the differences, including Euro-American societies[10] (Kuchiba, 1979).

When compared with Japan, the bilinear society of Southeast Asia can be said to be strongly individual-oriented but not as strongly as that of America. The social harmony is valued highly among individuals in Southeast Asia, so that the value of performance or achievements is not as much emphasized as in Japan or America. Again, in Southeast Asia, although particularistic dyadic relations and harmonious relations are highly valued, they do not have the strong group-oriented character of kin as in China or of families and villages as in Japan. These characteristics seem to be related to the peculiar character of a village community in most Southeast Asian ethnic groups. They permeate into any social organizations, including business and government. The looseness of their

[10]These are the relationships that emphasize personal attachment established *ad hoc* between two individuals with respect to different activities or occasions.

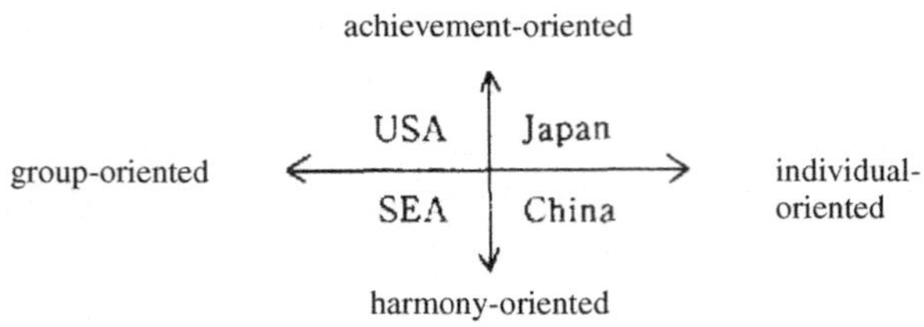

Fig. 3. Types of Social Organization.

social cohesion has important implications for economic development. M. Kuchiba used Figure 3 in Kuchiba (1979) characterize the social organizations in the world in terms of two axis: achievement-oriented *vs* harmony-oriented and group-oriented *vs* individual-oriented. His remarks in Kuchiba (1979) may be applicable, with slight modifications, to business or government organizations.

"The need for a multi-purpose farmers' cooperative is emphasized in Southeast Asia but it is not formed smoothly. In Japan, the self-governing body of a hamlet is often capitalized as a sub-unit of a cooperative organization. In this way, loyalty to the village becomes, at the same time, loyalty to the cooperative organization. Withdrawal from a cooperative organization can easily be interpreted to be a sign of disloyalty to the village, so that even though joining is easy, withdrawal is difficult. Sometimes the strength of this type of group orientation may become a hindrance to the implementation of a programme which covers a broad farming area, such as field consolidation. In contrast, joining a cooperative organization is a personal matter and joining and withdrawal are simple in Southeast Asia. The social foundations for membership recruitment, entrenchment and perpetuation are weak".

In order to carry out a large scale of operation in any field, what Max Weber called bureaucracy in the broad sense is essential. The soft society does not offer the historic experiences needed to organize the personnel in this bureaucratic fashion. If, therefore, Southeast Asian organizations are expanded, as they often have to be, either in private enterprise or government offices, they tend to be fragmented and co-ordination of departmental activities becomes almost impossible. The cohesion of strict organizational orders, even if repeatedly enforced, gradually becomes loose, so that tasks are often left unaccomplished with no serious punishment. Planning or preliminary studies for the implementation of policies for appropriate technologies are no exception.

The shortage of key personnel often accompanies this organizational problem. For these reasons, implementation of a plan often encounters unexpected difficulties and requires quick and adequate revision. The resulting confusion sometimes leads to abandonment of the whole plan. All these considerations imply that *appropriate technology* in this context is the one that does not require a large organization and tight administration to group work (Merton *et al.*, 1952). From this point of view, policies for the development of small and medium-sized enterprises are recommendable in the Southeast Asian context.

The most fundamental organizational question to ask may be which is more suitable for such societies, a free, private enterprise system or socialist system. It would be interesting to ask how the difference in the economic system influences the choice of technology and the pattern of technological changes. However, we confine our discussion here to the market or mixed economies, so that we do not enter the problem.

In this connection, it must be remembered that the market mechanism, which is the backbone of the free private enterprise system, does not usually work fully in the developing world, for a number of reasons. To mention a few, infrastructure (e.g., communication, transportation, financial institutions, etc.) is under-developed, and the efficiency of the existing facilities is reduced by human factors (e.g., language barriers and antagonism among different ethnic groups). A proper price system is missing, and all kinds of governmental further complicated interventions the situation.

5. Choice of Industry and Technology

Within the broad institutional framework of the aforementioned social attitude and behavior patterns, decision makers at the levels of government offices, industry, enterprise, and plants (or establishments) take steps in adopting and implementing the technologies which they consider appropriate. Government officials preparing a national or regional development plan are usually concerned with the choice of (a) industries, (b) ownership of enterprises, (c) location and scale of plants, and (d) technology or capital equipment to install.

As for the choice of industries, the first consideration should be the pattern of economic structure that is appropriate for the country. The most important institutional issue in this connection relates to the co-ordination among various ministries and agencies. Unless the ministry or agency in charge of this co-ordination has the full support of the political leader, no systematic and rational choice of sectoral and industrial compositions can be expected. As we discussed in Section 3 in some detail, political considerations often distort the development plan that is supposed to maximize employment or reduce the income differentials among various local classes or regions.

At this level of decision making on development strategies, the ideological problem of physiocrat versus mercantilist often arises: the principle of "agriculture first" fighting against that of "industrialization first" (Livingstone, 1968). This has important implications in offering employment opportunities and basic human needs to the majority of the population and in maintaining balances between urban and rural areas.

Within the manufacturing sector, there is a certain standard pattern of growth of different manufacturing industries which depends on the scale of national economy and per capita income (Chenery and Syrquin, 1975). The cases of textile and basic metal industries may be mentioned here for illustration.

It is very important to observe the similarities and differences in their growth pattern of large countries, small manufacturing countries and small primary countries. For instance, the share of basic metal industry increases with per capita income in all three cases, but it starts declining beyond some $1,000 in the case of large countries. Unless the country's officials have a clear idea of this kind of pattern appropriate for their own country at each stage of development, the appropriate choice of industries cannot be made.

The choice of industry is important in our context because it has great bearing on the choice of technology and the labor intensity of adopted technologies. This is clear, for example, when one compares petrochemical plants with garment manufacturing or metal engineering.

The pattern of ownership of enterprises in developing countries is considerably influenced by government regulations on foreign investment, minimum wage, labor unions, etc. For instance, in the Philippines, all foreign investments below 30% of the total paid-in capital of joint ventures

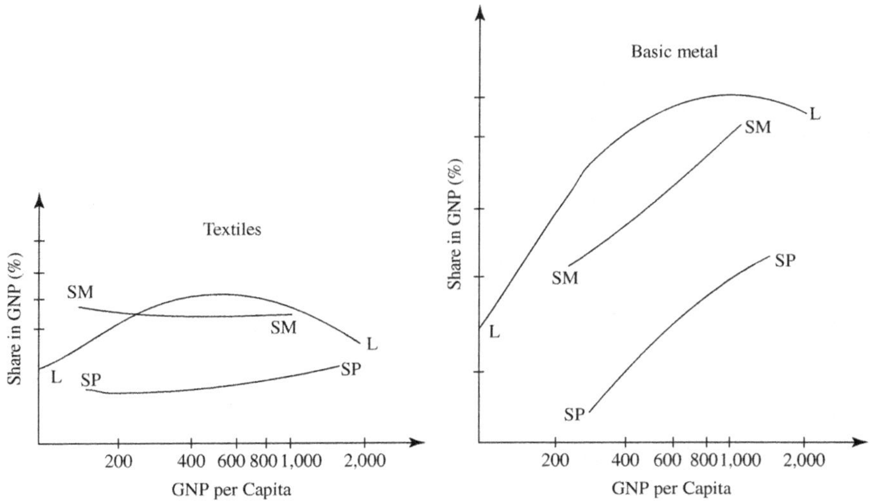

Fig. 4. The Shares of Textile and Basic Metal Manufacturing Industries in GDP by the Pattern of the Economy and by the Level of Per Capita Income.

Note: L stands for large countries. SM for small manufacturing countries and SP for small primary product producers.

Source: Bruton, H. J. 1979 [5]; H. Chenerv and L. Taylor, 1968 [7]; Chenery and Syrquin, 1975 [8].

are automatically approved. If the share is more than 30%, however, approval is not given easily unless the joint ventures are of pioneering types. In Thailand, the share of foreign capital must usually be kept below 50%. These regulations are to control the domination of foreign influence and foster the steady growth of indigenous entrepreneurs and domestic industries. Obviously, they reflect the value system of the society.

Whatever the criteria used in decision making may be, the foreign-local ownership composition and government regulations on it have an important bearing on the choice of technology. The technology is likely to be chosen by the foreign investors, because they tend to bring in the available technologies from their home countries.

In screening investment projects, the government has to assess the long-term effects of each project with respect to its development objectives: optimal use of natural and human resources, expansion of net foreign exchange earnings, increase in government revenue, consolidation of the economic base of political leadership, etc. How this assessment is done in, reality is a subject that merits empirical research. As regards investment by foreign firms, the criterion actually applied varies from one case to another, but the following seem to be among the common criteria: "first in first", "the most modern", "the best company at home", the political or personal connections between the decision makers and the investor, etc. How these criteria are reconciled with development objectives is a key question in the choice of appropriate technologies in these countries.

In the case of a multinational enterprise, its enormous scale of activities often scares local politicians and officials who worry about the nationalistic reaction of local people.[11] Pros and cons of multinationals must be studied carefully. In Southeast Asia, anti-multinational feelings have not been as strong as in Latin America, probably because of the relatively limited scale of their investment in this region, except for petroleum majors in Indonesia. This dose not necessarily mean that the happy situation will continue in the future.

Ownership may pose, in addition, another problem in terms of ethnic groups. In Malaysia and Indonesia, Bumi Putra policies give priority to indigenous ethnic groups in all kinds of economic activities and education. This will certainly contribute to the generation of techniques appropriate for the traditional sector and reduce dualism in the economy. For example, by supporting the participation of indigenous ethnic people in international joint ventures or subcontracting with them, their chance of learning modern technologies increases.

Another important issue pertaining to ownership concerns the public sector enterprises. Most enterprises owned by colonial powers have been taken over by the government and become state enterprises. Their size is often very large and they usually enjoy a monopolistic position. The technology adopted by them is often inappropriate from the viewpoint of the national economy. At the same time, with their monopoly power, the management is often inefficient or sometimes corrupt. One of such enterprises in

[11]There are many works that discuss merits of foreign investment and multinational corporations. For example, ÉCLA, 1968; Prebisch, 1963; Singer, 1975, 1977; Bhagwati, 1972; Dos Santos, 1970; Gough and Shama, 1973; Bagchi, 1973; Craft *et al.*, 1972; Vernon, 1970; Soedjatmoko, 1972.

Southeast Asia almost went bankrupt recently and caused a serious menace to the national economy. These public enterprises, with special protection provided by the government, often deprive private business groups of opportunities to generate more appropriate technologies, by occupying a dominant share of the market and making the cost of entry too high.

The location of large plants can change the regional distribution of economic opportunities, so that appropriate technologies for employment creation and improvement in income distribution may mean appropriate location of plants and enterprises. These considerations are particularly important in Southeast Asia. However, decisions on the location and scale of plants are very often at the mercy of political considerations, since the growth of prosperous private enterprises in one area changes the balance of economic power among various regions in the country and this, in turn, has great political implications.

To come to the choice of capital equipment, it is usually argued that the technology using more surplus labor or abundant resources is more appropriate. However, the question is not so simple. For example, the shortage of skilled labor and inadequacy of infrastructure sometimes necessitate the use of very advanced capital-intensive technology. Export requires a high standard of quality, which can only be achieved by modern machinery. These considerations often work as the factors against the wishes of many experts who advocate the need for "intermediate technology" in developing countries.

On the other hand, diffusion of modern technologies in a traditional society may encounter institutional obstacles. Technology is part of a culture, so that adoption of modern technology is not just a change in production function. It is a process of accepting modern civilization, which requires a change in the way of thinking and in the social order. For example, it may raise the social position of engineers and managers above that of the religious leaders, and this may not be acceptable in the traditional society. Consequently, new social conflicts may arise. Obviously, time is needed for the human mind to absorb a new cultural factor like modern machinery.[12] This is a slow process of adjustment and compromise.

[12]Many less developed country leaders like Onyemelukwe in Nigeria and others realized these problems (C. C. Onyemelukwe, 1974).

If technological choice is to be appropriate for factor endowment in less developed countries, there is undoubtedly a vast area of industries and service activities where labor-intensive technologies and expertise must be applied. This implies that there remain the traditional sectors that employ workers with poor capital equipment, while capital-intensive technologies are being introduced to the modern sectors. Hence, it is unavoidable to have a dual economy in any developing country. In this connection, the experience of Japan is suggestive.

In order to achieve industrialization along with the dual economy, the Japanese government played a positive role.[13] On the one hand, it has tried to foster new industries that would become export industries by various kinds of assistance, including its own effort to develop appropriate technology at the Agency of Industrial Technology.[14] On the other hand, it tried to help small- and medium-sized enterprises establish themselves. This helped solve the employment problem in the early stage of development and during the period of postwar recovery. The two-sided industrial policy made it possible for the Japanese economy to combine highly advanced technologies with relatively labor-intensive "intermediate" technologies of small and medium enterprises. This combination may have been the most appropriate approach, especially in connection with sub-contracting arrangements.

There are many successful cases of developing appropriate technologies also in other Asian countries. Some examples are related to Mudah Agricultural Development Authority (MADA) in Malaysia. It developed the Province of Mudah by introducing a new high-yielding variety of rice (HYVR) and simultaneously devising new cultivating machines that are different from the ones developed by International Rice Research Institute (IRRI). This seems to have been possible under the outstanding entrepreneurial leadership of the then director of MADA. He clearly saw the need for new types of smaller tillers and other farming machines.

[13]The Japanese Government's industrial policies are well documented.

[14]This is an agency which belongs to MITI and is specialized in the development of adaptation and generation of technology. It has about 4,000 staff, while the total number of staff of MITI itself is about 5,000. This illustrates the great importance MITI attaches to the problem of technology.

Requesting the cooperation of some Japanese firms and the government, he succeeded in initiating new designs for cultivating machines. The important factors then were the existence of an entrepreneurial leader and the organizational support to implement his ideas (Yamashita *et al.*, 1976).

Technology is not only embodied in machinery but also maintained or improved by personnel in enterprises. Its generation and dissemination in developing countries requires, therefore, a certain minimum number of engineers who are familiar with machines and tools and their production (Bruton, 1979). In order to secure the supply of such basic work force, it may be necessary to develop domestic capital goods industries in the early stage and to learn from similar experiences in other less developed countries. The latter is particularly important in adaptation of foreign technologies to local conditions and modification of traditional technologies to slightly more advanced ones (Stewart, 1977).

Government's policies are often considerably influenced by religious leaders, and the latter's recommendations may not always be compatible with the development goal of mass employment creation and elimination of poverty.

6. Concluding Remarks

On technological innovations and on institutional problems in the developing world, a fair amount has been written, but very little is known about the inter-relationships between the two. Based on the limited knowledge of the author, the paper explored this difficult domain of study. In many ways, however, it has ended merely in identifying problem areas. In order to verify the author's interpretations and establish the relative importance of various influential factors, a large-scale amount of fieldwork is necessary. This is the case with respect to each of the stages described in Section 3: collection of information, social attitude, decision-making and adjustment/implementation.

For the successful formulation and implementation of appropriate technology policies, this kind of empirical research is indispensable. At present, however, even the little and, in many ways, crude knowledge summarized in earlier pages has not been put together for policy makers, although many of them are aware of the issues and often have their own views on the questions. These views of decision-makers must be collected and analyzed. Government policies of developing countries, particularly those of most seriously underdeveloped countries, will greatly benefit from such studies in those countries, because it is in those countries that institutional and cultural factors pose especially serious obstacles to the implementation of appropriate technologies and to the satisfaction of basic human needs.

References

[1] Akamatsu, K. (1965). *Sekai Keizai Ron* (The World Economy). Kunimoto Shobo, Tokyo.

[2] Bagchi, A. K. (1973). "Foreign capital and economic development in India: A schematical view," in K. Gough and H. P. Sharma (ed.), *Imperialism and Revolution in South Asia*, Monthly Review Press, NY.

[3] Benda, H. (1958). *The Crescent and the Rising Sun: Indonesian Islam Under The Japanese Occupation: 1942–45*, The Hague.

[4] Bhagwati, J. N. (ed.) (1972). *Economics and World Order*, London.

[5] Bhalla, A. S. (ed.) (1979). *Towards Global Action for Appropriate Technology*. Pergamum Press, Oxford.

[6] Bruton, H. J. (1979). "On the production of appropriate technology," World Employ Programme Research Working Paper. WEP 2-22/WP 49, ILO, Geneva, June.

[7] Chenery, H. and L. Taylor (1968). "Development patterns among countries over time," *Review of Economics and Statistics*, November.

[8] Chenery, H. and M. Syrquin (1975). *Patterns of Development: 1950–1970*, Oxford University Press, New York.

[9] Craft, J. D. *et al.* (ed.) (1972). *Dependence and Underdevelopment*, New York.

[10] Dos Santos, T. (1970). "The structure of dependence," *American Economic Review*, May.

[11] ECLA (1968). *ECLA and Analysis of Latin American Development*, Santiago do Chile.

[12] Embree, J. F. (1950). *Thailand: A Loosely Structured Social System.* American Anthropologist, Vol. 52.

[13] Eyers, H.-D. (ed.) (1969). *Loosely Structured Social Systems, Thailand in Comparative Perspective*, Yale University Southeast Asia studies, Cultural Report Series. No. 9.

[14] Geertz, C. (1978). *Religious Change and Social Order in Suharto's Indonesia*, Asia, Autumn.

[15] Griffin, K. (1974). *The Political Economy O/ Agrarian Change*, Macmillan, London.

[16] Herrera, A. O. (1979). "The generation and dissemination of appropriate technologies in developing countries — a methodological approach," World Employment Programme Working Paper, WEP 2-22/WP 51. ILO Geneva, October.

[17] Hibino, T. (1977). *Kakyo* (Overseas Chinese). Nihon Hose Kyokai. Tokyo.

[18] Hibino, T. (1975). *Kakyo no Kazoku Seikatsu* (family life of overseas Chinese). Ajia Bunka (Cuitura Asiatica), March.

[19] Hufbauer, G. C. (1966). *Synthetic Maternal and the Theory of Informational Trade*, London.

[20] Hufbauer, G. C. (1970). "The impact of national characteristics and technology on the composition of trade in manufactured goods," in R. Vernon (ed.), [50].

[21] Ichimura, S. (1974). "Japanese entrepreneurship in early stage of economic development," *The Pacific Profile*.

[22] Ichimura, S.Y., Tsubouchi *et al.* (1974). "The socio-economic behavior of peasants in central Java and central Thailand — A summary report," in *Southeast Asian Studies*, December.

[23] Ichimura, S. (ed.) (1980). *Nippon Kigyo in Ajia* (Japanese joint-ventures in Asia), Toyokeizai Shimpo-sha, Tokyo.

[24] International Development Research Center (1976). *Science and technology for development: main comparative report of the science and technology for policy instrument project*, Ottawa.

[25] Ishii, Y. (1973). "Buddhism and nationalism in Thailand" in T. Takahashi (ed.). *T'onan Ajia no nattonalism to Shukyo* (Nationalism and Religions in Southeast Asia), Institute of Developing Economies. Tokyo.

[26] Ishii, Y. (1978). "Buddhism and Socialism in Southeast Asia," in K. Yanagawa (ed.), *Gendai-shakai no nanmondai to Shukyo* (Contemporary Society and Religion), Inst. for the study of Eastern Philosophy, Tokyo.

[27] Johnston, B. F. (1970). "Agriculture and structural transformation in developing countries: A survey of research," *Journal of Economic Literature*, June.

[28] Klonglan, G. and W. Coward (1970). "The concept of symbolic adoption: A suggested interpretation," *Rural Sociology*.

[29] Kojima, K. (1972). *Sekai Boeki to Takokuseki Ktgyo* (The world trade and multinational corporations), Sobunsha, Tokyo.

[30] Kuchiba, M. (1979). "Introduction: Problems and approaches from comparative perspective," in [31].

[31] Kuchiba, M. (ed.) (1979). *International Comparative Study of Rice-Growing Villages in Asia*, report to the Toyota Foundation.

[32] Livingstone, I. (1968). "Agriculture versus industry in economic development," *Jamal of African Studies*, March.

[33] Mansfield, E. (1968). *The Economics of Technical Change*, Norton and Co., NY.

[34] Mansfield, E. (1969). *Industrial Research and Technological Innovation — An Econometric Analysis*, Longmans. Green and Co., NY.

[35] Merton, R. K., A. P. Gray, B. Hockey, and H. C. Selvin (ed.) (1952). *Reader in Bureaucracy*, The Free Press, NY.

[36] Mizuno, K. (1975). "Family and religion in Thailand," in *Ajia Bunka* (Cultur Asiatica), March.

[37] Mori, M. (1978) *lsuramu ni totte no Kindai* (The modern age to Moslems), Chuo.Koron, Tokyo, December.

[38] Nishihara, M. (1976). *Tonan Ajia no Seiji-teki Fuhai* (Political corruption in Southeast Asia), Sobun-sha, Tokyo.

[39] Onyemelukwe, C. C. (1974). *Economic Development*, London.

[40] Posner, M. V. (1961). *International Trade and Technical Change*, Oxford Economic Papers.

[41] Prebisch, P. (1963). *Haia una dinamica del americano*, Mexico.

[42] Sachs, I. (1976). *The Discovery of the Third World*, MIT Press, Cambridge, MA.

[43] Singer, H. W. (1975). *The Strategy of International Development*, London.

[44] Singer, H. W. (1977). "Appropriate technology and a basic human needs strategy," *Informational Development Review*, 2

[45] Soedjatmoko (1972). *Technology, Development and Culture*, the Institute for Religion and Social Change, Tokyo, April.

[46] Stewart, F. (1977). *Technology and Under-development*, MacMillan, London.

[47] Tarde, G. (1903). *The Laws of Imitation*, Holt, Rhinehart and Winston, New York.

[48] Tsuchiya, K. (1979). *Tonan Ajia no Nogyo Hatten to Tobata Riron* (Agricultural development in Southeast Asia and the Tobata Theory). *Southeast Asian Studies*, September.

[49] Vernon, R. (1966). International investment and the product cycle. *Quarterly Journal of Economics*.

[50] Vernon, R. (ed.) (1970). *The Technology Transfer in International Trade*, NBER, NY.

[51] Watanabe, S. (1980). "Institutional factors, government policies and Appropriate Technologies," *International Labor Review.*
[52] Weitz, R. (1971). *From Peasant to Farmer Revolutionary Strategy for Development.* Columbia University Press, New York.
[53] Yamashita, M., S. Jegatheesan and W. C. Yoong (1976). *Agro-Economic Studies in the Mudah Project Area,* Alor Setar, MADA, Malaysia.
[54] Yamklingfun, P. (1974). Family, religion and socio-economic change in Thailand. *East Asian Cultural Studies.*

Chapter 11

The Choice of Appropriate Technologies II — Survey Findings in Indonesia, Thailand, and the Philippines

1. Introduction

1.1. *The Design of the Survey and Report*

Few studies on appropriate technologies for the Third World are based on empirical evidence from these countries.[1] My first article "Institutional factors and government policies for appropriate technologies in Southeast Asia" presented a conceptual framework for field research in this relatively unexplored area.[2] Our survey was designed on that basis to examine primarily the behavior of business corporations with regard to the adoption of technologies and the role of the government in promoting the application of *appropriate technologies* in three countries: Thailand, the Philippines, and Indonesia.

The survey was conducted with the questionnaire schedule prepared to ask business managers the questions on which they must have made decisions in the process of accepting new technologies, as my previous paper discussed. The fundamental scheme of this process of search, adoption, adaptation, and generation of economically appropriate and socially acceptable technologies are presented here as Figure 1.[3] In each step of this process, businesspersons decide on some problems. For instance,

---

[1]Literature on communication and diffusion of new technologies are surveyed in E. M. Rooers and R. Floyd Shoemaker (1971). *Communication of Innovations*, New York, The Free Press, but even this outstanding work offers only limited observations on contemporary conditions in developing countries.

[2]It was available as S. Ichimura, WEP 2-22/VP.66 and reprinted as a chapter of S. Ichimura, *Political Economy of Japanese and Asian Development*, Springer-Verlag, 1998.

[3]A. Robinson (1979). "Introduction" in *idem* (ed.), *Appropriate Technologies for Third World Development*, McMillan, London.

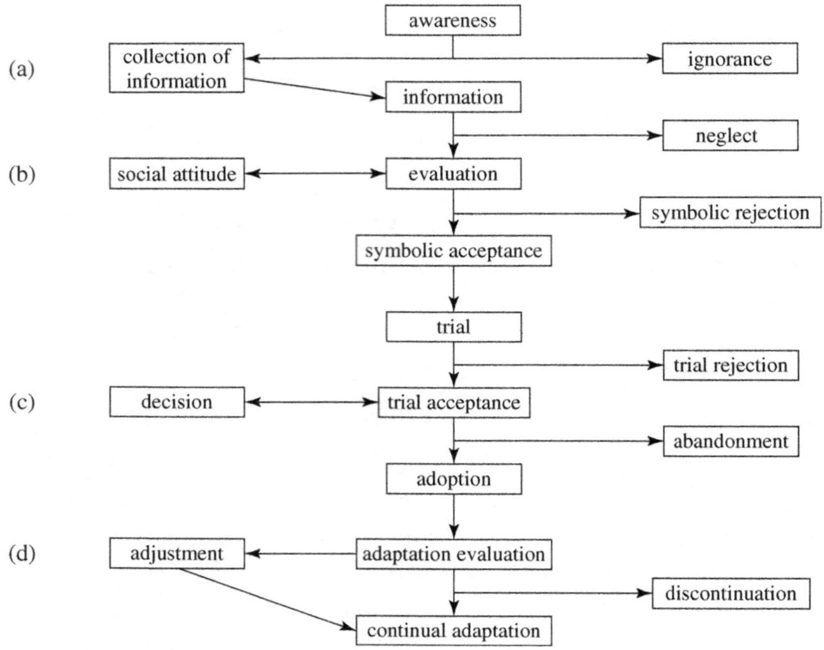

Fig. 1. Flow Chart of Adopting Process of New Technologies.

collection of information on new technologies must be made in one way or another. How it is done in practice or whether or not businessmen are satisfied with the prevailing way of obtaining information is an empirical question. It can be found out by a questionnaire survey.

There must be many questions of this nature. Only on the basis of the answers to such questions, we can see how this process actually proceeds in business management and try to conceive better policies for the government implementing appropriate technologies.

The questions are classified into eight broad problem areas: (1) basic information, (2) general issues on technologies and enterprises, (3) economic and social considerations in adoption, (4) trial and experiment, (5) adaptation, (6) diffusion, (7) impact of ethnic and religious factors and government policies, and (8) market and social organization. As Appendix shows, about 10 questions are asked on each issue. They are primarily meant to find out the practice of business enterprises in the process of accepting modern technologies and considerations behind the decisions. In formulating questions, particular attention was paid to the difficulties faced by the enterprises in the Third World, and effort was made to search for better policies or better ways of implementing the government policies for *appropriate technologies*.

These three countries are chosen, because they are distinctively different in their cultural background, historical heritage, and social organization, so that in comparison of survey findings from the three countries, it is hoped to be able to show how those cultural and institutional factors affect the implementation of their government's technology policies. The questionnaires used in the three countries are slightly different from the standard form in order to suit the local conditions. Moreover, in Thailand and Indonesia, they were produced in the local languages.[4]

The survey was conducted by our local collaborators. They not only tabulated the replies to the questionnaires but also wrote the reports mainly based on those replies *plus* respondents' answers to the open-ended questions. The observations and analyses of these reports are integrated in this report. The major findings will be discussed under the headings of this Survey Schedule after explaining our survey methods.

1.2. *How the Survey was Conducted and Organized*

The survey covered 25 textile companies and 25 electrical appliances and electronics companies in each of the three countries. These two industries were chosen because they have been established long enough in all three countries.

The companies surveyed were chosen from the lists of the manufacturing industries. They were based on the information from the Securities and Exchange Commission Board of Investments like *SEC Weekly Bulletin*, *List of Top 1,000 Philippine Corporations*, *Monthly Reports*, and other non-governmental sources like the ones prepared by Daily Newspaper Corp. in Manila, Bangkok, and Jakarta. They classify the companies into about 30 sub-sectors of manufacturing industries. A choice was made to distribute the selected companies evenly from the beginning to the end of the lists. Tables 1-1–1-4 show the scale distribution of the enterprises surveyed in the Philippines in terms of the paid-up capital, the relative share of local and foreign capital, the number of employees, and the amount of sales in

[4]Interested reader can obtain the Thai or Indonesian version from the author.

Table 1. The Scale of Enterprises Surveyed: The Philippines.

1-1. Paid-up Capital, 1970 and 1980 (million pesos).

	1970			1980		
	Textiles	Electric	Total	Textiles	Electric	Total
0–1	3	1	4	5	—	5
1–5	5	3	8	—	2	2
5–10	—	1	1	—	1	1
10–15	1	2	3	—	3	3
15–20	—	—	—	2	1	3
20–40	—	—	—	2	—	2
40–60	—	1	1	—	—	—
60–100	—	1	1	2	—	2
100–200	1	—	1	—	1	1
200–300	—	—	—	—	1	1
No information	15	16	31	14	16	20

1-2. The Share of Local and Foreign Capital.

	1970						1980					
	Total		Textiles		Electric		Total		Textiles		Electric	
	50		25		25		50		25		25	
Inter-views	Local	Foreign	Local	Foreign	Local	Foreign	Local	Foreign	Local	Foreign	Local	Foreign
21–30%	—	3	—	1	—	2	—	1	—	1	—	—
31–40	—	6	—	4	—	2	—	8	—	4	—	4
41–50	1	2	—	—	1	2	3	3	—	—	3	3
51–60	2	—	—	—	2	—	1	1	—	—	1	1
61–70	5	—	4	—	1	—	6	—	4	—	2	—
71–80	2	—	—	—	2	—	2	—	—	—	2	—
81–90	1	—	1	—	—	—	1	—	1	—	—	—
91–100	19	2	14	—	5	2	17	2	14	—	3	2
No inf.	18	2	6	1	11	1	18	2	6	1	11	1

This table gives more answers than the total of interviewed companies, because some gave the shares of local and foreign capital. In most cases the shares of local capital may be taken as more reliable figures.

1970 and 1980. The next two series of tables (Tables 2 and 3) give similar data for Thailand and Indonesia.

The survey was conducted by personal interviews. Most companies cooperated readily. Only a few refused. It was difficult, however, to interview the right person who has the information on paid-up capital and

1-3. Number of Employees.

	1970			1980		
–100	Textile	Electric	Total	Textile	Electric	Total
101–200	9	8	17	8	1	9
201–400	1	3	4	1	2	3
401–1000	5	5	10	4	5	6
1001–2000	4	6	10	3	11	14
2001–3000	4	1	5	2	3	5
3001–	1	—	1	3	2	5
No information	—	2	2	4	1	5

1-4. The Amount of Sales (million pesos).

	1970			1980		
	Textile	Electrical	Total	Textile	Electrical	Total
–1	1	1	2	—	—	—
1–5	3	3	6	3	1	4
5–10	1	—	1	2	—	2
10–20	2	1	3	3	2	1
20–40	1	1	2	1	—	1
40–100	1	—	1	1	1	2
100–500	—	—	—	1	3	4
500–	—	—	—	—	—	—
No information	16	19	35	14	16	30

Table 2. The Scale of Enterprises Surveyed: Thailand.

2-1. Paid-up Capital (million baths).

	1970			1980		
	Textile	Electrical	Total	Textile	Electrical	Total
0–9	8	12	20	7	8	15
10–29	6	9	15	7	12	19
30–49	—	2	2	1	5	6
50–99	4	—	4	4	—	4
100–199	2	—	2	2	—	2
200–499	1	—	1	2	—	2
500–	1	2	3	2	—	2
No information	3	—	3	—	—	—

2-2. The Share of Foreign Capital (%).

	Japan	US	Netherland	Others
0–9	—	—	—	—
10–29	—	—	—	—
30–49	14	—	—	1
50–69	2	1	2	—
70–89	—	—	—	—
90–100	1	2	—	—

2-3. Number of Employees.

	1970			1980		
	Textile	Electrical	Total	Textile	Electrical	Total
0–99	5	12	17	2	7	9
100–199	1	5	6	3	4	7
200–499	3	4	7	6	10	16
500–999	5	1	6	2	3	5
1000–1999	2	—	2	8	2	10
2000–	—	—	—	0	0	0
No information	6	4	10	—	—	—

2-4. The Amount of Sales (million baths).

	1970			1980		
	Textile	Electrical	Total	Textile	Electrical	Total
0–9	2	2	4	—	1	1
10–49	3	7	10	2	6	8
50–99	3	2	5	4	5	9
100–299	2	2	4	4	4	8
300–499	1	—	1	5	2	7
500–999	—	1	1	—	2	2
1000–1999	—	—	—	—	1	1
2000–	—	—	—	—	—	—
No information	14	11	25	9	4	13

Table 3. The Scale of Enterprises Surveyed: Indonesia.

3-1. Paid-up Capital (million Rp.).

	1970			1980		
	Textile	Electrical	Total	Textile	Electrical	Total
0–99	2	4	6	2	1	3
100–499	2	3	5	5	6	11
500–999	—	4	4	—	1	1
1000–1999	—	2	2	2	6	8
2000–3999	—	4	4	2	5	7
4000–	—	3	3	3	2	5
No information	19	8	27	11	4	15

3-2. Number of Employees.

	1970			1980		
	Textile	Electrical	Total	Textile	Electrical	Total
0–99	1	7	8	—	6	6
100–199	2	5	7	3	9	12
200–499	4	4	8	7	5	12
500–999	—	—	—	2	1	3
1000–1999	1	—	1	5	1	6
2000–	—	—	—	2	—	2
No information	17	9	26	2	—	2

3-3. The Amount of Sales.

	1970			1980		
	Textile	Electrical	Total	Textile	Electrical	Total
0–99	—	2	2	2	2	4
100–499	2	1	3	2	1	3
500–999	—	2	2	2	3	5
1000–1999	—	—	—	—	1	1
2000–4999	—	—	—	2	2	4
5000–9999	1	—	1	1	—	1
10000–19999	—	—	—	2	1	3
20000–	—	—	—	2	—	2
No information	22	20	42	12	15	27

3-4. A Summary Table for Small Firms (1980).

	Philippines[a]	Thailand	Indonesia[b]
Textile	52	44	53
Electrical	32	80	91
Total	42	62	72

[a]For the Philippines, less than 400 employees. [b]Percentage of the total replies only in Indonesia.

sales for 1980. The figures of paid-up capital and sales must be interpreted cautiously, because they may not reflect the exact book values of the companies, as will be discussed later.

In terms of the number of employees, as Table 3-4 above shows, enterprises with fewer than 500 (1980) accounted for more than 50% of the sample companies. As most of the companies use small amount of paid-up capital per worker, it may be conjectured that the technologies in use at the plants are likely to be labor-intensive. Another noteworthy point of the sample is that the joint ventures or foreign enterprises occupy about one third in the Philippines and nearly a half in Thailand but more than half in Indonesia, as is clearly shown in Table 4.

1.3. *The Respondents*

The survey findings must be interpreted bearing in mind who answered (Table 5). Their positions in the companies are given in Table 5-3. In Thailand and Indonesia, the respondents were divided evenly between top executives and middle managers, but in the Philippines they were mostly younger middle managers, which made the answers less reliable.

As religious factor was expected to affect decisions, the respondents' religions were sought. But their relevance did not come out clearly in the survey, because many respondents were not decision-makers. The high percentage of Christians in Indonesia was surprising. In this respect, there was no discernible difference between top executives and middle level managers. Whether this is a typical picture of Indonesian management or not requires further study. If business is a profession preferred more by Christians than Muslims, their behavior certainly reflects Christian rather than Islam values prevailing in Indonesia. In the other two, the religious distribution of respondents is the same as the population.

Table 4. Origin of the Sample Firms.[a]

	Textile			Electrical			Total		
	Ph	Th	In	Ph	Th	In	Ph	Th	In
Local	24	15	2	16	12	14	30	27	16
Foreign	1	10	23	9	13	10	10	23	43
US	—	—	—	4	—	—	4	3	—
Japan	—	—	2	3	—	1	3	17	3
HK	1	—	—	1	—	—	1	—	—
Germany	—	—	—	1	—	4	1	—	—
UK	—	—	—	—	—	—	1	—	—
Australia	—	—	—	—	—	—	—	—	—
Other EU	—	—	—	1	—	—	1	2	—
Other	—	—	16	—	—	—	—	1	16
For. Venture	—	—	(3)	—	—	5	—	(2)	(8)
Gov. Enter.	—	—	2	—	—	1	—	—	3

[a]There are some contradictions between this table and another table showing the share of foreign capital, because the number of joint ventures exceeds that of multinationals in the Philippines. This is probably due to an understanding of multinationals only as giant companies. In Thailand the associated countries are known only for total. The 16 companies in the *other* category in Indonesia are perhaps *Chinese–Indonesian* companies, because *local* is interpreted as *indigenous*, which excludes Indonesians of Chinese origin.

Table 5. Profile of the Respondents.

5-1. Position in the Company.

	Textile			Electrical		
	Ph	Th	In	Ph	Th	In
Top executives	4	12	11	1	15	17
Middle managers	15	12	14	18	9	7
Engineers	—	1	—	—	—	1
Others	5	—	—	6	1	—

Since the central theme of this survey is concerned with technologies, it is certainly desirable for respondents to have some knowledge of them. But in a few cases did an engineer answer the questionnaire. Neither the interviewer nor the interviewee was necessarily familiar with the technologies in use and the alternatives available to the corporation when its technological choices were made. Consequently, in many interviews,

5-2. Age.

	Ph	Th	In	Ph	Th	In
<25	2	—	[a]	4	—	—
25–30	3	3	—	12	4	—
30–39	8	7	—	18	19	—
40–49	4	8	—	8	17	—
50–	8	7	—	8	10	—

[a]In Indonesia this information is missing.

5-3. Religion.

	Philippines			Thailand			Indonesia		
	Textile	Electric	Total	Textile	Electric	Total	Textile	Electric	Total
Catholic	20	22	42	2	2	4	4	2	6
Protestant	2	2	4	—	—	—	8	10	18
Hinduism	1	—	1	—	—	—	—	—	—
Buddhism	—	—	—	23	23	46	—	1	1
Islam	—	—	—	—	—	—	11	12	23
Other	1	1	2	—	—	—	2	—	2
None	1	—	1	—	—	—	—	—	—

only after a long discussion were the technological questions adequately understood and some judgement may be needed whether the technologies had been chosen on the basis of proper economic calculation or not.

1.4. *Definition of "Technology" and "New" Technology*

The most fundamental question in this survey is, of course, how to define "technology". In general, the term may be interpreted broadly, including not only mechanical or engineering technology but also managerial know-how. In this study, however, technology is interpreted narrowly in the engineering sense. "New technologies" imply, therefore, an introduction of new machines of some kind. This definition was adopted only to make the responses to certain questions in the survey clear-cut and in fact it was easily understood by almost all interviewees.

The next question concerns what is *new* technology. Some of the *new machines* in small companies were sometimes second-hand or built by themselves by copying the models that they had seen at other factories,

Table 6. Adoption of New Technologies within the Last 10 Years of Operation.

	Total			Textile			Electrical		
	Ph	Th	In	Ph	Th	In	Ph	Th	In
Adopted	49	50	47	24	25	22	25	25	25
Not adopted	1	0	3	1	0	1	0	0	0

abroad, or sometimes in business magazines. The owner of a small electric appliance factory in Thailand proudly described a machine which he had assembled using imported parts and referring to catalogues issued by different machine suppliers. It is also true that the adoption of new technology by small enterprises often implies a series of minor improvements of old machines. With this interpretation of *new* machinery, all our sample firms except one in the Philippines and three in Indonesia had acquired new equipment within the last ten years, as Table 6 shows.

The new technologies adopted were reported in the most concrete terms in the Philippines. The types of machines introduced by the Filipino textile and electrical industries during the past 10 years are shown along with the number of corporations which adopted them. *Textile Machines*: (9) spinning, (8) knitting, (5) finishing, (4) dyeing, (3) open-end spinning, circular knitting, weaving, texturing, winding, (2) compressor, mom-fort machine (pressing or ironing), interlocked knitting, high speed garment machine, drawing, stentering, sanforizing, etc.

Electrical Machines: (7) solder, testing equipment, (6) wire bonding, moulding peeze, (5) hydraulic cutting, (4) die attach, lathe, press brake, sheering, oven machine, (3) milling machines, compressor, air-compressors, mechanical press, air-conditioner, presser, welding, marking, trimming, vacuum pumps, grinding, deep shouldering, air-dryers, wafer saw, bender, nibbler, shaper, spot-welding.

2. Information on Technology

2.1. *Source of Information*

Where do the companies obtain the information on new technologies? Table 7 shows their sources of information. The eight most frequently mentioned sources are listed here in the order of frequency.

Table 7. Sources of Information on New Technologies.

	Total (49)			Textile (24)[a]			Electrical (25)		
	Ph	Th	In	Ph	Th	In	Ph	Th	In
Radio	17	0	9	13	—	1	4	—	8
TV	5	0	18	5	—	1	—	—	17
Newspapers	7	0	14	4	—	1	3	—	13
Magazines	34	22	23	22	13	9	12	9	14
Assoc. Co.	25	0	0	16	—	—	9	—	—
Trade journal	40	10	26	24	7	13	16	3	13
Suppliers	49	8	6	24	13	13	25	10	17
Licensors	21	4	4	5	—	2	—	—	17
Customers	31	9	15	10	5	10	21	4	5
Trade Co.	49	8	6	24	7	2	25	1	4
Fair domestic	13	2	23	1	2	6	12	—	17
Fair intern'l	18	4	20	—	3	15	18	1	5
Trip abroad	26	28	27	8	11	13	18	17	14
Parent Co.	9	19	15	—	9	4	9	10	11
Telefunken	3	—	—	—	—	—	3	—	—
Matsushita	2	—	—	—	—	—	2	—	—
Trade Assoc.	—	5	15	—	2	2	—	3	13
Gov. service	—	—	17	—	—	5	—	—	12

[a]One company in textile industry in each country did not give its reply to this question.

Joint-venture firms naturally benefit from their parent or associated companies. Technical information is passed on from parent companies. Thai managers and technicians reported that they had opportunities to receive technical training at the plants of the foreign parent companies abroad. Some companies had licensing or technical assistance agreement with foreign firms. Most company managers in Thailand and Indonesia learned about new technologies through trips abroad. Smaller companies seemed to rely on machine- or material-suppliers for information about the availability of new machines or materials more heavily than larger ones. Companies with highly educated technical staff make better use of technical books and magazines, or the technical conferences in which they participate. The government services were rarely mentioned as a source of information. Only in Indonesia it comes in the eighth place. But this does not mean that the government information services are unimportant in other respects; for example, as a source of information on successes and failures of other companies in the country (see Table 28).

There is no government which is not conscious of the importance of research and development (R&D) policy, but the degree of the government's involvement in R&D differs significantly from one country to another. Each of the three countries has some kind of government information centers to offer information on technology. In Thailand, there is a national Thailand Institute of Scientific and Technological Research. Its office of scientific and technological service not only offers documentary information but also experiments or tests with new technologies for private enterprises. It is reported that the Institute has been successful in promoting certain food processing and other technologies in Thailand and offered useful information on new technologies. There are similar technological information centers in the Philippines, but their services are not widely used. Since obtaining information is the first step in introducing new technologies, a lot more effort by governments may be desirable.

The important contribution a government can make through this kind of institute has been demonstrated by the Korean Institute of Science and Technology, and the various services of the Ministry of International Trade and Industry (MITI) in Japan. Not only have they provided the important sources of information on better technologies but developed new technologies by themselves applicable in practice. The objective of these institutes in Korea and Japan has been much more ambitious than those of similar institutes in Southeast Asian countries. They have been receiving stronger financial and personnel support from the governments. They were, therefore, able to stabs good contact with the best centers of technological innovations abroad and to undertake ambitious research projects. Without an incessant flow of information on technology which is constantly improving, alternative technologies cannot possibly be chosen in a way suitable for the companies needs. To illustrate some gap between the services provided by the government's institutes and the needs of enterprises, a manager of a big joint-venture firm in Thailand commented that technology used in his factory was much more advanced than the one taught in local training institutes.

3. Adoption of New Technologies

3.1. *Frequency of Technology Adoption*

As we shall see in Tables 8-1–8-3, almost all the companies surveyed had constantly adopted new technologies over the last 20 years. Such technological change had been gaining pace during the last five or six years in all three countries. The Filipino responses clearly indicate this, and the limited information from Thailand and Indonesia supports similar trends.

This is not surprising because installing new machines to expand production or replace old machines is a normal aspect of factory operation. Usually, new machines will be of designs different from the old ones. Their

Table 8-1. When Companies Adopted New Machinery — the Philippines.

(No. of replies)	Total	Textile	Electrical
<1 year ago	31	13	18
<2 years ago	83	31	52
<4 years ago	59	17	42
<6 years ago	47	15	32
<8 years ago	—	11	7
<10 years ago	12	4	8
<12 years ago	10	6	4
<14 years ago	3	3	—
<19 years ago	6	3	3
<22 years ago	1	1	—

Table 8-2. How often Companies Adopted New Technologies — Thailand.

(No. of replies)	Once	Twice	3 times	4 times	5 times
Textile	2	7	5	3	8
Electrical	4	3	4	2	12

Table 8-3. When and how often Company Adopted New Technologies — Indonesia.

	Before 1970	1970–1973	1974–1977	1978–1981	Once	Twice	3 times
Textile	7	7	9	7	9	5	4
Electric	—	—	3	7	4	1	2

installation can be regarded as an adoption of new technology according to our definition. However, most respondents could not tell how often they introduced a new technology, because improvement of the production process goes on all the time and takes place at various stages of production. New machines or modification have certainly been introduced many times during the past 20 years, particularly in large modern companies. In many cases, the reported number of new technologies adopted, therefore, relates only to the important technologies. On the other hand, as Table 8-1 shows, the predominance of adoption in recent years, particularly in electrical industries, suggests that they may be looked at as experimental in nature.

3.2. *Reasons for Adopting New Technologies*

Why do private businesses adopt new machinery? Tables 9-1 and 9-2 indicate that increase in profitability (items 1, 4 and 5) improvement of the quality of the product, and expansion of production capacity were the three most important reasons that our sample firms acquired their most recent machine. The order of importance, however, seems to differ from one country to another.

It is interesting to note that the quality of the product has been such an important consideration in introducing their most recent machine. Although improved quality contributes to the expansion of sales and thereby profit, this also seems to indicate that in the textile and electronics industries import

Table 9-1. Reasons why Company is Currently using the Last Machinery — Total.

Order of import	1		2		3		
Country	Ph	Th	Ph	Th	Ph	Th	In
1 Profitability	20	3	6	4	5	5	12
2 Product quality	13	21	16	12	4	3	23
3 Product capacity	7	6	7	5	4	9	3
4 Productivity/day	2	10	6	6	13	3	25
5 Unit cost down	1	5	4	12	10	7	17
6 Increase employment	0	0	4	2	3	5	9
7 Partner recom.	0	0	0	0	2	0	0
8 Diversify	0	0	0	0	0	0	0
9 Gov. recom.	0	0	0	0	0	1	2
10 Tax exemption	0	1	0	0	0	0	0

Table 9-2. The Purposes for Most Recent Acquisition of Equipment — Total.

	Textile							Electrical						
	1		2		3			1		2		3		
	Ph	Th	Ph	Th	Ph	Th	In	Ph	Th	Ph	Th	Ph	Th	In
1)	11	1	2	2	2	2	6	9	2	4	2	3	3	6
2)	5	9	9	10	2	1	12	8	12	7	2	2	2	11
3)	2	4	4	1	4	4	1	5	2	3	4	0	5	2
4)	1	7	2	3	5	3	8	1	3	4	3	8	0	17
5)	1	3	2	6	5	4	3	0	2	2	6	5	3	14
6)	0	6	6	0	0	4	2	0	0	4	3	3	1	7
7)	0	0	0	0	0	0	9	0	0	0	0	2	0	0
8)	0	0	0	0	0	0	4	0	0	0	0	0	0	5
9)	0	0	0	0	0	0	1	0	0	0	0	0	0	1
10)	0	0	0	0	0	0	0	0	0	0	0	0	0	0

substitution has been achieved through local production of better quality goods previously imported from abroad. The export-oriented firms reported that the quality of their products was the first thing they thought of in deciding on the acquisition of new equipment. So did big manufacturers of electric appliances, because their market was very competitive in contrast, small companies regard reduction of unit cost of production to be more important than improvement of the quality of products. Price competition seems to be greater among small companies. Some of them reported that they could not improve the quality of their products because they do not have sufficient resources to acquire the expensive machines required for that purpose. Often these machines become economical at a larger scale of production, while expansion of the existing production capacity is a less important motivation of capital investment, because the market is still small and because there are too many producers. (Needless to say, the objectives listed in Table 9 are not mutually exclusive.)

Managers of small companies often knew of new up-to-date machines but could not afford to acquire them. For example, an engineer at electric lamp manufacturer reported: the company still uses the old machines installed at the time of commencement of the company many years ago. The owner knows of more efficient models such as the ones used by a large local competitor. They are automatic and require fewer workers to operate, producing a much larger number of lamps of more regular quality per hour. But with limited resources, he can afford only a Taiwanese copy of more, expensive Japanese models.

The case of a zip manufacturer reveals a different problem. He reports: "New, automatic machines require the supply of very highly standardized metal tapes. The machines automatically reject poor materials. With older machines, however, the operators could use tapes even if they were not up to the standard. New machines force us to improve even the quality of the zip parts which we produce."

These two cases show that the choice of technology by small firms is influenced not only by the shortage of capital but also by competition with larger corporations in the same country which use more efficient technologies. Given an uneven distribution of capital among the firms and varied tastes or needs of customers, there is no single technology which is appropriate for the industry concerned.

Given a dualistic industrial structure where small producers co-exist with large companies by relying on the lower wages — often accompanied by the sacrifices on the part of owner-proprietors or their family members — and on the low unit capital cost, an appropriate technology which meets the double objectives of "efficiency" and "employment-creation" simultaneously may be realized on the industrial level through an appropriate division of labor between large and small corporations. Creation of a single *appropriate technology* for an industry is easier said than done. The cost and time involved in creating *the appropriate technology* for a particular industry imposes too heavy a burden on scarce capital and skills in most developing countries. The argument on *appropriate technology* needs to be re-examined in the context of a more realistic picture of contemporary developing countries.

In a dualistic economy, an important question is which of large or small enterprises can make more efficient use of scarce resource like capital. One evidence from the survey of the Indonesian textile industry shows that the scale of production and capital/labor ratio have a high correlation with the rate of return to capital. Table 10 demonstrates the relevant data in this case.

Figure 2 shows that the correlations between capital/labor ratio and the rate of return to capital calculated on the basis of sales minus wage payment divided by the amount of capital is distinctively different between large and

Table 10. Sales, Capital, and Labor in Indonesian Textile Industry (billion rupiah; thousand persons).[a]

Firms	Sales (S)	Capital (K)	Labor (L)	S/K	L/K	(S – wL)/K
1	57,677	38,750	1,307	29.60	0.033	1.235
2	48,000	35,000	6,000	5.80	0.172	0.540
3	14,000	7,500	460	16.30	0.061	1.839
4	4,895	3,000	270	11.10	0.090	1.150
5	5,500	1,375	1,200	1.10	0.909	3.091
6	323	300	350	0.86	1.162	−0.038
7	897	112	153	0.72	1.388	6.612
8	13	6	150	0.04	25.000	−23.000
9	383	164	225	0.72	1.388	0.912
10	11,300	3,400	2,538	1.33	0.724	2.576
11	41	150	470	0.32	3.125	−2.875
12	705	300	404	0.74	1.351	1.046

[a]The wage rate is assumed to be 5 for firms (1) to (4) and 1 for (5) to (12). These are hypothetical figures approximating the prevailing wages in large and snail companies around Jakarta in 1981. The data for firms (8) and (11) may be unreliable, because their rates of returns show the large negative values and L/K are too large to be realistic.

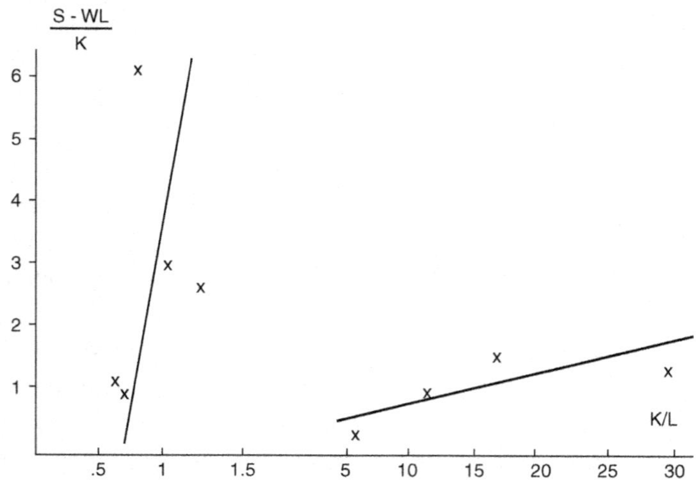

Fig. 2. Correlation Between Capital/Labor Ratio and Efficiency of Capital.

small enterprises. This implies that the same amount of capital allocated to smaller enterprises for whom capital/labor ratios are smaller can bring about more returns to capital, so that even if the wage differentials are not as much as 1 to 5, more investment in smaller enterprises seem to create more employment.

As we shall see later in Section 7, the government has not properly implemented its taxation policy to meet the needs of private enterprises despite the intention of the original plans. It still remains to be seen whether or not there is some room for the government to encourage an adoption of more appropriate technologies through taxation, subsidies, and technology policies.

3.3. *Economic Calculation and Other Considerations*

Needless to say, the entrepreneurs' choice of technology must be based ultimately on an economic calculation. But there may be some other considerations of secondary importance, although these may have indirect relevance to their economic calculation. This was asked in our surveys in Thailand and Indonesia, but unfortunately not in the Philippines. Table 11 gives the results. The five most important factors affecting differently their choice are shown below in the order of importance.

Thailand	Indonesia
1 Economic calculation	1 Economic calculation
2 Difficulty in managing workers	2 Relations with the government
3 Shortage of "middles"	3 Government regulations
4 Shortage of infrastructure	4 Social relations
5 Government regulations	5 Shortage of "middles"

Although it did not emerge explicitly in Tables 9-1 and 9-2, the government is very much in the minds of Indonesian businessmen, whereas in Thailand, the government does not take any position regarding the technologies to be applied in industries. The Thai government is interested in industrial development. Once in a while, the Thai Board of Investment announces the specific industries to be promoted, but the choice of technology is left to private investors. This is not the case in Indonesia. The government tries to guide private enterprises through various regulations.

Table 11. Relative Importance of Influential Factors on the Choice of Technologies.

	Textile						Electrical						Total					
Rank	(1)		(2)		(3)		(1)		(2)		(3)		(1)		(2)		(3)	
Country	Th	In	Th	In	Th	In	Th	In	Th	In	Th	In	Th	In	Th	In	Th	In
a. econ.cal.	19	17	2	6	2	1	20	14	3	9	2	2	39	31	5	15	4	3
b. lab.mang.	2	1	11	3	2	2	1	—	4	—	2	—	3	1	15	3	4	2
c. soc. relat.	—	1	—	4	—	3	—	—	—	4	—	5	—	1	—	8	—	8
d. gov.relat.	—	2	—	2	—	3	1	7	1	6	—	3	1	9	1	8	—	6
e. middle	1	—	5	3	5	—	1	—	4	—	5	2	2	—	9	3	10	5
f. milit. rel.	—	1	—	1	—	2	—	—	—	—	—	—	—	1	—	1	—	2
g. infrastruc	—	—	1	1	1	2	—	1	1	1	1	—	—	1	—	1	—	2
h. interna'l	—	—	—	—	—	4	—	—	—	2	—	—	—	—	—	2	—	4
i. gov.regul.	—	2	—	1	1	1	2	3	3	—	1	5	2	5	3	1	2	6
j. others	2	—	—	2	—	—	—	—	—	—	—	—	2	—	—	2	—	—

Note: Influential factors unabbreviated are: a. economic calculation, b. difficulty in labor management, c. social relations, d. relations with government, e. scarcity of middles, f. relations with the military, g. inadequate infrastructure, h. international relations, i. government regulations, j. other factors.

This difference between Thailand and Indonesia may be attributed to the following two factors.

First, there was no good engineering university in Thailand until very recently, whereas the Bandung Institute of Technology has supplied good engineers to Indonesian government offices. Second, on the whole, government intervention is much more prevalent in Indonesia. This may be explained by the following two facts:

(1) In Thailand, problems of overseas Chinese are not serious, whereas in Indonesia, promotion of non-Chinese businesses is an important political concern of the government.
(2) The private business sector is relatively weak in Indonesia partly due to governmental regulations and guidance's with subsidies and finances.

In Thailand, difficulty in managing workers is the second most important consideration. Since this problem concerns managerial know-how closely related to the nature of new technologies, it will be taken up

Table 12. Impact of Social Reactions.

	Total			Textile			Electrical		
	Ph	Th	In	Ph	Th	In	Ph	Th	In
Considered	32	43	29	14	22	19	18	21	10
Not considered	17	7	6	10	3	4	7	4	2
No answer	1	0	15	1	0	2	0	0	13
Total answers	49	50	35	24	25	22	25	25	12

later. What turned out to be generally important in both countries is securing well-trained operators of new machines and personnel for their repair and maintenance.

In adopting new technologies, the business enterprises are often obliged to take account of various social reactions to their choice of technology. (Table 12) Our survey discovered that the companies in Indonesia, Thailand, and the Philippines consider such extemal factors in adopting new machines, and those factors' importance is the greatest in Indonesia and the least in the Philippines. It is not accidental that this ordering corresponds to the relative importance of foreign corporations in these three countries, as was shown in Table 4.

One interesting question to be checked by our survey is whether people in the three countries show any significant degree of resistance or objection to the "foreign nature" of technology or product as is often argued with reference to "coca-cola culture". In the countries surveyed, there did not seem to be any serious problem in this respect. We did, however, identify some cases in which there were objections to the choice of a certain foreign technology. Foreign technologies of old vintages or second-hand machines are often objected to even when their price is low enough to justify the application of such machines economically. One respondent in the textile industry and two in the electrical appliances industry in the Philippines replied that they had encountered objections to an introduction of foreign technologies on the grounds that local substitutes were available. Perhaps when indigenous development of new technologies becomes noticeable, the preference for national over foreign technology will grow stronger.

3.4. *The Role of the Government in Technology Adoption*

There are a number of ways that the government influences the adoption of new technologies by private corporations (Table 13). For example, usually the latter must obtain permits from appropriate government offices to introduce foreign technologies. In our survey 7 companies — 3 in the textile and 4 in the electrical appliances industries — answered affirmatively when they were asked specifically whether their choice of technology had been influenced by the government. Despite a contrary impression given from Tables 9-1 and 9-2, it seems reasonable to say that the indirect influence of government is not negligible. Particularly relevant are the government policies related to taxation, various incentive measures taken to promote private investment, public works aimed at development of infrastructure throughout the country, and training programs. These policies will be discussed in Section 8.

The government offices that have relatively large influence on businessmen's decision-making may be identified by examining which of them were contacted at the time of adoption of new technologies. As Tables 14a–c indicate, the role played by the Board of investment is very important in all these countries. The Ministry of Industry is important only in Thailand and Indonesia. In the Philippines, financial institutions are contacted instead.

Table 13. Whether Influenced/not Influenced by Government in Adoption.

	Total	Textile	Electric
Influenced	7	3	4
Not influenced	42	21	21

Table 14. Government Offices Contacted.

(a) Thailand[a]

	Total	Textile	Electric
1 Board of Investment	25	14	11
2 Ministry of Industry	27	15	12
3 Others	—	1	2

[a]Some respondents gave more than one answer.

(b) The Philippines[a]

	Total	Textile	Electrical
Not contacted	26	12	14
Contacted	23	12	11
1 Board of Investment	18	11	7
2 Central Bank of the Philippines	11	6	5
3 Development Bank of the Philippines	3	3	—
4 Ministry of Industry	2	1	1
5 Ministry of Labor	2	—	2
6 Bureau of Customs	2	1	1
7 Bureau of Internal Revenue	1	1	—
8 Ministry of Trade	1	—	1
9 City Engineer's Office	1	—	1
10 Technical Resources	1	—	1
11 Tariff Commission	1	1	—
12 City Government	1	—	1

[a]Some respondents gave more than one answer.

(c) Indonesia[a]

	Total	Textile	Electrical
1 Dept. of Industry	29	13	16
2 Dept. of Commerce and Coop.	8	4	4
3 Board of Investment	14	5	9
4 Institute of Textile Industry (ITT)	8	8	—
5 Bandung Institute of Technology	3	3	—
6 Dept. of Trade	11	—	11
7 Dept. of Labor	1	—	1
8 Indonesian Institute of Science	2	—	2
9 International Telecommunication Agency	4	—	4

[a]Some respondents gave more than one answer.

3.5. *Contributions to the Development of National Economy*

Needless to say, the choice of new technology can influence economic development of a nation and thereby the pace of nation-building. How conscious are the business leaders of this fact? How much influence does this nationalistic consideration have on their decision-making concerning new technologies? Almost all respondents were very conscious of their

Table 15. How Companies Contributed to National Development: Indonesian Views.

	Textile	Electrical
1 Increasing employment	13	13
2 Paying tax	—	7
3 Producing goods cheaply	10	—
4 Improving the quality of products	7	—
5 Improving the standard of living	3	1
6 Contributing to GDP	7	3
7 Improving workers' skills	2	1
8 Improving technological standard	2	1
9 Conserving energy	—	3

contribution to national development. Unconscious of this were only two in the Philippines, three in Thailand, but none in Indonesia. This minority of respondents belonged to the electrical industry, and their companies were small and quite independent of any government policies.

Table 15 indicates the ways in which businessmen in Indonesia felt that their companies were contributing to national development.

Data obtained in Thailand and the Philippines, however, did not permit such quantitative assessment. The answers were generally the same. Typical answers in these two countries were:

(1) increasing employment opportunities,
(2) improving skills of local workers,
(3) import substitution and export promotion,
(4) increasing GDP,
(5) paying more tax to the government,
(6) improving the quality of products and offering better commodities at lower prices to consumers,
(7) helping other industries obtain domestic products more cheaply than imports,
(8) helping develop the local textile factories,
(9) providing the company's employees with higher wages and better welfare, schemes.

Thus, the leading industrialists were seemingly very conscious of and confident in their contributions to the national development. They did not fail to point this out in the survey, although of course this does not mean that their vested interests did not coincide more or less with the optimal path of the national economic development. On the other hand, some respondents were aware of conflicts between employment and new technologies. Some reported that the new machines had replaced a number of workers but added that they had been re-employed by other factories. Only some large textile manufacturers openly conceded that new machines had been introduced for the purpose of reducing the number of workers employed. Owners of a small company — often a household enterprise — were very modest in claiming their contributions to national development. They were seriously concerned about their own survival, which required their behavior on the basis of a purely economic calculation. If the levels of technologies at small and medium scale enterprises can be regarded as close enough to the appropriate technologies from the view-point of national economy, then the governmental subsidies to those enterprises might be compatible with national development goals. This was precisely the outcome of Japanese Industrial policy.[5]

Many companies including medium-sized ones were very proud of offering training opportunities to the students at technical schools and universities. They complained, however, that the graduates from technical schools always needed several months or even a longer period of further training before they became fully useful in the factories, while engineers fresh from university tended to look down upon manual work and to have difficulty with graduates from technical schools and manual workers. These findings seem to indicate the need for the government to improve the quality of education and training in technical or vocational schools and to change the attitude of graduates from the engineering departments of universities.[6]

[5]See S. Ichimura (1979). "Japanese industrial restructuring policies," Kyoto CSEAS Discussion Paper No. 106 (Kyoto); reprinted as Chapter 10 in S. Ichimura, *Political Economy . . . , op. cit.*; S. Ishikawa, "Appropriate technologies: some aspects of Japanese experiences", in A. Robinson (ed.), *op. cit.* pp. 75–132.

[6]See G. Myrdal (1968). *Asian Drama*, Princeton University Press, New York, pp. 71–126.

4. Trial and Experiment

4.1. *Practice of Trial*

It goes without saying that if trials or experiments are made before adopting a new technology, the adopted technology is more likely to be appropriate for the company. Surprisingly, however, quite a few of the companies surveyed in the three countries had chosen technologies without any trial or experiment (Tables 16 and 17).

Joint ventures, however, need no experiments or trials, because their technologies have already been in use in the parent companies. Usually foreign technicians of parent companies are sent to plan the production process, recommend the types of machines to be used and teach native workers how to operate the machines. Sometimes native workers are sent for training at an overseas factory of the parent companies. As was the case in a big electric appliance company in Thailand, choice of machines is sometimes made jointly by Thai and foreign partners. If a local entrepreneur can observe the operation of a machine at his foreign partner's factory, he can get better ideas than the latter as to whether the machine is appropriate in Thai conditions. For this purpose, most or the small companies surveyed sent their engineers abroad. In most cases, experimentation is not done in

Table 16. Test of Machinery before Adoption.

	Total			Textile			Electrical		
	Ph	Th	In	Ph	Th	In	Ph	Th	In
Experimented	24	39	44	9	21	23	15	18	21
Not experimented	25	11	4	15	4	1	10	7	3

Table 17. The Location of Machinery Test.

	Total			Textile			Electrical		
	Ph	Th	In	Ph	Th	In	Ph	Th	In
1 At company's plant	11	9	5	5	2	7	8	7	8
2 Elsewhere in the country	—	8	9	—	5	8	—	2	1
3 Abroad	14	31	27	3	17	13	9	14	14

their home country. The companies cannot afford to buy machines just for the purpose of experimentation.

More than half of the enterprises surveyed in the three countries relied exclusively on their parent companies' technologies. This raises a number of questions. First, technologies offered by the parent companies in industrialized countries may not have enough versatility to meet the needs and conditions in the developing countries. But alternative technologies may be available from other enterprises in the receiving countries. Thus, the process of checking and finding more appropriate technologies from the view-point of individual companies needs to be improved. Second, the technologies chosen on the basis of economic calculation by individual companies may still leave something to be desired from the view-point of saving capital and increasing employment for the national economy. In these respects, the governments as well as international organizations have an important role to play in collecting and disseminating information concerning technologies available and experience of successes and failures in importing those technologies into the Third World.[7]

It would be extremely useful, if such information could be supplemented with the knowledge regarding how to adapt them to local factor endowments and processes. In this connection, the South–South exchange of technological information is highly desirable. But at the same time, this may give rise to a new form of competition among developing countries at similar stages of development.

4.2. *Effects of Trials or Observation*

A crucial question is whether or not some of the technologies offered by the partner companies are sometimes rejected after observations or trials. In fact, there are many cases where companies have rejected the new technologies. Table 18 shows that the ratio of rejection is as high as 54% in Thailand, although in the Philippines and Indonesia, it is 14% and 19%, respectively. This clearly demonstrates that the effect of trials and observations is particularly marked in Thailand.

---

[7]A. Robinson, Introduction, *op. cit.*

Table 18. Result of Experimentation.

	Total			Textile			Electrical		
	Ph	Th	In	Ph	Th	In	Ph	Th	In
1 Rejected	3	21	6	2	11	3	1	10	3
2 Not reject.	13	18	26	6	10	21	12	8	5

Table 19. Reasons for Rejection.[a]

	Total		Textile		Electrical	
	Th	In	Th	In	Th	In
a Technology too advanced	11	8	6	10	5	3
b Hard to operate	5	19	2	9	3	11
c Too expensive	16	30	6	11	10	19
d Others	10	5	6	5	4	—

[a]This question was not asked in the Philippines. Many gave more than one reason.

The most frequent reason for rejection was the high cost of the machine under examination (Table 19). The second most common reason was the technological gap between the skills of engineers and workers available in the factories and those required by the machines. If these were the main reasons for rejection, one may say that the general direction of technological choice has been correct even from the view-point of the national economy. Within the menu of alternative technologies, they rejected those which required more capital and highly skilled labor, both of which were scarce locally. However, this does not mean that the technologies adopted have been sufficiently suitable to be called *appropriate*.

This point may be verified by checking the adoption of machinery after trials and observations (Table 20).

Compared with Tables 9-1 and 9-2, profitability and production cost items appear more important. In the final stage of adoption and the initial stage of operating new machines, the role of foreign engineers is often crucial. They usually discuss with native engineers about the machines to choose before making the final decision. When new machines arrive, they usually come to install. The foreign engineers run the machines teaching

Table 20. The Reasons for Adoption after Experimentation.

	Textile		Electrical	
	Thailand	Indonesia	Thailand	Indonesia
1. Profitability	12	17	12	18
2. Quality of product	20	12	16	22
3. Productivity/day	17	12	17	17
4. Unit cost reduction	17	16	14	18
5. Increase employment	5	8	3	17
6. Increase production capacity	13	12	11	10
7. Diversified	2	9	1	3
8. Dev. recommend.	—	7	—	13
9. Dev. Subsidies	—	1	—	3
10. Tax exemption	1	4	—	4
11. Foreign partner recommends	6	2	3	2
12. Others	—	6	2	7

local workers how to operate them initially for a few months and go home. In the joint ventures, their role is more active, staying in the new factory longer. One company representative said, one of the reasons for keeping foreign technicians is that unlike Thai technicians they carry more authority with workers. But there is no doubt that the primary objective is to benefit from the foreign engineers know-how that is related to similar machines. The government's policy to limit employment of foreign engineers in these countries is intended to promote the transfer of technology from foreign to native technicians as quickly as possible. Both foreign and local partners often complained that such policy was applied inflexibly without considering the real conditions of the factories. A breakdown of a machine could disrupt the operation of their plant for a long period, causing a loss far greater than the foreign engineers' salaries saved and that earning opportunities were lost.

5. The Modifications Required

5.1. *Technical Modifications*

The survey found that a substantial percentage of the machines adopted had required some modifications to suit the needs of the companies. Broadly,

Table 21. Modifications to Machinery.

	Total			Textile			Electrical		
	Ph	Th	In	Ph	Th	In	Ph	Th	In
Needed	23	22	27	10	10	19	13	12	8
Not needed	26	28	17	14	15	2	12	13	15

Table 22. Implementation of Needed Modifications.

	Total	Textile	Electrical
Modified	13	5	8
Not modified	10	5	5

three kinds of modifications were mentioned: scaling down of the capacity (e.g., by changing the speed of the machine), conversion of specialized machines into multi-purpose ones, and simplification of the design for easier operation and maintenance. It should be noted that even when the need for specific modifications was recognized, these were not always implemented. Our survey in the Philippines confirmed it (Tables 21 and 22).

Hence, one may conclude that ordinarily many enterprises make considerable efforts to modify the foreign-made machines and make them more appropriate for local conditions. Often, they cannot carry out the required modifications. Most interviewees in the Philippines attribute this failure to the lack of technical know-how and capable engineers.

5.2. *Adaptation to Social Conditions*

It is not unusual for firms to consider also some non-economic factors in choosing certain types of modifications, however minor they may be. The survey found that entrepreneurs were conscious of the social, especially local, reaction to the location and activity of their plants.

Needless to say, local employment opportunities depend primarily on the location of factories. At the same time, certain technological adjustments may also be required to adapt to the local conditions.

From Tables 23 and 24, it is clear that external consideration weighs heaviest in Indonesia, then Thailand and the least in the Philippines.

Table 23. Whether/or not Company Considered the Community's Attitude Towards the Location and Activity of the Plant.

	Total			Textile			Electrical		
	Ph	Th	In	Ph	Th	In	Ph	Th	In
Considered	6	5	47	3	2	23	3	3	24
Not considered	7	45	2	2	23	1	5	22	1

Table 24. Whether or not Company Considered Employment of Local Workers in Modifying Machines.

	Total			Textile			Electrical		
	Ph	Th	In	Ph	Th	In	Ph	Th	In
Considered	10	25	49	4	14	24	6	14	25
Not considered	3	22	0	1	11	0	2	11	0

This is consistent with observations of other aspects. In Java, Indonesia employment and underemployment are so serious that no plant director can ignore the problem. In order to provide job opportunities for local people. Labor-intensive methods are often adopted in peripheral processes like material handling and product-packing. In Thailand, industrial development concentrated mainly around Bangkok, because economic calculation does not justify the location of industrial plants further away from this city. Thus, regional considerations hardly enter into the minds of Thai businessmen. Even so, slightly over one half of the Thai businessmen in our survey were conscious of the importance of employment of workers in neighboring localities. The interviewees reported that there was no difference in the quality of labor whether workers came from nearby areas or the remote country-side. Workers seem to come all the way to Bangkok from various regions in Thailand. Industrial plants are widely dispersed. Sooner or later, urbanization may become intolerable in Thailand. This must be one of the areas where government actions are very much needed. What is surprising is the much less attention given to this problem in the Philippines. This may correspond to what G. Ranis found in his comparison of Filipino and Taiwanese industrialization: namely, the Filipino industrialists disregard the need for decentralization.[8] This seems to be more deeply rooted in the geographic distribution of economic resources, wealth and infrastructure in the Philippines than in inadequate government policies, to which Ranis attributed the problem. In order to change the whole configuration of economic geography, the government will have to re-examine the matter from many different points of view.

5.3. *Diffusion of New Technologies*

Once new technologies are introduced either in their original foreign form or in a modified form, they will be diffused sooner or later to the other companies. The speed and extent of diffusion have a critical bearing on the efficiency of the national economy as a whole. Some companies lead, and others follow. Our findings show some interesting differences among the three countries and between the two industries. This result may reflect differences in the stage of development of the two industries in each country. It seems that the followers are more numerous in the Philippines than in Thailand. This might be supported also by Table 25. To find quick followers is more difficult in the Philippines than in the other two countries. One may suspect that this may have something to do with the limited financial assistance offered by the government to the small and medium-scale enterprises and rather strict restrictions on financial activities of foreign banks in the Philippines. The Filipino regulations on foreign investment are more strict than the Thai, in permitting a share of paid-up capital beyond 30% only to pioneering foreign companies but only up to 30% to the followers. In contrast in Thailand, foreign capital

Table 25. Whether Company Adopted Machinery before or after Others.

	Total			Textile			Electrical		
	Ph	Th	In	Ph	Th	In	Ph	Th	In
Before	11	19	26	3	3	15	8	11	11
After	38	21	24	21	13	10	17	8	14

[8] G. Ranis (1979). "Appropriate technology in the dual economy: Reflections on Philippine and Taiwanese Experiences," in A. Robinson (ed.) *op. cit.*, pp. 140–159.

Table 26. How Soon Other Companies Followed in Adopting Machinery.[a]

	Total			Textile			Electrical		
	Ph	Th	In	Ph	Th	In	Ph	Th	In
a Very quickly	1	5	5	1	4	3	—	1	2
b Fairly soon	4	7	9	1	3	9	3	4	—
c Slowly	1	3	—	1	1	—	—	2	—
d Much later	1	—	19	—	—	10	1	—	9
e Not at all	3	2	1	—	—	1	3	2	1

[a]There are some inconsistencies between the numbers of replies in Table 25 and those in Table 26; particularly for Indonesia. Here they are left uncorrected.

Table 27. How Soon You Followed Others.

	Total			Textile			Electrical		
	Ph	Th	In	Ph	Th	In	Ph	Th	In
a Very quickly	7	4	3	6	2	2	1	2	1
b Fairly soon	17	9	3	7	8	3	10	1	—
c Slowly	9	6	5	5	2	2	4	4	3
d Much later	3	2	18	1	1	6	2	1	12

share permission up to 50% is almost automatic in most industries. These policies and regulations must have slowed down the speed of diffusion in the Philippines.

Similar observations can be made about Indonesian corporations. Many of them remain "slow followers", as Table 26 shows. This must also be due to the shortage of capital and technical skills. As for the followers, Table 27 indicates the speed of their catching-up. From the results shown in this table, Thai businessmen seem to be a little more responsive to other companies' success than Indonesian businessmen. By the same token, the Filipino businessmen do not seem to be slower in following up than Thai businessmen.

5.4. *How to Discover the Success of Other Companies*

The responsiveness of businessmen depends firstly on how easily they can obtain the information about the success or failure of others and secondly on how quickly they will respond to it. The following two tables (Tables 28 and 29) show the survey findings on these questions. It must be noted that the sources of information about other companies' success are rather different from those of information about new technologies quoted in Table 7. What appears to be particularly important in the former case is the role of customers or buyers, in addition to the sources mentioned in the case of new technologies. The government's role is important in Indonesia but not in the other countries.

Table 28. Company Undertakes New Ventures before or after Others.

	Total			Textile			Electrical		
	Ph	Th	In	Ph	Th	In	Ph	Th	In
Before others	27	25	18	10	14	12	17	11	6
After others	18	7	28	10	5	10	8	2	13
Cannot tell	4	13	2	4	6	2	—	7	—

Table 29-A. How Company Learnt about Others' Successes — Thailand and Indonesia.

	Total		Textile		Electrical	
	Th	In	Th	In	Th	In
1 Newspapers	2	13	5	1	13	1
2 Magazines	16	11	4	8	7	8
3 Radio	—	12	1	—	11	—
4 TV	—	26	3	—	21	—
5 Trade journals	—	—	—	—	—	—
6 Associate co's	14	24	12	11	21	3
7 Suppliers, mach.	14	23	13	7	10	7
8 Licensors	3	5	—	—	5	3
9 Customers	19	16	14	10	7	9
10 Trading co's	6	12	7	6	5	—
11 Trade associa'ns	9	14	4	6	10	3
12 Fairs, domestic	2	17	9	2	18	—
13 Fairs, intern'l	3	4	2	3	2	—
14 Gov. services	—	13	2	—	11	—
15 Parent co's	16	12	6	7	6	9
16 Travel	11	4	3	7	9	4
17 Others	13	7	1	6	—	7
18 No answer	—	—	—	—	—	—

Table 29-B. How Company Learnt about Others' Successes — Philippines.

	Total					Textile					Electrical				
	①	②	③	④	⑤	①	②	③	④	⑤		②	③		
1 Newspaper	8	3	—	3	1	4	3	—	1	1	4	—	—	2	—
2 Magazines	3	2	5	2	2	1	2	3	2	1	2	—	—	2	—
3 Radio	1	—	—	—	—	—	—	—	—	—	1	—	—	—	—
4 TV	—	1	—	—	—	—	1	—	—	—	—	—	—	—	—
5 Trade journ	1	2	—	1	5	—	—	—	—	—	1	2	—	1	2
6 Assoc co's	2	5	4	8	1	1	1	2	6	1	1	4	2	2	—
7 Suppliers	3	5	3	3	4	2	4	1	1	3	1	1	2	2	1
8 Licensors	1	1	1	2	—	—	—	—	—	—	1	1	1	2	—
9 Customers	10	6	7	2	3	8	4	4	—	2	2	2	3	2	1
10 Trading co	2	2	3	1	3	1	1	2	1	3	1	1	1	—	—
11 Trade ass	—	—	—	—	—	—	—	—	—	—	—	—	—	—	—
12 Fairs, dom	—	2	1	—	1	—	—	—	—	—	—	2	1	—	2
13 Fairs, inte	3	1	1	1	—	—	—	—	—	—	1	1	1	1	—
14 Gov. Serv	—	—	—	2	1	—	—	—	—	—	—	—	—	2	1
15 Travel	—	1	6	5	5	—	1	3	3	2	—	—	3	2	3
16 Parent co'	—	—	—	—	—	—	—	—	—	—	—	—	—	—	—
17 Others	2	3	1	1	4	2	—	—	—	—	—	3	—	1	3
18 No answer	3	5	7	8	8	2	4	6	7	7	1	1	1	1	1

Responses are particularly positive among Thai textile producers and least positive among Indonesian electrical appliances manufacturers. This seems to coincide with the timing of the development of these industries in the three countries. Joint ventures are often important not only to introduce new technologies but also to diffuse them because partners abroad try to follow quickly the success of fellow companies in the same industry and to introduce similar technologies into new joint ventures. They certainly have an advantage in learning the technical know-how and obtaining the necessary resources from the parent companies so that they are usually very quick in catching up. Often they are equipped with the latest models of machines, which are even better than those used by their parent companies in home countries, as some Thai and Indonesian managers reported. However, this process of introducing new technologies is not really diffusion to other companies in the country. It is merely a series of adoptions of new technologies by one company after another. It is not like Case I, but Case II. There is no easy way of discerning the two different cases from the observations or the survey reports. There are more companies of Case I, but large companies are likely to be in the Case II category.

Almost all small companies admit that their technologies are way behind the technologies of big corporations, and some are pessimistic about keeping up with the advances made by others. But from the view-point of employment, the technologies used by these companies must be kept efficient enough to be competitive for a number of products demanded by the mass of consumers. The government policies to promote joint ventures between small and medium-size enterprises in Japan and those in Southeast Asia must be highly recommended. It is said that the success of many companies in the textile industry in South Korea and Taiwan is due to their good contact with Japanese counter parts of similar scale. One characteristic of Japanese technicians frequently mentioned in the survey reports is that they hold regular meetings among themselves and exchange information on new technologies, even though they are competitors.

Many companies rely on machine or material suppliers for information concerning new technology and the success of others. The suppliers usually claim that others have already utilized their products. Customers and buyers are also important sources of information, particularly about textiles. They often show the companies the samples of fabrics, colors, and designs.

5.5. *The Role of the Government in Technology Diffusion*

One additional factor in the process of diffusion is the role of the government, because a government permits often required for the adoption of new technologies. Unless a permit is given promptly, the diffusion process will be delayed (Tables 30 and 31).

The government's policy is, however, somewhat different from one country to another. For instance, the Thai law does not require any

Table 30. Government's Permit is Needed/or not to Introduce New Machines.

	Total			Textile			Electrical		
	Ph	Th	In	Ph	Th	In	Ph	Th	In
Need	27	17	47	17	13	24	10	4	23
No need	22	33	2	7	12	1	15	21	1

Table 31. Whether Permit was Granted Promptly or Slowly.

	Total			Textile			Electrical		
	Ph	Th	In	Ph	Th	In	Ph	Th	In
Very quickly	17	1	10	9	—	2	6	1	8
Satisfactory	10	12	38	8	10	22	2	2	16
Very slowly	—	4	2	—	3	1	—	1	1

governmental approval when a company wishes to introduce a new technology. The Ministry of Industry encourages a use of certain new technologies but controls only the construction of new factories and the expansion of existing ones. Installation of new machines is regarded as an internal matter of the companies. If, however, it implies enlarging production capacity of the factory, a permit must be obtained. Except for the spinning and weaving factories, a permit is usually given in due time without requiring much "extra effort". The present government's policy to allow no expansion of spinning and weaving capacity is intended to preserve the employment opportunities in the small factories, but this policy goes against the interest of large textile manufacturers. They are exporters and want to replace existing machines with newer models which can produce higher quality fabric. The problem is that these new machines usually require more than 10 hp, which the government considers an expansion of capacity. Under the existing policy, it cannot be allowed. Clearly, it is a trade-off between export promotion and employment. Export promotion must be pursued, keeping in mind the sub-contract by large corporations with small firms to maintain employment.

Business executives often have to make a "special effort". Tables 32–34 of our surveys illustrate the kinds of "extra efforts" exerted to acquire a government permit or approval in the Philippines and Indonesia. These may not exhaust all that they had to do.

It might be noted that the role of business associations seems to be very important. In fact, some semi-official permits are delegated to the secretariat of the associations. This is perhaps an excellent way of improving the process of diffusion. As Table 35 shows the time required to obtain a permit is often very long, so that this must be a considerable hindrance to the quick diffusion of technologies as the amount of investment increases.

Table 32. Whether or not Effort Exerted to Obtain Government's Permit.

	Total			Textile			Electrical		
	Ph	Th	In	Ph	Th	In	Ph	Th	In
Yes	11	7	34	6	5	16	5	2	18
No	15	10	15	11	8	8	4	2	7

Table 33. Extra Effort Exerted to Obtain Government's Permit — Philippines.

	Total	Textile	Electric
	11	5	5
a. Follow-ups by frequent tel. calls	4	4	—
b. Personal visit to the man in charge	4	1	1
c. Documents of co's finance and study qualification	2	2	—
d. Further documents as gov. offices requires	2	—	2
e. Acquired permit from suppliers	1	—	1
f. Agreed to get needed manpower to run mach.	1	—	1
g. Changed the channel of request	1	1	—

Table 34. "Extra Effort" Exerted to Obtain Government's Permit — Indonesia.

	Total	Textile	Electric
a. Through exhibition	3	3	—
b. Through friends	9	4	5
c. Other procedures	4	1	3
d. Through associations	3	3	—

It is by no means exceptional for it to take two to three months to get any kind of permit.

6. Religious and Ethnic Problems

6.1. *Religious and Ethnic Heterogeneity*

The Philippines is a Christian country, Thailand is a Buddhist country, and Indonesia is predominantly a Muslim country. Does this affect in any way

Table 35. Length of Time Needed for Obtaining Permit.

	Total		Textile		Electric	
	Ph	In	Ph	In	Ph	In
<one week	2		2		—	7
<two weeks	2	14	—	1	2	
<one month	3		2		3	6
<3 months	7		6	9	1	
<5 months	1	23	—	6	1	7
<7 months	3		2	1	1	

the process of transfer of new modern technologies? How conscious of religion are the businessmen in these countries? Our survey attempted to elicit their views on this difficult question. The findings are by no means satisfactory but seem to show certain ways of thinking of Southeast Asian businessmen about the relations between material welfare and spiritual nemeses.

The business world in Southeast Asia has several other creeds besides those three mentioned above. Most westerners are Christians, but there are Japanese, Chinese, and Indians, etc. They bring in other religious and additional ethnic problems. Moreover, the business enterprises in Southeast Asia are often joint ventures with overseas Chinese. The ethnic problems related to overseas Chinese come up along with other anti-foreigner problems. The Indonesian government policy called "bumi putra" or "puribumi" in particular tries to provide preferential treatments for non-Chinese ethnic groups. There may be also some antagonism against westerners or Japanese which may or may not affect the decisions on adopting new technologies. The survey findings seem to show significant differences among the three countries with regard to the mode of decision making.

First, Thai and Indonesian businesses introduced new machines almost entirely by contacting foreign companies, whereas some Filipino businesses seemed to introduce new technologies without such contact. About 7 out of 24 in textile and 4 out of 25 in electrical appliances industries had no contact. Second, the nationalities contacted show that Japanese, American,

Table 36. Foreign Businessmen Contacted in Introducing New Machines.

	Total			Textile			Electrical		
	Ph	Th	In	Ph	Th	In	Ph	Th	In
1 Japanese	26	32	41	11	18	19	15	14	22
2 American	26	15	11	10	5	4	18	10	7
3 European	20	16	12	12	10	9	8	6	3
4 Chinese	11	15	11	3	8	5	8	7	6
5 Australian	2	—	—	—	—	—	2	—	—
6 Indian	1	—	—	1	—	—	—	—	—
7 Taiwanese	1	3	—	1	2	—	—	1	—
8 Korean	1	—	—	1	—	—	—	—	—
9 Singaporean	1	—	—	—	—	—	1	—	—
10 Indigenous	—	1	28	—	1	14	—	—	14

Table 37. Religious Backgrounds Influencing Specific Business Decisions.[a]

	Total			Textile			Electrical		
	Ph	Th	In	Ph	Th	In	Ph	Th	In
1 Prop to cumulate capital	28	39	13	24	22	8	4	17	5
2 Attain happy through business	9	28	10	2	11	8	7	17	2
3 Contrib. to national devel.	14	28	32	8	17	12	6	11	20
4 Save poverty via business	15	26	25	8	16	6	7	10	19
5 Competition contributes	13	37	12	8	19	12	5	18	—

[a]Those who did not admit the influence are the remaining number out of 25 in each industry and 50 in total. For instance, in the Philippine textile industry, I did not admit any influence of religion on his propensity to accumulate wealth. In the case of Thai textile industry, it is 3 etc.

European, and Chinese come out much to the fore. This is shown in Table 36. It is admitted by almost all partners in the three countries that the contact with foreign companies was very useful in introducing new technologies, regardless of their nationality. Table 37 gives our findings on the decision-makers awareness of the influence of their religious belief on their economic behavior.

Christians in the Philippines — all but 30 of the interviewees were Christians — admit the relevance of religious belief to economic behavior

Table 38. Influence of Religions or Ethnic Consciousness on Work Ethics.

	Total			Textile			Electrical		
	Ph	Th	In	Ph	Th	In	Ph	Th	In
1 Strong	7	—	17	5	—	—	2	—	11
2 Weak	9	—	9	1	—	5	8	—	4
3 Irrelevant	33	50	23	18	25	13	15	25	10
4 Other	1	—	1	—	—	1	1	—	—

much less than Buddhists in Thailand or Muslims in Indonesia. Thais are more conscious of the relevance than the other two, and Indonesians are more emphatic about the influence of religion on the national development and social contributions. In Indonesia, religious teachings emphasize contributions to the national economic development as well as individual happiness. The ways in which religion influences economic decisions positively or negatively must be further investigated.

What about the influence of religion or ethnic consciousness on work ethics among workers? The data on this point contained in Table 38 seems to show a somewhat different picture. It shows that Buddhism in Thailand, which was admitted to have a strong influence on managerial behavior (see the Thai columns in Table 37), does not seem to have much influence on laborers' work ethics. This is a rather unexpected finding. Perhaps, the former statement in Prof. Prasert Yamklinfung's country survey report needs to be modified. He himself suggests: "according to the respondents it has no effect on workers' work ethics whether they happen to be religious-minded or not. No respondent consulted Buddhist monks or fortune-tellers about their decision to invest, though many held religious ceremonies inside the company ground to commemorate important days or events in the company calendar. They were intended to bolster the morale of workers. A manager of a small company held religious ceremonies after a series of machine breakdowns in his factory, hoping that this would bring good luck to the company. There was nothing irrational about this, because the indirect effect was to recover the self-confidence on the part of workers."

Their relevance of religion to decision-making in respondents' answers does not mean that it really has no effect on businessmen's attitudes. How we can determine the actual behavioral relations is an interesting topic which needs a separate study and requires us to get at the religious beliefs and feelings at a deeper level. Furthermore, ethnic and regional differences among Buddhists do exist in Thailand, but they do not pose any serious problem in connection with the issues discussed here unlike those in Indonesia and the Philippines, because the Buddhists and Thais are absolute majority in Thailand and minority groups are little involved in industrial activities. Businessmen of Chinese origin think in terms of furthering their ethnic or regional interests in pursuing risky undertakings. They are conceded most importantly with their own profitability.

6.2. *The Role of Churches and Temples*

The churches, temples, or mosques may have some influence through their preaches or documents, but this does not seem to be the case in the Philippines and Thailand. No one in Thailand admitted it, whereas only one respondent in the Philippines admitted any positive role (Table 39).

But the Indonesia situation appears to be completely different. The respondents there admit the positive role played by the mosques. Some admit also that there are cases in which their role is negative. This seems to indicate that the religious teachings at mosques in Indonesia have a fair amount of bearing on businessmen's and people's activities. Some are not in accordance with business requirements. Table 40 gives the replies to the open question in our survey.

Table 39. The Role of Mosques in Indonesia.

	Total	Textile	Electrical
1 Positive	26	10	16
2 Negative	2	2	—
3 Neural	22	13	9

Table 40. Specific Aspects of Mosques' Influence in Indonesia.

Textile		Electrical	
1. Enhancing work ethics	5	1. Emphasize discipline in working	9
2. Decrease daily want	3	2. Decrease daily want	4
3. Buildings places for prayers	3		

It seems that economic ethics are taught at the mosques, and that religious or pedagogical teachings are effective in forming the desirable behavior pattern. One may wonder why this is so noticeable only in Indonesia, and what kind of teachings are made to the public in Thai Buddhist temples or Philippine churches.

6.3. *The Influence on Government Policies*

The influence of religion on the government's economic policies can hardly be direct in modern society. Is it so in the developing countries? According to Prof. Prasert Yamklinfung, "the question of religion and ethnic influences seems to be irrelevant in the Thai social setting. Buddhism in Thailand is not concerned with the policies and operations of the government or private businesses. It has no influence at all on government pouches toward new technology." It is, however, not so in the other two countries, as Table 41 shows. This is not surprising if one remembers the ethnic heterogeneity in Indonesia and, to a lesser extent, in the Philippines. The ethnic problems are very important in these two, and the role of religion is also more significant than in Thailand.

6.4. *The Behavior of Business Concerning Risk and Uncertainty*

Investment is made always with some degree of risk, and how such actions reconsidered in the context of religious or spiritual circumstances is important for perceiving the thinking of entrepreneurs in these countries. The survey findings on the issues show something of the psychology of

Table 41. Influence of Religion and Ethnic Consideration on Government Policies of R&D and Technology.

	Total			Textile			Electrical		
	Ph	Th	In	Ph	Th	In	Ph	Th	In
1 Strong	4	—	15	3	—	4	1	—	11
2 Weak	3	—	7	—	—	7	1	—	—
3 Irrelevant	40	50	35	20	25	12	20	25	13
4 Other	2	—	—	1	—	—	1	—	—

Table 42. The Role of Religion in Making Risky Investment.

	Total			Textile			Electrical		
	Ph	Th	In	Ph	Th	In	Ph	Th	In
1 Strong	—	1	19	—	1	16	—	—	9
2 Weak	2	6	5	—	2	3	2	—	2
3 Irrelevant	47	43	25	24	22	13	23	21	12

Table 43. Perceived Causes of Success in Businesses.

	Total			Textile			Electrical		
	Ph	Th	In	Ph	Th	In	Ph	Th	In
1 Luck	15	23	21	8	13	8	7	10	13
2 Effort	36	47	33	17	25	16	19	22	17
3 Good judgment	41	47	35	20	24	15	21	23	20
4 Other	70	5	—	32	6	6	38	5	—

businessmen. Here again Indonesian businessmen seem to be influenced by religious factors much more significantly than those in Thailand and the Philippines. From these observations, it seems safe to presume that Islam in Indonesia has closer relations with economic affairs than Buddhism in Thailand and Catholicism in the Philippines (Table 42).

Another aspect of religion's influence on economic action concerns the conception of success or failure in business. This may be influenced by the nature of religions or their teachings, for example, whether the religion is submissive to fate or emphasizes nemesis. How businessmen perceive their business successes can be seen from Table 43.

There seems to be a general consensus in attributing success to good judgment and effort in all three countries. None chose — in Thailand the order of importance was asked — luck as the first reason, and very few as the sole reason. Perhaps this implies that as respondents felt, they had some control over their success or failure.

The reasons for success given as "other" by the Filipino respondents are of some interest, because some of them are regarded as more important than "luck". Particularly, the first two are as indicative as any of good judgment and effort. The figure given indicates the number of respondents who gave each factor both in the textile and electrical appliance industries. For more details, see the following table.

a. Good and dynamic management	21
b. Good labor-management relations	17
c. Improved sales and the like	10
d. Better technologies and the like	9
e. Sufficient capital and finance	6
f. Other	7

Thus, introducing new technologies can only be successful if it is accompanied by good and dynamic management with good industrial relations. The reasons for failure are the reverse of the causes of success. The findings in the Philippines are given in Table 44.

The relative importance of "luck" is slightly less for failure, but in the case of textiles, the weight of luck is rather high. This may be because it is exposed to recessions and severe competition with other companies at home and abroad which is beyond the control of the company. Respondents' "other reasons" in the survey are also revealing.

a. Poor management	12
b. Poor labor-management	3
c. Sales or marketing problems	16
d. Inadequate technologies	5
e. Financial problems	11
f. Other	7

It is natural for the failure in sales promotion and financial difficulty to be important. Two respondents mentioned smuggling as a reason for

Table 44. Causes of Company's Failures in the Philippines.

	Total	Textiles	Electrical
1. Bad luck	7	4	3
2. Poor judgment	25	9	16
3. Lack of effort	21	8	13
4. Other	54	29	25

success, and two others attributed their failures to the same factor. There was also one in each case who attributed his success or failure to government taxation policy.

7. Market and Social Organization

7.1. *Joint-Ventures and Royalty Payments*

In the free private enterprise system, new technologies are usually imported through a joint-venture type investment or by buying patent. The royalty payment is more frequent in Thailand than in the other two (Table 45).

Many Thai companies have been relying on the parent corporations abroad. They started their manufacturing activities on the basis of turn-key contracts with foreign firms which not only designed the whole production process but also purchased and installed the machines to operate the factories in the initial period. Royalties were paid for a certain period. The companies took over the operation, however, when they became more confident in the operation or when they became dissatisfied with the amount of royalties they had to pay. As Thai managers became more familiar with the production operation, they sometimes found the prices of materials charged by their partners too high, and they obtained those more cheaply elsewhere. The amount of royalties often became too high as sales increased. Joint ventures and quality conscious local manufacturers usually pay royalties for technologies as well as for the right to use the foreign companies' trade marks, There are several ways of calculating the amount of royalties. The simplest method is to pay 1 to 4% of total sales. Sometimes, it depends on the value of the contents of particular products made by the local company, because not all of the materials are purchased from the parent company. Royalties are not added to the value of materials

Table 45. Royalty Paid/not Paid for Last Machinery Adopted.

	Total			Textile			Electrical		
	Ph	Th	In	Ph	Th	In	Ph	Th	In
Paid	2	24	9	—	9	7	2	15	2
Not paid	47	26	30	24	16	9	23	10	21

purchased from the parent company for the obvious reason that the latter has made some profit already from selling these materials to the local company. For high technology products like color TV, however, an initial fee of a fixed amount also has to be paid to the parent company besides ordinary royalties.

There are some important taxation problems in connection with royalty payments. The Thai government, for instance, is beginning to adopt more strict policies about the payment of royalties, because some companies took advantage of the present customs duties law to pay less duties by under-declaring the value of imported merchandise and compensating foreign exporters with royalty payments which are tax-exempt. The government has closed this tax loop hole by ordering importers to include royalties in the declared value of the imported merchandise, and duties are levied on this basis. Honest manufacturers complain that this change will subject them to a kind of double taxation. This means that they have to pay more for imported technology.

7.2. *Negotiation with Machine Suppliers*

If negotiations are made with the suppliers of technologies about the types of technologies to be introduced or the modification of original designs, the technologies adopted may be come more appropriate. The survey shows in Table 46 that extensive negotiations take place.

It is not true at all that foreign technologies are introduced straight away. They are carefully examined and selected by the businesses concerned. One of the important considerations in introducing machines is how many workers will be displaced, unless the level of production of the company increases sufficiently (Table 47).

This question was asked in the survey except for Thailand, where the question was mistaken as the one concerning workers' attitude toward

Table 46. Whether or not Company Negotiated with Suppliers.

	Total			Textile			Electrical		
	Ph	Th	In	Ph	Th	In	Ph	Th	In
Negotiated	34	26	37	15	13	21	19	13	16
Not negotiated	15	21	7	9	12	—	6	12	7

Table 47. Whether or not Employment Associated with Machines was Considered as Important Factor.

	Total			Textile			Electrical		
	Ph	Th	In	Ph	Th	In	Ph	Th	In
Considered	43	—	40	23	—	17	23	—	23
Not considered	4	50	3	2	25	3	2	25	—

Table 48. Size of Workforce Found Hard to Manage.

	Total			Textile			Electrical		
	Ph	Th	In	Ph	Th	In	Ph	Th	In
20	13	5	—	4	4	—	9	3	—
50	0	3	3	0	3	1	0	0	2
100	3	13	13	2	11	5	1	2	8
200	1	4	7	0	1	5	1	3	2
400	3	4	5	1	1	3	2	3	2
1000	10	5	5	5	1	2	6	4	3
Total	30	35	33	12	21	16	19	14	17

machines. Considerable attention was paid to this problem. In Thailand, some workers seemed to be unwilling to learn the new skills required for new machines. Some complained that they had to work harder than before because the new machines moved faster. But most respondents did not regard these as serious problems because after a while workers adjusted well to the change.

7.3. *Difficulties in Managing Workers*

As the scale of production increases with the introduction of modern machinery, the number of workers in plant or factory increases (Table 48). Did the managers in these countries find it difficult to manage them? If so, what was the number of workers of which problems began to appear?

This problem is related to the type of social organization of different ethnic groups as well as the entrepreneurs' ability to manage. The findings of the survey are rather interesting. Although there were quite a few companies that did not admit any difficulty in managing workers even beyond 1,000, some small companies started having difficulties even with 20 workers. The number of workers should be interpreted as the number of all the workers in one plant, but there is always some ambiguity in its meaning some respondents may have interpreted it as only the number under their supervision. This may have been the reason why such a small number as 20 was given. So far, as the number of workers under one supervisor is concerned. Many replied that up to 50, there was no problem if the workers were doing the same kind of work, e.g., assembly. But a group of skilled workers, as many admitted, had to be smaller, requiring much closer supervision. Beyond 100, some difficulty is admitted by many of respondents.

This seems to support the view that the optimal choice of technology varies with the scale of production and the managerial ability of the companies. Needless to say, so far as the technology remains relatively simple and requires no precise coordination of the work of many employees with specialized skills, this interaction of labor with management does not come into play. In such a case, appropriate technology for a firm can be considered only with respect to the scale of production and the direct cost of capital depreciation and the proportional labor cost associated with the use of the machines. If, however, the difficulty of management comes into the picture, then the managerial indirect cost may go up or efficiency may go down. Hence the scale of production must be determined by optimizing the rate of return on the new machines to be introduced. This is nothing but the standard textbook case of the long-run cost survey. There is another way of looking at this managerial problem. It is concerned with the number of levels of supervision or administration between the top management and individual workers. The more levels, the more difficulty is to organize the workers. If workers and other staff are difficult to organize, the levels of supervision will be fewer. As a result, the scale of production must be smaller, and the machinery must be adjusted to that scale. It seems that the levels most frequently practiced are four and five. The survey findings in Thailand and Indonesia are shown first in Table 49.

In the case of the Philippines, the question was asked more specifically to give the positions of these levels. The answers gave the following patterns as the most typical type: (1) President, (2) Vice-president, (3) Managers, (4) Department head, (5) Supervisors, (6) Section chiefs, and (7) Supervisors.

Table 49. Levels of Supervision in the Company.

	Total		Textile		Electrical	
Levels	Th	In	Th	In	Th	In
3	2	4	2	—	—	4
4	15	20	8	9	7	11
5	23	15	8	10	15	5
6	6	7	3	6	3	1
7	2	—	8	—	—	—
8	1	—	1	—	—	—
Other	1	—	1	—	—	—

This seems to imply that the levels of supervision in the Philippines are more like those in developed countries. Thai and Indonesian business administration seems to have fewer levels. It may be too hasty to conclude there from that it may be a reflection of their types of social organization, because the size of sampled enterprises in the Philippines is larger. There are, however, some Filipino companies which do not have "department heads" and "section chiefs". They have only five levels which coincide with the other two countries cases. These are typically small enterprises with fewer employees. Therefore, overall one may say that supervision hierarchy in these countries tends to be of smaller scale than the typical in advanced industrialized countries.[9]

7.4. *Work Rules and their Enforcement*

The third aspect of labor management, which has some relevance to the choice of technology, is the enforcement of work rules. Modern technologies are usually a system of machines which requires not only a well-organized group of workers but also certain work rules to be observed. All companies have some work rules based on stipulations of the labor law. Some have additional rules depending on their particular needs and problems of the companies such as rules about safety measures, company

[9]L. M. Hanks (1977). "The corporation and the encourage: A comparison of Thai and American social organization," in S.W. Schmidt, C. H. Lande, and J. C. Scott (eds.), *Friends, Followers, and Factions*, University of California Press, Berkeley, pp. 161–165.

Table 50. Difficulties in Enforcing Work Rules in the Philippines.

	Total			Textile			Electrical		
Work rules ↓ difficulty →	Very	Fairly	Not	Very	Fairly	Not	Very	Fairly	Not
1 Absenteeism	14	14	20	8	6	10	6	9	10
2 Tardiness	12	14	23	5	8	11	7	6	12
3 Reporting breakdown	3	12	34	2	5	17	1	7	17
4 Over time	—	8	41	—	3	21	—	2	20
5 Other	3	9	52	—	5	28	3	3	24

Table 51. Difficulties in Enforcing Work Rules in Thailand and Indonesia.

	Total		Textile		Electrical	
	Th	In	Th	In	Th	In
1 Very difficult	6	—	4	—	2	—
2 Fairly diff.	12	12	9	7	3	5
3 Not diff.	32	24	12	16	20	13

uniforms, telephone use, smoking and eating during working hours, etc. In the Philippines, our surveyed required about what rules the companies had and whether they found it difficult to enforce them or not. Table 50 presents the responses.

Clearly, some work rules are difficult to enforce. The most notable ones are absenteeism, tardiness, reporting breakdown, overtime, securing permit for leave, and attention to the work performed. Some companies could enforce them; the difficulty is not too much (Table 51).

In Thailand and Indonesia, the survey findings are as follows. Enforcement seems more difficult in Thailand than in Indonesia, and it appears that in the Philippines it is even more difficult than in Thailand. This seems to be explicable in terms of the careful supervision observed at the lower levels of labor management in the Philippines.

7.5. *Work Incentives*

The survey findings show the following measures effective to overcome the various difficulties and improve the efficiency of work (Table 52).

Table 52. Incentives to Work.

	Total			Textile			Electrical		
	Ph	Th	In	Ph	Th	In	Ph	Th	In
1 Higher wages	45	19	18	17	13	9	28	6	9
2 Better human relation	26	29	43	14	15	20	12	14	23
3 Better working cond.	27	13	38	13	10	15	14	3	23
4 Fringe benefit	36	31	25	18	18	13	18	13	12
5 Other	30	5	8	12	1	7	18	4	1

It is noteworthy that Indonesians better regard human relations distinctively as an important determinant of incentives more than the other countrymen. They are more like the Japanese workers for whom the business enterprises are like extended families. Filipinos and to a less extent Thais are relatively more concerned with pecuniary rewards. In the context of introducing new technologies, however, the ability of managers to keep good human relations may be difficult to find in Indonesia, where different ethnic groups co-exist in the same urban area. This may impose another difficulty in enlarging the scale of production unless the new technologies to be introduced can increase production by mechanization.

As for other incentives, particularly in the Philippines, some profit-sharing bonus or payment schemes are found to be very effective. Introduction of a merit system of promotion is also reported to be important. If these economic incentives required accompanying the adoption of new technologies, they are not too difficult for large enterprises to introduce. Big companies can afford to have a higher pay scale or at least pay minimum wages which are rather high. But this creates problems for small companies. Some companies emphasize better working conditions in the plants. This condition cannot also be easily provided by small companies with poor resources. They are often engaged in the production processes which expose workers to heat and other hazards. All companies claim that they already have the fringe benefits and welfare measures of some kind. But the details vary from one company to another. The improvement cannot be easily made in many small companies even if it is required to give incentives to workers.

8. Government Policies and their Implementation

8.1. *Government versus Business*

We have already discussed in passing the role of government in the process of accepting new technologies and choosing *appropriate technologies*. Some specific questions must be examined carefully. We already found that the government's influence is rather weak in the Philippines and Thailand but very strong in Indonesia. The government's request, if not regulations, to private businesses is presumably based on considerations of national economy but may not coincide with the private business' stake. How are those cases handled?

The conflicts or contradictions are especially frequent in Thailand (Table 53). The complaints detected in the interviews reveal that respondents are concerned about the structure and rate of taxation, lack of coordination among government offices and poor implementation of industrial policies. They are not necessarily relevant directly to technological issues, but as they pose difficulties for the growth of enterprises, technology transfer is hindered. In order to resolve these problems, most Thai companies rely on the Thai Industry Association which is very active and presents their cases to the appropriate government offices. But most Thai businessmen are very pessimistic about the Probability of changing government policies, regulations and practices in their favor.

(a) import duties are unduly high .... (1)
(b) foreign staff utilization is restricted too much .... (1)
(c) more basic materials must be imported .... (2)
(d) export certificates must be given more easily .... (2)
(e) government should listen more to positive suggestions .... (3)

Table 53. Whether or not Conflicts between Government's Requests and Company's Interests are Experienced.

	Total			Textile			Electrical		
	Ph	Th	In	Ph	Th	In	Ph	Th	In
1 Experienced	5	26	10	2	10	9	3	16	9
2 Not experienced	44	25	35	22	15	13	22	9	14

Table 54. Ways of Resolving the Conflicts in Indonesia.

	Total	Textile	Electrical
1 Through association	8	4	4
2 Direct contact with gov.'s offices	2	2	—
3 Compromising with gov. practice	7	3	4
4 Adjusted to the situations	2	—	2

In Indonesia, conflicts are not so serious as in Thailand, because businessmen are ready to coordinate their decisions with the government requests. Nevertheless, there are still conflicts according to the replies to the open questions in the survey. The figures in parentheses indicate the numbers of cases reported. There are also complaints about too flexible applications of government regulations. Businessmen, however, seem to overcome these conflicts as Table 54 shows.

8.2. *Government Involvement in Technological Choice*

The government is sometimes directly involved in choosing or promoting a certain type of technology. The survey finds these issues in the three countries as in Tables 55 and 56.

Only in Indonesia is the government directly involved in choosing technologies. In three cases in Thailand, the government requested companies to employ more workers. In Indonesia, however, the government makes specific suggestions on technologies, which reveal the underlying ideas concerning technological choice on the part of responsible government officials. By "appropriate" technologies, the Indonesian government seems to mean technologies which (a) increase labor productivity, (b) yet employ

Table 55. Whether or not Government Suggested Machinery for Company.

	Total			Textile			Electrical		
	Ph	Th	In	Ph	Th	In	Ph	Th	In
1 Suggested	—	3	46	—	3	23	—	—	23
2 Not suggested	49	47	—	24	22	—	25	25	—

Table 56. Government's Request on Technological Choice in Indonesia.

	Total	Textile	Electrical
1 Employ more workers	13	10	23
2 Save capital	14	4	10
3 Save resources	17	14	3
4 Save energy	6	2	4
5 Save foreign employees	10	6	4
6 Increase labor productivity	36	16	20
7 Produce more cheaply	2	1	1
8 Improve quality of products	27	12	15
9 Use more domestic input	31	11	20
10 Other	4	4	—

more workers, (c) produce better quality of goods, and (d) preferably rely less on foreign personnel.

This is certainly an ideal type of technology. To what extent these conditions are met, however, depends on the available menu of technologies offered to the decision-makers, and on whether the interests and judgment of government coincide with those of the decision-makers.

8.3. *Businessmen's Interest in New Ventures*

The businessmen who make decisions have their own interest and attitude towards the government or the outside world. The survey findings tell the following story on this matter. It is not self-evident that the business enterprises are run with their own company's interests as the primary motivation, because their owner may have several companies under his control and try to maximize the sum of their profits. If the company is in ownership of one proprietor, then the primary concern of the company may be his or his family's interest. Such seems to be the case with some textile companies in the Philippines (52%), Thailand (20%) and Indonesia (8%). In the case of electrical appliances industry, however, such a case is rare in all the countries (Table 57).

Another notable finding is businessmen's great concern about the national interest. This is particularly true in the electrical appliances industry, probably because unlike the textile industry, this is an industry which has been newly developed with great support from the government.

Table 57. Specific Factors Considered Important in Undertaking New Ventures.

	Total						Textile						Electrical					
Rank	1			2			1			2			1			2		
Interest ↓	Ph	Th	In	Ph	Th	In	Ph	Th	In	Ph	Th	In	Ph	Th	In	Ph	Th	In
1 Own fam.	16	3	2	4	12	3	13	3	2.	2	6	7	3	3	—	2	6	1
2 Co's	22	38	34	16	7	9	8	18	19	11	4	3	14	20	15	5	3	6
3 Ethnic gr.	1	—	2	1	—	3	—	—	2	—	—	3	1	—	—	1	—	—
4 Spec'l gr.	—	—	1	3	—	3	—	—	1	1	—	2	—	—	—	2	—	1
5 National	9	4	10	22	27	19	3	2	1	9	15	7	6	2	9	13	12	12
6 No inf.	1	—	—	1	1	3	—	—	—	1	—	—	1	—	—	2	—	4

In Thailand and Indonesia, the national interest was indeed ranked in second place in the minds of businessmen who undertook new ventures. Certainly the government can use this as leverage and promote technological progress in such industries. In these cases the conflicts between the private sector and the government tend to be more frequent. As was observed in Table 53, conflicts were more frequent and serious in the electrical appliances than in the textile industry.

8.4. *Taxation*

Conflicts with government policies are often related to tax laws and their application. At the same time, the government can influence the direction of industrial composition and choice of technologies by taxation policies. Many respondents complained of the negative effects of the tax structure and tax rates on the future industrial development of the countries concerned. Various comments on taxation made by Thai businessmen are quoted here to illustrate the specific problems.

(1) The tax structure and rates are unfavorable particularly for electrical appliance assemblers. For example, the duties on the materials and parts necessary for local assembly are high, whereas the duties on complete sets imported are lower. As a result, the locally assembled sets become more expensive than imported sets contrary to the intention of government policies for import substitution.

(2) The government tries to promote export of industrial products by granting the tax refunds for exports. But the procedure is complicated, conditions are hard to satisfy and it takes a long time to get any actual return. The result is that businessmen are discouraged rather than encouraged to produce for exports.

(3) The Thai government's recent decision to levy duties on royalties including even those paid abroad, increases the cost of local manufacturing. The government's new method of assessing income tax on companies' profits also requires re-examination. On the whole the tax structure needs to be constantly readjusted in the light of industrial policies at each stage of economic development of the country.

Naturally business circles complain of heavy taxes. Remember that government budgets in developing countries almost always suffer from serious deficits, which is a main cause of secular inflation. The three countries surveyed are no exception. The government's capability of collecting taxes without causing any serious social unrest is often critical in maintaining political stability. In addition, there are several ones associated with the development of import substitute industries. The familiar ones are:

(1) smuggling of complete sets of electrical appliances, etc,
(2) inefficiency or corruption of customs offices,
(3) regulations concerning tax holidays.

They will be discussed in turn. In order to develop import-substitution industries, the governments usually impose higher import tariffs on complete sets than on parts or materials, and levy a consumption tax proportional to the value of the product whether it is domestically produced or imported. In order to make the industries competitive, the period of protection and phasing down of protective rates must be carefully designed. Smuggling, of course, disturbs all the rational calculations. It is, however, so prevalent in reality that the government's effort to suppress it is absolutely necessary. Inefficiency of customs houses and other related government offices is a serious obstacle to any rational economic policies. Prof. Prasert Yamklinfung reports, "criticism of the government sometimes centers out right on the corruption of some government officials in the customs and revenue departments. Instead of rendering services, these officials have become a serious obstacle to the efficient running of business. They are alleged to be arbitrary in their attitudes and slow in performing their duties. Manufacturers who produce for export market usually have to wait several months before they can get the tax returns, although the government promises to return them as incentives to exporters. Some respondents are pessimistic about the possibility of change in the government's efficiency in this regard."

The income tax holiday for exporting enterprises in *promoted status* needs to be reconsidered. As Dr. Hing Sarn Santikarn argues in her excellent research on *Technology Transfer*,[10] two criteria are applied to determine the period of tax holidays:

(a) *value added criterion*

Share of value-added in annual sales	Exemption period
Less than 30%	5 years
31–40%	6 years
41–50%	7 years
over 50%	8 years

(b) *Employment criterion*

Number of workers	Exemption period
fewer than 200	5 Years
200–400	6 Years
401–600	7 Years
Over 600	8 Years

The employment criterion certainly inhibits the employment objectives of the government. As we have already seen, many firms employ fewer than 200 workers, so that they will be treated unfavorably in comparison with larger corporations. This is not desirable in the light of the evidence that was shown in Table 10 and Figure 1 in Section 2. On the contrary, smaller companies must be given more favorable tax holidays so long as they satisfy the same value added to capital ratios in direct subsidies in the form of tax exemptions or cheaper capital particularly in favor of large corporations will make the capital/labor ratios in manufacturing industries higher than otherwise.

[10]M. Santikarn (1981). *Technology Transfer: A Case Study*, Singapore University Press, Singapore, pp. 42–46.

In Thailand, where export promotion of the textiles has become very important, the government may have chosen deliberately the promotion of exporting enterprises but the overall implications of such taxation policy needs more careful reconsideration. All these tax policies suffer from difficulties to implement. For example, the Board of Investment is supposed to give privileges like tax exemption to those making worthwhile investment. But the coordination between the Board of Investment and the Customs Department is so bad that the promotional privileges are hardly appreciated by businesses.

8.5. *The Minimum Wage Law*

It has become almost fashionable to enact a minimum wage law in the developing world. The countries under study are no exception. In Thailand prior to 1973, wages were left completely free to be fixed by the market mechanism. A 1971 survey of 401 manufacturing establishments in Greater Bangkok area gave the average monthly earnings of unskilled workers as 670 bahts for males, 446 bahts for females, and 224 bahts for children.[11] On the basis of 26 working days, the daily wages were 25.8, 17.1, and 8.6 bahts respectively.[12] The consumers' price index rose by 11.7% in 1973 and 23.3% in 1974 respectively. Wage increases were demanded and 297,508 and 723,000 working days were lost by industrial disputes in 1973, 1974, and 1975 respectively. The minimum wage law was enacted in these circumstances in April 1973 and wages were subsequently adjusted as follows:

1. April, 1973	12 baht	Greater Bangkok
2. January, 1974	16 baht	Greater Bangkok
3. June, 1974	20 baht	Greater Bangkok and suburbs
4. October, 1974	16 baht	Whole Thailand
5. January, 1975	25 baht	Greater Bangkok

[11] N. K. Sarkar, "Industrial Structure of Greater Bangkok" quoted by [10] in Chapter 10, p. 48.

[12] But the official estimate given by the Department of Labor is lower than this survey estimate. N. Chantharawithun's *Thai Labor and Industry* (*Raeng-Ngan Thai kap Utsahakam*, Samakhek Sangkhomsat Haeng Prathet, Thai 1972) gives an estimate between 10 and 15 bahts per day and 8 to 10 bahts a day for the preceding two decades.

It should be noticed here that in almost two years, the rate of wages in real terms at the minimum level as is required by the law, rose by more than 100%. Since the labor productivity could not increase so much in two years even at large corporations, the businesses began to feel the impact in 1974 and 1975. There have been a number of labor disputes around Bangkok since then, and they were more or less related to the enforcement of the minimum wage law. The minimum wages set by the government tend to be too high. They cannot be afforded by many companies. The government often cannot assess possible implications of a minimum wage rate beforehand and consequently is obliged very often to change the rate. It is very important, therefore, to introduce the law with caution to ensure that the long-run effects on the rest of labor, particularly the unemployed, do not more than compensate the temporary favor given to a group of workers with stronger bargaining power. On the basis of the argument above, it may be safe to assume that minimum wage law tends to make the adoptable technologies less labor-intensive and introduce uncertainty into business conditions.[13]

It is true that our survey findings showed weak effect of the government regulations on private enterprises' decisions especially in Thailand, and that this perhaps applies to the minimum wage law as well. Since, however, it is enforced rather strictly in big cities, especially with respect to foreign enterprises, its influence on their choice of technologies may not be negligible.

In implementing the minimum wages law, some practical problems are often encountered. They will be explained in relation to Indonesia. The minimum wage rate in Indonesia varied from 450 Rp to 875 Rp in 1981 (615 Rupiah = 1$). It was argued that if determination of the wage rate was left to free bargaining between workers and employers, it would tend to

---

[13]There is a theoretical analysis of minimum wages in the Third World, which maintains that the effective minimum wage regulation always lowers the growth rate of national economy. (J. I. Drabiscki and A. Takayama (1982). "Minimum wage regulation and economic growth," *Journal of Economics and Business*, pp. 231–240.) In reality, however, one should not hastily conclude that this conclusion holds, and minimum wage law necessarily decreases employment opportunities, especially if saving ratio is significantly positive in the country and if foreign investment is not discouraged.

Table 58. The Minimum Wages in June–September, 1980.

	Cost	Manuf.	Food process	Plantation	Farm work
1 Jakarta	750	400	—	—	—
2 West Java	—	518	—	700	250
3 Central Java	500	265	—	700	250
4 East Java	500	250	—	700	250
5 Sumatra	—	—	500	—	—
6 South Sumatra	1300	350	1000	—	—
7 South Sulawesi	750	750	—	—	—

Table 59. Sectoral Wage Differentials Per Month.

	Farming	Mining	Manufacturing	Services
Max (a)	191,411	569,535	413,044	322,339
Min (b)	67,080	67,080	39,775	32,795
a/b	11.1	8.5	10.4	9.8

be too low and make employment unstable. The workers would tend to do "job-hopping" and lose opportunities of training on the job. This means that an introduction of minimum wage rate at a steady rate could have a desirable aspect. The minimum wage in practice differs very widely from one region to another and from one industry to another. Our survey in Indonesia[14] shows this gap as in Table 58.

Diffrentials in the minimum wages are great. The gaps between large and small enterprises are extremely big. The Ministry of Transmigration gives the following information of the gap between the highest and the lowest wages in different industries (Table 59).

Another relevant aspect of wage payments is the importance of wages in kind and fringe benefits. The money wages quoted above tend to exaggerate the wage differential. This is particularly complicated in Indonesia. Often the wages in kind include rice, sugar, uniforms, lunch and medicines, and fringe benefits cover supplementary support for transportation, housing,

[14] Nihon Rodo Kyokai (Japan Labor Association) (1981). *Indonesia no toshi rodosha* (*Urban workers in Indonesia*), Nihon Rodo Kyokai, Tokyo.

medicare, social insurance, and bonus.[15] The low wages in small businesses or in the informal sector are often supplemented by the atonalistic care offered by the proprietor and his family. Under these conditions, if the minimum wage law were really enforced — this is scarcely the case in small towns or rural areas — the impact would be very serious to small enterprises and almost intolerable to those whose job opportunities would be reduced.

8.6. *Industrial Policies*

As the relative weight of manufacturing industries becomes greater, the coordination of various industrial activities with government policies becomes increasingly important. The first consideration is the relation between agriculture and manufacturing industries or that between the rural and urban residents. In particular, the income differentials between the two areas should not be too large, because if they are large, then transmigration from rural to urban areas will create the serious conditions in urban slums. The support of producers' price for rice as well as the subsidies to consumers' rice price is one of the typical policies for this purpose. In order to avoid too rapid urbanization, new capital construction must be made more in rural or local areas. An important consideration in investment decision-making is, as our survey found, availability of infrastructure. The second consideration is the relation between large and small enterprises. This chapter already dealt with this problem to some extent. It must be kept in mind also that a large manufacturer sometimes plays a role of skill accumulation which may be important in developing new industries or introducing new technologies. This benefit may be tied in with training programs or R&D expenditure of the government. In this context, distinction between large and small enterprises is not necessarily critical for some industries particularly in the tertiary sector.

The third consideration is the relation between foreign capital and domestic capital. There is no doubt that various government policies like tax holidays are meant to promote the inflow of foreign capital. Several

---

[15]*cf.* C. Manning "Fringe benefits in manufacturing: Efficiency or welfare?" *Bulletin of Indonesian Economic Studies*, July 1980.

problems will be discussed in later sections but it may be pointed out here that the benefit of foreign capital investment must be evaluated carefully in terms of the employment opportunities that it has created.

The fourth consideration is the relation between the private sector and the public sector. In this sense, government policies to strengthen the position of business associations are highly commendable in Thailand as well as in other countries. It may also be desirable to increase the degree of communication among various business associations like the Japanese Chamber of Commerce, the Overseas Chinese Economic Association, the American Chamber of Commerce, the Thai Chamber of Commerce, etc. They may be able to exert more influence jointly and to change government policies in their favor and thereby resolve many of the conflicts between movement policies and business interests as well as among themselves.

8.7. *Science and Technology Policy*

Government policies in this field, at least until very recently, hardly existed in Thailand and the Philippines and were not very effectively implemented in Indonesia. It is highly desirable that each government's development plan spells out the national objectives in promoting science and technology, provides guidelines for disseminating technologies and implementing R&D policies. This will probably have a direct impact on private companies' behavior in technological transfer in Indonesia. In the other two countries what is more sectors or corporations where technological transfer of appropriate kind is likely to be carried out or has been carried out efficiently by private enterprises.[16]

Sometimes it is argued that the royalty payment for trade marks or brand names cannot be supported. It must be recognized, however, that use of such names may be economizing the resources required to promote exports, although excessive payment of royalties in connection with local subsidiaries of foreign companies needs to be re-examined. The government must regulate the excessive amounts given to the suppliers of technologies by setting limits to the amount or duration of royalties. But at the same time,

[16]UNCTAD: *Draft outline of an international code of conduct development of industrial technology in Asia and the Pacific* (Bangkok, 1976), and C. Himawan (1980). *Foreign Investment Process in Indonesia*, Gunung Agung, Singapore.

they must prevent restrictive practices like terminating production upon expiration of contracts or unilateral obligation for purchasers to furnish all information on product improvements. The role of government in checking the process of technology transfer is very important. Foreign patents registered and expired must be communicated to the relevant businesses as soon as possible. It is highly desirable that as soon as the government recruits the necessary engineering staff, it experiments with appropriate technologies and suggests the private sector any means of creating and adopting socially desirable technologies.

The government may directly undertake training programmers, or grant subsidies to training or research activities in private companies. It should be recognized that small manufacturers or farmers can hardly afford to develop or learn new technologies. Yet their prosperity is crucial to increase employment. The domestic supply of materials for industries must also be developed. Ideally, the cotton growing and textile industry should develop side by side. The residential permit for foreign technicians even if they are badly needed for operating the new technologies in the textile industry, is very difficult to obtain and almost impossible to extend once it expires. But these technicians often have to stay on; otherwise, the factories do not function efficiently. In order to meet this frequent request, the government offices will need to employ technical experts who can understand the practical problems of modem technologies.

8.8. *Control of Foreign Ownership and Competition*

Probably, a fair statement about control of foreign capital is what Dr. Mingsarn Santikarn wrote at the end of her dissertation: "as long as the government promotes a competitive environment, strengthens tax administration and collection and regulates technology transfer by effective registration, there seems to be no need for further special control on foreign investment.[17]" On the other hand, there may still be scope for policies to promote the transfer of technologies from foreign to local firms. Nevertheless, the government has been seriously worried that by so doing it may lose control over production and pricing of industrial products. For example, a resolution of the Cabinet on January 22, 1974

[17]Mingsarn santikarn, *op. cit.*, p. 253.

makes it mandatory for foreign investors in Indonesia to have local partners. Moreover, the Foreign Capital Investment Law of 1967 (Article 27) requires that foreign investors gradually increase the Indonesian capital share.

The requirement of "equity participation" often contradicts the desire to promote foreign capital investment and the support of "puribumi" policies. It is unavoidable that as a result the transfer of appropriate technologies slows down. Some suggestions to improve government policies in this regard are as follows:[18] The concepts of "foreign company" and "national company" must be defined clearly. Otherwise, "compulsory equity participation" may be interpreted by foreign investors as camouflaged nationalization policy. In the Philippines, for example, an enterprise is classified as "national" if 60% of its capital is in the hands of Filipinos. In Indonesia, there is no clear definition offered by the government, but the definition adopted by Andean countries seems to appeal to some officials. They define the identity of a company not on the basis of capital ownership but the identity of the personnel holding effective control.[19] This will prevent the so-called "Ali Baba" (i.e., nominally Indonesian but *de facto* foreign firms), but it will also make investment in Indonesia less attractive. At any rate, leaving some grey area between foreign and national enterprises — in the case of Argentina, between 51 and 80% — usually has the effect of raising the upper limit to 80%. What is important is not to leave any uncertainty in calculating the cost and return on investment abroad. It is also related to the question of whether national enterprises are free from the restrictions imposed upon foreign enterprises. There is a need for defining clearly "puribumi" and "non-puribumi". Since many regulations in Indonesia refer to this distinction[20] and wish to treat "pruibumi" Indonesians more favorably, clearer ways of identifying them are desirable. Particularly, if so many restrictions are to be imposed upon the economic activities of non-puribumi, the loose definition may have a negative effect on the influx of foreign capital and the associated transfer of modern technologies.

Restrictions on the sales of shares might also deserve re-examination. Many existing companies have restricted the sales of their shares to

---

[18]As for the excellent discussion on legal aspects of these problems. See Himawan, *op. cit.*, pp. 278–297.
[19]R. Danino (1876). Andean Code after five years — 8 lawyers of the Americas, p. 646.
[20]For example, the decision of the National Stabilization Council, January 22, 1974.

particular individuals and related corporations. There are several reasons for this practice. An organized capital market, for example, did not exist in Indonesia until December 27, 1976. But even thereafter, the lack of experience and shortage of capital on the part of the general public has kept the equity participation rather low. The Indonesian government envisages that it should reach 51% of all foreign investment enterprises by 1984. This seems to be too ambitious, because one study[21] shows that local people's equity participation in joint ventures (foreign invest intent), totaling 4.6 billion dollars in 1974, was only 8.5%; 63.3% comprised foreign loans, and 28.2% was actual foreign equity capital. The industrial breakdowns are as follows:

Metal	21.8	Transportation	13.7
Recreation	20.5	Basic Metal	12.7
Construct	19.0	Farming	9.6
paper	18.6	Hotel	8.7
Trade	17.5	Forestry	7.8
Machinery	17.3	Textiles	7.5

In the case of Indonesia, it may be possible to increase local equity participation by spending oil dollars. It will require very careful planning to administer the joint ventures which have higher participation ratios in so many sectors what is needed is a plan of bringing up the capable entrepreneurial businessmen as fast as equity participation increases. In other countries, it will take a longer time perhaps more reasonable is, as in Bolivia and Ecuador to reach 51% in 20 years or so.

Some attention might be given to the lending policy of the banks. Bank loans should be extended to national corporations not only on the basis of available collateral but the credibility of companies' profits. Otherwise, the shortage of national capital will prevent the influx of foreign investment due to the lack of counter parts. This will be a serious hindrance to the transfer of technologies associated with direct foreign investment in these developing countries.

[21] S. Iskandar (1975). "Meningkartan peranan modal nasional dalam Projek projek PMA" (increasing the role of national capital in Foreign Capital Investment Projects), *Kompas*, September 6.

Appendix: Questionnaire Form for Survey on Appropriate Technologies and Development Policies

I. Basic Information		
1.1.	Reporter ______________________	(age) __________
1.2.	Religious affiliation ______________	
1.3.	Name of Company ______________________ (address)	
		(Commencement Year)
1.4.	Position	
1.5.	Type of work:	
1.6.	Company's line of business	
1.7.	National or joint venture?	
	a) foreign venture	
	b) joint venture	(Which country's?)
	c) government enterprise	
	d) indigenous group's	
	e) other	
1.8.	The amount of sales, capital and the number of employees	

	Sales	Capital	(foreign %)	Employees
1970*				
1980				

*If commencement was later than 1970. The first full year for the company's activities.

II. General Questions	
2.1	During the last 20 years, have you ever adopted any new technologies* in your factory? **Technology* in this questionnaire means the *techniques* related to *machines* and the new information directly connected with the machines or their running. In other words, it is *hard-wares*, not *soft-wares*, or simple improvement of management. (*If your answer is "Yes", skip the questions from 2.1 to 2.8.*)
2.2	Have you ever felt the needs for improving the technologies in your factory? Yes: __________ No: __________
2.3	Have you known any new technology which you wanted to adopt? Yes: __________ No: __________ (*If your answers are "no" to (1–3) questions, then ask the following.*)
2.4	Have you ever tried to obtain any information of new technologies? Yes: __________ No: __________

2.5	Through what means did you try to obtain any information of new technologies?			
	a. radio	________	i. trading co's	________
	b. TV	________	j. trade associations	________
	c. newspapers	________	k. domestic trade fairs	________
	d. magazines	________	l. international trade fairs	________
	e. associated co.'s	________	m. trips abroad	________
	f. mach. or material supplier	________	n. government services	________
	g. licensors	________	o. 'parent co's	________
	h. customers or buyers	________	p. others	________
	(If "No" to Q 2.4, then			
2.6	Why didn't you try?			
	a. no resources to do any better	________	d. no interest	________
	b. no access to information	________	e. other	
	c. useless for us	________	(________________)	
	If "yes" to 2.3 and 2.4, then			
2.7	How do you characterize the type of technologies that you considered for your factory?			
	a. labor-intensive	________		
	b. capital-intensive	________	h. requires skilled workers	________
	c. energy-saving	________	i. requires no skilled workers	________
	d. fairly modern	________	j. requires foreign engineers long	________
	e. traditional	________	k. requires foreign engineers short	________
	f. requires high level technology	________	l. requires domestic engineers only	________
	g. requires medium level technology	________	m. others (specify ________________)	
2.8	Why didn't you adopt it? (Order the items according to the importance.)			
	a. shortage of capital	________		
	b. didn't have engineers	________		
	c. didn't have technical *know-how*	________		
	d. hard to find skilled workers	________		
	e. not much chance to increase sales	________		
	f. government regulations or intervention	________		
	g. objection of the society	________		
	h. other — specify ( )	________________		

2.9	How many times and when have you introduced new technologies for the past 20 years? What types of technologies were they? Year Type of Technologies 1. 19 ____ ________________ 2. 19 ____ ________________ 3. 19 ____ ________________ 4. 19 ____ ________________ 5. 19 ____ ________________
2.10	Through what means did you obtain the information of new technologies? a. radio ________ i. trading companies ________ b. TV ________ j. trading associations ________ c. newspapers ________ k. domestic trade fairs ________ d. magazines ________ l. international fairs ________ e. associated companies ________ m. trips abroad ________ f. suppliers of machines or materials ________ n. government services ________ g. licensors ________ o. *parent* companies ________ h. customers or buyers ________ p. others- specify ________
2.11	What were the reasons for adopting them? Choose as many as you wish. Give the order of importance. (the order of importance: 1, 2,) a. to increase profitability (________) b. to improve the quality of products (________) c. to increase the productivity per day (________) d. to decrease the unit cost of production (________) e. to increase the employment opportunities (________) f. to increase the production capacity of the company (________) g. to diversify the activities of the company (________) h. government recommended (________) i. government gave subsidies (________) j. government gave tax-exemptions (________) k. foreign partners recommended (________) l. nothing else was available (________) m. others (________) (Specify. ________________)

	III. *Economic and Social Consideration in Adoption of New Technologies*
3.1	In adopting new technologies or building new plants with old technologies, did you consider the various reactions outside and inside the factories, besides the companies' business interests? Yes: __________; No: __________
3.2	If "Yes", what kinds of consideration did, you make? Please mention up to three! 1. ____________________ 2. ____________________ 3. ____________________
3.3	Was there any sentimental objection to introducing "foreign" technologies into your factory? Yes: __________; No: __________
3.4	Have you encountered any difficulty in utilizing the new machines in practice? If you have, please mention the technical or human difficulties up to three. 1. ____________________ 2. ____________________ 3. ____________________
3.5	Have you received any influence of the government authorities in adopting or rejecting the new technologies? If so, how did it come about? Please explain. ____________________ ____________________
3.6	What government offices have you contacted in the process of adopting new technologies? 1. Board of Investment _______ 2. Ministry of Industry _______ 3. Technology Information Center _______ 4. other — specify _______ 5. ____________________
3.7	Have you thought that by introducing the new technologies you made contributions to national development or nation-building in your country? Yes: __________; No: __________
3.8	In what ways, do you think, you made contributions? Please mention up to three. 1. ____________________ 2. ____________________ 3. ____________________
3.9	In what way, do you think, you can contribute to the needs of your country's nation building? Please mention up to three. 1. ____________________ 2. ____________________ 3. ____________________

IV. Trial and Experimentation	
4.1	Have you tried or observed the experiment of the technologies before adopting them? Yes: ________; No: ________
4.2	Where was the experiment performed? 1. in your plant ________ 2. elsewhere in the country ________ 3. abroad ________
4.3	Have you rejected some technologies as the result of trial or experimentation? Yes: ________; No: ________
4.4	If rejected, what was the reason? a. technically too advanced ________ b. difficult to practice ________ c. too expensive ________ d. other (specify________)
4.5	How did you find out that it was not appropriate from your point of view? (For example, by cost a/c. friends' advices, etc.) Please explain. ________________________ ________________________ ________________________
4.6	If you accepted the new technologies after trial or experiment, what was the criterion for your decision of acceptance? a. increases profitability ________ b. improves the quality of products ________ c. increases productivity per day ________ d. decreases unit cost of production ________ e. increases employment opportunities ________ f. increases the company's production capacity ________ g. diversifies the company's activities ________ h. government recommended ________ i. government gave subsidies ________ j. government gave tax-exemption ________ k. foreign partners recommended ________ l. nothing else was available ________ m. others ________ (specify: ________________________)

V. Adaptation	
5.1	After adopting them, did you have any need for modifying or adjusting them to suit the needs of your factory in any way different from the original design or instructions? Yes: __________; No: __________
5.2	If "yes," how did you modify them? (____)
5.3	In making the adjustments, have you considered the peoples' or villagers' attitude toward the location or activities of your plant? Yes: __________; No: __________
VI. Ethnic Problems and Religion	
6.1	Whom or what companies have you contacted in connection with introducing new technologies into your company? a. American ________ b. Japanese ________ c. European ________ d. Overseas Chinese ________ e. Indigenous other businesses ________ f. Others (specify______) ________
6.2	Did you find the contact useful for accepting new technologies? Yes: __________; No: __________
6.3	In what way did they offer the positive contributions in introducing new technologies to your factory? Please explain. (____ ____)
6.4	In your field what type of companies or business groups are particularly important or positive in accepting new technologies? 1. ____________________ 2. ____________________
6.5	Do you think that your religious background (or social consciousness) has influenced in any way the approaches to new, foreign technologies when you had to make decisions? a. in the propensity to accumulate wealth ________ b. in attaining spiritual happiness through business ________ c. in contributing to national development ________ d. in helping the poor via businesses ________ e. in the attitude toward competition ________ f. other (specify ______________) ________
6.6	Do you think that religion or ethnic consciousness plays a significant role in determining work ethics among workers? a. strong influence ________ b. weak influence ________ c. irrelevant ________ d. other comments ________

6.7	Have the temples, churches, or mosques played any role, positive or negative, in the approaches to modern, new, foreign technologies in your country? a. positive ________ b. negative ________ c. neutral ________
6.8	Can you give one or two examples that religion or ethnic considerations have affected the attitude toward technologies? 1. ________________ 2. ________________
6.9	Do you think that religious or ethnic considerations have affected the government policies on R&D policies and technology development plans? a. strongly ______ b. weakly ______ c. irrelevant ______ d. other ______
6.10	In undertaking risky decision or investment, does your religion or fortune-telling play any role, besides rational economic calculation? a. strongly ______ b. weakly ______ c. irrelevant ______ d. other ______
6.11	When you fail or succeed in your own business, do you think that you are primarily lucky or due to your effort? Please rank the following causes. (1, 2, 3 etc.) a. luck ______ b. effort ______ c. good judgment ______ d. other ______
6.12	If somebody succeeds, do you attribute it to luck, effort, judgment or anything else? a. luck ______ b. effort ______ c. good judgment ______ d. other ______
	VII. Government Policies
7.1	When you undertake new ventures, which factor has priority in your calculation? Please rank them (1, 2, 3 . . .) according to the importance in your mind. 1. your own interest ______ 2. your family's interest ______ 3. your company's interest ______ 4. your ethnic group's interest ______ 5. your regional interest ______ 6. your country's interest ______
7.2	Do you have any experience of finding a conflict between government policies and your company's interest? Yes __________ No __________
7.3	Please explain the nature of conflicts. 1. ________________ 2. ________________ 3. ________________
7.4	Did you make any compromise to resolve it? Please explain. ________________
7.5	Did the government authorities suggest a certain type of technologies as appropriate or desirable? Yes __________ No __________

7.6	How did they describe it? Mark what, you believe, they requested to consider. 1. employ more workers ______ 6. more productive per worker ______ 2. save capital ______ 7. produce output more cheaply ______ 3. save resources ______ 8. better quality of product ______ 4. save energy ______ 9. more domestic input ______ 5. employ less foreign personnel ______ 10. other ______
7.7	Did you have to depend on foreign engineers at the beginning in installing and running the new capital equipments? Describe the type of technology in us A. ______ B. ______ C. ______
7.8	How long did you need them? 1) less than one year ________ 2) less than 2 years ________ 3) longer than two years ________
	VIII. Diffusion
8.1	Did you adopt the new technology before anybody else or after somebody did so? a) before anybody else ________ b) after somebody did ________
8.2	If "a", how did others follow you? 1) very quickly ____ 2) fairly soon ____ 3) slowly ____ 4) much later ____ 5) none ____
8.3	If "b", how did you follow them? 1) very quickly ____ 2) fairly soon ____ 3) slowly ____ 4) much later ____
8.4	By what means did you learn about the success of the other companies? a. radio ____ b. TV ____ c. newspapers ____ d. magazines ____ e. associated companies ____ f. suppliers of machines or materials ____ g. licensors ____ h. customers/buyers ____ i. trading co's ____ j. trade associations ____ k. domestic trade fairs ____ l. international trade fairs ____ m. trip abroad ____ n. gov. services ____ (specify ________) o. parent company ____ p. other ____ (specify ____________)
8.5	Which do you prefer in undertaking new ventures, before others or after many succeeded? a. before others ____ b. after others ____
8.6	Did the government support the new ventures with new technologies? Yes __________ No __________
8.7	Did you need the government's approval or permit for introducing new technologies? Yes __________ No __________
8.8	How soon was it given? a. very quickly __________ b. satisfactory __________ c. very slow __________

8.9	Did you have to make special efforts for obtaining the government's support? Yes ________ No ________
8.10	What kind of efforts did you make? ________
8.11	How long did it take to obtain the government's permit or support? ________
	IX. Market and Social Organization
9.1	Did you pay royalties for the new technologies you introduced? Yes ________ No ________
9.2	How much did you pay? (Type of Technology) (the amount of royalty) A. ________ ________ B. ________ ________ C. ________ ________
9.3	Nave you ever negotiated with the suppliers of new technologies about the types of technologies to introduce or the modification of the original designs? Yes ________ No ________
9.4	When you introduced the new technologies, did you consider the number of workers to employ as an important factor? Yes ________ No ________
9.5	Do you find it difficult to manage, if the number of workers (employees) exceeds any following number? a. more than 20 ________ d. more than 200 ________ b. more than 50 ________ e. more than 400 ________ c. more than 100 ________ f. more than 1000 ________
9.6	How many levels of supervision do you have between top-executives and individual workers? 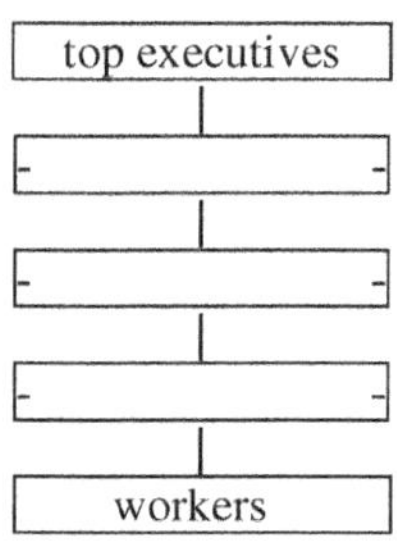
9.7	What "work rules" do you have? If you have any written rules, please give us those. Or describe it briefly below. ________ ________ ________

9.8	Do you have any difficulty in enforcing the work rules in your factory? a. very difficult __________ c. not difficult __________ b. fairly difficult __________ d. other comment: __________
9.9	How do you give workers incentives to work harder? a. higher wages __________ d. fringe benefit __________ b. better human relations __________ e. other __________ c. better working conditions __________ (specify ________________)
9.10	When you made a choice of technologies, which factors were relatively more important according to your experiences? (Please give ranking of importance as 1, 2, 3 *etc.*) a. economic calculation: __________ b. difficulty in managing workers: __________ c. social relations __________ d. relations with the government __________ e. shortage of "middles" __________ f. relations with the military __________ g. availability of external infrastructure __________ h. international relations __________ i. government regulations __________ j. other: __________ (specify ____________________)
9.11	What do you want for the government to do for promoting an introduction of more appropriate technologies? ____ ____

Chapter 12

The Socio-Economic Behavior of Peasants in Central Java and Central Thailand*

Shinichi Ichimura†, Koichi Mizuno†, Yoshihiro Tsubouchi†,
Toshio Asano‡, Prasert Yamklinfung§, Akin. Ra. Bibhadana¶,
Yut S. Akdejayont¶ Mubyarto|| and Masuri Singarimbun**

1. Introduction

This is a comparative study of the village lives in Central Java and Central Thailand to find the differences as well as similarities in the villagers' socio-economic behaviors. Three sample villages were chosen from Central Java and the Bangkok Plain respectively as those representing the characteristics of natural environments in each area. They were already discussed in earlier papers. The villages in Central Java were chosen from volcanic fan area (Klaten Village), coastal plain (Demak Village), and limestone plateau (Gading Village), while those in Thailand were from delta area (Pathum Thani Village), flood plain (Ayutthaya Village), and fan area (Saraburi Village). The volcanic fan areas have been the center of traditional paddy cultivation in Central Java, while the delta area has been developed since the 19th century to form the present rice bowl of Thailand. Thus, Klaten Village and Pathum Thani Village are characterized by advanced and commercialized paddy cultivation. Gading Village and Saraburi Village are

*This was published in *Southeast Asian Studies*, Vol. 12, No. 3, December 1974. The authors are affiliated with the following institutions.
†The Center for Southeast Asian Studies, Kyoto University; ‡Primate Research Institute, Kyoto University; §Department of Sociology, Faculty of Political Science, Chulalongkorn University; ¶Faculty of Liberal Arts, Thammasat University; ||Faculty of Economics, Gadjah Mada University; **Institute of Population Studies, Gadjah Mada University.

newly opened villages located in the marginal zone of cultivation. Demak Village and Ayutthaya Village are placed in-between.

About 30–50 households were randomly chosen in each village among those with male household heads of 25–59 years of age and primarily engaged in agriculture. The exact number of the sample households in each village is as follows: Klaten 30, Demak 33, Gading 30, Pathum Thani 49, Ayutthaya 33, and Saraburi 41.

A questionnaire schedule like the one in Appendix[1] to this chapter was prepared for this research. Its main items are the following: (1) peasants' evaluation of natural environments, (2) attitudes toward agricultural innovation, (3) attitudes toward labor, and (4) attitudes toward saving. University senior students with the supervision of participating researchers in July and August 1973 conducted interviews. The duration of interview was about one week in each village. Table 1 gives the average acreage of land owned and cultivated by sample households in each village. A marked difference in the scale of cultivation is found between Thai and Javanese villages.

2. Natural Environments and Peasants' Response

Water is critically important for paddy cultivation. The three sample villages in Java differ in the way of controlling water. Klaten Village is located in the

Table 1. Average Area of Landholding.

	Area owned per sample household (ha)		Area cultivated per village household (ha)		
Villages	Mean	SD	Mean	SD	Percent of owned to cultivated
Klaten	0.71	0.54	1.12	0.51	63.2
Demak	0.69	0.20	0.89	0.75	77.6
Gading	0.49	0.40	0.56	0.48	87.8
Pathum Thani	2.56	4.16	6.67	4.43	38.3
Ayutthaya	4.35	3.65	6.85	4.59	63.4
Saraburi	4.40	3.76	4.88	2.83	90.3

[1]The questionnaire schedule in Appendix is translated from the Japanese one used for comparative purposes and almost identical with the original used in this survey.

volcanic fan area, where small streams are numerous and easy to manage. Peasants themselves had traditionally controlled the water but the Dutch government improved it. In contrast, Pathum Thani is located in delta, where the water control became possible recently through a large scale of canal schemes. In other areas, an efficient control of water has been impossible with existing level of technology and an available amount of capital. As a result, villages on a limestone plateau or on a fan like Gading and Saraburi often suffer from drought, whereas villages on a plain like Ayutthaya suffer from flood. Villages on a coastal plain like Demak suffer from both flood and drought.

Evaluation of water control in each sample village by the specialists in our team and evaluation of irrigation efficiency by villagers seem to reflect the above situation (see Table 2). Evaluation of irrigation by Ayutthaya villagers, however, seems to be unduly higher than that of specialists. For the question asked not about water control in general but only about irrigation. Table 3 shows farmers' evaluation of rainfall in each village. Klaten and Ayutthaya have the highest scores. This evaluation may reflect the fact that both villages seldom suffer from water shortage. The actual rainfall in the area may be not evaluated as such. Table 4 shows specialists' and villagers' evaluation of soil fertility in each village. The villagers' grading finds no significant difference among three villages in Thailand in spite of the existing difference evaluated by specialists. In Java, villagers' grading shows the highest value at Klaten where specialists found the poorest quality of soil. Villagers' grading seems to be influenced by the high yield in the village owing to good irrigation system and extensive application of fertilizer.

Table 2. Evaluation of Water Control.

Villages	Specialist's	Villagers'
Klaten	5	3.6
Demak	3	2.7
Gading	1	No irrigation
Pathum Thani	4	3.7
Ayutthaya	2	3.7
Saraburi	2	No irrigation

Notes: 5 = Very good, 4 = Good, 3 = Ordinary, 2 = Poor, 1 = Very poor.

Table 3. Evaluation of Rainfall.

Villages	Specialist's	Villagers'
Klaten		3.5
Demak	No	3.0
Gading	information	3.0
Pathum Thani		2.6
Ayutthaya		3.3
Saraburi		3.1

Notes: 5 = Very good, 4 = Good, 3 = Ordinary, 2 = Poor, 1 = Very poor.

Table 4. Evaluation of Soil.

Villages	Specialist's	Villagers'
Klaten	2	3.6
Demak	3	2.6
Gading	4 and 2	2.8
Pathum Thani	3	2.9
Ayutthaya	2	3.1
Saraburi	1	3.0

Notes: 5 = Very good, 4 = Good, 3 = Ordinary, 2 = Poor, 1 = Very poor.

Judging from this observation, it may be assumed that ordinary farmers do not duly appreciate the quality of soil, unless the soil is extremely poor. The following tables show evaluation of water control, rainfall, and soil.

The mean and median amounts of harvest in the best, ordinary, and worst years are shown in Table 5. The highest harvest among all sample villages is found at Klaten Village on the volcanic fan in Java. In Thailand, Pathum Thani on delta shows the best harvest. These two villages are characterized by their good water control systems. The annual fluctuation of harvest indicated by (Best harvest – Worst harvest)/(Ordinary harvest) is also relatively small in these two villages. The ordinary harvests in other two villages in Java are lower than those of Thai villages, though the range of annual fluctuation is smaller. Considering the scale of cultivation at the same time, we can say that the characteristics of paddy growing in the marginal Thai villages is its uncertainty of crops, whereas that of marginal Javanese villages is its self-consuming subsistence existence.

Table 5. Average Yield of Paddy (ton/ha).

	(1) Mean amount of harvest (t)				(2) Median amount of harvest			
Villages	Best	Ordinary	Worst	Fluctuate	Best	Ordinary	Worst	Fluctuate
Klaten	7.1	5.5	3.4	0.67	7.2	5.7	3.8	0.60
Demak	1.4	1.0	0.6	0.80	1.4	1.2	0.5	0.75
Gading	1.1	0.8	0.5	0.75	1.4	0.8	0.7	0.88
Pathum Thani	3.5	2.8	1.5	0.71	3.7	3.2	1.8	0.59
Ayutthaya	2.6	2.0	0.4	1.10	2.8	2.3	0.4	1.04
Saraburi	2.0	1.5	0.5	1.00	2.2	1.8	0.5	0.94

Table 6. Major Causes for Bad Crops (%).

Villages	Flood	Drought	Insects	Diseases	Rats
Klaten	0	0	100	20	87
Demak	67	18	64	82	45
Gading	3	50	33	17	20
Pathum Thani	6	0	35	39	80
Ayutthaya	94	0	0	0	6
Saraburi	0	98	7	0	0

Table 7. Bad Crop Year for Most Respondents.

Klaten	1 year ago	63%
Demak	2 years ago	45%
Gading	5 years ago	20%
Pathum Thani	2 years ago	27%
Ayutthaya	4 years ago	94%
Saraburi	1 year ago	93%

Table 6 shows the main causes of bad crops in each village. The villages with poor water control suffered mainly from floods or droughts. The villages with adequate water control suffered only from secondary disasters such as insects, diseases, and rats. Table 7 shows that the bad crops caused by floods or droughts in Thailand tend to occur in a specific year. This confirms the above-mentioned gamble-like character of paddy growing in those villages.

The countermeasures taken against the damage from disasters are particularly noticeable in the commercialized paddy-growing villages that

Table 8. Countermeasures Against Crop Damages.

	% of those trying countermeasure	Kind of countermeasure applied	Evaluation of effect[a]
Klaten	90	Insecticide, poison	100
Demak	36	Insecticide	50
Gading	30	Insecticide	100
Pathum Thani	93	Poison, insecticide	84
Ayutthaya	38	Small earth bank	100
Saraburi	5	Pump	50

[a]Percent of those who gave positive answer to those who tried any countermeasure.

are free from both flood and drought. Table 8 shows that they find the application of chemical insecticide or poison especially effective against diseases and rats. On the other hand, the villagers suffering from flood or drought seem to find their individual efforts effective only for the limited area of paddy fields (Ayutthaya), or almost beyond human control so that very few try to get water through pumps (Saraburi).

As for the improvement of the methods to avoid damages, farmers suffering from flood suggest to build small earth banks by themselves (Ayutthaya) or to build permanent banks or dams through government budget (Ayutthaya, Demak). Farmers suffering from drought suggest to observe the climate carefully (Gading) or to apply artificial rains (Saraburi), although the effect of such methods is in fact dubious at present. Only villagers suffering from insects, plant diseases, and rats are able to find an effective way of preventing damages through individual or community effort: to apply chemicals (Demak, Gading) or chemicals and poison collectively by all villagers (Klaten, Pathum Thani).

3. Adoption of Recommended Varieties — An Aspect of Agricultural Innovation

The process of adopting recommended varieties of paddy, an aspect of technical innovation was examined in each village. Table 9 shows the acceptance of the varieties. No marked difference exists between Thai and Javanese villages. However, this table needs a careful interpretation in the light of field observations. First, Gading Village must be put aside, because

Table 9. Acceptance of Recommended Varieties.[a]

Village	Use		Not use	
Klaten	18	60.0	12	40.0
Demak	13	39.3	20	60.7
Gading	25	83.3	5	16.7
Pathum Thani	49	100.0	0	0.0
Ayutthaya	35	75.7	8	24.3
Saraburi	1	2.5	40	97.5

[a]Number of households and the percentages are shown.

Table 10. Adoption of Recommended Varieties.

	0–2	2–4	4–6	6–8	8–10	10–12	12–14	14–16	16–18	18–20	20–22	22–24	24–
Klaten	3	12	3	—	—	—	—	—	—	—	—	—	—
Demak	3	8	2	—	—	—	—	—	—	—	—	—	—
Gading	4	7	3	1	3	2	2	1	—	—	—	—	2
Pathum Thani	1	20	26	1	—	—	—	—	—	—	—	—	1
Ayutthaya	—	—	2	3	6	2	6	6	—	—	—	—	—
Saraburi	—	—	1	—	—	—	—	—	—	—	—	—	—

it is a new settlement; and Klaten Village percentage should be interpreted as unduly low because the survey conducted during the wet season when IRRI variety is suitable would have shown much higher percentage of adaptation. Accordingly, the degree of acceptance of recommended varieties, in the order of better adoption, Pathum Thani and Klaten that are both provided with well-controlled irrigation system constructed by national governments; lower scores in the villages of Ayutthaya and Demak, where water control is not so efficient. Lastly comes Saraburi Village which has no large-scale irrigation but some simple devices provided by local community. Marketing conditions unfavorable for new varieties are also intercepting the acceptance in this village. Overall, water control and marketing conditions are two decisive factors for villagers actually to adopt the recommended high-yielding varieties of paddy.

Table 10 shows the number of respondents for the year when they adopted recommended varieties for the first time, and Table 11 the same

Table 11. Information on Recommended Varieties.

	0–2	2–4	4–6	6–8	8–10	10–12	12–14	14–16	16–18	18–20	20–22	22–24	24–
Klaten	13	2	3	—	—	—	—	—	—	—	—	—	—
Demak	9	3	1	—	—	—	—	—	—	—	—	—	—
Gading	—	8	6	2	—	2	2	3	—	—	—	—	2
Pathum Thani	2	36	11	—	—	—	—	—	—	—	—	—	1
Ayutthaya	—	2	6	5	1	7	—	—	—	—	—	—	—
Saraburi	—	—	1	—	—	—	—	—	—	—	—	—	—

Table 12. Average Time-lag between Information and Actual Adoption.

Village	Information	Adoption	Time-lag
Klaten	2.277	1.611	0.666
Demak	2.384	1.153	1.231
Gading	9.120	8.240	0.880
Pathum Thani	3.666	3.041	0.625
Ayutthaya	8.760	7.240	1.520
Saraburi	—	—	—

for the year when they obtained the information about these varieties. Tendencies are that Pathum Thani and Klaten have concentrated in a few years between 2 to 4 years and 2 to 6 years before, whereas Ayutthaya has a scattered form. Demak Village resembles somewhat Klaten, and Saraburi is insignificant because there was only one respondent whoever tried to adopt a recommended variety. The most interesting is Gading that gives an extremely wide range of distribution in contrast with other villages. It covers almost 30 years since its foundation up to the present day. A possible interpretation is that this village does not have a long history of development yet for villagers to establish a stable and suitable variety of paddy. The villagers of Gading have been trying, therefore, over these years to find eagerly the best variety among those recommended by the authorities. On the other hand, Saraburi villagers have already established the local varieties most suitable for the village during the 80 years since its foundation.

In Pathum Thani and Klaten, introduction of new technology seems more active than in other villages. Table 12 proves this on the speed of

Table 13. Number of Inquisitive Persons.

Villages	Type I.	Type II
Klaten	4	0
Demak	3	2
Gading	5	1
Pathum Thani	2	0
Ayutthaya	2	1
Saraburi	0	0

Notes: Type I are those who show innovative attitude in Question 16 (see Table 14) and 17 (see Table 15). Type II is those who show innovative attitude in Question 16 but not 17.

introducing new varieties. The time lag between information and actual adoption is the shortest in Pathum Thani and Klaten where governmental effort is very intensive, whereas it is longer in Ayutthaya and Demak where such effort is less ascertainable.

Referring to the way in which the varieties have spread, we could reasonably assume that each village holds a few persons who were rather inquisitive in their character at the first moment of introduction. See Table 13. These persons together with other village leaders served as pioneers and introduced the recommended varieties to the villages. Other villagers adopted them under the influence of village headmen or some influential persons nearby. Table 14 shows the general pattern.

It may be noted that the villagers with the most innovative attitude (item A in Table 14) are superseded in number by the most innovative villagers (item A in Table 15), except for Gading Village. This is an interesting observation and may be a result of their previous success in adopting new varieties. It is also worth noticing that among three sample villages in each country, Klaten and Pathum Thani are the most positive villages, because there is none in the villages who does not show any interest in governmental introduction of new varieties.

Slight differences are discernible, however, between Pathum Thani in Thailand and Klaten in Java. First, according to Table 14, the Klaten farmers were more strongly influenced by government or village headman than Pathum Thani farmers were, whereas the latter were more strongly

Table 14. Reasons for Adopting Recommended Varieties.

Villages/Reasons	A	B	C	D	E	F
Klaten (18)	4(22%)	11(61)	6(33)	—	7(39)	1(15%)
Demak (13)	5(38)	7(54)	8(61)	2(15)	1(8)	2(15)
Gading (25)	5(20)	6(24)	16(64)	2(8)	—	3(12)
Pathum Thani (49)	2(4)	17(35)	24(49)	3(6)	—	5(10)
Ayutthaya (25)	2(8)	8(32)	10(40)	1(4)	2(8)	2(8)
Saraburi (1)	1(100)	—	—	—	—	—

Notes: A = worth trying anything new; B = recommended by governments or village heads; C = seeing results of neighbors; D = seeing results in surrounding villages; E = seeing results in extension farm or village seeds plots; F = others. Multiple answers were permitted.

Table 15. Attitude Toward New Varieties Recommended by the Government.

Villages/Attitudes	A	B	C	D	E	F
Klaten (30)	11(37%)	10(33%)	12(40%)	—	—	—
Demak (33)	8(24)	2(6)	20(61)	4(12)	3(9)	1(3)
Gading (30)	6(20)	16(53)	6(20)	3(10)	—	—
Pathum Thani (49)	37(76)	—	7(14)	—	5(10)	—
Ayutthaya (33)	17(52)	—	12(36)	3(9)	—	1(3)
Saraburi (41)	11(27)	—	28(68)	2(5)	—	—

Notes: A = I would plant it before anybody else; B = I would try to plant it after it has been tested at village's seeds plots; C = I would plant it if somebody else succeeds; D = I would not be interested in it; E = others; F = unknown. Multiple answers were permitted in Java.

influenced by neighbors than the former. This difference may be an outcome from their headmen's idiosyncratic personality's variation or an effect of their different socio-cultural patterns of village organization. Second, the villagers of Pathum Thani and Ayutthaya in Thailand are more positive than those of Klaten and Demak in Java are. The meaning of this difference seems to be understood by the existence of very progressive or rational farmers in Pathum Thani Village. They are those five, classified as "other", persons and asserted that they would decide only after they have tried the new variety and compared its productivity with those of the varieties they had ever used.

From these observations, the following conclusions on agricultural innovations may be drawn. First, water control is the most important limiting factor for adopting new varieties. Second, commercialization of paddy cultivation seems to reinforce peasants' incentives to adopt recommended varieties. Third, government's effort of introducing new varieties tend to be concentrated and well accepted in those commercialized areas equipped with good water control system. Lastly, along with these similar tendencies in both countries, the differences exist between Thai and Javanese peasants in their attitude towards government and spontaneous action to adopt new varieties of rice, which requires a farther investigation.

4. Farming as an Occupation — Obstacles and Incentives

Farmers were asked to respond to each of the following eight factors whether they regard it as bothering their farming or not: (a) crop's dependence on weather, (b) hard work under the sun and hot weather, (c) irrigation, (d) soil, (e) hard work with small revenue, (f) instability of price, (g) dangerous working condition, and (h) high rent. Figure 1 shows the results.

Not many respondents feel the climate as an obstacle to efficient working in any one of six sample villages. No significant difference exists

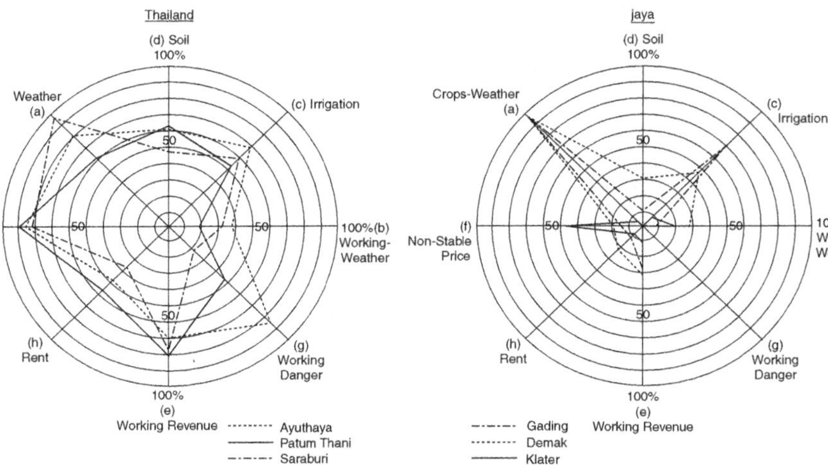

Fig. 1. Factors Bothering Farmers.

between Thai and Javanese villages; though a slight difference is detected, reflecting the severer climatic conditions in Thailand. Danger in farming is felt to a certain extent in Thai villages, whereas no one feels so in Javanese villages. The strongest danger is felt in Ayutthaya Village, where the danger of poisonous snakes is reported. Thai farmers seem to be more exposed to the uncontrolled nature than Javanese farmers are.

Dependence of harvest on weather bothers the farmers in the villages with poor control of water supply. The farmers in Klaten, for example, have no problem on this matter. In the village, irrigation is also not a problem. The farmers in Pathum Thani Village, where water control system is well established, still have some problems on irrigation. The farmers in all Thai villages and Demak Village in Java sense some problem in soil fertility. Klaten villagers, on the contrary, feel no problem on the part of soil. Since they have increased the harvest by applying modern technology, they have been able to neglect soil problems so far. In Gading Village, actual farming seems to be well established according to the traditional classification of soil, and this fact may be the reason for relative easiness felt by villagers on soil problems.

Remarkable differences appear, however, between Thai and Javanese farmers with regard to economic difficulties. Thai farmers feel the difficulties more keenly than Javanese farmers do. However, difference is not so much among the villages within the same country.

Table 16 shows the farmers' attitude toward work and income. They choose one of the two statements concerning attitude toward labor: "'the same income but less working hours" or "more income with more working hours". Although there is some difference in attitude even among three villages in the same country, Thai villages as a group gained a significantly higher percentage than Javanese villages as a whole in choosing the

Table 16. Attitude Toward Work and Leisure.

Village	Klaten	Demak	Gading	Pathum Thani	Ayutthaya	Saraburi
A	12(40.0)	17(53.0)	10(33.3)	5(10.0)	9(27.0)	7(1.0)
B	18(60.0)	16(47.0)	20(66.7)	44(90.0)	24(73.0)	34(83.0)
Total	30	33	30	49	33	41

Notes: A = same income but less working hour; B = more income with more working hour.

attitude "more income with more working hours". This, however, does not necessarily imply that Thai villagers are likely to work harder than Javanese villagers are.

Since Thai villagers have more chances of favorable non-agricultural labor than Javanese villagers do, the former are more likely to conceive work in terms of income than the latter. Thai villagers are more pragmatic in this respect. Hence, when they were asked which they would prefer, "the same income but less working hours" or "more income with more working hours", they were quick to respond to the latter. However, Javanese villagers with fewer opportunities to work for pecuniary income may not have been ready to respond spontaneously to "more income with more working hours". Thus, more of the farmers were inclined to respond to "the same income but less working hours".

We tried to find some factors that would explain this difference between Thai and Javanese farmers' attitude by cross-tabulations, but it has proved that we cannot assume any significantly patterned correlation between this subject and other factors such as age, land ownership, cultivated land, villagers' innovativeness, attitude toward paddy farming, or degree of satisfaction. This tendency may be related to a larger scale of cultivation in Thailand than in Java. Almost all the respondents in Gading and Demak in Java regard paddy cultivation as good in terms of income. In these two villages, paddy cultivation does not constitute the exclusive economic activity because of severe conditions of the physical settings. Thus, their strong desire for paddy cultivation might have caused those responses. The farmer's responses were cross-examined by age, land ownership, and cultivated land acreage employing t-test. Our findings are shown as Table 17. As a result, the following significant differences were detected.

(1) In terms of income:

(a) the mean age at Klaten Village (46.26 years for "good"; 51.45 years for "not good": $t = 2.1015$, $d.f. = 28$),
(b) the mean age at Ayutthaya village (44.53 years for "good"; 38.50 years for "not good": $t = 2.0698$, $d.f. = 29$),
(c) the mean area of cultivation at Ayutthaya Village (5.81 ha for "good"; 3.17 ha for "not good": $t = -2.0537$, $d.f. = 29$).

Table 17. Evaluation of Paddy Cultivation.

In income	Klaten	Demak	Gading	Pathum Thani	Ayutthaya	Saraburi
Good (%)	20	30	17	29	35	32
Good	43	67	83	18	13	32
Not good (%)	7	3	0	49	39	20
Not good	30	0	0	4	13	17
Good	63	97	100	47	48	64
(Ignore) (%)	27	33	17	78	74	52

(2) In terms of labor:

(a) the mean age at Pathum Thani Village (42.34 years for "hard"; 48.73 years for "not hard": $f = 2.1068$, $d.f. = 47$).

In Pathum Thani and Saraburi, older farmers tend to regard paddy cultivation as good in terms of income, though no significant difference is detected. Note that in all Thai villages, older farmers tend to regard paddy cultivation as good in terms of income, and that the reverse is true in Klaten of Java. It may lead to new findings if an investigation is made further into the effect of age on farmer's evaluation of paddy cultivation.

A question dealing with perception of relative happiness of being a farmer in comparison with a non-farmer was asked in Thailand and Java. Factory laborer and government employee were chosen as representatives of non-farmer in Thailand and in Java respectively. The difference in these representative occupations might have caused some difference in peasants' responses in two countries, making the comparison somewhat meaningless. The result is shown in Figure 2.

In Thailand, more than 60% of the respondents chose farmer as a happier status than laborer. The most important reason for this choice is the

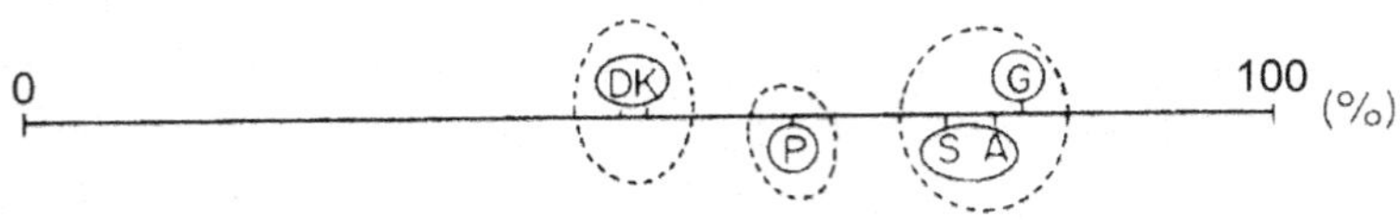

Fig. 2. Percentage of those who Chose Farmer as Happier Occupation.

Note: The circles indicate homogeneous groups of villages based on statistical results by x^2-test at 1% level and 5% level.

freedom on the part of farmers throughout three villages. In Pathum Thani Village, the percentage is lower than in Ayutthaya and Saraburi. Accessibility to better jobs as well as knowledge of them in Pathum Thani which is closer to urban districts than other two villages seem to be related with the respondents' lower appreciation of farming. A higher percentage of tenants in Pathum Thani Village offer another reason for the respondents' choice for non-farmers. The most important reason for choosing non-farmers in Pathum Thani Village is income and followed by less worry and more comfortable working conditions. In two Javanese villages (Klaten and Demak), about a half of the respondents chose farmer as happier than government employee. The most important reason for this choice is freedom as it is in Thailand. Income and security are the most important reasons for respondents choosing government employees in Klaten and Demak respectively. A different pattern of answers appears in Gading, where 80% of the respondents appreciate the farmer's life. The reasons of their choosing farmer are not only freedom but also income. The fact that chances to get good status as a government employee are very limited in this newly opened remote village might be related with this type of responses. A few people who have chosen government employees as happier in this village put their emphasis on security and physical working conditions rather than income. As a general trend, the farmer's life is fairly well appreciated in connection with freedom they enjoy, especially in the villages located far from urban districts.

5. Saving and Success

5.1. *Saving*

A question was asked about the balance between income and expenditure. It looked strange that in relatively poorer villages of Gading and Demak, a higher percentage of respondents were found with income and expenditure in balance, and that in richer Klaten and Ayutthaya, expenditure exceeded income. Thus, what is important for balancing income and expenditure seems to be not the absolute amount of income but the pattern of villagers' expenditure.

The next question asked was whether the farmers are satisfied with present amount of income or not. The answers show similarity in differences among six villages (see Figure 3). The same tendency seems rather

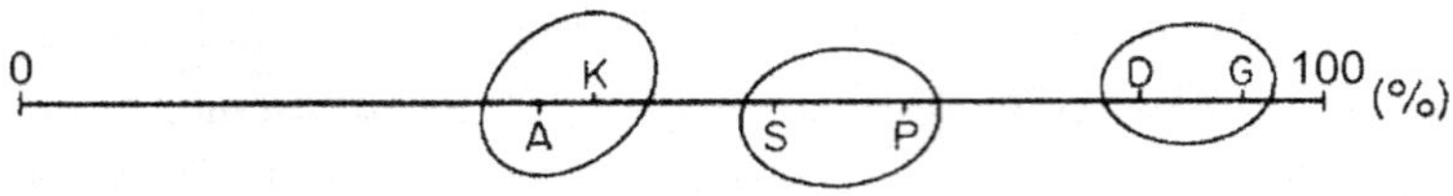

Fig. 3a. Percentage of those with Balanced Income and Expenditure.

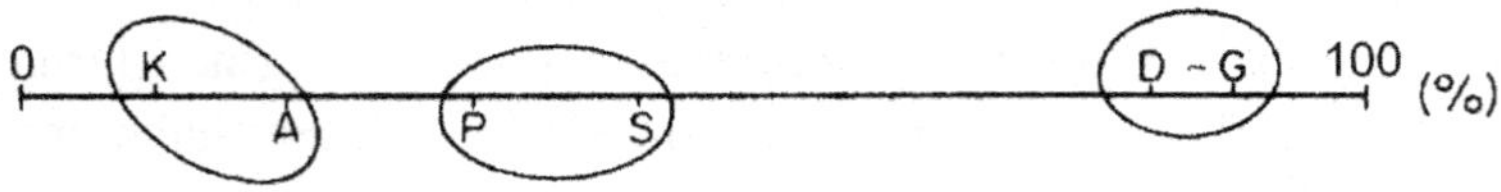

Fig. 3b. Percentage of those Expressed Satisfaction with Present Income.

Table 18. Character of the Satisfied and the Unsatisfied.

	% of samples			Average age of Respondents		Average acreage of land holding		Average acreage of cultivation	
	Yes	No	Not included	Yes	No	Yes	No	Yes	No
Klaten	13	87	0	47.00	48.35	0.74	0.70	1.15	1.12
Demak	82	18	0	40.56	41.83	0.69	0.71	0.91	0.85
Gading	90	10	0	45.07	38.33	0.49	0.50	0.57	0.50
Pathum Thani	35	65	0	49.35	40.81**	3.85	1.87	9.07	5.40**
Ayutthaya	21	71	9	39.57	42.30	5.28	4.48	7.89.	7.10
Saraburi	44	54	2	45.56	41.05	4.02	4.63	5.95	3.93

*Significant by *t*-test at 5% level.
**Significant by *t*-test at 1% level.

exaggerated. This exaggeration is caused by the two inconsistent responses: (1) dissatisfaction in spite of balanced income and expenditure and (2) satisfaction in spite of excess of expenditure over income. These inconsistencies may be interpreted as some indicators reflecting the discrepancies between farmers' aspiration level and realized consumption.

Table 18 shows the householder's average age, the average size of landholding, and the average scale of cultivation for those who expressed satisfaction with the present income (yes) and for those who did not (a). *t*-test was applied to see if the difference between two groups is statistically significant. In Demak and Gading, most respondents express their satisfaction regardless of their scale of landholding and cultivation.

This suggests that aspiration for consumption is not yet playing an important role in the value system of all the villagers there. A reverse situation is found in Klaten and Ayutthaya: most farmers are not satisfied with their present income regardless of their landholding and cultivation size. In these villages, aspiration for consumption seems important for all the villagers and almost all of them always feel the gap between aspiration and realized consumption. In Pathum Thani and Saraburi, the farmers cultivating a large acreage of land tend to be satisfied, whereas those cultivating a small area were not. In these two villages, where more income through more working hours is strongly desired as shown before but agriculture is a major source of income, the scale of cultivation rather than income is directly correlated with the farmers' psychological satisfaction or dissatisfaction.

The major forms of keeping surplus money in each village are shown in Table 19. Saving at bank is found only in Thai villages, reflecting the relatively developed stage of commercialization in rural Thailand. Keeping money in cash is found in all the villages of both countries except for Saraburi, which is not safe enough against robbers. The traditional method of saving in precious metal or stone is still important in Javanese villages. It is noteworthy that this form shows the highest percentage even in Klaten Village which is the most commercialized of three Javanese villages. Distrust in bank notes is still unforgettable among Javanese farmers who experienced a serious postwar inflation. Among Thai villages, this form of

Table 19. Methods of Keeping Surplus Money.

Method/Village	Klaten	Demak	Gading	Pathum Thani	Ayutthaya	Saraburi
1 Cash	○	◎	○	○	◎	—
2 Bank deposit	—	—	—	○	◎	◎
3 Precious metal and stone	◎	○	◎	—	—	○
4 Land	○	○	○	—	○	○
5 Cattle or fowls	—	○	◎	—	—	—
6 Paddy or dried cassava	○	◎	○	—	—	—
7 Boat or motor cycle	○	◎	—	—	—	—
8 Lending out	—	—	—	—	○	—
9 Mutual aid	—	—	—	—	—	—

Note: ◎ indicates high percentage; ○ means a holder or second owner.

Table 20. Three Most Important Purposes of Savings.

	(1)	(2)	(3)
Klaten	Better farming	Education	Children
Demak	Emergency	Old age	Children
Gading	Old age	Better farming	Emergency
Pathum Thani	Better farming	Education	Emergency
Ayutthaya	To buy land	Better farming	Emergency
Saraburi	Emergency	Better farming	To buy land/old age

savings is found only in Saraburi — the most remote village. Investment in land is practiced in all the villages of both countries except for Pathum Thani. The land around this village has become too expensive for the local people to invest in, because it is already the object of investment by urban speculators. Miscellaneous devices of investment such as raising cattle or fowl, keeping paddy or dried cassava, or buying boats or motorcycles to lend out are found mainly in Javanese villages.

Three important purposes of farmers' saving in each village are shown in Table 20. It is noteworthy that better farming and education are considered as the first two motivations in Klaten and Pathum Thani, the most advanced and commercialized village in each country.

5.2. *How to Become Rich*

Two related questions were asked to identify the factors for becoming rich: (1) about those interviewed themselves and (2) about those who were more successful than the interviewed. Villagers gave very pragmatic answers to both questions. The number of those who regarded "good faith or making merit" as a key to success was smaller than we expected in both countries. However, the difference between Thais and Javanese is of great interest. In Javanese villages, a number of respondents chose "working hard" and "luck" as the important factors in both questions, whereas in Thai villages, they chose "working hard" and "not to do anything luxurious". This difference suggests that pragmatic attitude is more prevalent among Thai villagers, while Javanese villagers feel dominated by something unmanageable by human effort. Particularly, in Klaten and Demak of Java, "not to do anything luxurious" is regarded as a more important factor by the interviewee himself, but "good judgment" as a cause of success for other successful villagers. In Ayutthaya Village of Thailand, on the other hand, only a small number of villagers marked "working hard" for other successful persons, and 30% of the respondents considered "inheritance" as the main factor of success.

To summarize the above observations on saving and success, we may say as follows. (1) Involvement in commercialization seems to cause an imbalance between income and expenditure. The advantageous physiographic conditions, therefore, is not directly combined with attitude toward more saving. (2) Yet, the modern way of economic thinking is more or less penetrating into the lives of villagers at advantageous location. (3) Thai and Javanese peasants show somewhat different ways of thinking concerning the factors to become rich. Thais are rather pragmatic, and Javanese are rather fatalistic. These conclusions can be observed by Tables 21 and 22 and summarized by Figure 4.

6. Some Cultural Premises

The final part of our interview was to ask villagers to give one or two proverbs or mottoes that came to their mind as those which they are fond of and therefore have a preference to follow. We did not force them to do so, but many villagers responded positively to this request. We could collect more expressions than we had expected. Previous questions were primarily concerned with the socio-economic behavior of farmers, but the proverbs

Table 21. Factors Related to Becoming Rich for the Interviewed Himself.

Factors		A	B	C	D	E	F
Village	Respondents	No. (%)	No. (%)	No. (%)	No. (%)	No. (%)	No. (%)
Klaten	30	15(50)	21(70)	4(13)	1(3)	7(23)	18(60)
Demak	33	20(61)	19(58)	1(3)	2(6)	1(3)	25(76)
Gading	30	22(73)	12(40)	2(7)	1(3)	3(10)	20(67)
Pathum Thani	49	38(78)	24(49)	17(35)	1(2)	5(10)	11(22)
Ayutthaya	33	24(73)	16(48)	10(30)	2(6)	4(12)	8(24)
Saraburi	41	27(66)	17(41)	3(7)	0	8(20)	16(39)

Notes: A = Working hard; B = not to do anything luxurious; C = education; D = good judgment; E = good faith or making merit; F = luck.

Table 22. Factors Related to Becoming Rich for the Most Successful Farmer in the Area.

Factors / Village/Respondent		A No. (%)	B No. (%)	C No. (%)	D No. (%)	E No. (%)	F No. (%)
Klaten	25	17(68)	8(32)	0	14(56)	6(24)	13(52)
Demak	31	22(71)	4(13)	0	5(16)	4(13)	27(87)
Gading	27	22(81)	11(41)	0	2(7)	7(26)	12(44)
Pathum Thani	35	27(77)	20(57)	13(37)	5(14)	0	7(20)
Ayutthaya	26	8(31)	11(42)	0	0	0	10(38)
Saraburi	37	29(78)	19(51)	4(11)	2(5)	8(22)	0

Notes: A = Working hard; B = not to do anything luxurious; C = education; D = good judgment; E = good faith or making merit; F = luck.

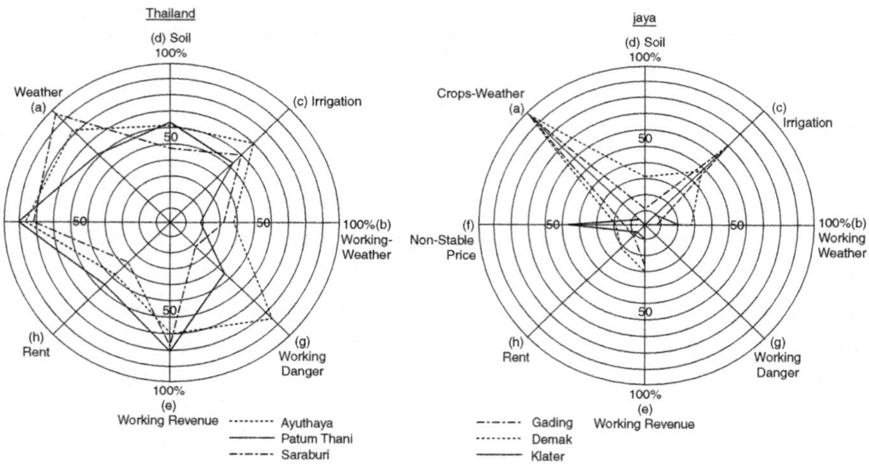

Fig. 4. The Most Important Factor to become Rich.

are hoped to reveal some aspects of the contemporary native culture, which have been inculcated in villagers' mind.

The rate of respondents to the total number sample is 96% (89 out of 93 persons) in Java and 61% (75 out of 123 persons) in Thailand. The differential ratio is significant at 1% level by χ^2 tests ($x^2 = 44.915 > x^2_{0.01} = 6.635$; $d.f. = 1$). This suggests that the verbal statements transmitted over generations play a more important role in Javanese villages than in Thai villages.

The expressions collected were originally written in vernacular languages, and then translated word for word into English by the native participants in each country. Rejecting free translation, we preferred this method because we wanted to avoid any bias which might enter the process of free translation, and also we wanted to define a particular meaning of each word in its context. In the analysis, similar expressions were grouped together into a single representative statement in such a way that each statement represents other similar verbal expressions. Thus, we acquired 25 statements from Thai villagers and 27 statements from Javanese villagers. Table 23 presents a list of these statements arranged under three categories of "working", "sociality" and "way of life". In order to make this arrangement,

Table 23. List of Proverbs and Mottoes Collected from Villagers.

Thailand	Java
[A: On Working]	
O Forbearing and hard work can overcome any obstacle. (P3 A6 S3)	O Ever health, everyday work hard. (D2, K1) Work hard and believe in God. (D1)
1. When you arc used to anything, you don't feel it is difficult. (Al) Perseverance, delight. (Al) Delight will make you better, (S1)	1. Health, safety is always prayer to God. (D1) Safety hygiene and eat enough. (D5) Work hard to want enough food, better home, to build a better living. (K5, D1, G5)
2. I want to be rich, even if I have to work hard. (AI, S1) Working in honest occupation. (P4) Good payment induces people to work hard. (Pl) Money is work, work is money. (S1)	2. If you need something, you have to do something too. (K4, G2); You have to do something hopeful. (K1) You have to do honestly. (K1); Living is for hard working. (G2) The man must receive according to his work, and then the man always has to exert oneself. (G1)
	3. We can only try, and God will make decision. (K1) Work hard and don't care for the result. (K1) Life is like a wheel. Sometimes it's up and sometimes it's down. (K1)

(Continued)

Table 23. (*Continued*)

Thailand	Java
[B: Sociality]	
O One can depend only on oneself. (P4 AI S3) Help each other; conscious of merit-demerit. (S1) 1. Don't give difficulties to other people. Rely on yourself. (Pl) 2. If you wouldn't help someone to do something, you shouldn't interrupt his work. (SI) Diligence, saving, good friend; right way of living. (Al)	O Unity makes strength, so you have to do mutual aid. 1. Come together, whether one can eat or not. It is very difficult for the people to move to other areas. (D3) Farmer is the foundation of the nation. (K1) Farmer must progress. (K1) To be a farmer, have to live simple life to be a good farmer. (G1) 2. Work together, shoulder by shoulder. (D2)
[C: Way of Life]	
O Be honest. (P5 A1) Merit making, one's luck and further life depends on one's past life. (P4 S1) Try to save quarters until one baht. (P5) 1. Good deed leads to good result. Evil deed leads to evil result. (P3 A2 S6) Must be honest. An honest man always have, a dishonest man is rich only for a while. (Al) Five Buddha teachings. (AI S1) 2. Take it when you have the opportunity. (PI AI S2) 3. If you have little money, you cut down your eating. (Pl) Don't spend more than the money you have. (Al)	O If you want to become rich, you must be economical. If you want to become clever (skilful), you must be diligent. (K3 G1) If you do a good thing, you will receive a good reward, but if you do a bad thing, you will receive a bad disaster. (K3 G1) 1. If some day you become rich don't forget when you were still poor, So don't be proud of your richness. (K1)
[D: Miscellaneous]	
One should beat children, just like one's cattle, because we love them. (P2) Do everything for my children. (Al) Follow the elders' foot step. (S1)	Living gladly, quiet, save. (D2) Happiness does not come from wealth (richness) or from social status. (K1) While ducking under water, drink water. (K1)

we first sorted all the statements into groupings by a key word in each statement and using it as a clue. Then, if every statement was assigned a core- or sub-status and all the statements in a group make up a meaningful set, we acknowledged the groupings as categories. Core statements are those which substantially explain the keyword in the statement. In Table 23, core statements are shown by O on the first line of the statements of each category. Underlined are the words that we treat as keywords; the capital letter next to the statement indicates the village where the expression was collected; and the number shows the frequency in which they were uttered by interviewees. From both statements, we tried to infer cultural premises, which would shape the behavior pattern of villagers.

In Thai villages, the most frequently stated theme on working is, "forbearing and hard work can overcome any obstacle". As sub-statements imply, working is regarded in terms of money, and it should be in honest occupation. Work as such, however, is "hard in nature" since it is something for a man to "forbear". But one should conceal the hardship in a mental state of "delight". These cultural premises on working display an emphasis put on occupational conditionality and self-control of emotion. In contrast, in Javanese villages, work is valued somewhat for its own sake, not as a measure for getting money as in Thai villages. The main theme is "one should work hard everyday", and "health" is valued for this purpose. Furthermore, working has culturally a specific value as shown in a statement: "one has to always exert oneself".

The most frequently stated theme on sociality in Thailand is: "one can depend on oneself", which implies belief in self-reliance. This does not mean that "mutual help" is devalued, but on the contrary, it constitutes one of crucial elements of social organization both in actual and ideal levels. These two premises may seem contradictory at a first glance, but in fact, they limit each other so as to make a good balance. Thus, as is shown in sub-statements, at occasions one should help each other in such a way as it reinforces his self-support, but not in such a way as it gives him any importunity, interference, or interruption. This is the way that villagers are getting along with others. Thus, we may assume that Thai villagers are more individualistically oriented and to each individual social entity is felt as a network of dyadic relations which extend centering upon him. Javanese theme is contrasted with the above Thai view of individual existence in society. "Unity makes strength so you have to do mutual aid (*gotong-royong*)" is a favorite statement of Javanese villagers. "Mutual aid" is valued because it brings people unity or force which emerges from being together and doing something shoulder by shoulder. In this sense, although dyadic relations may be still one of characteristics of Javanese social organization as it is for Thais, Javanese villagers are more socially oriented and are likely to perceive themselves as a social group to be called farmers.

Figures 5 and 6 schematically summarizes their ideas on working.

Figures 7 and 8 schematically summarizes sociality in Thailand and Java.

One important difference between Thai and Javanese cultural premises concerns with notion of "luck". To the mind of Thai villagers, any creature, whether it is an animal, human being, or super natural being, can live a lengthy cycle of lives. One's good luck in the present life is considered as

(Buddhist Teaching)
→ (Honest occupation)
→(Working)→(Money)
↓
(Hard)
↓
(Perseverance)
↓
(Delight)

Fig. 5. Working (Thailand).

Pray to God
↑
Safety, hygiene, eat enough → Ever health → (Work hard)
→ (Need something, do something hopefully)
↓
(Don't care the result, Life is like a wheel)
↓
(Living is for hard working)

Pray to God
↓
(Believe in God decision)
↓
(Enough food, better living)
↓
(Always, exert oneself.)

Fig. 6. Working (Java).

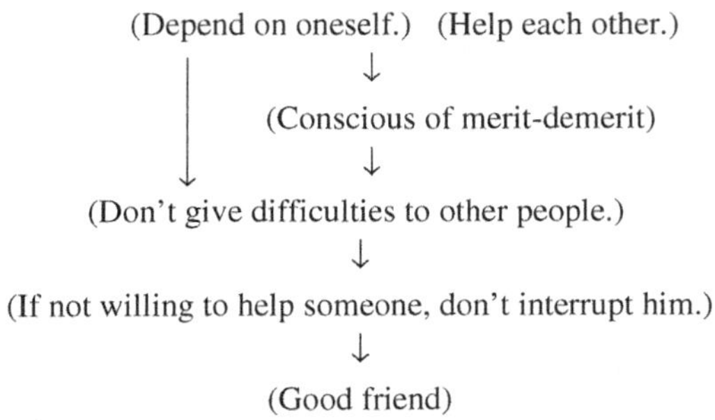

Fig. 7. Sociality (Thailand).

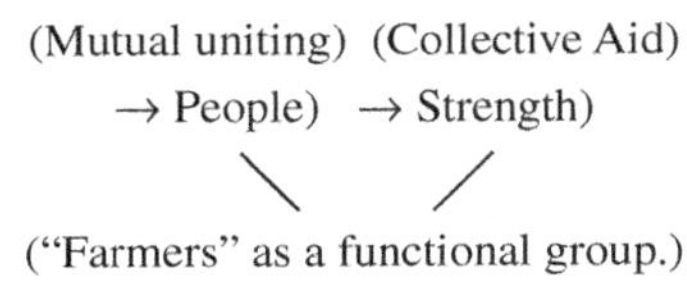

Fig. 8. Sociality (Java).

a result of what he did in his past life, and his good luck in the next life depends on what he does in this life. On the other hand, for the Javanese villagers, luck is endowed by the judgment of God, so long as we rely on a villager's single statement saying "only try and God will make decision". Another interpretation of luck is that the traditional Javanese society was hierarchically ordered so well that an individual's effort was not easily rewarded in terms of higher economic status. In either way, however, to wait for luck without doing anything is devalued, and "one should do something if he wants to have something". These cultural characteristics in Thailand and Java are summarized in Table 24.

Appendix. Questionnaire Schedules

I. *Our Design and Practice of the Surveys in Southeast Asia and Japan*

The empirical findings reported in this chapter were based on the surveys conducted in Thailand, Java, and Indonesia. Furthermore, a similar survey was conducted at two villages in Niigata and Shiga prefectures, Japan for comparitive purposes. The synthetic report in Japanese was published in

Table 24. Cultural Characteristics of Thai and Javanese Farmers.

Thailand	Java
[Working]	[Working]
Occupational conditionality to working.	Cultural acceleration for working.
Direct relationship between money and working.	Result is a decision of God.
Basically, work is hard.	Working itself has a value.
Self-control of emotion.	Body conditions for continuous working.
[Sociality]	[Sociality]
Individually oriented (self-reliance).	Socially group oriented.
lisping other's self-support.	Mutual aid to get strength.
Dyadic relationship.	Collective strength.

1975 as *Rice-growing and Farmers*: S. Ichimura (ed.).[2] The three villages in Thailand and Java were chosen as representative ones in the areas, and the farming — exclusively or almost exclusively — households were chosen among those with male heads of age around 25–59. Choice was made at random from a list of farmers households prepared in each village by the village head. The original questionnaire schedule was prepared in English first, and then translated into Thai, Javanese (not Indonesian), and Japanese for Japan. Questions were carefully formulated as much as possible by referring to some quantitative aspects of farming to avoid any misunderstanding. Some questions were modified particularly for specific alternative choices in each country mainly to suit the local conditions. In addition, a face sheet contained some questions about the farmer's household: family members' age, schooling, occupations, owned land, and cultivating acreage.

As for practical interview, in Southeast Asian villages, two students asked the farmers directly in local dialect (in Javanese in Java) while one native researcher and another Japanese researcher accompanied them. In Japan, one or two researchers visited the home of each interviewee and explained the purposes and the contents of the studies and left the

[2]It was *Ine to Nomin*: Center for Southeast Asian Studies, Kyoto University. Contributors were Hayao Fukui, Koichi Takaya, Yoshihiro Tsubouchi, Yoshio Asano, and Koichi Mizuno. It was more comprehensive in some aspects than the chapter here and refers to the differences in rice-growing farmers between Southeast Asia and Japan.

questionnaire schedule with them, which were collected later. Both in Southeast Asia and Japan, the rate of returns was always more that 90% in any village.

Meeting with interviewees was carefully arranged in each country. In Thailand, a village head took the interviewers to each sample farmer's house and explained the purposes to every interviewee. In Java, each farmer was called to assemble in a meeting house in the village, where the village head explained the purposes. In Japan, notification was often made by wired broadcasting and mailed to each sample household. Intermediation of village heads may have caused some semi-official influence but interviewers tried to avoid it as much as possible.

II. *Questions*

Q1. Which year in the past five years did you get the worst harvest?

[Year]

Q2. How much was the harvest then? [Paddy kg/10a]

Q3. Which year in the past five years did you get the best harvest?

[Year]

Q4. How much was the harvest then? [Paddy kg/10a]

Q5. What caused the bad harvest? Please check any reasons.

a. Flood	Yes	f. Rats	Yes
b. Drought	Yes	g. Cold weather	Yes
c. Insects	Yes	h. Sunshine shortage	Yes
d. Disease	Yes	i. Others	Specify
e. Birds	Yes		

Q6. What cause was the most serious one?____________________

Q7. Did you take any measures to overcome the bad harvest?

② No

② Yes, ; specify

(In case, you did something,)

Q8. Was it effective? [No] [Yes]

Q9. Do you know any better measures now than before?

[No] [Yes]

If yes. Please specify.______________________________

Q10. How do you evaluate the quality of soil in your paddy field?

Very bad | Bad | Average | Good | Very good

Q11-(1). How do you evaluate the irrigation system around your paddy field?

Very bad | Bad | Average | Good | Very good

Q11-(2). How do you evaluate the drainage system around your paddy field?

Very bad | Bad | Average | Good | Very good

Q12-(1). How do you evaluate the precipitation around your paddy field?

Very bad | Bad | Average | Good | Very good

Q12-(2). Which influences more on the harvest around here, temperature or precipitation?

[a. Temperature] [b. Precipitation]

Q13. Which variety of rice seeds did you use this year?

[1.] [2.] [3.]

Q14. In what year did you use those seeds? If more than one, choose only the newest one. (Q15 and 16 too.) [Year]

Q15. In what year did you get the information about that variety?

[Year]

Q16. What motivates you to adopt that variety?

- a. Anything new is worth trying
- b. Agricultural cooperative recommended
- c. Having seen the success of neighbors
- d. Learning the success in nearby villages
- e. Official specialists recommended
- f. Others: Specify______________________

Q17. How do you respond if the local government or cooperatives recommend a new variety?

- a. I adopt before anybody else
- b. I adopt if somebody else succeeds.
- c. I am not interested in it.
- d. Others: Specify______________________

Q18. About working and income, which of the following do you prefer?

- a. Income remains the same, but working hours are less.
- b. Income increases but working hours increase also.

Q19. Do you want to have some second job in your slack seasons?

- a. I already have a second job.
- b. Yes, I want.
- c. No, I don't.

Q20. How do you evaluate rice-growing agriculture in comparison with other occupations?

a. In terms of Income:	1. Good	2. Not good
b. In terms of labor:	1. Hard	2. Not hard

Q21-(1). Do you feel any suffering in rice-growing from the following items?

a. Income depends so much on harvest or weather.

1. We suffer	2. We don't

b. We must work hard on very hot or cold days.

1. We suffer	2. We don't

c. Irrigation

1. We suffer	2. We don't

d. Land

1. We suffer	2. We don't

e. Hard labor but poor revenue

1. We suffer	2. We don't

f. Crop prices are unstable.

1. We suffer	2. We don't

g. Danger in farming labor

1. We suffer	2. We don't

h. Farm rent is too high.

1. We suffer	2. We don't

Q21-(2). Do you have any other items from which farmers suffer?

Specify ______________________________

Q22. Who do you think is happier, farmers or factory workers?

a.	Farmers
b.	Factory workers
c.	Cannot tell

Q23. Why do you think so?

a. Revenue	
b. Freedom	
c. Work conditions	: Specify ______________________
d. Others	: Specify ______________________

Q24. Do you have enough revenue to save? [1. Yes.] [2. No.]

Q25. In what forms do you keep your savings?

a. Cash	e. Land
b. Deposits	f. Shares
c. Precious metals	
d. Precious stones	

Q26. For what purposes have you saved?

a. Education	f. Preparation for sickness
b. Marriage	g. Prepare for calamities
c. Other family ceremonies	h. For the future of children
d. Farm improvements	i. For possible change of jobs
e. Preparation for old age	j. Others

Q27-(1). If you could unexpectedly earn 1 million Yen, how would you spend it? Prepare a budget for your use.

____

____

Q27-(2). If the unexpected earning is 10 million Yen, how would you spend it? Prepare a budget.

____

Q28. Are you satisfied with the present level of revenue?

[1. No.] [2. Yes.]

Q29. What do you think is important for a farmer like you to become rich?

[a. Work hard] [d. Judge sensitively the benefit and loss of activity]

[b. Not be too luxurious.] [e. Hold religious creeds]

[c. Be well-educated] [f. Good luck]

Q30. Can you name a very well-off farmer in this neighborhood?

____

Q31. Can you select the main two reasons why he has been so successful?

a. Work very hard	d. Judgment is sensible and quick
b. Not too luxurious	e. Holds firm religious creeds
c. Well-educated	f. Was lucky

Q32. Do you believe that you too can do the same as he did?

1. Yes, I can
2. No, I cannot

Why not? State the reasons. ____________________

____

Q33. Please quote the proverbs, mottoes, maxim or sayings that you like.

____

____

Chapter 13

Japanese-style Management in Asia — Introduction*

1. Sequential Relationship to Our Earlier Study of Japanese Firms in Asia

This research was undertaken as a sequel to our earlier works on Japanese enterprises in Southeast Asia. It constituted part of a comprehensive project on Culture Conflicts in Asia.[1] The main objectives were first to collect the observations of the managers of Japanese joint ventures or subsidiaries in Southeast Asia and analyze the issues raised by anti-Japan demonstrations then. The first method used was mainly interviews and questionnaire survey of the managers who had experiences of managing the joint ventures in Asia but were back to Japan. The study was perhaps the first of its kind in the sense that the companies chosen were a systematic random sample representing the population, and the questions were carefully prepared to analyze the experiences and behavior of Japanese enterprises and their managers. The questions covered the managers' personal lives in addition

---

*This was published in *Southeast Asian Studies*, Vol. 22, No. 4, March 1984.

[1]This project on Culture Conflicts covered all the aspects — cultural, political, and economic — of conflicts or accords arising from past and contemporary contact between the different cultures of various races and nations. In conducting survey work abroad, we have greatly benefited from the unusually generous cooperation of many agents, their staff and many other kind individuals in all of the Asian countries covered by this study. We all consider ourselves under a debt of deep gratitude to their kindness, without which this research would have never been accomplished.

The participants in our project this time include not only those who have written the papers in this special issue of *Southeast Asian Studies* but also several other scholars: Kuniyoshi Urabe (Kobe University), Takenori Inoki (Osaka University), and Hideichiro Nakano (Kwansei Gakuin University). All of us wish to express our hearty gratitude for the generous support of the Kansai Economic Research Center, Osaka and the Ministry of Education for this research project over a period of five years.

to business matters. The main findings were reported in *Nihon Kigyo in Asia* (*Japanese Firms in Asia*), edited by S. Ichimura, Toyokeizai Shimpo-sha, Tokyo, 1980 and its English summary: "Japanese Firms in Asia" was published in *the Japanese Economic Studies*, 1982.

One serious criticism of our first report was that it did not include the responses of local staff to the Japanese-style management and Japanese managers or families. The local state of affairs was observed only from the Japanese side. The same situations might have looked quite different from the viewpoint of natives. No doubt, in order to analyze the relations or conflicts between Japanese firms or businessmen and local staff, the opinions of local staff must be taken into account. However, it is very difficult to obtain such observations with the approval of management and still minimize bias. The primary motivation of this research was to remedy this shortcoming of our earlier study. For this purpose, two questionnaires[2] were prepared; one addressed to top managers, who are usually Japanese, and another addressed to middle managers who are exclusively natives of the countries where the plant is located.

Another important comment was that the business environment and practices in the five ASEAN countries differ from those in the three East Asian countries that might point up new issues. Since Japanese direct investment in Korea, Taiwan, and Hong Kong is no less important than that in ASEAN, we decided to include the three newly industrializing countries in the present study. Southeast Asia here must be interpreted in the broad sense to include the ASEAN plus 3.

In Southeast Asia Japanese, capital constitutes less than 50% of total capital in most joint ventures so that their presidents are often non-Japanese. However, actual management of these companies is often entrusted to Japanese vice-presidents. Our questionnaire to top managers was distributed, therefore, to Japanese vice-president as well as president in each company except in South Korea, where Korean presidents actually manage the joint ventures. Therefore, two kinds of questionnaires to top-managers were prepared; one in Korean, addressed to Korean presidents

[2]In preparing the questionnaires, Prof. Kuniyoshi Urabe made the greatest contribution, which all the members of the team acknowledge with gratitude. Those two questionnaires are appended at the end of this chapter.

and another in Japanese addressed to Japanese top-managers, which was the same as the one used in all the other countries.

The companies usually chose the middle managers who received and filled out questionnaires but in most cases, they mailed the questionnaires directly to the local offices that generously accepted our request for cooperation in sending out and receiving the questionnaires. This approach certainly produced a certain bias toward the choice of pro-company employees but, after examining the processed results of their responses, we do not believe that this bias is strong enough to invalidate any fair interpretation of our findings.[3] Our findings must, however, be interpreted carefully, and our interpretations may be open to criticism. It would be impossible to conduct this kind of questionnaire survey without the cooperation of enterprises and their top management. This was just about, as far as we could go in this research.[4]

2. The Japanese Style of Management and Labor Relations

In this research project, we narrowed the coverage of the survey and interviews and focused on the Japanese style of management and labor relations to enrich our analysis of Japanese businessmen's behavior. However, the questionnaires were designed not only to obtain first-hand knowledge of Japanese management but also to learn about the responses

[3]The offices that cooperated with us in distributing the questionnaires were: (Indonesia) Japanese Overseas Enterprises Ass., c/o JETR0, Jakarta; (Singapore) Japanese Overseas Enterprises Ass., c/o JETR0, Singapore; (Malaysia) JETR0, Kuala Lumpur; (Thailand) Japanese Overseas Enterprises Ass., c/o JETRO, Bangkok; (The Philippines) Japanese Chamber of Commerce, Manila; (Hong Kong) Japanese Chamber of Commerce, (Taiwan) Japanese Chamber of Commerce, Taipei; (Korea) Japanese Chamber of Commerce, Korean Chamber of Commerce, Korean Institute of Economics and Technology, Seoul, and Japanese Chamber of Commerce, Pusan. To all of them, we are most grateful.

[4]To reduce the degree of bias, we requested the top manager to distribute two or three questionnaires to "average" middle managers, and also in the design of questions we included some checking. For example, respondents were asked, instead of replying: "satisfied" or "dissatisfied," to reply "very satisfied," "a little satisfied," or "dissatisfied." The intention was that those who chose a little satisfied would be regarded as really dissatisfied but not daring to say so. When we reported our preliminary findings to top managers in several countries, they were often surprised by their subordinates' opinions frank, understanding and even critical. They were all very appreciative of this research.

of local staff to Japanese management practices in Southeast Asia. The prevailing style of business management in ASEAN countries and Hong Kong has been English or American. The so-called Japanese style of management drew attention, first in the United States business community and then in Europe, in the early postwar years. But in Southeast Asia, where Japanese companies began direct investment around 1960 which became significant in the 1970s, their style of management has gradually permeated into the business community through the activities of Japanese joint-ventures only in very recent years. The findings of our studies, therefore, may be revealing the initial experiences of and responses to Japanese management in Southeast Asia. In Korea and Taiwan, however, the business environment is very different. The fact that some businessmen in Korea and Taiwan would consider the so-called Japanese-style management to be, rather, the Asian-style management, proves the general practice of similar management styles.

The definition of the Japanese style of management is, however, not common to all students of business management. For this study, we simply adopted the following characteristics of Japanese enterprises as the definition and tried to investigate their adaptation to business conditions in Southeast Asian countries.[5]

(1) *Lifetime commitment or employment:* management is based on the assumption that once employees are properly employed, they commit themselves to their company for the rest of their working lives, so that stable employment is taken for granted and job rotation or on-the-job training becomes routine.

---

[5]There are many works on Japanese management. References may be found in (1) Urabe, Kuniyoshi: *Nihon Teki Keiei-o Kangaeru* (Consider Japanese Management), Chuokeizai-sha, 1981; (2) Ouchi, W. G.: *Theory Z*, Addison Wesley, 1981; (3) Urabe, Kuniyoshi, and Omura, Kihei: Nihon-teki Roshi-Kankei-no Tankyu (*Inquiry into Japanese Style Labor Relations*), Chuokeizai-sha, 1983.

An international comparison of Japanese and American management systems was undertaken using a questionnaire survey similar to ours by four management scientists and published as: Kagono, T., Nonaka, I., Sakakibara, K. and Okumura, A.: *Nichi-bei Kigyo-no Keiei Hikaku* (*Comparison of Management Systems in Japanese and American Enterprises*), Nihon keizai Shimbun-sha, 1983.

(2) *Seniority system*: seniority-based promotion and wages/salaries are widely adopted as essential parts of lifetime employment. They combine not only seniority in terms of age but also graduation year and level of schooling. At the same time, it should be remembered that evaluation of personal merit is strictly practiced in Japanese-style management.
(3) *Humanistic principles*: human relations in the company are greatly stressed and regarded almost like those in the family or local clans in feudal times, with common objectives. Thus, the objectives of the company are often set by the founder and emphatically taught to employees. Mensualization — which means to reduce the status difference between managers and workers — is accepted as a matter of principle. It is quite common, therefore, for example, for even section chiefs to work with their subordinates in one large room. Welfare benefits within the company are strongly emphasized.
(4) *Groupism*: group decision-making, group responsibility, the "ringi" system, and flexible management are well-known now all over the world as characteristics of Japanese management. They constitute some aspects of groupism.

First, we studied the actual practice of Japanese management in Southeast Asia via top-managers' replies to our questionnaire. Then, we investigated the local middle managers' responses to Japanese management in the same way. The number of replies in each country in our survey is shown in Table 1.

These answers were processed by a computer's program SPSS (Statistical Package for Social Sciences) to compute averages or totals depending on the questions. The processed results are interpreted together with the results of the interviews conducted by each author in the country for which

Table 1. Interviewed Top Executives and Middle Managers

	In	Si	Ma	Th	Phil.	HK	Tw	Kr[a]
Top executives	67	49	52	58	40	44	58	59 (40)
Middle managers	129	210	82	90	134	36	90	83

[a]Top executives figure for Korea in parentheses is the number of Korean executives.

he is responsible. The details of the findings may be left to the country reports.[6] Emphasis here is placed on the interpretation of the survey findings in relation to institutional and cultural factors in the countries studied. An overall statistical analysis of these findings will be undertaken as a separate research project in the future.

3. Some Remarks on International Comparison

A general picture of the business conditions of Japanese joint ventures or subsidiaries can be seen in Appendices I and II, which summarizes the findings in comparative tableaux. Some brief remarks are offered here to facilitate a comparative understanding of our survey findings.

The founding year of a representative joint venture is in the early 1970s, so that most of them are only about 10 to 15 years old. The scale of operation in terms of the number of employees is about 400, smaller in Hong Kong and bigger in Korea. Since enterprises with less than 300 employees are regarded as medium or small enterprises in Japan, these joint ventures are not very big in scale. The Japanese share of paid-up capital is above 50% except in the Philippines, where regulations on foreign share is more restrictive. Indonesia and Thailand have rather restrictive regulations, and they have become more so in recent years. The leading role of Japanese managers, however, seems more important than capital share implies, partly because the financial assistance given to the companies is often arranged through the Japanese managers.

The percentage of parts procured locally reflects the degree of balanced industrial development in each country. It is particularly low in the Philippines and Indonesia, where manufacturing industries are not highly developed yet. Japanese managers are dissatisfied in these countries and in

---

[6]An interim report is available: *Nikkei Goben-Kigyo no Keiei to Roshi-Kankei* (*Management and Labor Relations in Japanese Joint-Ventures*), Kansai Economic Research Center, Osaka, September, 1983. Its contents are: (1) Tomita, Teruhiko, "Japanese management and labor relations in the Philippines". (2) Urabe, Kuniyoshi, "Japanese management and labor relations in Singapore". (3) Nakano, Hideichiro, "Japanese management in Malaysia". (4) Imaoka, Hideki, "Japanese management and labor relations in Malaysia". (5) Ichimura, Shinichi, "An international comparison" (6) Questions and Answers; Appendix: Questionnaire and Survey Findings.

Korea. Manufacturing industries in Korea seem rather highly dependent on imported intermediate products, in spite of the development of some highly technical industries.

As for basic management policy, "localization" has been adopted in all the countries, but more so in Thailand, Malaysia, Indonesia, and Korea. The actual practice of Japanese management, as revealed in the answers to the question of promoting Japanese management (Question 18), was in general least emphasized in the Philippines and the most comprehensive in Korea. There are significant differences among the countries with respect to which aspects of Japanese management are emphasized. In every country, employment stabilization and management, philosophy and objectives are most promoted, but there are some differences with regard to the third most important aspects: Philippines (human relations), Singapore (human relations), Malaysia (human relations), Thailand (seniority-based wages and human relations), Indonesia (seniority-based wages and human relations), Hong Kong (human relations), Taiwan (human relations), and Korea (human relations).

Emphasis on human relations can be clearly seen, and the percentage of companies which emphasized these seems to reflect, more or less, the extent to which human relations are seen to be problematic; thus, from highest to lowest: Singapore, Taiwan, Korea, Indonesia, Hong Kong, Malaysia, Thailand, and the Philippines. Problems with partners (Question 17) are most frequent in Korea, Taiwan, Indonesia, and Thailand in that order. Similarly, the problems with unions are most frequent in Thailand, Korea, and Indonesia. Thus, studies on partnerships and labor relations are particularly important for these four countries.

The responses of local middle managers to Japanese management differ significantly from one country to another. Negative answers to the questions on working relations with their company (Questions 15 and 16 in Questionnaire II) for example, reveal as in Table 2.

It may be surprising to find that definitely more than half of middle managers in Korea, Taiwan, and Hong Kong are not very proud of working in Japanese joint ventures, whereas the converse is true in the ASEAN countries. Nevertheless, there does not seem to be any significant gap in the commitment of middle managers between the ASEAN and East Asian countries.

Table 2. Middle Managers are Not Proud of Nor Committed to Japanese Co's.

	HK	Tw	Kr	In	Si	Ma	Th	Ph
1. % of middle managers not very proud of working for their co's.	72	69	60	39	32	25	18	18
2. % of middle managers not feeling committed to the co's.	39	27	28	49	40	25	32	30

Table 3. Barriers between Japanese Managers and Local Staff.

	Ph	SI	Ma	Th	IN	HK	Tw	Kr
1. Language	1	1	1	1	1	1	1	2
2. Value difference (2, 3, 4)	2	4	4	2	4	3	2	1
3. Non-social (6, 7)	4	2	2	4	3	2	4	4
4. Business decision-making (5, 8)	3	3	3	3	2	4	3	3

As for barriers between Japanese managers and local staff (Question 20), the language barrier comes first in all countries except for Korea, where differences in customs, values, and management geared to head offices in Japan are equally important. The order of importance in all countries is shown in Table 3.

These differences must be explained not just by the cultural differences between Japan and other Asian countries but, more precisely, by the differences in cultural gaps between Japan and each of Asian countries, or the differences in mutual modes of social interaction. For example, the cultural gap between Japan and Indonesia is not the same as that between Japan and Korea. Japanese behave toward Indonesians differently from the way they do toward Koreans. Such careful analyses remain for future research.

The original questionnaires in eight countries are reproduced here as Appendices with the findings to show the bases of our arguments.

Appendix I. Questionnaires to the Top Japanese Managers.

Questionnaire	Ph	Sin	Mal	Th	Ind	HK	Tw	Kr
1. Respondent's name _______ Age __	42.3[a]	43.6	43.5	44.8	48.5	43.6	48.4	48.3
2. Co's name _______ Respondent's position								
3. Co's address First Year of operation	1976	1974.6	1971	1969.7	1974.1	1971.8	1970.3	1972.1
4. President's name								
5. Amount of capital	30,029[b]	18,878	25,030	45,591	3,990	2,947	2,039	19,672
6. Japanese equity share (%)	49.5	87.1	62.4	50.9	60.7	95.4	74.8	62.8
7. Products a. b. c. d								
8. Destinations a. b. c. d.								
9. Business Performance	Ph	Sin	Mal	Th	Ind	HK	Tw	Kr
1977 1978 1979 1980								
Sales	93,834[c]	34,559	47,887	531,900		19,914	9,828	22,596
Profit/sales (%)	8.6	7.4	5.5	5.0		21.3	6.0	8.8
10. Employees Total	454	380	374	394	434.8	155.1	443.4	671.7
Racial composition a. Japanese	3.8	7	9.4	8.7	7.4	7.3	5.3	3.1
b. Chinese	0.9	267	80	77	5.4	143.6	447	
c. Indigenous	359	112	260	374	387			614.6
d. Others	0.2	73	66	75	10.9	10.0		
(*Management Policy*)								
11. Composition of Board Members (number)								
Japanese Local Total								
Full time, Part time, Total								

(*Continued*)

Appendix I. (*Continued*)

Questionnaire	Ph	Sin	Mal	Th	Ind	HK	Tw	Kr
12. Is localization your management policy? Yes: _______	28.5[d]	33	39	42	53	28	61	46
No _______ (Our policy is the same anywhere)	8.5	11	6	5	9	6	17	8
13. Up to what high level are locals promoted? Personnel manager/ Manager/Supervisor (in number)	1.9/13.1/ 31.6	1.4/9.1/ 23.4	2.1/7.5/ 14.1	1.3/7.6/ 23.9	1.5/8.0/ 17.1	0.9/0.9/ 8.9	1.9/6.8/ 7.2	
Japanese	0.6/2.8/ 0.8	0.8/4.9/ 1.5	1.0/3.2/ 1.3	1.0/3.3/ 0.4	0.4/3.4/ 0.6	1.0/1.1/ 4.2	0.6/1.8/ 1.3	0.5/1.3/ 1.3[e]
14. Please give the information for employees.	Ph	Sg	My	Th	In	HK	Tw	Kr
1. Average years of employment	4.0	2.5	4.1	6.9	4.8	4.5	5.2	5.0
2. Attendance rate	94.2	95.3	93.5	94.7	94.5	97.5	95.8	
3. Separation rate (per month)	1.5	4.9	3.1	0.8	1.5	2.1	3.1	3.9
4. Average salaries (managers)	3,518[f]	1,691	1,396	12,370	355.1	7.3	25.2	617.6
5. Average salaries (workers)	1,135	491	390	3,951	75.9	2.8	11.3	208.6
15. What % of parts are locally procured?								
1. Percentage	39.4	46.7	47.2	50.4	39.3	43.5	50.0	48.0
2. Satisfied	12	12	22	21	18	10	34	15
3. Not satisfied	22	31	30	22	42	2	43	34

(*Continued*)

Appendix I. (*Continued*)

Questionnaire	Ph	Sin	Mal	Th	Ind	HK	Tw	Kr
16. Policy on Transfer of Technology and Management?	Ph	Sg	My	Th	In	HK	Tw	Kr
1. We recruit technicians and managerial staff from outside.	12 (27)[g]	12 (27)	14 (27)	12 (23)	10 (16)	7 (21)	18 (22)	15 (26)
2. We train them within the company.	41 (91)	41 (91)	44 (84)	52 (90)	59 (94)	27 (82)	79 (95)	53 (95)
3. We have an engineering department.	11 (24)	16 (36)	6 (11)	8 (14)	6 (10)	7 (21)	28 (34)	18 (32)
4. We have a research and development department	6 (13)		3 (6)	4 (7)	4 (6)		14 (17)	13 (24)
5. Others		3 (7)	5 (10)	3 (6)	3 (5)	1 (3)	7 (8)	3 (6)

Questionnaire	Ph			Sg			My			Th			In			HK			Tw			Kr		
17. Have you had troubles with your partner on management? How serious? a: serious, b: small, c: none	a	b	c	a	b	c	a	b	c	a	b	c	a	b	c	a	b	c	a	b	c	a	b	c
1. Personnel policy		18	22		2	16	1	7	27		12	36	2	17	37		1	6	4	17	42		15	29
2. Promotion	1	12	24			18		6	27		9	39		15	40		1	6	2	13	48		13	32
3. Salaries	2	13	24	1	3	14		7	26		10	38	1	14	41		2	5	2	14	46	3	8	34
4. Bonus and welfare	1	11	26		2	16		3	30	1	5	42	2	8	44		2	5	1	12	48	1	8	36
5. Remunerations to directors		4	21			17	1	3	27	2	2	42	3	6	43		2	5		3	52	2	6	31
6. Dividends		6	28			16	2	4	21	2	13	31		9	45		2	5		11	45	1	11	28
7. Investment plans	3	12	13		2	15	1	7	23	2	10	34	1	16	37		2	5	4	9	43	2	12	31
8. Technology transfer		8	29			16		2	30	1	10	35		11	43		2	5	3	11	40	3	15	26

(*Continued*)

Appendix I. (*Continued*)

Questionnaire	Ph	Sin	Mal	Th	Ind	HK	Tw	Kr
9. Sales policy	1 13 24	1 16	2 8 23	3 9 3	4 13 42	1 5	6 16 37	1 11 34
10. Pricing policy	2 8 26	1 16	1 4 26	2 10 34	1 11 44	2 5	5 14 41	1 12 33
11. Purchasing policy	9 26	17	2 1 30	3 8 36	3 8 42	2 5	2 10 46	1 13 31
12. Others (explain others.)	7 17	9	1 19	4 28	3 5 26	4	2 5 30	4 3 14
18. Which features of Japanese management did you adopt?	Ph	Sg	My	Th	In	HK	Tw	Kr
1. Employment stability	23 (50%)	41 (81)	34 (71)	36 (64)	50 (79)	36 (75)	66 (81)	37 (68)
2. Seniority-based wages	15 (33%)	24 (48)	22 (46)	27 (48)	40 (64)	18 (45)	37 (45)	33 (61)
3. Seniority-based promotion	13 (28%)	19 (38)	17 (35)	16 (29)	30 (48)	10 (24)	28 (34)	28 (52)
4. Job-rotation	18 (29%)	23 (46)	16 (33)	14 (25)	21 (33)	8 (20)	32 (39)	20 (37)
5. Emphasis on management philosophy and objectives	33 (72%)	28 (56)	29 (90)	36 (54)	39 (62)	15 (37)	68 (83)	38 (70)
6. Little dependence on job manual (flexible management)	16 (35%)	26 (52)	11 (23)	12 (21)	23 (37)	13 (32)	31 (38)	21 (39)
7. Group decision-making	20 (43%)	22 (52)	19 (40)	15 (27)	23 (37)	9 (22)	26 (32)	24 (44)
8. Group responsibility	8 (17%)	9 (18)	7 (15)	5 (9)	17 (27)	2 (5)	18 (22)	14 (26)
9. Emphasis on smooth human relations	21(46%)	37 (74)	25 (52)	27 (48)	40 (64)	25 (31)	58 (71)	36 (67)
10. Ringi	15 (33%)	10 (20)	8 (17)	11 (20)	16 (25)	8 (20)	35 (43)	35 (65)
11. Minimization of status differences	13 (28%)	24 (48)	14 (29)	6 (11)	14 (22)	8 (20)	25 (20)	17 (32)
12. Others		3	4	1	4	16	4	3

(*Continued*)

Appendix I. (*Continued*)

Questionnaire	Ph	Sin	Mal	Th	Ind	HK	Tw	Kr
19. Which measures for employment stabilization, did you adopt?	Ph	Sg	My	Th	In	HK	Tw	Kr
1. Better welfare facilities	18 (42)	18 (37)	22 (47)	26 (46)	40 (60)	7 (17)	43 (51)	29 (50)
2. A pension scheme	11 (26)	3 (6)	14 (30)	24 (43)	17 (25)	11 (26)	37 (44)	14 (24)
3. Seniority-based wages	24 (30)	23 (47)	27 (57)	32 (57)	46 (69)	25 (60)	39 (46)	37 (64)
4. Compensation for long service	16 (37)	34 (69)	24 (51)	33 (57)	34 (51)	10 (24)	56 (66)	43 (74)
5. A scheme to help employees buy houses	3 (7)	1 (2)	5 (11)	2 (3)	17 (25)	5 (12)	1 (1)	8 (14)
6. Job rotation	11 (26)	19 (39)	11 (23)	7 (12)	15 (22)	9 (21)	21 (25)	15 (26)
7. Internal promotion	30 (70)	38 (78)	40 (85)	34 (61)	51 (76)	26 (61)	55 (65)	41 (71)
8. Smooth human workers-managers relations	25 (58)	33 (67)	26 (55)	31 (55)	43 (64)	23 (55)	55 (65)	35 (60)
9. Small group activities	12 (28)	24 (49)	11 (23)	11 (20)	17 (25)	5 (12)	37 (44)	32 (55)
10. Continuous training	28 (65)	26 (53)	23 (49)	19 (34)	43 (64)	12 (29)	51 (60)	37 (64)
11. Efficiency reward wages	16 (37)	15 (30)	13 (28)	16 (29)	17 (25)	11 (26)	23 (27)	11 (19)
12. Others	3 (7)	2 (4)	5 (10)		6 (9)	1 (2)	5 (6)	3 (5)
20. Which measures of small group activities did you adopt to improve productivity?	Ph	Sg	My	Th	In	HK	Tw	Kr
1. Suggestion scheme	29(85)	24 (50)	14 (50)	24 (44)	30 (73)	10 (30)	54 (79)	49 (91)
2. Zero defect movement	3 (9)	3 (6)	5 (18)	4 (7)	2 (5)	1 (3)	4 (6)	3 (6)
3. QC circles	16 (47)	22 (46)	17 (61)	25 (46)	12 (29)	5 (15)	45 (60)	43 (80)
4. Others	1 (3)	4 (8)	8 (2*)	2 (4)	9 (22)	2 (6)	8 (12)	4 (7)

(*Continued*)

Appendix I. (*Continued*)

Questionnaire	Ph	Sin	Mal	Th	Ind	HK	Tw	Kr
21. Are wages of your workers basically fixed or dependent on the outcomes?	Ph	Sg	My	Th	In	HK	Tw	Kr
1. Fixed	22	30	38	46	45	30	52	47
2. Depends on outcomes		1	3			1		
3. Combination of both	23	17	8	11	22	9	33	11
22. How are your workers rated for wages?	Ph	Sg	My	Th	In	HK	Tw	Kr
1. Hourly rated	3	3.7	1		1		3	5
2. Daily rated	4	10.2	6	1	8	2	12	10
3. Combination of (2) and 4)	11	17.0	16	26	26	8	44	30
4. Monthly salaries	14	28.2	26	30	30	32	26	12
5. Others	12	9.0						1
23. On what criterion do you determine the wages?	Ph	Sg	My	Th	In	HK	Tw	Kr
1. Job category	7	6.5	8.5	2	13	6	22	14
2. Merit	5	5.0	7.0	3	12	6	7	6
3. Seniority		3.0	5.0	4	2	2	2	8
4. Overall rating	23	31.5	28.5	46	36	27	52	29
5. Others	10		1.0	2	1	1		1

(*Continued*)

Appendix I. (*Continued*)

Questionnaire	Ph	Sin	Mal	Th	Ind	HK	Tw	Kr
24. Do you differentiate the wages of those in the same position on the basis of job evaluation?	Ph	Sg	My	Th	In	HK	Tw	Kr
1. Yes	39	40	42	52	62	36	17	41
2. No	7	9	4	5	5	4	8	16
25. Of the fringe benefits,	Ph	Sg	My	Th	In	HK	Tw	Kr
1. Annual leave days/year	13.7	11.0	14.0	11.9	12.6	11.4	17.8	10.4
2. Sick leave days/year	14.3	19.6	19.9	32.4	143.7	46.5	23.9	36.1
3. Marriage leave days/year	3.3	3.7	3.4	4.5	3.4	5.3	6.7	5.2
4. Maternity leave days/year	44.7	58.6	51.4	38.5	74.2	52.6	50.9	38.8
5. Birth, and funeral leave days/year	2.7	4.1	2.6	4.8	2.5	3.1	5.8	5.0
6. Overtime % extra	40.2	59.5	59.9	72.2	117.3	36.5	41.5	72.7
7. Relief allowance % extra	12.0	23.7		10.0	36.0		30.5	69.3
8. Family allowance								
9. Food allowance								
10. Transportation allowance								
11. Inflation allowance								
12. Others								

(*Continued*)

Appendix I. (*Continued*)

Questionnaire	Ph	Sin	Mal	Th	Ind	HK	Tw	Kr
26. Do you have retirement benefit system?	Ph	Sg	My	Th	In	HK	Tw	Kr
1. We do not have	8	34	17	4	12	13	8	1
2. We give a lump sum at retirement time.	28	8	22	42	50	20	69	52
3. We have a pension scheme.	5		3	5		3	3	5
4. Others	3	2	5	2	3	2	4	1

[a]The figures are averages for Questions 1, 5, 6, 9, 10, 13, 14, 15(1), 25, and 38. The figures for the rest of questions are the number of respondents.

[b]The monetary unit of Questions 5 and 9 is 1,000 pesos for the Philippines, S$1,000 for Singapore, 1,000 Ringgits for Malaysia, 1,000 Baths for Thailand, US$1,000 for Indonesia, HK and Taiwan, and one million Won for Korea.

[c]Sales in Question 9 are for 1980.

[d]In a few cases, the number of respondents is not given as an integer, because even if the reply should be a single choice, some chose several, so that in such cases ($1/n$) was assigned to each reply, where n is the number of choice given by the respondent.

[e]For Korea, the second category is "production technology manager", and the third "other managers".

[f]The monetary unit: the Philippines, peso: Singapore: S$, Malaysia: Ringgit, Thailand: Baht, Indonesia: US$, Hong Kong: 1,000 HK$, Taiwan: 1,000 NT$, Korea: 1,000 won.

[g]Unless specified otherwise, the figures in parentheses are percentages. For item i in Question j, $\% = 100\ X$ (the number of respondents who chose item i)/(the number of respondents who answered question j).

Appendix II. Questionnaires for Local Middle Managers.[a]

(Basic Information)	Ph	Sin	Mal	Th	Ind	HK	Ta	Kr
1. Respondent's name _______ Age _______	34.[b] 5[c]	31.8	36.5	39.2	41.4	38.5	44.3	41.7
2. Co.'s name Dept.								
3. Position (e.g., sales manager, prod. supervisor)								
4. Education								
Univ.	163	57	35	51		11	63	69
Pol.tech.	2	33	7	21		5	21	1
High sch.	4	39	30	12		4	54	7
Others		5	6	4		14	4	1
5. How long have you been with this co.? _______ years	4.9	4.9						
6. Have you worked with other co,'s before?	Ph	Sin	Mal	Th	Ind	HK	Tw	Kr
1. Yes	150	153	62	53	93	32	120	58
2. No. (Go to Q. 11.)	20	51	17	36	32	4	24	23
7. If yes, how many times have you changed? Times	2.6	2.2	2.3	2.1	2.2	2.6	2.3	1.8
8. What type of company was your employer before this?								
1. Japanese company	15	34	5	15	17	7	18	9
2. European company *foreign includes joint venture	8	37	16	12	17	6		1
3. American company	28	33	10	15	6	5	8	4
4. Local Chinese company	22	33	17	15	26	13	72	
5. Local indigenous company	59	4	10	14	40	3		39
6. Government office	17	22	9	13	24	5	23	8
7. Others (specify _______)	40	22	14	6	20	2	19	

(Continued)

Appendix II. (*Continued*)

(Basic Information)	Ph	Sin	Mal	Th	Ind	HK	Ta	Kr
9. What was your position or job title in previous co.?								
10. What was your main reason to leave previous co.?	Ph	Sin	Mal	Th	Ind	HK	Tw	Kr
1. Irrational management	24	26	14	7	20	4	13	11
2. Bankruptcy or pull-out	14	13	3	11	16	3	9	12
3. Low salary or wages	47	21	10	11	18	6	6	3
4. Bad human relations	14	13	8	3	6	3	6	7
5. Unstable employment	21	21	12	6	13	1	10	3
6. Poor prospect for advancement	65	54	31	17	41	9	10	6
7. Little chance of learning new technology	39	40	13	12	28	9	31	5
8. Others (specify _______)	49	42	26	17	39	11	62	18
11. How did you come to know of this company?	Ph	Sin	Mal	Th	Ind	HK	Tw	Kr
1. A relative was a manager of this col	4	1	4	6	19	3	12	8
2. My friends work in this co.	34	33	18	21	32	12	35	7
3. My school recommended it.	1	7		5	9	1	3	5
4. Newspaper advertisement	62	118	39	19	23	14	52	22
5. Public employment offices	1	3	5	2	2	1	2	
6. Others (specify _______)	71	50	20	43	51	5	44	42
12. What were the main reasons why you chose the co.?	Ph	Sin	Mal	Th	Ind	HK	Tw	Kr
1. Higher salary or wages	46	27	14	22	21	8	21	7
2. Higher position or status	56	33	19	21	17	16	30	5
3. Better working conditions	38	49	21	19	37	13	77	31
4. More chances of learning new technologies	104	118	42	48	48	19	80	23

(*Continued*)

Appendix II. (*Continued*)

(Basic Information)	Ph	Sin	Mal	Th	Ind	HK	Ta	Kr
5. Stable employment	54	78	36	40	28	14	46	21
6. Good reputation of the co.	53	62	31	31	24	13	73	13
7. Better prospects for advancement	113	108	45	40	63	12	22	19
8. Others (specify _______)	22	48	24		27	9	19	26
13. Did the co. send you to Japan for training?								
1. Yes	61	107	45	54	64	19	86	53
2. No	112	101	35	35	58	17	55	29
3. If yes, how long? _______	3.0	3.5	2.5	3.8	4.0	2.2	2.6	
14. What kind of training do you want in Japan, if the opportunity is given?								
[Working Conditions with the company]								
15. Are you proud of working with this co.?	Ph	Sin	Mal	Th	Ind	HK	Tw	Kr
1. Yes, very much	141	144	60	73	76	10	44	34
2. Yes, a little	31	62	20	16	45	22	68	414
3. No.		4			3	4	31	8
16. Would you say that you are committed to this co.?								
1. Yes, definitely	126	122	61	60	63	22	105	60
2. Yes, somewhat	42	71	19	28	37	13	34	23
3. No.	4	10	1		23	1	4	
17. Do you feel participating in managing this co.?								
1. Yes, very much	130	82	50	49	87	11	53	21
2. Yes, a little	34	109	27	38	35	24	80	48
3. No.	8	18	4		2	1	11	13

(*Continued*)

Appendix II. (*Continued*)

(Basic Information)	Ph	Sin	Mal	Th	Ind	HK	Ta	Kr
18. What style management prevails in this co.?								
1. Authoritarian	48	110.5[d]	49	16	74	17	74	25
2. Participatory	100	92.5	29	61	47	18	64	56
19. Any communication barriers between Japanese and local staffs?	Ph	Sin	Mal	Th	Ind	HK	Tw	Kr
1. Yes	93	119	43	55	54	22	85	48
2. No (Ic no, go to Q. 21.)	72	89	34	35	72	14	57	31
20. If yes, mark three main factors for barriers.	Ph	Sin	Mal	Th	Ind	HK	Tw	Kr
1. Language know	65	85	31	36	45	18	76	29
2. Custom difference	52	30	13	9	15	13	29	28
3. Value difference	39	40	17	35	16	5	41	30
4. Religious difference	3	0	3	0	2	0	0	0
5. Japanese stay short in SEA	19	22	14	9	12	8	19	6
6. No personal contact with Japanese outside	20	45	15	18	17	10	2218	9
7. Japanese staff tend to form a closed circle	22	47	19	20	21	8	44	4
8. Japanese managers geared too much to Japan	41	47	14	25	29	7	8	30
9. Others (specify _______)	7	7	5	6	6	2		2
21. Do you think that Japanese staff are willing to transfer new technology and management knowhow?	Ph	Sin	Mal	Th	Ind	HK	Tw	Kr
1. Yes, very much	111	93	42	21	50	15	80	26
2. Yes, a little	51	103	32	59	71	16	46	45
3. No.	5	9	4	8	3	4	14	11

(*Continued*)

Appendix II. *(Continued)*

(Basic Information)	Ph	Sin	Mal	Th	Ind	HK	Ta	Kr
22. Do you observe job-hopping among your friends?	Ph	Sin	Mal	Th	Ind	HK	Tw	Kr
1. Very often	35	42	17	6	23	4	25	10
2. Occasionally	86	135	45	35	77	11	58	66
3. Rarely	47	31	19	45	27	19	58	6
23. How do you think of job-hopping?								
1. Perfectly natural and OK	25	13	5.5	2	9	9	67	
2. Undesirable but justified	58	91.5	36.5	16	62	15	44	22
3. Too much is not good.	64	61	30	11	35	8	20	52
4. No good.	9	59.5	10	59	23	2	7	8
[*Morale*]								
24. Are you satisfied with your pay?	Ph	Sin	Mal	Th	Ind	HK	Tw	Kr
1. Yes, very much	35	41	10	11	31	7	34	9
2. Yes, a little	98	126	53	69	75	21	87	44
3. No	37	40	17	8	21	8	21	29
25. Are you satisfied with your job responsibility?								
1. Yes, very much	115	112	47	36	82	15	52	36
2. Yes, a little	47	86	32	52	43	17	80	44
3. No	10	9	2	1	4	3	10	2
26. Are you satisfied with your relations to chief?	Ph	Sin	Mal	Th	Ind	HK	Tw	Kr
1. Yes, very much	125	130	53	28	87	18	61	25
2. Yes, a little	39	74	24	58	41	21	75	50
3. No	4	2	3	3	1	2	8	7

(Continued)

Appendix II. (*Continued*)

(Basic Information)	Ph	Sin	Mal	Th	Ind	HK	Ta	Kr
27. Are you satisfied with your relations to peer groups?								
1. Yes, very much	114	130	50	37	110	15	48	30
2. Yes, a little	53	69	27	49	18	20	90	48
3. No	2	7	3	3		1	6	4
28. Are you satisfied with your prospects of advancement?	Ph	Sin	Mal	Th	Ind	HK	Tw	Kr
1. Yes, very much	73	77	35	29	65	10	53	17
2. Yes, a little	78	103	39	57	52	17	67	51
3. No	17	16	5	3	11	9	20	14
29. Do you attend management meetings?								
1. Regularly	114	108	49	50	59	13	97	22
2. Occasionally	51	44	21	18	41	13	29	24
3. Rarely	24	52	11	14	19	9	16	35
30. How many times a month?	5.6							
31. Have you ample chances to comment on management?	Ph	Sin	Mal	Th	Ind	HK	Tw	Kr
1. Regularly	82	56	38	41	66	16	88	17
2. Sometimes	74	100	34	35	41	13	41	49
3. Rarely	15	47	10	8	16	6	11	17
32. Have you group meetings with subordinates?								
1. Yes	114	110	42	34	62	11	61	39
2. Yes, irregularly	50	88	37	46	48	15	68	39
3. No	7	10	1	6	11	8	11	4
If yes, how many times a month?	1.6	2.2	1.5	2.0	1.2	2.0	2.1	2.0

(*Continued*)

Appendix II. (*Continued*)

(Basic Information)	Ph	Sin	Mal	Th	Ind	HK	Ta	Kr
33. What are the primary purposes of group meetings?	Ph	Sin	Mal	Th	Ind	HK	Tw	Kr
1. Goal setting	150 (89)[e]	153 (76)	69 (84)	54 (60)	80 (69)	13 (39)	85 (60)	44 (44)
2. Problem-solving	167 (99)	189 (94)	79 (96)	78 (87)	106 (91)	30 (91)	126 (89)	64 (82)
3. One way communication	51 (30)	50 (25)	20 (24)	58 (64)	34 (30)	2 (6)	26 (18)	34 (44)
4. Socialization	67 (40)	72 (36)	33 (40)	42 (47)	27 (24)	6 (18)	60 (42)	23 (30)
5. Others (specify ______)	32 (19)	43 (21)	14 (17)	25 (28)	20 (17)	4 (12)	12 (9)	7 (9)
34. Should group meetings be held within working hours?	Ph	Sin	Mal	Th	Ind	HK	Tw	Kr
1. Yes	25	60	11	24	47	17	59	4
2. Not necessarily	135	140	70	62	73	10	37	75
3. No	5	6	1			6	42	3
35. Do you encourage team work to achieve a group objective rather than individual performance?	Ph	Sin	Mal	Th	Ind	HK	Tw	Kr
1. Yes	169	206	81	82	116	30	140	81
2. No	1	2	1			1	2	
36. If you are asked unexpectedly to look after your fellow manager's work due to his sickness, which attitude do you take?	Ph	Sin	Mal	Th	Ind	HK	Tw	Kr
1. Will do so, because it is part of my job	62.5	146	60	62	98	28	103	72
2. Happy to help my friend in emergency	88	47.5	14	20	23	7	34	6
3. Will do so, if paid	0		1				5.6	3.1
4. It is not my duty	2					1		
5. Others (specify ____________)	18.5	15.5	7	5	6	1	7	4

(*Continued*)

Appendix II. (*Continued*)

(Basic Information)	Ph	Sin	Mal	Th	Ind	HK	Ta	Kr
[*Motivation for efficiency*]								
37. What kind of incentives are important, do you think, to motivate local workers to improve productivity? Mark two items.	Ph	Sin	Mal	Th	Ind	HK	Tw	Kr
1. Money incentives	114	116	42	39	53	21	71	29
2. Promotion	47	40	16	62	22	15	22	6
3. Good human relations	74	116	45	43	61	13	19	44
4. Excellent leadership	78	86	35	21	81	10	92	31
5. Self-managing work group	11	5	1	10	11	1	21	21
6. Job-enrichment or making job interesting	68	68	28	16	54	9	56	29
7. Others (__________)	6	4	6	5	12	2	6	1
38. Do you think that even in the case of workers, pay increase or promotion should be based on individual appraisal rather than mere seniority?	Ph	Sin	Mal	Th	Ind	HK	Tw	Kr
1. Yes	161	199	73	85	122	33	131	54
2. No	8	7	8	4	5	3	10	27
39. Do you offer friendly counseling to your subordinates over their private affairs as well as job-related matters?	Ph	Sin	Mal	Th	Ind	HK	Tw	Kr
1. Yes	165	183	73	86	107	34	143	64
2. No	2	24	8	1	17			6
3. (If yes, how often a month? (______) times	4.5	2.7	4.2	9.7	2.5	1.8	2.0	

(*Continued*)

Appendix II. (*Continued*)

(Basic Information)	Ph	Sin	Mal	Th	Ind	HK	Ta	Kr
40. If you find an employee incapable of, or unfit for, performing a job assigned, what would you do?	Ph	Sin	Mal	Th	Ind	HK	Tw	Kr
1. Will transfer him to another job in co.	115	168	53	54	113	23	107	58
2. Will try to find him a job in another co.	5	5	4		1		17	3
3. Will press him to resign	13	5	3	1	1	1	3	
4. Will fire him.	7	8	3	1	5	5	3	
5. Others (specify ______________)	49	39	22	37	21	12	25	
[*Mensulation*]								
41. Managers should be given the private offices, do you think?	Ph	Sin	Mal	Th	Ind	HK	Tw	Kr
1. Yes	81	51	37	45	23	17	39	1
2. No	91	154	42	42	99	17	101	82
42. Do you like to participate in games or club activities with general workers?	Ph	Sin	Mal	Th	Ind	HK	Tw	Kr
1. Yes	143	184	66	81	94	24	117	64
2. Not much	26	21	16	5	25	10	25	16
3. Not at all	4	3			3	2		2
43. Do you like to participate in an annual dinner party sponsored by the company or a recreation committee?								
1. Yes	150	191	77	81	108	31	137	64
2. Not much	17	18	5	5	17	4	6	13
3. Not at all	3							4

(*Continued*)

Appendix II. (*Continued*)

(Basic Information)	Ph	Sin	Mal	Th	Ind	HK	Ta	Kr
44. Do you have lunch with workers at the company canteen?								
1. Yes	152	168	61	69	76	18	120	76
2. No	18	32	17	15	46	14	18	6
45. Managers should be provided with a company restaurant separated from the canteen for workers, do you think?	Ph	Sin	Mal	Th	Ind	HK	Tw	Kr
1. Yes	19	5	4	12	23	2	6	4
2. No	154	201	77	75	100	33	134	78
[*General Impression*]								
46. Do you think that the job descriptions specifying each post's authority and responsibility in detail should be given to locals?	Ph	Sin	Mal	Th	Ind	HK	Tw	Kr
1. Yes	145	150	50	75	112	33	126	72
2. No	26	56	30	11	14	3	13	7
47. What are very satisfying points in this company's management? Please point out as many as you wish in the list.	Ph	Sin	Mal	Th	Ind	HK	Tw	Kr
1. Very small status difference between managers and workers.	60	102	39	36	39	8	47	52
2. Even top managers mix with workers	100	104	43	41	40	18	70	32
3. No lay-offs.	39	57	32	25	22	3	35	27
4. No severe punishment for mistakes.	33	63	25	20	19	13	30	27

(*Continued*)

Appendix II. (*Continued*)

(Basic Information)	Ph	Sin	Mal	Th	Ind	HK	Ta	Kr
5. Good human relations between Japanese and local staffs	102	97	41	41	89	23	66	38
6. Good chance to learn technology and knowhow	130	99	48	45	89	15	67	34
7. Good chance to career advancement	98	69	32	35	77	5	21	19
8. Good team spirit prevails	94	76	36	46	95	16	62	19
9. Others (specify ______________)	13	6	6	15	9	1	6	2
48. What are weak points in this company's management? Please point out as many as you notice in the list.	Ph	Sin	Mal	Th	Ind	HK	Tw	Kr
1. Slow decision-making	60	92	28	27	34	10	45	37
2. Poor chances for promotion	36	14	18	12	29	7	21	27
3. Poor training opportunities	39	71	28	29	49	6	47	28
4. Poor management system	20	45	11	17	10	8	35	14
5. No clear responsibility for individuals	63	91	32	44	39	10	62	33
6. Others specify ______________)	41	31	15	23	20	9	12	8
49. Do you welcome consensus to decision?								
1. Yes	153	179	75	75	109	27	124	76
2. No	13	17	3	5	9	2	12	6
50. Do you welcome opportunities for job rotation to become a generalist rather than one type professional?	Ph	Sin	Mal	Th	Ind	HK	Tw	Kr
1. Yes, very much	141	130	52	53	103	31	128	71
2. Not so much	28	59	24	26	17	3	18	8
3. Not at all	1	15	5	2				1

(*Continued*)

Appendix II. (*Continued*)

(Basic Information)	Ph	Sin	Mal	Th	Ind	HK	Ta	Kr
51. Should even workers be given the chance for job-rotation?								
1. Yes	151	167	67	82	92	25	117	60
2. No	19	36	11	5	32	9	25	20
52. Please note any new experiences in this company's management or running the factory after working here. Specify (_______)								

[a]This English version was used for Malaysia, Singapore, and the Philippines, but for the rest of five countries it was translated to the national languages.
[b]The figures are averages for Questions 1, 5, 7, 13 (3), 30 and 39 (3). The figures for the rest are the number of respondents.
[c]If two or more (n) answers are chosen in a question which requires one item, then 1/n is assigned to each answer.
[d]Figures in parentheses are %. For item i, for example, % = 100 × (the number of respondents who chose item (i) ÷ (the total number of respondents).

Chapter 14

Japanese-style Management in Singapore*,†

1. Job-hopping in Singapore

The greatest problem in Singapore that Japan-affiliated companies confront is "job-hopping". Singaporean workers change their employer as soon as they find a position in a different company with better pay. The labor turnover rates being very high there, some companies showed even more than 100% in their annual separation rates.

Great many advertisements for workers occupy a lot of space in Singaporean newspapers and magazines. Even in commuting buses, which many companies operate for their own employees, similar advertisements are conspicuous. At reception offices, a number of job applicants are often waiting for an interview. It is not rare that when you visit a factory you meet several workers who are just starting new jobs. Every day, many workers get employed and many leave in Singapore. This is a phenomenon seldom seen in many companies in Japan, which employ fresh graduates on fixed dates.

As was shown in the previous issue of *Southeast Asian Studies*, Vol. 22, No. 4, Appendix: Questionnaires for Top Japanese Managers and Questionnaires for Local Middle Managers, local workers employed by Japan-affiliated companies continued in their service for 2.5 years on the average in Singapore, but 4 years in the Philippines, and 4.1 years in

*This was published in *Southeast Asian Studies*, Vol. 23, No. 1, June 1985.

†The author Urabe Kuniyoshi (1920–1986) of this chapter was Professor of Business Administration, Kobe University for many years and was a Professor at Matsuyama University when he wrote this paper. He was an outstanding scholar in the field, making an essential contribution to our study of Japanese style management in Asia. I have kept this article in my volume to record his contribution in English (SI), with Mrs Urabe's consent.

Table 1. The Length of Continuous Service of Employees.

	Less than 1 year	1–2 years	2–3 years	3–4 years	4–5 years	More than 5 years
Numbers	319	75	112	63	49	80
%	45.7	10.7	16.1	9.0	7.0	11.5

Malaysia (Question No. 14). Thus, the average length of service is very short in Singapore; the separation rate is 4.9% per month and reaches about 60% a year. In other words, in a company employing 100 local workers, approximately 60 of them leave every year. As was mentioned before, there are some companies where the annual separation rate is over 100%.

Table 1 shows the numbers and percentages of local employees classified by the lengths of continuous service in a certain Japan-affiliated company in Singapore. Those who leave the company within one year after being employed account for as high as 45.7%. The higher the separation rate is, the shorter the period of continuous service becomes. Such a high separation rate naturally induces heavy expenditure on recruitment and training new employees and leads to a high percentage of inferior goods.

It requires time for new employees to achieve optimum efficiency even in simple work. Thus, a high separation rate serves as a negative factor in terms of both expenditure and the quality of products. Among the advantages of companies in Japan are increases in productivity and quality, which are attributable to rises in learning and experience curves.

The learning curve represents the degree of proficiency in a job. As one becomes more proficient in a job, learning productive efficiency increases. In addition to this, an increase in productivity due to a rise of the experience curve is also attracting attention: as the accumulative output increases, the cost of production shows a proportionate, rapid decrease.

As the effect of the experience curve, when the accumulative output doubles, the cost of production decreases by 20% to 30%. Not merely does a worker's skill increase in proportion to learning but an increase in the accumulative output leads to new ideas for improvements of working processes, tools, and equipment. As a result, quality greatly improves, and the proportion of inferior goods decreases. Thus, a rise of the experience curve greatly contributes to a reduction of production costs.

Compared with large companies in the U.S. and Europe, those in Japan, which are stable in terms of employment due to the lifetime employment, have remarkable characteristic by using the experience curve to the best advantage. They continuously make use of the effects of the experience curve for improvements, progress and innovations, which raises productivity and quality.

In the case of companies with a very high annual separation rate of 60% or so, short-term employment caused by the high separation rate makes it impossible to take full advantage of the effects of the experience curve. Hence, if the effects of the experience curve are to use, job-hopping must stop. Until job-hopping stops, the Japanese-style management cannot prevail, and *vice versa*.

2. Promotion of Japanese-style Management

A few years ago, the Singaporean government began enthusiastically to promote Japanese-style management. It established *the Japanese Style Management Promotion Committee*, which includes leading members of Japan-affiliated companies, as an advisory organ directly responsible to the President. It broadcast also the slogan "learn from Japanese-style management" on radio and television.

Here are a few of the suggestions advanced for the promotion of Japanese-style management by the above-mentioned committee. One is the suggestion to remove the ceiling set on bonuses. Until then, bonuses had been limited to the amount equivalent to three months' pay as part of the government's incomes policy. The bonus system in which bonuses are paid not only to management members of a company but also to its employees in general is one of the characteristics of Japanese management. This system has the advantage of fostering loyalty to the company by making the payment of bonuses take on the character of distribution of profits or sharing of achievements. It is notable that the adoption of the Japanese bonus system has been suggested as a step toward fostering workers' loyalty to their companies.

Another proposal advanced by the committee was related to the government's policy concerning a social welfare fund called the Central Provident Fund. In this social welfare system, each employee was obliged to put 22.5% of his or her income into the fund and, what is more, each company had to put 22% of the total wages to pay into the fund. In other words, an amount equal to almost half of the total salaries was allotted for this social welfare fund. The ample funds thus raised were assigned for, among others, retirement annuities, housing loans, and the construction of multistorey apartment houses for workers. Especially, the construction of multistorey apartment buildings in the vicinities of their factories was enthusiastically promoted, for the government had adopted a policy of the adjacency of one's job site and residence.

In relation to this social welfare system, from 1982 onward, the committee advanced a reform that companies reserve half of the sum they pay into the social welfare fund (that is, 11% of the total wages to be paid), and that the interest revenue coming from that fund be invested for the improvement of intra-company welfare facilities like company apartments or sports facilities for their workers. This proposal aimed at enhancing corporate solidarity among workers by means of companies' direct investment in intra-company welfare projects in place of the government projects and, thereby, at preventing job-hopping.

The underlying idea was to heighten the employees' loyalty to their companies and increase the rate of labor immobility by making companies themselves responsible for their own welfare policies for the employees after the example of Japanese-style management rather than by making the government entirely undertake the nation's social welfare policy after the British style.

A third proposal made by the committee was related to the reform of the education system. The practice of job-hopping and the high separation rate can be attributed in part to the fact that Singapore was long a colony of Britain and has adopted various aspects of British culture. The population of Singapore consists of about 75% Chinese, 20% Malays, and 5% Indians. The people of this multiracial nation have a strong sense of individualism and have a marked concern to pecuniary return.

These aspects and the adoption of British culture are reflected in the educational system. For instance, reflecting the British idea that universities are institutes for training the elite, there are only two in all — the National University of Singapore and Nanyang University.

As a foundation for promoting Japanese-style management, the Singaporean government adopted a policy to reform the educational system. For example, they have decided to establish a new technological university. Furthermore, they plan to introduce collective education into elementary, junior and senior high schools; Japanese school customs and events such as athletic meetings and morning assembly are to be adopted for junior and senior high schools as part of the collective training.

Thus, the policy of the Singaporean government is to actively promote Japanese-style management. In reality, however, it is not so easy to implement. One of the six Japan-affiliated companies I visited happened to be refurbishing its office premises. The refurbishment was for the express purpose of constructing a private office for the native manager, for native managers are liable to leave without a private room. The other five companies adopted the policy of large, unpartitioned rooms for all office workers including managers, which is one of the characteristics of Japanese management. Some hesitation persists among Japanese managers about whether they should push the Japanese style of management or adapt themselves to the local way of management.

In relation to this, I would like to show some of the results obtained through the questionnaire mentioned at the beginning of this report. The answers to Question No. 12 tells us that 75% of the Japan-affiliated companies in Singapore, which answered the questionnaire, are adapting themselves to the local way of management, while the remaining 25% are implementing Japanese-style management. This would indicate that those companies of the acclimatization type overwhelmingly outnumber those of the other type. In practice, however, the former include companies adopting Japanese-style management more or less. In other words, some companies are actually implementing Japanese-style management, though adjusting to local practices to some extent instead of adopting entirely the same management system as is taken in Japan. The answers to some of the other questions will be helpful to comprehend this. Here, I would emphasize that the companies classified as the acclimatization type (75%) actually include those adopting Japanese-style management to some degree or the other.

Five of the six Japan-affiliated companies I visited were actively carrying out Japanese-style management, though they differed slightly in degree. One of the decisive factors, which determine a company's policy as to whether to adopt Japanese management or not is the distinctiveness of its products. When a company succeeds in the product differentiation and therefore has an advantageous position in the market, it is easy to implement Japanese-style management. When, however, its products are not differentiated and the company faces keen competition, it is difficult to carry out. This is the case with one of the above-mentioned six companies. This company produces vinyl pipes, which makes product differentiation difficult, and has decided on a policy of adapting itself to the demand of the local managerial personnel for private office room. Another decisive factor is the type of ownership; that is, whether a company is owned jointly or unilaterally. It goes without saying that when a company is a joint venture and the local side has the right of management with a local owner installed as president, it is most difficult to implement Japanese-style management. When a company is a joint venture and its management is entrusted to the Japanese side with Japanese appointed as president, the active promotion of Japanese-style management is possible to some extent. When a company is entirely owned by Japanese enterprise, Japanese management can be most easily carried out. In view of this, Japan-affiliated companies in Singapore tend to change their ownership structure to that of a wholly owned subsidiary. Among the few companies, which have recently made this change, is Seiko's subsidiary in Singapore.

3. Evolution of Japanese-style Management in Overseas Enterprises

The Japanese-style management, which is now being implemented overseas, certainly shares some of the characteristics of Japanese management described by James Abegglen, who did research into the Japanese companies of the 1950s. Among them are the lifetime employment system, the wages system based on seniority, the seniority promotion system, and the company's own welfare system. But it is also true that Japanese-style management developed in Japanese enterprises overseas has some different characteristics; that is, aspects considerably different from those that J. Abegglen characterized as the Japanese lifetime employment system. In other words, a new or modernized Japanese-style management is being developed in the Japanese companies overseas. I would like to examine from an evolutionary standpoint the actual development of Japanese-style management being carried out in Singapore.

3.1. *Separation of Ownership from Management*

One of the characteristics of Japanese-style management is the separation of ownership and management. In Southeast Asian countries, local companies are usually small in scale and many of them are family concerns. Furthermore, the stock markets are still at an underdeveloped stage. Accordingly, it is not usual for capital and management to be separated. This means that when a joint venture is undertaken, capital and management can easily be linked together; the local owner more often than not holds the right of management and, as a result, the actual management style takes on a capitalistic feature. In contrast, Japanese-style management is characterized by the separation of ownership and management, entrusting management to a managerial expert; that is, the professionalization of managerial function. Based on this separation of capital and management, other factors of Japanese-style management are incorporated. For instance, in the case of a joint venture formed by Mitsubishi Electric Co. and a Singaporean owner, Mitsubishi's share accounted for only 35% of the capital of the company, but the local owner entrusted management to Mitsubishi Electric Co. after a failure due to mismanagement. In the beginning, a Singaporean president headed the joint venture was by, and Mitsubishi afforded technological and managerial support. With the local owner as president, however, the capitalistic management could not produce satisfactory results. After a Japanese managerial expert assumed president, it began to make a better showing.

Culture and conditions in Southeast Asia make it difficult for companies there to separate capital from management, and a capitalistic management is apt to prevail. Without the separation of capital and management, however, Japanese-style management could never be carried out. The professionalization of managerial function is an indispensable basis for the realization of Japanese-style management. The Japanese enterprises overseas in Singapore tend to change their ownership structure from joint ownership to a wholly owned subsidiary for implementing the Japanese-style management.

3.2. *Stable Employment Policy*

Industrialization of Singapore is rapidly advancing, and many foreign companies are extending their business here. In view of the sellers' market for labor, the lifetime employment is not highly evaluated. In 1981, the Singaporean government carried out a policy of a drastic pay raise. It aimed at reforming the industrial structure of Singapore to cope with the rapid industrial growth of South Korea and Taiwan. As a result, salaries almost doubled in two years. The reform of the industrial structure meant shifting labor-intensive industries out of Singapore to other countries and inviting technology-intensive industries to take their place. Because of this, a subsidiary of Matsushita Electric Co., for example, discontinued the production of inexpensive popular audio products in Singapore and moved its production to the Philippines. To take its place, they decided to manufacture rather high-grade audio products requiring higher technology in Singapore. Owing to this strategic decision, Matsushita subsidiary was obliged to suspend operations about two months. However, some 200-factory employees were not laid off but allowed to remain for study and training or conducting miscellaneous affairs. The Japanese-style employment policy was practiced.

The policy of not laying off employees is not necessarily economically disadvantageous to the company, for expenditure is required to employ and train new workers until they master the specific skills required. Nevertheless, the fact remains that even Japan-affiliated companies cannot help reducing personnel in some cases, for instance, when a structural depression in business causes the company semi permanently to be overstaffed. In the case of American-affiliated companies in Southeast Asia, for instance, it is not unusual to dismiss employees who have not been able to achieve expected results. However, Japan-affiliated companies seldom, if ever, dismiss employees because they have attained unsatisfactory results or are inefficient. Instead, they retrain or relocate such employees, thereby ensuring the continuity of their employment in the company.

Thus, Japanese-style management today can be credited more with a stable employment policy, as opposed to an employment policy characterized by "firing after a disappointing performance". It aims at ensuring employment as stable as possible from the viewpoint of human interests. Some local workers emphasize that Japan-affiliated companies treat them as human beings. One of the merits of contemporary Japanese-style management lies in the embodiment of this philosophy of treating the company employees as human beings.

3.3. *The Internal Promotion System (Career Management System)*

In general, Singaporean companies have been strongly influenced by British industrial culture, and usually employ managerial officers such as chief accountants or personnel managers by advertising in newspapers. In Britain and the U.S., it is customary to employ experienced people even for managerial positions from the labor market outside the company.

In contrast, the Japanese system employs fresh graduates who have no managerial skills or experience and trains them within the company. After some length of service, they are promoted to managerial positions including those of personnel manager or chief accountant. This is referred to as *the internal promotion system*. It can also be described as a *career management system*. This system contributes not only to an increase in the rate of immobility of labor, allowing long-term employment, but also to intensification of employees' loyalty to the company. Furthermore, it leads to the accumulation of the enterprise-specific skills and, in turn, serves as a major factor in bringing about an improvement in quality and cost-effectiveness. Thus, the company loyalty and managerial efficiency is built upon the internal promotion system.

Most Japan-affiliated companies in Singapore intend to implement this internal promotion policy, though in practice, the policy does not always work well. For instance, Matsushita Electric Co.'s subsidiary in Singapore successfully trained an employee as a personnel manager at considerable cost. But he soon left the company for a better-paid position, which forced them to employ an experienced manager from the outside to fill the vacant position immediately. This company makes it a rule to educate and train local prospective managers, supervisors, and chief engineers in Japan for three and a half months on the average. With this program, the company aims at not merely cultivating technical skills but at inculcating the Japanese culture, sense of values, and way of thinking into local prospective managers. They are expected to play central roles in Japanese-style management when they return to Singapore. For the future advancement of Japanese-style management, it is necessary to further promote the educational and training system within the company.

The seniority promotion system was pointed out by J. Abegglen as one characteristic of Japanese-style management. Today, however, in view of the modernized system of the Japanese management recently developed, it would be more appropriate to replace this term with *the internal promotion system or career management system*. The old promotion system in which promotion is based merely on length of service is today utterly opposed in Singapore. But even in this new *internal promotion system*, length of service is taken into account for promotion to one degree or another. Therefore, although this system is helpful in increasing the rate of immobility of labor, it causes complaints among local employees, who claim "promotion is slow in Japanese companies".

3.4. *Seniority Wage System and Personnel Evaluation*

The seniority wage system is another characteristic of Japanese-style management, which J. Abegglen pointed out. But some Japanese scholars like Prof. K. Koike maintain that the seniority wage system is not limited to Japanese companies but adopted by American companies as well on the basis of the seniority rule stipulated in the labor agreement between labor and management. However, I would like to stress that the seniority rule in the U.S. or Britain is completely different from the seniority wage system or seniority promotion system in Japan.

For example, in the case of the joint venture which was established by the acquisition of Mitsubishi Electric Co., a Western-style wage agreement is concluded between the management and the labor union. The agreement stipulates wages per hour for each different job and also the rates of increase in wages after one-year and two-year continuous service. The wage system is literally based on length of service. But it should be noted that this system is a manifestation of the seniority rule demanded by the labor union. The seniority rule which is characteristic of labor agreements in Britain and the U.S. does not contain the concept of personnel evaluation but rather means automatic pay raises merely on the basis of length of service.

This is also true of promotion when the British- or American-style seniority system is laid down, promotion is decided on according to length of service without giving consideration to personnel evaluation, that is, to each employee's work efficiency and attitude. The conclusion of an agreement of the British- or American-style seniority system results from the union's claim and is helpful in forging loyalty to the union, not to the company.

In contrast, the seniority promotion system and the seniority wage system in Japan are institutionalized for the purpose of increasing loyalty to the company. In the Japanese system, pay raises and promotion are decided on the basis not only of length of service but also of personnel evaluation of such aspects as service efficiency, service record, and cooperativeness. In this sense, it would be inappropriate to maintain, as Prof. K. Koike did, that the seniority system in Britain and the U.S. is the same as the seniority promotion and wage systems in Japan.

On the other hand, subsidiaries of Matsushita Electric Co., and Seiko in Singapore are carrying out a policy to decide on wage raises and promotion by taking the result of personnel evaluation as well as length of service into consideration even in the case of factory workers. As a contemporary characteristic of Japanese-style management, the seniority system is intermingled with the ability principle as reflected in the personnel evaluation system. This helps to heighten employees' willingness to work and loyalty to their companies.

Some kind of personnel evaluation forms are used by almost every Japan-affiliated company in Singapore. There are three kinds of evaluation forms: those for factory workers, for managers, and for staff. As is indicated by these forms, Japanese-style personnel evaluation is marked by the amount of importance attached to personal aspects such as attitude and personality as well as to ability to perform one's duties.

3.5. *Enterprise Unions*

(1) *Unions in Singapore*: The rate of formation of unions in Singapore is not high. It was 33% in 1980 and decreased to 28% in 1982. In the case of manufacturing industries, the rate went down to 19% in 1982. Union members in Singapore number about 220,000 in all, and unions whose members total 210,000 belong to the National Trade Union Congress (NTUC).

The unions are composed mainly of industrial, craft, and general unions. However, it deserves attention that enterprise unions have been recently organized. Among the industrial unions are United Transport Workers' Union (UTWU), United Workers of Electronics and Electric Industries (UWEEI), Metal Industries Workers' Union (MIWU), and Chemical Industries Workers' Union (CIWU). Among those classified as craft unions are

Stevedore and Seamen Unions (SSU) and Sea-Vessels Workers' Association (S-VWA). General unions are those organized regionally irrespective of types of industry or craft.

Recently, however, a new trend to organize enterprise unions as part of the reform to implement Japanese-style management has appeared. Among the companies which have formed enterprise unions are Robin Shipbuilding Company affiliated with Hitachi Shipbuilding Co., Jurong Shipyard, Metal box Company, and National Steel Company.

(2) *Cooperative Labor-management Relationships*: The secretary-general of NTUC recently stated, "Harmony between labor and management would enable them to successfully meet the needs of the new economic age. For this purpose, a cooperative labor-management relationship is *a necessity*".

In Singapore, strict union control is exercised through NTUC and a labor-management conciliation policy is being carried out. Not a single strike was staged since 1978. A labor agreement was concluded in 1978 between Robin Shipbuilding Company affiliated with Hitachi and the Pioneer Industries Union. It is interesting to note that the agreement contains clauses related to labor-management cooperation. Article 3(B) of the agreement reads as follows.

> Labor and management
>
> 1. shall actively carry out all procedures devised for increases in productivity and efficiency, and
> 2. shall encourage all company employees to make the utmost effort to increase productivity, and shall cultivate the spirit of close cooperation between labor and management concerning every aspect, especially the effective use of time, materials and facilities.

The agreement also stipulates the establishment of productivity and safety committees each consisting of representatives of both labor and management as well as union participation in management in conformity with the spirit of labor-management cooperation.

In the case of industrial unions, however, their cooperation with the managerial side and their participation in management have limits. The leading members of branches of industrial unions have not necessarily been employed by the companies concerned but are usually people outside the companies. They tend to limit their scope of interest to such matters as negotiations for pay raises and amendments of labor agreements. But it is not surprising that they show little interest in the practical promotion of labor-management cooperation as stipulated in labor agreements. As the industrial unions officers are outside of companies concerned, they have little of the working knowledge indispensable for increasing productivity. In addition, why should they positively promote labor-management relations when they lack a sense of unity with the companies? The formation of enterprise unions by some companies including Robin Shipbuilding Co. was underlain by the idea of overcoming the limitations of the industrial unions.

4. Modernization of the Lifetime Employment System

In making a comparative analysis of management in Japanese and Western companies as of today, those aspects of the Japanese lifetime employment system which have been modernized since the end of World War II cannot be ignored. Contemporary companies in Japan are at the stage of internationalization and setting up their factories overseas with a view in part to solving the problem of trade friction. In this situation, the comprehension of the essential qualities of the modernized lifetime employment system would be necessary for an accurate understanding of the characteristics of Japanese-style management practiced by Japanese companies overseas.

4.1. *Equalization of Status*

Every business organization forms a hierarchy in terms of power and responsibility: men holding different positions have different competence and responsibilities and are accorded different salaries, status, and treatment. This is almost the same in every country. Business organizations always have a hierarchical status system. In companies, especially those in capitalistic nations, there is class distinction in status between staff members and factory workers within the company. This is true of companies in the U.S. and Europe even today. The same situation existed in Japan before World War II.

After the war, however, humanization of the lifetime employment system developed in Japan in line with the abolition of class distinction in status within the companies. The movement was triggered by claims for democratization of industries by postwar radical labor movements, and it was accompanied by a change in the ideology underlying the Japanese management through the postwar abolition of paternalism in prewar days to the philosophy of humanization. The abolition of class distinction in status within the company was a major reform in the social structure of the Japanese company and made an undeniable contribution to alleviating class confrontations between labor and management.

In the lifetime employment system in prewar Japan, new employees had been classified into two status groups, that is, office staff and factory workers on the basis of their educational background, and class distinction had been made between the groups in treatment and promotion. After the abolition of the two-class status system through postwar democratic reforms within the company, factory workers, too, were paid monthly salaries and given bonuses. In addition, they were allowed to share the companies' welfare facilities, such as the canteens, dormitory, and recreation facilities with staff members on an equal basis. In prewar years, the promotion ladder for workers was limited to the foreman level. In postwar years, the limit was abolished. In other words, in prewar Japan, while staff members were considered to be the company's regular employees, factory workers were not necessarily so. But after postwar democratic reforms, all employees including factory workers were treated as full members of the company.

In European and American companies, there remains class distinction in status between staff members and factory workers within the company. It is true that Japanese business organizations, which are after all hierarchical organizations, also have a system in which employees standing in a vertical hierarchy are accorded different responsibilities, power, and salaries. In this sense, status distinctions do remain; it would be practically impossible for any business organization to carry out equalization of status in the literal sense of the word. But there is no class distinction in status in Japanese organizations like there is in the U.S. and Europe, and status differentiation has been further reduced in Japanese companies. This is what is meant by an evolved characteristic of the Japanese management system. Society in the plants set up overseas by Japanese companies, compared with their American and European counterparts, is strongly characterized by the features of status equalization.

For instance, in Japan-affiliated companies in Singapore, Japanese presidents and plant-superintendents wear the same uniform as local workers inside the plants and take meals together with local workers in the company canteens; they often visit work sites and are ready to talk to workers; the Japanese executives, mixing with local workers, take part in the companies' sports day, and other sports activities like volley ball and soccer. The policy of status equalization shown by these facts contributes to increasing mutual understanding between labor and management and to easing labor management confrontation. This is one attractive quality of Japanese-style management that local workers highly appreciate. Status egalitarianism like this is seldom witnessed in European- or American-affiliated companies.

4.2. *Human Relations Policies*

In the 1950s and 1960s, human relations theories advanced in the U.S. had a great influence on and played an important role in the postwar modernization of the Japanese management system. In Japan, there is an old expression "An enterprise depends entirely on human beings." This expression is indicative of the Japanese philosophy of management that more importance should be given to the administration of human resources than to any other resource. The human relations policy comprised a cardinal factor of Japanese management, in which the spirit of harmony was traditionally thought most important.

Therefore, the traditions of Japanese management already had a conceptual conformity with the managerial philosophy unfolded in the human relations theory formulated in the U.S. As a result, various human relations policies taken on the basis of these theories were actively incorporated into the postwar Japanese management system, and contributed to its evolution.

According to the human relations theory, employees' morale is a decisive factor in enhancing productivity, and improvements of human relations are indispensable in raising their morale. Some of the human relations policies incorporated into the evolved Japanese management system are as follows:

1. promotion of better communication;
2. employees' suggestion system;

3. interviewing program;
4. personnel counseling;
5. education of foremen and super-intendments; and
6. recreational activities.

How far these human relations policies are diffused in Japanese companies needs no explanation. Japanese enterprises overseas, when compared with their American or European counterparts, are noticeably distinguished by the substantiation of human relations policies.

In the case of Matsushita Electric Co.'s subsidiary, it is an established rule to hold a 10-minute meeting in each workshop every morning before work starts. At the meeting, the superintendent gives instructions necessary for the day, a worker whose turn it is to make a speech expresses his opinions, and all the workers sing the company song together at the end of the meeting. Other Japan-affiliated companies in Singapore also mostly hold a morning assembly every day, though they may not go so far as to have their employees sing their company songs. The morning meeting is instrumental in promoting better mutual understanding and group solidarity, and is a realization of the human relations policy.

On the contrary, a similar meeting is seldom held in the companies affiliated with European or American corporations. Probably, this is due partly to the fact that workers in the West generally regard labor power as a commodity and lack a sense of loyalty to their companies. They would be presumably reluctant to leave their homes 10 minutes earlier for a morning assembly. Japan-affiliated companies in Singapore hold such annual events as sports day and a year-end party. Often referred to as an annual party in Singapore, the year-end party is attended by all employees as well as the president and executives. Year-end parties held by some companies are attended by as many as 1,000 or so. Events like this are also significant in the sense of practicing human relations policies, for they are helpful for promoting better mutual understanding between labor and management through human contact and eventually for strengthening their spiritual bond.

In the case of a corporation in Singapore affiliated with Sekisui Chemical Company, the Japanese plant manager often holds informal drinking parties, inviting assistant managers of different nationalities such as Indians, Chinese, and Malaysians. The effort he makes to bring mutual understanding among people of different color, customs, and languages may touch some of them. This is another example of practicing human relations policies.

Still another typical example is seen in Singapore Time Company, Seiko's subsidiary. In this company, a number of club activities are promoted for the employees, ranging from sports such as baseball, soccer and volleyball to arts and crafts including photography.

4.3. *The Adoption of New Human Relations Policies*

The human relations policies mentioned above have their limitations. Under these policies in which top priority is given to establishing good human relations, employees are liable either to give more consideration to harmonious relations with their colleagues than to the work itself, or to be content to follow others' ideas. Thus, they tend to fall into the habit of merely aligning themselves with others and lose their own individualities, independence, and their challenging quality. How to activate these innovative qualities in the work group in harmony with the group solidarity is a great problem, which the Japanese management system faces.

Employees', too, began to feel dissatisfied with merely good human relations after rises in income and educational standards which followed the high growth of Japanese economy. Even labor unions came to demand that employees' needs for self-actualization should be satisfied in the workplace. It was the advent of new human relations theory that provided a theoretical support in solving the problem of how each individuals needs for self-actualization could be satisfied without disrupting group harmony. Among these new theories were the XY theory advanced by D. McGregor, the participative management theory of R. Likert, and the hygiene motivations theory of F. Herzberg. In the new theories, importance was placed on satisfying employees' desire for self-actualization, while the earlier human relations policies aimed at satisfying employees' desire to belong to a group.

The employees' need for self-actualization will be satisfied by the formation of the autonomous work group. In line with the advent of new human relations theories, activities in small groups were widely adopted by Japanese companies in the 1960s and 1970s in the forms of the ZD (zero defects) campaign and the organization of work improvement teams and QC circles, and they took root as an important aspect of the evolving Japanese management system.

4.4. *Small Circle Activities*

Small group activities have the principle of self-management. Small groups of workers are organized and the leader of each group is elected. Each group holds discussions to decide on its own targets concerning product quality and improvements of operations on its own judgment. Then the group is responsible for its own administration.

Small group activities are not a product of mere collectivism but they aim at raising employees' morale and at improving quality and productivity by satisfying their desire for self-actualization while activating their sense of challenge within limits not prejudicial to group harmony. The ZD campaign has its origin in a U.S. space plan, for the fulfillment of which related industries were called upon to carry out a campaign to make defectives zero. This drive is conducted based on autonomous management by small groups of workers.

The QC circle method, which is now attracting global attention, is also based on autonomous management by small groups. Originally devised by the Japan Scientific Technological Federation, it has become widespread in Japanese companies.

The idea of small group activities came originally from the new human relations theories mentioned before and a theory of group dynamics advanced in the U.S. However, the method of small group activities is more widely spread among companies in Japan than in America. The reason for this can be explained as follows.

In American companies, duties are specialized and each employee assumes responsibility only for a specific duty. His wage is commensurate with his specific duty. Therefore, he shows little interest in other duties. Furthermore, the high rate of labor turnover and short-term employment naturally make the length of the employee's service in a specific company short. These factors are disadvantageous to the effectiveness of the method of small group activities, for the immobility of labor is necessary in order for employees to be able to make use of their service experience to improve quality or operations by this method.

Still another factor, which has made diffusion of autonomous group activities difficult in American and European companies, is the relatively hostile relations between labor and management. In the U.S., where labor management relations are dominated by collective bargaining, not only introduction of new apparatus but even changes in the method or speed of their operation are regarded as alterations of working conditions, and they are subject to collective bargaining in addition to wages and working hours. The shop rules stipulating methods and speeds of operations form a part of the labor agreement. Therefore, improvements in quality and operations through their autonomous work group would be regarded as changes in methods and processes of operations, which must be subject to collective bargaining as the alteration problems of labor agreement. As a result, it is hard for the method of small group activities to take hold. It is not only in the U.S. but also in Britain as well that labor management relations in which collective bargaining are frequently resorted to serve as a great barrier to the improvement of productivity and quality by the autonomous work group's activities. In contrast, the effectiveness of small group activities among companies in Japan is attributable first to employees' strong sense of unity with or loyalty to their companies which results from the lifetime employment system.

Another reason is employees' experiences in various jobs through job-rotation during their long-term service: their varied experiences are helpful in providing solutions to the problems of improving quality and operations in their workplaces.

A third reason is the high educational and intellectual standards of Japanese factory workers: nowadays, senior high school graduates are accounting for a higher and higher percentage of workers.

A fourth reason is a cooperative relation between the management and the enterprise union which was organized under the Japanese lifetime employment system. It seldom occurs in the Japanese labor management relations that alterations in operation methods and speeds are subject to collective bargaining or that an article to this effect is stipulated in the labor agreement. Therefore, the existence of unions does not serve as an obstacle to daily improvement of work methods by small group activities. Still another reason is the fact that there are not such antagonistic or hostile relations between the foremen and workers as are seen in the workplaces of the U.S. companies. In the case of Japanese enterprise unions, foremen and workers are both union members and are on senior–junior terms. The former are in the position of providing friendly protection to the latter while the latter support the former. In the small group activities, the foreman acts as a friendly adviser to the workers' group. The supportive relationships thus formed between foremen and workers in factories are contributing to the effectiveness of small group activities among Japanese companies.

Small group activities can be considered a by-product of the Japanese lifetime employment system and today they are one of the distinctive features of evolving Japanese-style management. Whether small group activities are effectively practiced or not is one criterion for judging the degree of infiltration of the Japanese management system in Japanese enterprises overseas.

References

[1] Abegglen, J. C. (1958). *The Japanese Factory; Aspects of its Social Organization*, Free Press, New York.

[2] Abegglen, J. C. (1973). *Management and the Worker. The Japanese Solution*, Sophia University, Tokyo.

[3] Cole, R. E. (1971). *Japanese Blue Collar, The Changing Tradition*, University of California Press, Berkeley.

[4] Cole, R. E. (1979). *Work, Mobility and Participation — A Comparative Study of American and Japanese Industry*, University of California Press, Berkeley.

[5] Dore, R. (1973). *British Factory-Japanese Factory: The Origin of National Diversity In Industrial Relations*, University of California Press, Berkeley.

[6] Marsh, R. M. and H. Mannari (1977). *Modernization and the Japanese Factory*, Princeton University Press, Princeton.

[7] Urabe, K. (1978). *Nihonteki Keiei o Kangaeru* (A thought on Japanese Management), Tokyo Chuo Keizai Sha, Tokyo.

[8] Urabe, K. (1979). "A critique of theories of the Japanese style management system," *Japanese Economic Studies*, 7(4), 33–35.

[9] Urabe, K. (1984). *Nihonteki Keiei wa Shinka Suru* [Japanese Management Does Evolve], Tokyo Chuo Keizai Sha, Tokyo.

[10] Yoshino, M. Y. (1976). *Japan's Multi-national Enterprise*, Harvard University Press, Cambridge.

Note: The references include some works not cited in the text, but perhaps the author wished the reader to learn the best references on the issues discussed. I have kept the references here as he did.

Chapter 15

Japanese-style Management in Indonesia*

1. Difficulties of Japanese Business Management in Indonesia[1]

The management of Japanese joint ventures in Indonesia is not easy. Of the eight countries our survey covered, namely, Korea, Taiwan, Hong Kong, the Philippines, Thailand, Malaysia, Singapore, and Indonesia, only Korea and perhaps Thailand presented greater difficulties to Japanese managers. This may be surprising to many Japanese non-businessmen, because many Japanese who have been to Indonesia talk fondly about their stay and personal contact with Indonesian people. But those who have had any serious working relations with Indonesian businesses or government offices usually have a different view.

Almost all the Japanese top managers interviewed reported a variety of serious problems with employees; for instance, they often had to give elementary industrial training to newly employed workers. Some managers with experience in other ASEAN countries had no hesitation in saying that

---

*This was published in *Southeast Asian Studies*, Vol. 23, No. 1, June 1985. The two articles of Urabe's and mine succeed this journal's last issue (Vol. 22, No. 4) on Japanese-style management in Southeast Asia.

[1]I thank Mr. Kiyoshi Onozawa (then Japan Overseas Enterprise Association in Jakarta; now Associate Professor of Tokyo University of Foreign Studies) and Mr. Masayasu Ichiki (Japan Indonesia Businessmen Association) for their help in conducting this survey, and Mr. Junker Tamba (Chief, Information and Computation Bureau, BAPPENAS) for his translation of the questionnaire into Indonesian. It was not easy, because some technical words had to be translated for the first time. Without their help this survey would not have been completed so quickly with such limited resources.

difficulties were more serious in Indonesia than elsewhere. This has several implications.

(1) Most workers have little experience of working in modern industrial factories where standard discipline is taken for granted.
(2) Japanese joint ventures in Indonesia often build factories and plants for new manufacturing industries, so that novice workers have to learn the new types of production processes even if they have come from other modern establishments.

Although per capita GDP has risen considerably in Indonesia, this is largely due to the contribution of the oil sector. The manufacturing industries are still underdeveloped.[2] One question in our questionnaire shows that Indonesia has the lowest percentage of locally procured parts among eight countries, and that the Japanese top managers are very dissatisfied with this low percentage situation as Table 1 shows.

For this reason, new managers have to run not only their own establishments but also build up the external conditions for business transactions. In other words, it also has to prepare the infrastructure for business. This lack of infrastructure for business at present characterizes some difficulties facing Japanese management.

Japanese managers experienced also other difficulties in conflicts with partners and labor relations. The former seemed particularly serious among four Asian countries: Taiwan, Korea, Indonesia, and Thailand. This is clear from the replies to Question 17 in our questionnaire survey to top managers. Respondents who had troubles, both minor and serious (figures in parentheses), with partners on management policies exceeded 20% in

Table 1. Percentage of Local Procurement and Dissatisfaction.

	In	Ma	Ph	Sg	Th	HK	Kr	Tw
% of local parts	39.3	47.2	39.7	46.7	50.4	43.5	48.0	50.0
% of dissatisfied managers	70.0	57.7	64.7	72.1	51.2	16.7	69.4	55.8

[2]Recent Indonesian economic development is surveyed by two excellent works: Booth and McCawley (1981) and Thee Klan Wie (1984) (Japanese).

Table 2. Main Causes of Trouble with Partners.

	Personnel	Sales	Purchases	Pricing	Investment	Tech. trans.	Dividend	Wages	Bonus
Tw 158	21 (13)	22	12	19	13	14	11	16	13
Kr 146	15 (10)	12	14	13	14	18	12	11	9
IN 153	19 (12)	17	14	12	17	11	9	15	10
Th 118	12 (10)	11	11	12	12	11	5	6	4

Note: The figures in parentheses are the percentages of the companies which experienced trouble with partners; the total number of troubles in each country is given right of it.

Table 3. Main Sources of Trouble.

	No. 1	No. 2	No. 3	No. 4
Tw 158	Sales	Personnel	Price	Wages
Kr 146	Tech. Transfer	Personnel	Purchase =	Investment
IN 153	Personnel	Sales =	Purchase	Investment
Th 118	Dividend	Personnel =	Price =	Investment

Note: Those linked with = are of the same ranking; e.g., in Indonesia sales policy and purchase policy were sources of trouble at the same number of companies.

these four countries: Taiwan, 27.0 (4.8); Korea, 25.9 (3.4); Indonesia, 24.0 (3.1); Thailand, 21.5 (2.9). Among the ASEAN countries, Indonesia is foremost in this respect. The partners of Japanese joint ventures in Indonesia are typically Chinese Indonesian or government offices, because most of the *puri bumi* (indigenous Indonesian) businessmen lack the capital to match Japanese investment and cover the 51% of the total paid-up capital. The types of trouble in partnership seem to reveal underlying tensions between Japanese management and their counterparts. Table 2 shows the breakdowns for the four countries. It may be instructive to observe the major sources of trouble as Table 3 shows.

The reasons for the contentious nature of personnel matters and sales-purchase policies in Indonesia seem to be related to the kinds of partnership prevailing there. Government offices often take advantage of a partnership by demanding high positions in the company for their old staff. Japanese managers do not necessarily appreciate the abilities of these personnel, although they sometimes play crucial roles through their contact with government offices.

Government offices may demand to expand the dealings with *puri bumi* companies, but many Japanese managers are often compelled by the reality of business conditions in Indonesia mainly to purchase materials from and sell products to Chinese Indonesian merchants. If the partners are Chinese Indonesian, then conflicts may arise between the government's demands — or the Japanese managers' attempt to comply with such demands — and the Chinese partner's view of reality.

Troubles with workers or trade unions are also significant in Indonesia among Asian countries. Japanese manager's report that of the ASEAN five countries, Indonesia is only next to Thailand by a small margin in having troubles with labor unions. Besides these two countries, Korea and Malaysia seem to be the places where Japanese managers frequently face the labor troubles. The percentage of such companies that reported whether they had troubles with unions or not is as follows: Thailand 26/40 (65%), Korea 29/45 (64%), Indonesia 32/53 (60%), Malaysia 17/30 (57%), the Philippines 8/19 (42%), Singapore 12/31 (39%), Taiwan 19/52 (37%), and Hong Kong 3/12 (25%).

Managers in Indonesia find it hard to deal with labor unions. Perhaps to the surprise of the general reader, the Indonesian percentage of such companies: 75% is the highest and followed by Taiwan with 54% only, as Question 33 shows. A number of the managers interviewed reported that they faced unreasonable — from their point of view — demands from labor union leaders. The causes for troubles with labor unions in Indonesia show certain clear characteristics (see Table 4).

Table 4. Main Causes of Trouble with Labor Unions.

	Wages	Welfare	Personnel	Promotion	Work hour	Holidays	Others
Thailand	19 (73)	11 (42)	5 (19)	4 (159)	5 (19)	3 (12)	3 (12)
Korea	20 (69)	9 (31)	5 (17)	5 (17)	1 (3)	2 (7)	6 (21)
Indonesia	23 (72)	4 (13)	10 (31)	0	1 (3)	4 (13)	10 (31)
Malaysia	8 (47)	9 (3)	6 (35)	1 (6)	2 (12)	3 (18)	4 (24)

Note: The figures in parentheses are the percentages of the causes for trouble in the total number of companies with trouble. Since most companies marked two causes, the sum of the percentages does not add up to 100.

(1) The dominant cause is wages and salaries. This is common to Thailand and Korea, but in Indonesia, there is less concern with welfare programs. That item is the second main causes in Thailand and Korea.
(2) The second main cause is personnel matters. This is very different from Thailand and Korea but common to Malaysia.
(3) The third cause is holidays. This is not so important in Thailand and Korea but similar to Malaysia.
(4) Working hours and promotion seldom become issues in Indonesia, but as Table 4 shows, they are rather important in Thailand and Korea.

All these observations indicate that Indonesia is rather unique in ASEAN five countries from the viewpoint of management. Other studies given in references at the end of this chapter confirmed similar findings.

2. Some Characteristics of Japanese Management in Indonesia

We conducted the questionnaire survey for this article in 1983 and processed in the same year. There were slightly over 200 Japanese joint ventures in Indonesia then. Questionnaires were mailed to all the companies known to the Jakarta Office of the Japan Overseas Enterprise Association or Himpunan Usahawan Indonesia Jepang (Japan Indonesia Businessmen Association) in Jakarta. The questionnaire schedules for top managers in Japanese (Questionnaire I) were sent to Japanese representatives in the respective companies, whereas the questionnaire schedules for middle managers (Questionnaire II) were prepared in Indonesian and mailed to each company with the request that they be given to average middle managers. These questionnaires and the summary of responses were appended to the previous special issue of *Southeast Asian Studies*.

Replies came back from 80 companies. 67 top managers replied and 130 local middle managers gave responses. This is an unusually high percentage of returns for this kind of questionnaire survey in Indonesia. The survey did not include the trading companies or bank branches that are not engaged in productive activities, because the purpose of our study was primarily to examine the applicability of the Japanese style of management in manufacturing activities. Respondents may be biased toward the larger enterprises in Indonesia, because the average number of employees in each company: 435, seems to be larger than the mean size of all the Japanese joint ventures in Indonesia. This does not seem to affect, however, the findings of our survey on Japanese-style management in Indonesia.

The first characteristic of Japanese management in Indonesia is that workers stay with the companies longer than they do in other countries. Despite the relatively short period since establishment, most workers have stayed almost five years with the companies. Job-hopping is almost non-existent.

This is, first, a consequence of the shortage of employment opportunities as well as the Japanese style of management. The interviews with workers reported in Japan Overseas Enterprise Association (1981) revealed that most Indonesian workers view employment by foreign joint ventures as a privilege and that they would never think of leaving their companies, except in the unlikely event that they were offered a substantially better chance. Even then, however, their wages or salaries are often not high enough for them to support their families and other dependents. They gladly work over-time whenever the chance is offered.

Second, there are government regulations on dismissal in Indonesia that require the negotiations with and the consent of labor unionist and local and central labor committees. This has made it more difficult for Japanese joint ventures to dismiss the Indonesian employees if they wish to dismiss despite their normal style of lifetime employment.

Third, one should not forget that the practice of Japanese management in Indonesia puts greater emphasis on stable employment. This is clear in the high percentage of the companies emphasizing stable employment and seniority-based wages and promotion (see Questions 18 and 19 in Questionnaire I). It may be interesting to learn that as a measure of employment stabilization, 25% of Japanese joint ventures have adopted schemes to assist workers to buy houses, which is much higher than in any other Asian country. This may be a policy reflecting and adapted to the poor living conditions of Indonesian workers.

The second characteristic is that the internal training of workers or staff rather than recruitment from outside receives much more emphasis than in any other country (see Question 16 in Questionnaire I).

The shortages of skilled and semi-skilled workers coexist with an abundance of unskilled workers in Indonesia as in any other underdeveloped country. In Indonesia, among the ASEAN countries, this is especially serious so that internal training and promotion must be more widely practiced. Such practices as job-rotation cannot yet be used effectively for training. Indeed, 64% of the companies emphasize continuous training and good human relations between workers and managers, but only 22% practice job-rotation, and 29% QC circles, for which the figures are more than 46% in other countries.

The third characteristic is that the reward system and promotion in Indonesia put more emphasis on the evaluation of individual merit than in other Asian countries. This is clear in the replies to Question 24, on differentiation in the wages of workers in the same post owing to job evaluation, Question 30, on promotion, and Questions 31 and 32, on training. On-the-job training is very much emphasized, and despite the distance, training in Japan is offered to the same extent as in Taiwan or Korea. This may be a device, matching to a greater variation in workers' abilities to bring up their capacities to the required level in shorter time. On the other hand, welfare programs are much more generous in Indonesia than in other Asian countries. This may be necessary to compensate the lack of social welfare and business infrastructure mentioned above.

3. Labor Relations in Japanese Joint Ventures

Labor relations in Indonesia seem to be rather unique among those in Asian countries. This observation coincides with another study conducted by the Institute of Social Problems that was established by moderate Japanese labor unions (see Ajia Shakai Mondai Kenkyusho, 1984). Table 5 shows the replies to the question: to which country's labor relations are your country's labor relations similar.

Table 5. To Which Country's Labor Relations are Your Country's Similar?

	In	Ma	Ph	Sg	Th	HK	Kr	Tw
Japan	1.9	9.3	11.5	26.3	1.9	0	10.7	16.3
US–EC	25.0	46.6	42.5	18.4	40.7	29.3	3.6	11.6
Asian	0	18.6	36.1	10.5	25.9	17.1	32.1	11.6
Unique	59.6	7.0	3.3	36.9	25.9	53.6	26.8	44.2

Note: The remaining percentage account for "no answer" and "do not know".

It is clear from Table 5 that union leaders themselves recognize the labor relations in Indonesia as unique rather than similar to any other countries' unions. Since, however, labor relations in Indonesia are still in the formative stage, they may undergo changes in the future, as manufacturing industries develop and the supply of semi-skilled and skilled workers increases. Any managers interviewed could not tell how they change. At any rate, labor disputes are very frequent in Indonesia as well as in Thailand. Another finding of the same study (Ajia Shakai Mondai Kenkyusho, 1984) is instructive in revealing the different attitudes of Japanese managers toward labor unions in different countries (Table 6).

The difference between Indonesia and Thailand in the Japanese managers' attitudes toward labor unions is very significant. Thai union leaders are much more critical of management. However, the replies to the next question asking the reasons why the company's attitude toward unions is unfavorable reveal a surprising fact; that is, the company's unfavorable attitude is primarily attributed to the local partners' lack of understanding about the activities of labor unions rather than Japanese managers themselves or Japanese enterprises' policies. In this point, Indonesian and Thai views coincide. Thus, it must be recognized that

Table 6. Japanese Managers' Attitudes Toward Labor Unions.

	In	Ma	Ph	Sg	Th	HK	Kr	Tw
Favorable	51.9	20.9	23.2	63.9	14.8	21.9	12.5	18.6
Neutral	26.0	74.4	32.1	22.2	20.4	56.1	10.7	53.5
Unfavorable	9.6	2.3	44.7	13.9	63.0	4.9	23.2	18.6
Do not know	9.6	2.3	0	0	0	17.1	33.9	9.3

Note: The remaining percentage account for "no answer".

Table 7. Why Company is Unfavorable Toward Unions.

	In	Ma	Ph	Sg	Th	HK	Kr	Tw
Against co's policy	15.4	60.5	16.4	13.9	29.1	17.1	23.2	34.9
Partner's lack of understanding	50.0	30.2	36.1	50.0	54.6	4.9	55.4	30.2
Trouble making	25.0	4.7	24.6	25.5	14.5	36.6	1.8	14.0

Note: The remaining percentage account for "no answer" and "do not know".

the role of partners is so important. Perhaps, the shortage of appropriate partners lies at the core of these troubles. This amounts to a shortage of entrepreneurship in the developing countries.

4. Responses of Local Middle Managers to Japanese Management

The local middle managers who replied to the questionnaire had changed the jobs on average 2.2 times in the past. While this is true of the middle managers in other Asian countries, those in Indonesia stayed with the Japanese joint-ventures two to three years longer than their counterparts in other ASEAN countries — see Questions 5–7 in Questionnaire II — and come closer to the period of stay in Northeast Asian countries. This is undoubtedly related to the shortage of employment opportunity discussed in Section 2 and may be related to the character of their group consciousness in Indonesia, which we observed in our village survey before.[3] It is interesting to note that Malaysian workers seem to show the same tendency compared with Singaporean or Philippine workers.

The motivations for leaving previous employers and moving to Japanese joint ventures in Indonesia seem to be the same as those in other Asian countries: the first is the better prospect for advancement; the second is the better chance of learning new technologies. This is a strong characteristic of Japanese joint ventures. Despite criticism of the slow transfer of technology in Japanese joint ventures, their effort to provide the middle level managers or engineers with good learning opportunities is recognized by their own employees.[4]

---

[3]The survey Ichimura *et al.* (1974) included a study of group consciousness by collecting the proverbs remembered by farmers in the villages surveyed. The one remembered by most farmers was: Unity is strength, so you have to help each other.

[4]In the questionnaire survey (Ichimura, 1983) concerning technology transfer in Indonesia the influence of government policies is much stronger than in other Asian countries, so that initiatives come less from the private sector. Another important aspect of management related to technology transfer is the number of levels between the top and the workers. In Indonesia a typical style is four levels, whereas in the Philippines a typical style is five levels. This proves that managing workers is more difficult in Indonesia than in the Philippines. See Ichimura (1983: 71–77).

Table 8. Pride and Commitment.

	Indonesia	Malaysia	Philippines	Singapore	Thailand	Hong Kong	Korea	Taiwan
Proud	61.3	75.0	82.0	68.6	82.6	27.8	41.0	30.8
Commit.	51.2	75.3	73.3	60.1	68.2	61.1	72.3	73.4

Note: The remaining percentage account for "no answer" and "do not know".

Table 9. Opinions on Job-hopping.

	Perfectly all right	Justifiable	Too much is no good	No good
In	7.0	48.1	27.1	17.8
Sg	5.8	40.7	27.1	22.5

Information about companies is obtained by word of mouth in Indonesia rather than through newspapers, which is more important in other countries (Questionnaire II). A certain degree of nepotism is noticeable in Indonesia and seems the strongest in Asia.

Indonesian middle managers are, however, less proud of working for their companies than those in other ASEAN countries. What Table 8 shows may be surprising? The proportion of middle managers who were proud of working for their companies or definitely committed to their companies were lowest in Indonesia of five ASEAN countries, and commitment was even less than in the three Northeast Asian countries (Questions 15 and 16).

One surprising finding (Question 23), shown in Table 9, may explain this fact. The question on job-hopping revealed that Indonesian middle managers find nothing objectionable in this practice. Compared with their counterparts in Singapore, where job-hopping is notorious, Indonesian middle managers fundamentally accept job-hopping even more positively. If, therefore, the chance arises, they will think nothing of leaving their companies. This may seem to be contradictory with the group-consciousness mentioned above in connection with village life. It merely shows, however, that the sense of community among the Japanese joint ventures' employees in Java is still weak, although group-consciousness is stronger than in other ASEAN countries. Such a strong sense of identity with the companies as the one among Japanese employees in Japanese enterprises has not been fostered yet in Japanese joint ventures anywhere in Asia. It remains to be seen if such solidarity in business enterprises can grow outside Japan.

In this connection, it may be instructive to observe that the percentage of middle managers who regard the type of management as "authoritarian" (top-down) rather than "participatory" (bottom-up) is highest in Indonesia and Malaysia among all Asian countries: Malaysia 62.8, Indonesia 61.2, Singapore 54.4, Taiwan 53.6, Hong Kong 48.6, the Philippines 32.4, Korea 30.9 and Thailand 20.8. This seems to show that the standard Japanese style of participatory management is practiced less in Indonesia or is so perceived by Indonesian middle managers. This seems to imply that in Indonesia the initiatives do not come from middle managers. Indeed, Japanese top managers reported in interview that they were not necessarily satisfied with this aspect of middle management.

Nevertheless, the communication barriers between Japanese and local staff seem to be less severe in Indonesia than in other countries (Questions 19 and 20). Indonesia is the only country where more respondents denied rather than affirmed the existence of serious barriers. This is consistent with the general impression of many Japanese that they can get along well with most Indonesians in the personal sphere. Even in working relations inside the enterprises, the communication between Japanese and Indonesian staff is good. This seems to have little relations to the ease of learning Indonesian, because the same situation does not obtain in Malaysia where the language is the same; moreover, those who affirmed such barriers in Indonesia cite the language as the primary barrier to communication. In the opinions of the top managers interviewed, admission of less communication barriers between Japanese and Indonesian is mainly due to gentle nature of most Indonesians. One revealing finding on this matter may be the data shown in Table 6. Although the attitude of Japanese top managers must be more or less the same in all the ASEAN countries, Table 6 demonstrates that the reaction of labor union leaders to Japanese managers differs very much. Indonesians make a remarkable contrast with Thais in regarding the attitudes of Japanese managers as favorable for labor unions. This difference may be at least partly a reflection of the general public opinions toward Japan in these countries, which may in turn be influenced by the political climate. The political stance of the public opinions toward Japan in Indonesia is certainly better than in Thailand. It seems to require further

Table 10. Communication Barriers Between Japanese and Local Staff.

	Indonesia	Malaysia	Philippines	Singapore	Thailand	Hong Kong	Korea	Taiwan
Language	45 (28)	31 (25)	65 (25)	85 (27)	36 (23)	18 (26)	29 (21)	76 (31)
Value difference	36 (23)	33 (26)	94 (36)	70 (22)	44 (28)	18 (26)	58 (33)	70 (28)
Sociability	38 (24)	34 (27)	42 (16)	92 (29)	38 (24)	18 (26)	13 (10)	40 (16)
Comp's policies	41 (26)	28 (22)	60 (23)	69 (22)	34 (22)	15 (22)	36 (27)	63 (25)

Note: "Value differences" includes: difference in customs, value differences and religious differences; "sociability" includes: a lack of personal relations outside the workplace between Japanese and local staff and a tendency of Japanese staff to form a closed and exclusive circle; "company's policies" includes: the short duration of stay by Japanese staff in Southeast Asia, and the gearing of Japanese management too much to the head office in Japan.

The figures in parentheses are the percentages of the factors in the total number of factors given in the replies. Each respondent was asked to point out three factors.

studies how these public relations are reflected in the intra-firm relations. The factors responsible for communication barriers between Japanese and other Asian staff in each country (Question 20) are summarized by Table 10.

In every country except for Korea, language is the most important single factor cited as a barrier to communication. However, if similar factors are grouped together as in the table, then the relative weight of language differs in each country. In Indonesia, language is still the most important factor, and the other three main categories of factors have more or less the same weight. But in other countries, the relative weights of the different factors vary greatly. Differences in values seem to be the most important factor in Korea, the Philippines and to a lesser extent Thailand. Sociability is not important in Korea, Taiwan and the Philippines.

The second most important factor after language in Indonesia is the perception that "Japanese management is geared too much to the head office in Japan". Even some Japanese top managers also pointed out this factor. Various issues unique to Indonesia may not be understood at the head offices in Tokyo or Osaka so that Japanese and local staff share common grievances against the head offices.

In general, dissatisfaction with wages and salaries in Southeast Asia is naturally very strong. Indonesian middle managers do not express exceptionally high dissatisfaction, but neither are they satisfied. They are satisfied with their job responsibility, in which respect Korean, Taiwanese, and Thai middle managers expressed more dissatisfaction. The top managers interviewed were fairly, but not very, satisfied with the performance of middle managers in their companies. They report a constant struggle to maintain morale in their companies. This remark may correspond to the findings (Question 37) about the incentives needed to motivate the local workers. The middle managers themselves reply that the following incentives are important in this order (the figures show the number of respondents' marks):

1. excellent leadership that encourages teamwork......... (81)
2. good human relations .... (61)
3. job-enrichment, or interesting work.................. (54)
4. monetary incentive.................................. (53)
5. promotion... (22)
6. self-managing work group .... (11)

The emphasis placed on non-pecuniary incentives is more conspicuous in Indonesia than in other countries. The main reason seems to be that careful and kind guidance and watchful attention given to workers, rather than pecuniary motivation to them, are essential in maintaining a constant, smooth flow of work in the factories. The same thing can be said about the effort required to keep up the morale of middle managers. According to our survey (Questions 26–28), human relations are very good and better than in other Asian countries. This must have contributed to high morale in Japanese joint ventures in Indonesia.

Groupism seems to be well accepted by Indonesian middle managers. They participate actively in-group meetings and express their opinions. They hold group meetings with their subordinates regularly or irregularly, on average about 1.2 times a month (Question 32), which is slightly less frequent than in other Asian countries. Such meetings are held mainly to solve problems and set goals (Question 33). Many of them (39%) think that such meetings should be held within normal working hours (Question 34). This percentage is considerably higher than in other countries. Overall,

Indonesian middle managers lack the initiative to "motivate" workers to greater efficiency, in comparison with their counterparts in other Asian countries. This may be another reason why the working of the Japanese style of management is difficult in Indonesia and why an adaptation to local conditions is necessary.

Mensualization, or egalitarian principles, in management seems to encounter subtle resistance in Indonesia, where it is less easily acceptable than in other Asian countries (Questions 41–45). Indonesians seem to have their own social class-consciousness. For instance, 82% of them accept that there should be "no private offices for managers", but do not necessarily wish to participate in the dinner parties or club activities sponsored by the companies. The percentage of middle managers who prefer not to have lunch with workers in the company canteen is considerably higher in Indonesia than in other Asian countries: Indonesia 38%, Thailand 18%, Singapore 16%, and Korea 7%. Indonesians seem to be much more position-conscious and class-conscious than other Asian nationalities. It remains for future studies to ascertain whether this is attributable to Javanese society, or there are significant ethnic differences in this respect.

General impression on Japanese management is rather favorable (Questions 47–52). Indonesian middle managers appreciate team spirit, good human relations with Japanese staff, good chance to learn technology and expertise, and the consensus approach, but as we just discussed, less so mensualization. Indonesian middle managers accept one standard practice of Japanese management, job-rotation, more than their counterparts in other Asian countries do but some object to applying it to workers. It is not clear yet whether this is another aspect of Javanese class-consciousness or it reflects their realistic recognition of the great variation in workers abilities.

Indonesian criticisms on Japanese management differ little from those in other countries. Surprisingly most managers (47%) criticize poor training opportunities. This may be an expression of a strong desire to learn more technology or management expertise. However, it should be remembered that about 20% of respondents made no criticisms at all. Then, it may be that we must perceive Indonesians' strong desire to explore potentials behind their gentle or only outwardly effeminate behavior and remarks.

References

[1] Ajia Shakai Mondai Kenkyusho [Institute for the Study of Social Problems in Asia]. 1984. *Ajia no Rodosha wa Nanl'o Kangaete lru ka* [What are Asian Workers Thinking of?], February.

[2] Booth, A., and P. McCawley (eds.) (1981). *The Indonesian Economy during the Soeharto Era*, Oxford University Press, Kuala Lumpur.

[3] Ichimura, S. (1983). *Institutional Factors and Government Policies for Appropriate Technologies. Survey Findings in Indonesia, Thailand and the Philippines*. ILO Working Papers, WEP 2-22/WP. 110. January.

[4] Ichimura, S., K. Mizuno, Y. Tsubouchi *et al.* (1974). "The Socio-Economic Behavior of Peasants in Central Java and Central Thailand — A Summary Report," *Southeast Asian Studies*, 12(3), 322–343.

[5] Japan Overseas Enterprise Association (Koizumi; Nobuo: Research Coordinator). (1981). *Indonesia no Toshi Rodosha* [Urban Workers in Indonesia]. Nihon Redo Kyokai [Japan Labor Association] Research Document No. 98. March.

[6] Thee Klan Wie (ed.) (1984). *Antologi Ekonomi Indonesia* [Indonesia no Keizai]. Translated by Hiroshi Kanoh, Kosuke Mizuno and Yoshinori Murai, Mekonsha, Tokyo.

Chapter 16

Japanese-style Management in China — A Summary Report*

1. International Comparison of Japanese-style Management in Asia

This is a partial report of a large joint research project being undertaken by the authors. It is a continuation of joint research project with more collaborators by questionnaire survey and interview about the management styles of Japanese joint ventures in East Asian countries and area undertaken about a decade ago. Our earlier works were already published in two books (Ichimura, 1980, 1988). These studies covered Japan, Korea, Taiwan, Hong Kong, Thailand, Malaysia, the Philippines, Singapore, and Indonesia but not Mainland China. In the early 1980s, there were very few Japanese joint ventures in Mainland China. This time we have undertaken such a study in China to fill the gap. In this recent study, we conducted the surveys in three areas within China, namely, around Shanghai, Beijing, and Dalian. We have completed the surveys in these three areas and just finished a simple summation of the questionnaire returns around those three cities. This is the first interim report about our survey in three areas in China and gives only an exposition of some aspects of our findings.

2. Twelve Characteristics of Japanese-style Management

In our earlier study, the 12 features of management demonstrated in Table 1 characterized the Japanese-style management. It has been often thought

*The authors Shinichi Ichimura, Shoichi Ito, Nobuteru Kusanagi and Teruhiko Tomita are at International Center for the Study of East Asian Development, Osaka Prefecture University, Osaka International University and Shiga University respectively.

Table 1. The Practice of Japanese-style Management in Japan.

		Manufacturers			Non-manufacturer			Commerce		
	Industry	Small	Large	Total	Small	Large	Total	Small	Large	Total
1. Stable employment	86.0	60.0	90.5	84.6	83.3	90.3	88.4	77.8	84.6	81.8
2. Seniority wage	47.5	46.7	44.4	44.9	58.3	50.0	52.3	77.8	30.8	50.0
3. Seniority promotion	42.8	40.0	30.2	32.1	41.1	31.2	34.1	44.4	7.7	22.7
4. Job rotation	51.6	20.0	61.9	53.8	41.7	50.0	47.7	44.4	38.5	40.9
5. Emphasis on ideals	69.7	60.0	69.8	67.9	75.0	71.9	72.7	66.7	84.6	77.3
6. Flexibility management	48.4	60.0	49.2	47.4	33.0	34.4	34.1	33.3	38.5	36.4
7. Group-decision	42.6	40.9	49.2	47.4	33.0	34.4	34.1	33.3	38.5	36.4
8. Group responsibility	10.7	6.7	12.7	11.5	0	12.5	9.1	0	0	0
9. Human relation emphasis	57.4	40.0	68.3	62.8	33.3	53.1	47.7	33.3	46.2	40.9
10. Ringi system	82.8	60.0	84.1	79.5	83.3	90.6	88.6	100.0	92.3	95.5
11. Minimum Difference	36.9	33.3	76.2	67.9	33.3	65.6	56.8	33.3	46.2	40.9
12. Small group act	63.9	33.3	76.2	67.9	33.3	65.6	56.8	33.3	46.2	45.5
13. Others	6.3	0	6.3	5.1	8.3	9.4	9.1	11.1	7.3	9.1

Note: 1. Large implies the corporations with more than 300 employees; 2. small implies those with less than 300 employees; commerce is part of non-manufacturing industry.

as if they were practiced nearly 100% in Japan. But our findings by questionnaire survey in Japan showed that this was not the case, as is demonstrated by Table 1. The questions were asked to top managers whether they practiced each item very much (3), not so much (2), or not practiced (1). The percentage of those in (3) and (2) are taken as those practicing the Japanese-style management in our Table 1. The practice of the Japanese-style management in Japan measured in this fashion is far from 100%. Clearly, the degree of practice differs from one item to another. A simple average of those in all items is slightly above 50%. Please notice that some items are very highly practiced particularly by the corporations with more than 300 employees. Since the multinational corporations investing abroad

Table 2. Comparison of the Practice of Japanese-style Management in 8 Asian Countries.

	Lifetime employment	Human relations	Groupism	Seniority
Japan	69	55	46	40
Korea	53	56	44	57
Taiwan	60	58	44	57
Hong Kong	48	59	31	43
Singapore	49	59	31	43
The Philippines	40	49	32	31
Thailand	45	38	19	39
Malaysia	52	47	24	41
Indonesia	56	49	32	56

(a) Lifetime Employment	1. Stable employment, 4. Seniority promotion
(b) Humanism	5. Emphasis on ideals, 9. Emphasis on human relations, 11. Minimum differentials
(c) Groupism	6. Flexible management, 7. Group decision making, 8. Group responsibility, 10. Ringi system, 12. Small group activities
(d) Seniority	2. Seniority wage system, 3. Seniority promotion

are mostly the large ones, the management practice in Asia may be expected to be higher than in Japan. Our actual findings in Asia are reproduced here as Table 2 and Figure 1.

In Table 2, the scores of those 12 characteristics are aggregated into four major indices by simple arithmetic average as follows:

By comparing the indices of these four characteristics in other Asian countries with that of Japan, we can tell the degree of localization of Japanese-style management in Asian countries and areas. Figure 1 visualizes more impressively this fact. Clearly, some countries like Taiwan, Korea, and Singapore seem to show management styles similar to Japanese. How to analyze the fact must be carefully considered. The interested reader may be referred to the books given in references at the end.

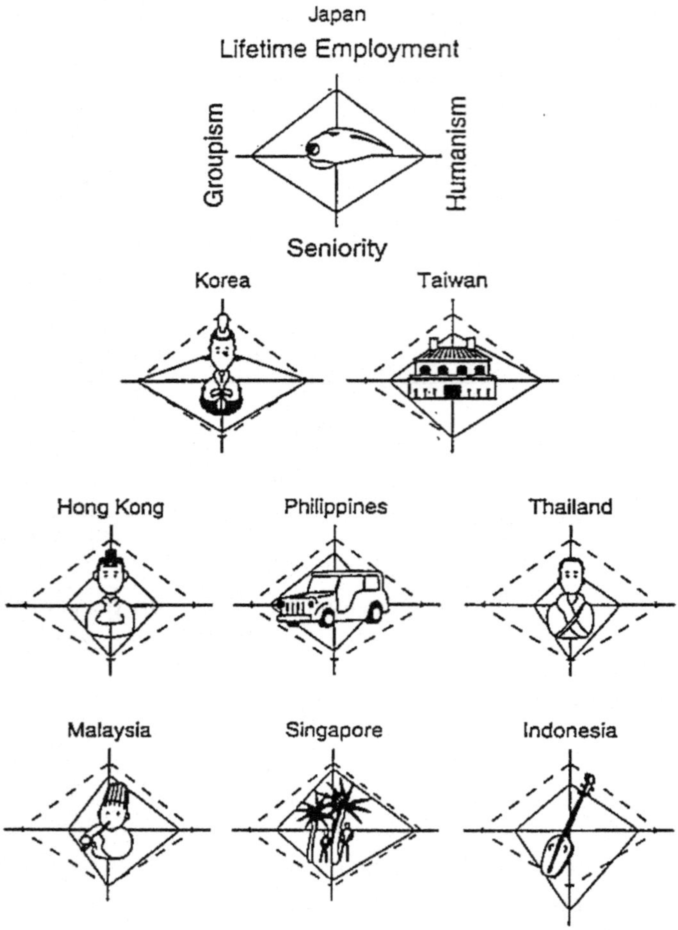

Fig. 1. Modification of Japanese-style Management in 8 Asian Countries in Four Characteristics.

3. Japanese-style Management Practice in Mainland China

In the recent studies for Japanese joint ventures in China, we improved the questionnaire schedules based on experiences in our earlier works. The items of characteristics of Japanese management listed in our questionnaire were increased from 12 to 32. The answers to our questions are sought for five levels: highly practiced (5), largely practiced (4), neutral (3), largely not practiced (2), and not practiced almost at all (1). The points given in the following tables are the average scores in the replies from the returns.

Table 3. Japanese-style Management in Beijing, Shanghai, and Dalian: Top-manager's Judgment on Degree of Practice.

New	Old	Characteristics	Shanghai	Beijing	Dalian
1	(5)	Emphasis on business ideals	4.1	4.5	4.2
2		Simultaneous employment	2.8	2.9	2.5
3	(1)	Stable employment	3.9	4.3	3.7
4		Continuous internal training	4.1	4.5	4.2
5		Primarily internal promotion	3.8	3.9	—
6	(9)	Human relations of labor management	4.1	4.2	4.3
7	(11)	Minimum differentials in labor management	3.5	3.4	3.3
8		Emphasis on team work spirits	4.1	4.4	4.1
9	(6)	Job flexibility	3.5	3.7	3.4
10		Sharing information	3.9	4.1	3.5
11		Emphasis on quality	4.7	4.8	4.7
12	(7)	Consensus decision-making	3.8	3.9	3.5
13	(10)	Ringi system	3.3	3.8	3.5
14	(12)	QC circles	3.4	3.9	3.3
15		Proposal system	3.4	3.5	3.6
16		TQC	3.5	3.7	3.4
17		Just-in-time system	3.1	3.1	3.3
18	(2)	Seniority wage system	2.6	2.7	2.7
19	(3)	Seniority promotion	2.6	2.6	2.7
20	(4)	Job rotation	3.0	2.9	3.2
21		Transfer positions	3.1	2.8	3.1
22		Emphasis on *Corporate Man*	3.1	3.1	2.8
23		Prize to long-time employees	2.9	3.2	2.8
24		Enterprise labor unions	3.3	3.2	3.0
25		Strengthening work	4.0	4.0	3.9
26		Emphasis on examiners	3.7	3.4	—
27		Big room offices	3.6	3.8	3.3
28		On-the-job training	3.8	4.1	3.9
29		Off-the-job training	3.2	3.1	3.2
30		Studying in Japan	3.9	3.9	3.5
31		Welfare benefit in corporations	3.8	4.0	—
32		Others	3.5	5.0	—

If the points are more than three, that characteristic of Japanese style is on the practiced side. The higher the score is, the more practiced that aspect of Japanese-style management is.

From Table 3, we can compare the practice of Japanese-style management on these 32 characteristics in three different areas of China, as evaluated by Japanese top managers themselves. Furthermore, by taking the percentage of 3+4+5 of the total, we can compare the practice in China with those in other Asian countries on those earlier 12 characteristics. The interested reader can find himself about many other aspects of Japanese joint ventures' practice in China from the summary given in Table 4 until we publish all of our findings and their analyses as a book (Ichimura, 1998).

Table 3 gives the following impression about evaluation of Japanese top managers:

1. The practice of Japanese-style management does not fundamentally differ from one region to another among three cities.
2. It is largely more prevalent in the order of Beijing–Dalian–Shanghai, and the difference between Dalian and Shanghai is negligible.
3. On the whole, the practice of management styles in both places are similar to the practice in Japanese joint ventures in Taiwan rather than in Hong Kong, and more so in Beijing than in Shanghai. Without this survey, one could not have expected this finding.

4. Differences in Native Middle Managers' Reaction to Japanese-style Management

Our survey included the one on native middle managers' reaction to the Japanese management practiced in each corporation. Table 4 gives a comparative summary of the findings in Beijing, Dalian, and Shanghai.

Clearly, in all of the three cities, the responses of middle managers are such that their evaluation of the degree of implementing Japanese-style management is less than the top managers'. It is interesting to notice that the middle managers are much more willing to accept the Japanese-style management than the degree of actual implementation in Japanese joint venture corporations. Careful interpretation may be necessary of this fact, however. Maybe, the middle managers chosen are those who are more willing to cooperate with management than the average or representative middle manager. Notice that the middle managers in Beijing are much more willing to accept the Japanese-style management than those in Shanghai. This fact corresponds to the actual practice remarked by the Japanese top managers in Shanghai and Beijing. This is just one of our observations on regional difference that one can make from our surveys.

Table 4. Top and Middle Managers' Judgment on Implementation and Willingness to Accept Japanese-style of Management in their Companies.

	Top's evaluation			Middle's perception			Middle's acceptance		
1. Management philosophy	4.5	4.2	4.1	3.3	3.7	3.7	3.7	3.7	3.8
2. Annual recruitment for all	2.9	2.5	2.8	2.8	2.6	2.8	3.2	3.5	3.2
3. Stable employment	4.3	3.7	3.9	3.7	3.7	3.4	4.0	4.2	4.2
4. Continuous in-house training	4.3	4.1	3.9	3.1	2.9	2.9	4.6	4.2	4.2
5. Harmonization between managers and the managed	4.2	4.3	4.1	3.5	3.6	3.9	4.3	4.0	4.2
6. Minimization status difference	3.4	3.3	3.5	3.1	3.3	3.3	3.9	3.7	3.6
7. Encouraging team spirit	4.4	4.1	4.1	3.9	3.8	4.2	4.4	4.6	4.4
8. Group meeting	—	—	—	3.4	3.2	3.6	3.9	3.9	3.8
9. Flexible management/job demarcation	3.4	3.4	3.5	2.2	2.8	2.8	3.0	3.5	3.7
10. Sharing objectives and information	4.1	3.5	3.9	3.3	3.4	3.3	4.4	4.1	4.0
11. Strong quality consciousness	4.8	4.7	4.7	4.0	4.3	4.2	4.7	4.8	4.6
12. No private office system	3.8	3.3	3.6	3.2	3.7	3.6	3.9	4.0	3.8
13. On-the-job training	4.1	3.9	3.8	3.7	3.1	3.5	4.6	4.3	4.2
14. Off-the-job training	3.1	3.2	3.2	2.6	2.0	2.4	4.4	3.5	4.0
15. Training in the head office	3.9	3.5	3.9	2.6	2.4	2.6	4.5	4.3	4.3
16. Consensus-based decision	3.9	3.5	3.8	3.6	3.1	3.0	4.1	3.7	3.9
17. Ringi system	3.8	3.5	3.3	3.6	3.6	3.5	4.1	3.9	3.9
18. QC circle	3.9	3.3	3.4	2.5	3.4	3.1	4.3	4.3	4.2
19. Suggestion system	3.5	3.6	3.4	2.9	3.3	3.1	4.4	4.1	4.0
20. Company-wide quality control	3.7	3.4	3.5	3.1	3.5	3.3	4.4	4.4	4.2
21. Just-in-time system	3.1	3.3	3.1	1.9	2.5	2.2	3.6	3.6	3.1
22. Length-of-service based pay raise system	2.7	2.7	2.6	2.9	3.2	2.6	3.8	3.9	3.6
23. Length-of-service based promotion system	2.7	2.7	2.6	2.6	2.7	2.4	3.9	3.7	3.4
24. Job reassignment	2.8	3.1	3.1	2.3	2.5	2.5	3.8	3.4	3.4
25. Job rotation	2.9	3.2	3.0	2.6	2.4	2.5	3.6	3.2	3.3
26. Inclination to foster "company men"	3.1	2.8	3.1	3.4	3.3	3.6	4.2	4.2	4.0
27. Recognition for long service	3.2	2.8	2.9	2.7	2.2	2.8	4.0	4.0	4.1
28. Inclination toward in-house union	3.2	3.0	3.3	2.3	2.7	2.5	4.1	3.3	3.7
29. Humane treatment of labor	4.2	4.3	4.1	3.5	3.8	3.6	4.5	4.4	4.3
30. Tight manning standard	4.0	3.9	4.0	3.2	3.6	3.6	4.5	4.1	4.1
31. Others	5.0	—	3.5	—	—	—		—	—

References

[1] Ichimura, S. (ed.) (1980). *Nihon Kigyo in Asia (Japanese Firms in Asia)*, Toyokeizai Shinpo-sha, Tokyo.

[2] Ichimura, S. (ed.) (1988). *Asia ni nezuku Nihonteki Keiei (Japanese Style Management rooting in Asia)*, Toyokeizai Shinpo-sha, Tokyo.

[3] Ichimura, S. (ed.) (1998). *Chuugoku kara mita Nihonteki Keiei, (Japanese Style Management viewed in China)*, Toyokeizai Shinpo-sha, Tokyo.

Part IV

Political and Cultural Problems of Asian Nations

Chapter 17

Nationalism and Asian Political Leaders

1. Introduction

This was a keynote speech[1] at the annual convention of Mito Historical Association at Mito city, 1995, and its latter half was published in its organ, *Mito History Review*, 1997. This chapter is a summary translation by the author on the discussions of the role of two great political leaders' nationalism in Asia: Sun Yat-sen and Sukarno.

2. Political Leadership for Nation-building

Part II already discussed the prerequsite for starting the construction of modern national economy in Asia. The minimum essential are national unification and economic take-off. They are not sufficient. On human side, the country needs great political leaders who can achieve not only national unification but also motivate the young people to devote their energy for idealistic nation-building and the enlightened intellectuals to offer new ideas to reform the old regimes and construct modern states. To express their ideals or political slogans, most Asian leaders used slogans such as nationalism, humanism, or democracy and coined some charming words of their own. In addition, some religious tradition such as piety to God

[1]The speech broadly covered the following topics: (1) First half of the 20th century and the latter half; (2) two trends of global affairs: integration and split; (3) nation-building in Asia; (4) independence war and civil wars; (5) the latter half of 20th century is the period of nation-building; (6) Hsin-hai revolution and Sun Yat-sen's three principles; (7) Indonesian Independence and Sukarno's Pancha Sila; (8) difficulties in nation-building; (9) some perspectives of Asia's future — the clash of civilizations and China's expansionism. This chapter translates primarily topics 6 and 7 and adds some notes.

and social fairness were also emphasized to unite all social groups in the nation-state. Let us see the history.

The first Asian nation that emerged as a modern state was Japan. Certainly, Japan needed the same kind of political leadership and spirits to modernize herself. There are so many similarities between what Japan achieved in the Meiji reform and what other Asian countries achieved later in the post-World War II independence movements or even earlier anti-colonial movements. My observations will be limited only to the roles of leaders and their spirits or the political ideals that guided their nations to modernize themselves.[2] Needless to say, the success of the Meiji reform and establishment of a new centralized government in Japan must have been a great precedent for many Asian political leaders, not only then but also later, and whether independence-oriented or anti-colonial. In the case of Japan, the greatest opening of the Meiji era was the official declaration of guiding principles of the new government, which took place in the formal Shinto style ceremony on 14 March 1868. The Emperor Meiji oathed the following *Oath in Five Articles*[3] with the government top leaders in front of the ancestorial gods.

(1) Deliberate assemblies shall be widely established and all matters decided by public discussion.
(2) All classes, high and low, shall unite in vigorously carrying out the administration of affairs of state.
(3) The common people, no less than the civil and military officials, shall each be allowed to pursue his own calling so that there may be no discontent.
(4) Evil customs of the past shall be broken off and everything based on the just laws of nature.
(5) Knowledge shall be sought throughout the world so as to strengthen the foundations of imperial rule.

---

[2]The history of Meiji reform is described very well in the classic work of N. Herman Norman, *Japan's Emergence as a Modern State*, 1940 (many editions later).

[3]This translation was taken from D. Keen: *The Emperor of Japan Meiji and his World, Columbia University Press, 2005.*

It is impressive that as early as 1868, Japanese political leaders recognized the guiding principles for the modern state so well as these five articles stated.[4]

3. Sun Yat-sen and Three Principles of the People

It goes without saying that this oath implies the same ideas as democracy, national unification, social fairness, etc. required for modernization. It was Sun Yat-sen (1866–1925) who could learn the recent events of the Meiji reform and got the impact.[5] He left many letters and writings admiring the performance of the Meiji reform and many patriotic warriors. Particularly after the Sino-Japanese War in 1894–1895, many Chinese students began to flow into Japan and started their own movements of anti-colonial and anti-Ch'ing in dynasty revolution.

The political ideas of Sun Yat-sen are the famous *Three Principles of the People*. Its exposition is usually taken from the book which is based on the lectures he gave on his last days. It is often translated as consisting of nationalism, democracy, and peoples' welfare (livelihood). Before reaching those three words as the essence of his ideals, however, he came through a number of Western and American thoughts. By looking back his ways of reaching the final conclusions, we can learn how those attractive three principles were coined in his mind.

When he was young, he and his colleagues at *the Revive China Society* had the slogans: *Four Basic Plans and Three Steps*. The former were (1) Drive out Evil Enemies, (2) Restore Great China, (3) Construct People's State, and (4) Fair Ownership of Land Property. The famous slogan of Meiji reform was "respect the Emperor, exclude foreigners". The first two of *Four Basic Plans* were exactly these, namely, nationalism. The third is democracy. The fourth was People's livelihood or economic

[4]The emperor of Japan, Showa, quoted this Oath in his imperial edict on New Year day of 1946 and re-emphasized in his interview with newspapers in 1977 that democracy was nothing new to Japan but what Emperor Meiji advocated in the Oath.

[5]This should not be interpreted that Sun Yat-sen was influenced by this Oath. Earlier, he was widely influenced by Western thoughts, particularly his education and travels in the U.S. He was a Christian in his creeds, although he had some very close friends in Japan like Toten Miyazaki and Tsuyoshi Inukai.

development.[6] He had these ideas already when he and his collaborators organized *the Revive China Society* but published in 1905 as an editorial of *Min Bao*.[7] Sun Yat-sen's ideology typically expresses the three aspects of almost all Asian nationalisms: (1) anti-foreign ideas and self-esteemed nation, (2) self-determination (no subjugation), and (3) improve peoples' living. These principles are common to the ideals of all the political leaders in Asia, including Sun Yat-sen, Sukarno, Jose Rizahl (1861–1896: Philippines), U Nu (1907–1995: Myanmar) and so on.

Three Steps meant that the Chinese revolution could not be achieved all at once, so that it must take three steps, namely, (1) military government, (2) training government, (3) constitutional government. For the ideal constitutional government like the U.S., government cannot be realized in China due to the low level of education and knowledge of the Chinese people now. People need more education and experiences of running the various organizations by themselves.

Even the contents of nationalism or democracy in three principles had to be changed as he faces reality in China after the success of revolution. For instance, Sun Wen first wanted to establish the new China mainly on the basis of Han ethnic group. But after Chi'ng (Qing) dynasty fell, he wanted to inherit the entire territory of Qing dynasty so that he needed the way of integrating different ethnic groups as minorities within the new Republic of China. There remained many other difficult problems of organizing the modern state in China which he and his collaborators could not solve in their lifetimes.

4. Sukarno and Pancha Sila

Sukarno (1901–1970) was the hero of Indonesian independence. His name is sometimes spelt as Soekarno in the Dutch way, and it is a full name in Javanese. He was born in Surabaya as a son of Javanese noble family

---

[6]This last item was referring to land ownership and administration of its rent and other remunerations. We do not enter the discussion on this point here. However, Maoists interpreted this idea according to Marxism–Leninism, and Nationalist Chinese interpreted as fair control of free private enterprise system.

[7]Sharman, L. (1968). *Sun-Yat-Sen, His Life and Its Meaning; A Critical Biography*, Stanford University Press.

and his mother was from a Bali Hindu family. He was Indonesia's first President in office from 1945 to 1967. He was already a prominent leader of Indonesian Nationalist Movement during the Dutch colonial period and had to spend in Dutch detention several times, altogether over a decade. It was the Japanese army forces (top commander was Hitoshi Imamura, a thoughtful Christian general) that released him from a Dutch prison as soon as they came in early 1942. They requested him and his collaborators' cooperation with the Japanese army to stabilize the livelihood of Indonesian population and the social order. There was a strong sympathy in the Japanese military with the indepencence movements in Indonesia, so that Japanese occupation army and the Indonesian nationalists' groups cooperated rather friendly, though there appeared many difficult issues later to resolve during the war. On 15 August 1945, the Japanese government officially accepted the Potsdam Declaration and surrendered. The news reached Sukarno and his group. They immediately decided to declare Indonesia's independence by themselves. After some consultation with the Japanese side, they drafted the Independecne Declarations. At the same time, a group of Indonesian leaders agreed on the five principles of founding a new independent nation: Indonesia. Pancha Sila were the Sanskrit words (Pancha = five, Sila = principles) expressing those principles. They are written as preamble in the final form of the Indonesian Consitution declared on August 17, 1945:

1. Belief in the divinity of God,
2. Just and civilized humanity,
3. The unity of Indonesia,
4. Democracy guided by the inner wisdom in the unanimity arising out of deliberations amongst representatives,
5. Social justice for all of the people of Indonesia.

These sentences were mostly taken from the so-called Djakarta Charter which Sukarno formulated his political ideologies developed for the past 20 years at BPUPKI[8] on June 1, 1945. They may express his original ideas

[8]Committee for preparing for Indonesian Independence, Badan Penjelidik Oesaha Persiapan Kemerdekaan Indonesia, a quasi-legislature consisting of 67 representatives from most ethnic groups in Indonesia.

more straightforwardly. The original Sukarno views were reported as the following:

(1) Nationalism, whereby a united Indonesian state would stretch from Sabang to Merauke, encompassing all former Dutch East Indies.
(2) Internationalism, meaning Indonesia is to appreciate human rights and contribute to world peace, and should not fall into chauvinistic fascism such as displayed by Nazis with their belief in the racial superiority of Aryans.
(3) Democracy, which, Sukarno believed, has been always in the blood of Indonesians through the practice of consensus-seeking (*musyawarah untuk maufakat*), an Indonesian-style democracy different from Western-style liberalism.
(4) Social justice, a form of populist socialism in economics with Marxist-style opposition to free capitalism. Social justice also intended to provide equal share of the economy to all Indonesians, as opposed to the complete economic domination by the Dutch and Chinese during the colonial period.
(5) Belief in God, whereby all religions are treated equally and have religious freedom; Sukarno saw Indonesians as spiritual and religious people, but in essence tolerant towards differing religious beliefs.

On June 22, Islamic elements of BPUPKI nationalists created a small sib-committee of nine, which formulated those Sukarno's ideas into the five point Pancha Sila in a document known as *the Jakarta Charter*; that is:

(1) Belief in one and only Almighty God with obligation for Muslims to adhere to Islamic Law.
(2) Civilized and just humanity.
(3) Unity of Indonesia.
(4) Democracy through inner wisdom and representative consensus-building.
(5) Social justice for all Indonesians.

It has concisely summarized Sukarno's ideas but made two important changes: (a) to put religious article to the front and (b) to make Indonesia the Islamic state to practice the Islamic Law (sharia). However, as was already quoted above, the final constitution accepted (a) but not (b), namely, it excluded the reference to Islamic Law for the sake of national unity. This was to resolve the important difference between Sukarno and Islamic elements including M. Hatta at the last critical moment. This points to the most critical issue in nation-building in almost all countries in Asia, because all the countries consist of many ethnic groups, and often each ethnic group has its own religious belief or some sects of a religion or religions. How to unite such people and form a modern state is the most critical matter. Certainly, Indonesia is no exception. About 75% of total population are Muslims, but there are many ethnic groups that are predominantly Christians like Bataks, those Hindus like Balinese, Budhists, or Taoists and so on. Sukarno has known all these from his childhood.[9]

It is clear that Panch Sila in the Constitution of Indonesia covers all the required causes needed for modern nation-building in Asia, as we mentioned at the beginning. It is also clear, however, that some requirements contradict themselves. In particular, three matters are important and they have shown up in Indonesia as well as China: (1) multi-ethnic country and national unification; (2) religious tolerance and multiple religious creed; and (3) free, private enterprise system (capitalism) and socialism (social fairness). Before concluding this chapter, some brief notes will be added on these matters.

5. Multi-ethnic and Multi-religious Country and National Unification

If there are several ethnic groups in the same nation, and they are *antagonistic* to each other, there is no choice but to subdivide the country into smaller countries with their own territories, because national unification is a necessary condition to form a nation-state. The British India was divided to Nepal, Butan, India, Pakistan, Bangladesh, Sri Lanka, and Myanmar for that reason. Similarly, the Balkan countries were separated from each other after the WWI, partially merged after the WWII, and separated again after the end of cold war.

---

[9]As for special conditions of religions in Indonesia, see Chapter 9.

If different ethnic groups are not mutually antagonistic, then several groups can form a nation like some European countries. Many of them educate the people in different languages (often French, Dutch, German, or Italian, etc.). This does not prevent them from forming one nation-state. The essential condition then is no antagonism and agreement on the rule of law.

In the countries with multiple religions, what is required for nation-building is religious tolerance or secularism — separation of religions from daily living of ordinary families. Religious antagonism can be very fierce. Modern nations have learnt by now that religious wars had better be avoided, so that almost all the consitutions of modern states admit the freedom of beliefs. There are two groups of countries in the world now that do not admit freedom of religion (or liberty of conscience): (1) some Islamic countries[10] and (2) some Communist countries.[11]

In the case of Soviet Union, as soon as the iron rule of Communist Party is removed around 1989, all the republics in the Soviet Union and the satellite countries sought independence. Clearly, there was no voluntary bondage to tie them together as the same country-men, nation, or even the allies.

6. Sympathy of Asian Nationalism with Socialist Countries

One characteristic of Asian political leaders is that most of them show somewhat, or sometimes strong, sympathy with Marxian socialism. Examples of such political leaders include Sun Yat-sen, Sukarno, U Nu, Nehru, and so on, although all of them are very religious persons in their own creeds. The reasons are the following. When they were students in the West or their own countries and learnt the western social thoughts, Marxism or similar socialist thinkings were fashionable in the university circles and journalisms, particularly in the midst of Great Depression in the 1930s. Moreover, Marxists attacked capitalism not only as a cause for depression in advanced Western economies but also as a cause for imperialistic

[10]Some Islamic groups admit other religions but not atheism and regard Communism as atheism. Massacre of communists took place in Indonesia and under Pol Pot for this reason.
[11]Under Communist Pol Pot regime, massacre took place for this reason.

colonialism to exploit the colonies in Asia and Africa. A march to socialism seemed to be on the road in dominant countries to the mind of young, immature mind from colonized countries. At the time of cold war, many Asian political leaders were attracted by the voices of Soviet and Chinese leaders until they realized and were disillusioned by what had really taken place in those two countries.

Chapter 18

Is the Clash of Civilizations or Nations?*

1. A Certain Bias of Huntington's Thesis

Huntington's book *The Clash of Civilizations* attracted an enormous attention among the political arguments in Japan as well as all over the world, perhaps because it gave an impression that the book correctly predicted the forthcoming wars in Iraq and Afghanistan. The book was a development of the author's sensational article in the *Foreign Affairs*, July 1993. His straightforward arguments in the article caused so many criticisms that he considerably modified and mitigated the original assertions. I myself recognized that the article had proposed an extremely important problem on the world affairs after the Cold War. I noticed, however, that as he had been so in his earlier writings on other subjects, he sharply pointed out a few important problems and their analyses, but at the same time, he committed some mistakes of bias and exaggeration. To my limited knowledge, he wrote the following two outstanding books and made great contributions in political science: *The Soldier and the State*, 1957, and *Political Order of Changing Societies*, 1968. The former dealt with the civilian control in the United States, whereas the latter argued on the issues of political instability caused by the success of economic growth in many developing countries. He based his arguments on the observations in Latin America. In both studies, his sharp proposal of important issues was very impressive but his methods and logics were imperfect and observations were not universal historically and regionally. His conclusions were biased or not necessarily right.

---

*This review article on Samuel P. Huntington, *The Clash of Civilizations* and *The Re-Making of the World Order*, Simon and Schuster, 1996, was published in AURORA (a quarterly organ of the Kansai 21st Century Association), Spring, 1999.

For instance, he argued that economic growth caused income inequality and led to social instability in Latin American countries. When, however, James Morley and I studied the Asian development, the contrary was true. I cannot help feeling that he did not know the real circumstances in Asia even in this study of *The Clash of Civilizations*.[1] I would take up some issues and critically review the book and his perspectives on the likely challenge to the United States in the 21st century.

2. A Sense of Crisis as Christians

Huntington's article in 1993 was not his own article but a report for the project commissioned to the John M. Olin Institute for Strategic Studies, at Harvard University just established under his directorship on July 1, 1989. The project was on what would be the national interest of the United States after the end of Cold War. To organize a research project on this theme right after 1989 was rather unusual. For after the fall of Berlin wall, optimisms prevailed that American superpower could dominate the world and keep peace so that one could talk about peace dividends, or some intellectuals like Francis Fukuyama trusted that the parliamentary democracy would dominate the political system anywhere in the world so that he entitled his book *The End of History*.[2] Samuel P. Huntington, however, believed that the serious world conflicts were likely to occur not on economic interests or ideologies but between different nation-states or social groups that belong to different civilizations. At first, I did not understand where from his worry came. While reading his article, I realized that his worry was the challenge of non-Christian civilizations or Islam–Confucius civilizations against Christian civilizations. Perhaps, when the project theme was given, he must have asked himself who would be challenging our Christian civilizations. Such a sense of crisis of the author shows up clearly in the paper. Would it not be too excessive to worry about such challenges despite the superpower of the US at its peak? Would it not lead to an over-reaction

[1]Morley, J. and S. Ichimura, "Varieties of Asian Growth and Political Change," in Morley, J. (ed.), *Driven by Growth*, The Sharp, NY, 1993.

[2]Fukuyama, F., "The End of History," The *National Interest*, Summer 1989, was the first article publishing his ideas and expanded as a book: *The End of History*, Free Press, 1992. The title often caused a misunderstanding of his views. He meant only the end of ideological differences on political system of governance. Even so, he was too simplistic.

of the US power if anything goes wrong in the new world? It is true that the Challenge of Communism implied to negate any religions freedom and private property but not necessarily all other non-Christian civilizations.[3]

3. What is Civilization?

A flood of critical opinions on S. Huntington's first article were sent into the editorial office of the *Foreign Affairs*, which seems to have led the author to modify and mitigate his provocative statements and became almost as moderate as the normal assertions on civilizations in the 1996 book. The crucial question in his thesis is to define more clearly, what civilization is, and the second question is more specifically to explain the actual ways for civilizations to clash. What actually clashes are the tight social organizations such as religious groups, nations, races, states, etc. He maintains, however, that to regard the conflicts, battles or wars in the coming world as clashes of inclusive units like civilizations is a better way of grasping the future struggles of many social organizations. He interprets Arnold Toynbee's words, "civilization is a comprehensive concept and cannot be included in something else", by quoting Mathew Melco's sentences to paraphrase.[4]

> Civilization is a totality. Civilizations have a certain degree of integration. Their parts are defined by their relationship to each other and to the whole. If the civilization is composed of states, these states will have more relation to one another than they do with states outside the civilization. They might fight more, and engage more frequently in diplomatic relations. They will be more interdependent economically. There will be pervading aesthetic and philosophic currents.

The borders of civilizations will be drawn by the common factors in languages, histories, living customs, and social institutions as well as

---

[3]In the European and Chinese histories of thought, the individual thinkers' nationalities, ethnic and religious backgrounds, and their childhood are far more important and complicated than the cases of Japanese scholars. For instance, to understand Marxism, it is essential to know that he was born as a son of rabbi. To understand great contemporary scholars like Kissinger, Brzezinski, and others, their family backgrounds are very important. It seems to me that S. Huntington's examination of North American civilization for its identity and characteristics suggests the importance of examining other civilization like Japanese in the same way.

[4]Malco, M., *The Nature of Civilizations*, Boston, Porter Sargant, 1969.

Table 1. Seven Civilizations in the World.

Civilization	Religion	Nations, ethnic group	Language
1 Western civilization			
1. West European	Protestant, Catholic	Scandinavian, German, Anglo-Saxon, France, Latin races	English, German, French, Spanish, Italian, etc.
2. North American	Protestant, Catholic, and others	*Op. cit.* plus negro, new immigrants	English, Spanish, French, etc.
2 Chinese civilization	Taoism, Confucianism, Buddhism, Communism,	Han, Mongol, Tibetan, and others	Chinese, Mongolian, and others
3 Japanese civilization	Shintoism, Buddhism, and others	Japanese and small minorities	Japanese
4 Indian civilization	Hindu and others	Many ethnic groups	Hindu and others
5 Islam civilization	Islamism	Middle and Near East, North African, and Iran	Arabian and others
6 Russian civilization	Russian orthodox,	Russian, Central Asian ethnic groups	Russian and others
7 Latin-American civilization	Catholicism	Original natives, Latin European, negro	Spanish, Portuguese, etc.

the subjective recognition of those. He summarized the seven important civilizations in the world as shown in Table 1.

Table 1 clearly shows that each civilization is characterized by its dominant religions. In this connection, S. Huntington was conscious of the possible mistreatment of an important religion Buddhism, as if it is a sub-culture of Chinese or Japanese civilizations. At the same time, he explains similarly, why the Jewish religion and Jews are not treated as one civilization despite its strong influence in the US. He asks, how about Jewish civilization? The majority of researchers on civilization do not refer to it. For its population is so small that it is not an important civilization. Toynbee once commented that it sprang from the early Syrian culture but could not grow smoothly afterwards. The Jewish religion was historically related to both Christianity and Islamism, but the Jewish people did not lose their own cultural identity amazingly in the midst of West European civilizations, East European orthodox churches, and Islamism for so many centuries. Now that Israel is founded as the State, the Jews are fully equipped with their religion, language, living customs, literature, social institutions, territory, and political homeland; namely, all objective factors needed for civilization. However, how about the subjective recognition of their own identity as such? The self-identity of the Jews living in the other civilizations seems to differ from the perfect identity with Israel to the perfect identity with the other civilizations of their own residences except for the nominal creeds. Many Jews in Western Europe are of the latter type."

Thus, except for two religions, Buddhism[5] and Judaism, all religions are the bases of civilizations in the world. At some places in the book, he mentions that the essential factors of civilization are religion and language. That is not an appropriate statement. Social groups that are likely to be formed with the same language may be called "nation" or "tribe" in English or may be identified with some ethnic group.[6] Civilization can be defined by religion as a primary cause so that its border is normally not as clear as nation — speaking the same language. His arguments often do not distinguish between the clashes of civilizations from the clash of nations. In Western Europe or American continent, that distinction was not so important, but in Eastern Europe, Middle East, Eastern Europe, Central Asia, China, and East Asia, the distinction is very important. Otherwise, sometimes one cannot distinguish civil wars from international wars. How complicated the mixture of religions and nations are in East Asia can be seen in Table 2.

If China, Russia, and Japan are added to this table, it will complete the configuration of East Asian countries. The wars likely to occur in East Asia will be the clash of nations rather than civilizations or religions. S. Huntington counts the Iraq war and the Afghanistan war as No. 1

[5]S. Huntington misses the essential information of Southeast and South Asia, where the majority of the peoples in many countries believe in Buddhism: They may be called *Buddhist nations* in the same sense that Western European countries are Christian nations. Sri Lanka, Myanmar, Thailand, Lao, Cambodia, Vietnam, Nepal, and Bhutan are like that. In all of them and some regions in India, Buddhism is not a sub-culture of anything.

[6]Social group organized by the same language as a prime cause is called in Japanese "*minzoku*," distinguished from race, States, tribe, or country.

Table 2. Religions and Nations in East Asian Countries.

Country	Religion	Nation, tribe	Language
1 North Korea	Confucianism, Communism	Korean	Korean
2 South Korea	Confucianism, Christianism, Buddhism	Korean	Korean
3 Taiwan	Confucianism, Christianism, Taoism, Buddhism	South Han tribe	Beijing Chinese, Fukien
4 Philippines	Catholicism	Many tribes	Taganrog, etc.
5 Vietnam	Buddhism, Communism	Vietnamese	Vietnamese
6 Laos	Buddhism	Laotian	Thai
7 Thailand	Buddhism	Thai and others	Thai
8 Cambodia	Buddhism	Cambodian, others	Cambodian
9 Malaysia	Islamism, Taoism, Christianism, others	Malay, Chinese, Tamil	Malay, English, and others
10 Singapore	Taoism, Christianism, and others	Southern Han, Malay, and others	English
11 Indonesia	Islamism, Hinduism, Christianism	Javanese, many tribes	Indonesian, etc.
12 Myanmar	Buddhism	Burmese and others	Burmese, etc.
13 Brunei	Islamism	Malay	Malayan

and No. 2 wars of civilizations. For several reasons, his argument is too unreasonable. One should remember that Iraq attacked Kuwait just before the Gulf war. Obviously, it had nothing to do with religion. There are many Islamic countries around Afghanistan. It is very hard to regard these wars really as caused for religious reasons.

4. Where and What Conflicts will Occur?

The fundamental ideas of S. Huntington are that the clash of civilizations will occur primarily between leading states of both civilizations and along the fault line. He writes "the fights between different civilizations would take two forms. At the micro level of regions, they will occur on the border of civilizations. It can either occur between neighbors of different civilizations or it can occur between social groups with different civilizations inside one country. As was the case in the Soviet Union or Yugoslavia, it can occur if after the ancient regime breaks down, a new force is born to initiate forming a new government. Conflicts on the border are likely to occur between Islamic and non-Islamic groups.

At the macro level of global affairs, the conflicts of heartlands are likely to occur between some powers in different civilizations. The issues are of classic types in international politics. A list of those follows:

1. The ways and means of global development; influence on the policies of World Bank, IMF, and other international organizations.
2. Relative military forces to show up in non-proliferation of nuclear weapons, disarmament, limits of military expansion.
3. Economic power shown in the debates on trade and direct investment and the related benefit and welfare.
4. Human right issues, including those of the same nationalities or races in different civilizations.
5. The issues related to values and cultures; conflicts caused by enforcing its own values of one civilization upon another.
6. Territorial issues: heartlands come out to the front.

The conflicts on these issues will lead to wars, if the balance of power between civilizations is lost. S. Huntington worries about Asia, because as some Asian countries side with stronger nations, the US India, or Russia may get involved in war against expanding China to maintain the balance of power. Another war he seriously worries is the clash of Western civilizations with the Islamic circles. He writes that this war will be far more serious than the war against Marxism–Leninism.

This argument seems to deny the possibility that various civilizations permeate each other systematically and influence constructively and eventually can coexist with the differences remaining to realize the world civilization. To say it more simply, his argument admits clash only, no coexistence at all. His first article certainly implied that assertion. I felt myself that it was a monotheist's simple-minded and dangerous conclusion. There must have been many similar criticisms. In the book, he replied to a criticism of Hayward Alkar by saying that, he would not deny the possibility that the world civilization would be born where all the nations could colive with the sense of solidarity.

If one pursues this point further, it would require a reconsideration of his theme itself, because the issue is what determines the clash or the coexistence of civilizations. I notice, however, that unlike his first article, the book makes many remarks that admit the coexistence of civilizations. He often warns against the self-righteousness of the US or Western civilization. The conviction that the Western values or institutions may be forced upon non-Western peoples is, as he writes in the book, something to be accused as immoral. He gives a warning: Western universalism may induce a large scale of war between heartlands. It is not only dangerous to the world but also to the West, because the West may be defeated. After the breakdown of the Soviet Union, the Westerners are convinced that they are in the dominating position, which nobody has ever attained. On the other hand, the weak Asian and Islamic societies are getting ever stronger. Then, we should not apply the famous logic of Brutus for the leader of a power.

> Our legions are brim-full, our cause is ripe.
> The enemy increaseth every day,
> We, at the height, are ready to decline.
> There is a tide in the affairs of men,
> Which taken on the flood, leads on to fortune;
> Omitted, all the voyage of their life
> Is bound to shallows and miseries.
> On such a full sea are we now afloat,
> And we must take the current when it serves,
> Or lose our ventures.

Thinking and acting that way, Brutus lost the battle of Philippi, which we should never repeat.

5. Consider Heartland vs Rimland and Land Power vs Sea Power

Now we as Japanese should ask ourselves what lessons we could learn from S. Huntington's outstanding work. Before reflecting on it, however, some elements of geopolitics[7] are necessary to learn, because Japan is so different from the US in some fundamental characteristics. First, we should

---

[7]Geopolitics was developed originally by Harcott J. Mackinder (1861–1947). His ideas were declared in "On the Scope and Methods of Geography," in *Proceedings of the Royal Geographical Society*, vol. 9, March, 1887 and recognized by "The Geographical Pivot of History," in *Democratic Ideals and Reality*, Washington, DC, National Defense University Press, 1996.

learn a size difference of Japan from China, Russia, or the US[8]; second, the distinction between sea power and land power; third, the one between heartland and rimland, as geo-politicians pointed out a long time ago.[9] From this geo-political viewpoint, Zbigniew Brzezinski argued in his *The Grand Chess Board*, 1998 about the geo-strategy of the US. He points out that only six heartlands exist in the world; namely, China, India, the US, Russia, Germany, France, whereas all others including Japan, UK, Indonesia are rimlands. Heartlands are all land powers, except for the US that is simultaneously a sea power. UK and Japan are sea powers. Z. Brzezinski repeated the classic proposition of N. Spykman that the US has its vital stake in protecting the interests of Western Europe: France and Germany in particular. From these points of view, Z. Brzezinski points out the border of two power groups — China and Russia vs the US and the rest of East Asia and the Pacific along Korean peninsula, the East China sea, the Taiwan strait, South China sea off the Vietnam coast. S. Huntington's arguments differ from Z. Brzezinski only where Russia is classified. If we consider the two scholars' points of view, Japan's position would be easier to understand. Japan is a rimland and sea power. As Huntington said, it is a singular civilization whose sphere of influence has shrank after the World War II. We Japanese must look at the world affairs from the viewpoint of such a nation's civilization.

6. Which Civilization Could Exert the Biggest Influence?

The US drove the world of 20th century. The sources of its power were:

1. military power,
2. economic power, and
3. superiority in socioeconomic and political institutions.

The other factors making American civilization attractive were:

4. political authority to control and influence the other nations,
5. superiority of cultural, scientific, engineering activities, and
6. higher levels of human and societal moral.

---

[8]Size here refers to territory. Japanese population is about the same as Russian.

[9]As for the United States, classic works are Nicholas J. Spykman, (1893–1943), *America's Strategy in World Politics*, Harcourt, Brace and co., NY, 1942 and *The Geography of the Peace*, Harcourt, Brace and co., NY, 1944.

When a nation or a group of nations plays a leading role among civilizations, those who could support the high-level civilizations as pillars are the individuals capable of carrying out the balanced conditions of those factors. If any nations have many such persons, they carry great authority to influence on other civilizations. To look back, the rise and the fall of civilizations from the viewpoint of such supporters of civilization were also done in both books but not enough. Japan in early 21st century is certainly smaller and relatively less than before in the above-mentioned six points. However, as she had done from late 19th century to early 20th century, we could do the same contributions perhaps in different ways in 21st century, if we try hard enough.

Appendix

List of Monographs and Collected Papers of Shinichi Ichimura

This is a list of monographs and main articles and essays by Shinichi Ichimura in the area of economics and related sciences on Japanese and Asian issues. In this list, the titles in non-English are translated into English. The original languages are indicated after the published year by the signs such as (J): Japanese; (C): Chinese; (F): French, (I): Indonesian, and (S): Spanish. Notes on author column: S-auth = single author = S. Ichimura; Co-auth = with other authors; Ed = edited and written by S. Ichimura; Co-ed = edited and written with others; Sp = supervised. The names of co-author or co-editor are given at the right-hand corner of the title column.

I. Monographs

No	Year	Title	Author	Publisher
1	1951 (J)	(*National Income and Resources*) (N. Kamakura)	Co-auth	Kobundo
2	1953	*An Inquiry into Nonlinear Theories of Economic Fluctuations*	S-auth	MIT Dissertation
3	1954 (J)	(*The Structure of Economic Circulation*)	S-auth	Sobun-sha
4	1957 (J)	(*The Structure of the Japanese Economy — Input–Output Analysis*)	S-auth	Sobun-sha
5	1957	*A Historic Development of Economic Dynamics*	S-auth	Japan Academy
6	1958-1 (J)	(*Japanese Economy and Regional Economy*)	Sp	Sobun-sha

(*Continued*)

(*Continued*)

No	Year	Title	Author	Publisher
7	1958-2 (J)	(*Applications of Interindustrial Study*)	Ed	Yuhikaku
8	1960-1 (J)	(*The Future of Japanese Economy*)	Ed	Yuhikaku
9	1960-2 (J)	(*The Future of Okayama Prefecture*)	Ed	Okayama Prefecture
10	1960-3	*Programming Techniques for Development* (J. Tinbergen *et al.*)	Co-auth	ECAFE
11	1962 (J)	(*Missions of Educators*)	Ed	Japan Education Association Series
12	1963 (J)	(*Euro-American Education and Japanese Education*)	S-auth	Sobun-sha
13	1965 (J)	(*The Japanese Economy in the World*)	S-auth	Chuokoron
14	1968-1 (J)	(*Books Recommended for Contemporary Students*) (Aida, Nagai, and Uno)	Co-auth	Kodan-sha
15	1968-2 (J)	(*Management Methods in Computer Age*) (Transl.)	Ed	Nihonkeizai
16	1969 (J)	(*Twenty Recommendations for University Reform*) (M. Kohsaka and T. Yoshida)	Co-ed	Sobun-sha
17	1970 (J)	(*How to Comprehend the Contemporary World?*)	S-auth	Kodan-sha
18	1970 (J)	(*Economic Power on Trial*)	S-auth	Nihonkeizai
19	1970 (J)	(*Readings in Econometric Models of Japanese Economy*) (M. Tatemoto)	Co-auth	Toyokeizai
20	1974 (J)	(*Thinking of Southeast Asia*)	Ed	Sobun-sha
21	1974-1 (J)	(*Southeast Asia: Nature, Society and Development*) [28] translated	Ed	Sobun-sha
22	1974-2 (J)	(*Economic and Political Trends in the Soviet' Bloc*) (M. Inoki)	Co-ed	Sobun-sha
23	1975-1 (J)	(*The Economic Development of East and Southeast Asia*) [24] translated	Ed	Sobun-sha
24	1975-2	*The Economic Development of East and Southeast Asia*	Ed	University Press of Hawaii
25	1975-3	*A Regional Economic Survey of South Sumatra Province* (K. W. Thee *et al.*)	Co-auth	LIPI, Jakarta
26	1975-4 (I)	(*Indonesia: Various Issues and Events*) (Koentjoronigrat)	Co-ed	Obor, Jakarta
27	1976 (J)	(*In the Stream of History*)	S-auth	Sobun-sha
28	1977-1	*Southeast Asia: Nature, Society and Development*	Ed	University Press of Hawaii

(*Continued*)

(*Continued*)

No	Year	Title	Author	Publisher
29	1977-2	*An Econometric Analysis of the Japanese Economy* (L. R. Klein *et al.*)	Co-auth	Japanese S. for AS^{+}
30	1978	*Econometric Models of Asian Countries I*	Ed	ADIPA*
31	1979 (J)	(*Economic Development of Communist China*) (translation of the book in fn. 1)	Ed	Sobun-sha
32	1980-1 (J)	(*Japanese Firms in Asia*)	Ed	Toyokeizai Shinpo
33	1980-2	*Econometric Models of Asian Countries II*	Ed	ADIPA*
34	1981 (J)	(*Japanese Education: Ideals and Sufferings*)	Ed	Sobun-sha
35	1985-1 (J)	(*Wishing to Normalize Japanese Education*)	S-auth	Sobun-sha
36	1985-2 (J)	(*Searching for the Course of Japanese Economy*)	S-auth	Sobun-sha
37	1985-3	*Econometric Models of Asian LINK* (M. Ezaki)	Co-auth	Springer Verlag
38	1988-1 (J)	(*Japanese Style Management Rooting in Asia*)	Ed	Toyokeizai shimpo
39	1988-2	*The Challenges of Asian Developing Countries*	Ed	APO^{++}
40	1988-3	*Indonesian Economic Development*	Ed	JICA*
41	1988-4 (J)	(*The Political Economy of Contemporary Japan*) (M. Kohsaka)	Co-ed	PHP Institute
42	1989-1 (I)	(*Indonesian Economic Development*) Indonesian Transl.←[40] (S. Odano)	Co-ed	Univ. of Indonesia Press
43	1989-2	*The Political Economy of Fiscal Policy* (Urrtia and Yukawa)	Co-ed	UN University Press
44	1993-1	*The Role of Japan in Asia*	S-auth	I C S Press
45	1993-2	*Econometric Models of Asia-Pacific Countries* (Y. Matsumoto)	Co-ed	Springer Verlag
46	1994-1 (C)	(*Japanese Economy, Development and International Relations*) (ed./Transl. Se Wen)	S-auth	Beijing UP
47	1994-2 (J)	(*Transitional Economies in Asia*) (K. Miyamoto)	Co-ed	OIU
48	1998-1	*Political Economy of Japanese and Asian Development*	S-auth	Springer Verlag

(*Continued*)

(*Continued*)

No	Year	Title	Author	Publisher
49	1998-2 (J)	(*Japanese Style Management in China*)	Ed	Toyokeizai Shinpo
50	1999	*East Asian Economic Development* (F. G. Adams)	Co-ed	Praeger Publisher
51	2000	*Econometric Modeling of China* (L. R. Klein)	Co-ed	WSPC
52	2001-4 (J)	*Foundation of Economics* (2001-4 text editions)	S-auth	Sobun-sha
53	2001-2 (J)	(*Prof. H. Aoyama's Studies and Education*)	Ed	Sobun-sha
54	2003-1	*Interregional Input–Output Analysis of Chinese Economy* (H. J. Wang)	Co-ed	WSPC
55	2003-2 (J)	(*Political Economy of Japan and Asian Development*) [48] translated by S. Nagao	S-auth	Sobun-sha
56	2003-3 (J)	(*Economics of Harbors and Regions*) (Author M. Doi)	Sp	Taga Shuppan
57	2004-1 (J)	(*Interregional IO Analysis of Chinese Economy*) [54] translated	Co-ed	Sobun-sha
58	2004-2 (J)	(*Asian Development and Decentralization*) {59} translated	Ed	Kitakyushu City
59	2004-3	*Development and Decentralization in Asia*	Ed	Kitakyushu City
60	2004-4 (J)	(*Asian Automobile India and China's Challenge*) (Liu, Findley)	Sp	Sobun-sha
61	2004-5 (J)	(*Who has Defended the Japanese Education*)	S-auth	Sobun-sha
62	2005-1 (J)	(*Econometric Modeling of China*) [51] translated	Co-ed	Sobun-sha
63	2005-2 (C)	(*Interregional IO Analysis of Chinese Economy*) Chinese transl. by Li Shanton	Co-ed	Zai-Kei, Beijing
64	2006 (J)	(*My Postwar 60 Years*)	S-auth	Naigai News
65	2008-1 (J)	(*Revised Fundamental Law of Education and Teachers Attitude*)	S-auth	Kogakkan University Press
66	2008-2	*Decentralization Policy in Asia Development* (R. Bahl)	Co-ed	WSPC
67	2009	*Transition from Socialist to Market Economies* (Sato and James)	Co-ed	Palgrave-McMillan

(*Continued*)

(*Continued*)

No	Year	Title	Author	Publisher
68	2010	*Macroeconometric Modeling of Japan* (L. Klein)	Co-ed	WSPC
69	2011 (J)	(*Macroeconometric Modeling of Japan*) Transl. ← [68]	Co-ed	Nihon Keizai Publishers
70	2012-1 (J)	(*Japan's Two Problems — Royal Law and the Long Recession*)	S-auth	Kokumin-kaikan
71	2012-2 (J)	(*Unless Royal Family Law is Revised, No Prince Will Be*)	S-auth	Fujiwara-Shoten
72	2013 (J)	(*Without Reforming Imperial Law, Royal Princes Will Disappear*)	S-auth	Fujiwara-Shoten
73	2015	*Japan and Asia* (in print)	S-auth	WSPC
74	2015 (J)	(*Benevolent Teachers and Beneficial Friends*) (in prep)	S-auth	Sobun-sha
75	2016	*Japan and China* (in prep)	S-auth	—

[1]T. C. Liu, A. Eckstein and W. Galenson (eds.), *Economic Trends of Communist China*, Aldine, Chicago, 1969.
[+]Japanese Society for Asian Study; [*]Association of Development Research Institutes in the Pacific and Asia; [++]Asian Productivity Organization.

II. Articles and Essays — 1949 and 1950s

No	Year	Titles of articles	Published places
1	1949 (J)	(Hicks' Theory of the Firm)	*Studies in Modern Economic Theory*, I
2	1951-1	A Critical Note on the Definition of Related Goods	*Review of Economic Studies*
3	1951-2 (J)	(Changes in Taste and Demand — J. R. Hicks vs O. Lange)	*The Economic Review*, May, 67-4/5
4	1951-3 (J)	(The Multiplier Analysis of Changing Process)	*The Economic Review*, September, 68-1/2/3
5	1953-1	A Note on the Concept of Consumers' Surplus	*Econometrica*, July, Vol. 21-3
6	1953-2	A Tentative Non-Linear Theory of Economic Fluctuations in the Purely Competitive Economic System I, II	*The Economic Review*, October
7	1954-1	Toward a General Nonlinear Dynamic Theory of Economic Fluctuations	Published in ①

(*Continued*)

(*Continued*)

No	Year	Titles of articles	Published places
8	1954-2 (J)	(From Analyzing Dependence on Trade to Nonlinear Programming)	*The Economic Review*, April, 5-2
9	1954-3 (J)	(The Determination of National Income Level Recondered)	*The Economic Theory*, May, No. 19
10	1954-4 (J)	(Three Notes on Non-linear Cycle Theory)	*Economic Studies Quarterly*, 5-1/2
11	1954-5 (J)	(Economic Growth Theory — Introduction)	Published in ②
12	1954-6 (J)	(On Economic Growth Theory)	*The Economic Theory*, May, No. 21
13	1954-7 (J)	(Fundamental Disequilibrium of the Japanese Economy and the Structure of World Trade)	*Economic Analysis* (MITI), 16
14	1955-1 (J)	(Three Notes on Interindustrial Analysis)	*Economic Studies Quarterly*, 6-2
15	1955-2	Notes on Non-Linear Business Cycle Theories	*Osaka Economic Papers*, March
16	1955-3 (J)	(A Critical Note on Hicksian Business Cycle Theory)	*Economic Theory*, May, No. 25
17	1955-4 (J)	(Three Notes on Input–Output Analysis)	*Economic Studies Quarterly*, December, 6-1
18	1956-1 (J)	(Some Calculated Findings of IO Analysis of Japanese Economy)	*The Statistical Research Association*
19	1956-2 (J)	(Shortage of Resources and Nation's Capacity)	*The Economic Theory*, No. 25
20	1956-3 (F)	(Expansion Economique et Cycles)	Published in ③
21	1957-1 (J)	(Economic Growth and Business Cycles)	Published in ④, August
22	1957-2 (J)	(An Analysis of Reinvestment Cycles)	*Osaka U Economics*, November, 7-3
23	1959	Factors Proportions and Foreign Trade: the Case of Japan (M. Tatemoto)	*Review of Economics and Statistics*

Notes: Most departments of economics in Japanese Universities publish the journals of their own: Kyoto University: *The Economic Review*; Wakayama University: *The Economic Theory*; and so on.

① K. Kurihara (ed.), *Post-Keynesian Economics*, Rutgers University Press, New Brunswick, 1954.

② Y. Takata (ed.) (J), *Studies of Economic Growth*, Vol. I, Yuhi-kaku, Tokyo, 1954.

③ CNRS (ed.) (F), *Les Modeles Dynamiques en Econometrie*, Paris, 1957.

④ Y. Takata (ed.) (J), *Studies of Economic Growth — Growth and Stability*, Vol. III, Yuhi-kaku, Tokyo, 1957.

1960s

No	Year	Titles of articles	Published places
24	1960-1	The Structure and Growth of the Japanese Economy (S. Miyano)	ISER DP, Osaka University
25	1960-2 (J)	(The Structure and Growth of the Japanese Economy)	Published in ①
26	1962 (J)	(Demand and Supply Functions of Money)	*Economic Studies Quarterly*, 12-2
27	1963-1	A Dynamic I-O Model of Japanese Economy	ISER DP, Osaka University
28	1963-2 (J)	(To Improve the Long-Term Forecast of Japanese Economy)	Published in ②
29	1964/3-1	A Quarterly Econometric Model of Postwar Japanese Economy: 1951–1959*	*Osaka Economic Papers*
30	1963-2 (J)	(Japanese Export Functions: 1952–1959)	*Economic Studies Quarterly*, 14-2
31	1964-3 (J)	(On Identities in the Monetary Sector)	*Economic Studies Quarterly*, 14-2
32	1964/7-4	A Quarterly Econometric Model of Postwar Japanese Economy: 1952–1961*	*Osaka Economic Papers*
33	1964/9 (J)	(An Estimation of the Demand for Water in Tokyo)	Sangyo Keikaku Kaigi
34	1964-5 (J)	(Fundamental Problems of Economic Growth)	Published in ③
35	1964-6 (J)	(The Interwar Period of the World Economy and Analysis)	Published in ④
36	1965	A Model of Regional Planning	Published in ⑤
37	1966-1	An Econometric Model of Domestic Migration and Regional Economy	*The Regional Science A. Papers*
38	1966-2 (J)	(A Comment on the Relations Between Price and Money Wages)	Published in ⑥
39	1967/6	Dynamic Properties of the Osaka Econometric Model of Postwar Japanese Economy: 1952–1961 (L. Klein)	*ISER Discussion Paper*
40	1968	Factors for Rapid Economic Growth	Published in ⑦
41	1969-1 (J)	(A Comment of Ono's Measurement of Philipp's C.)	Published in ⑧
42	1969-2	An Econometric Analysis of Postwar Japanese Economy-III: Detailed Discussion of the Osaka Model	Kyoto University, *CSEAS Discussion Paper*, 4
43	1969-3	An Econometric Analysis of Postwar Japanese Economy-II: Outline of the Osaka Model	Kyoto University, *CSEAS Discussion Paper*, 5

(*Continued*)

(*Continued*)

No	Year	Titles of articles	Published places
44	1969-4	*An Econometric Analysis of Postwar Japanese Economy-VI: Compilation of Data**	*CSEAS Discussion Paper*, 7

* All these papers are the products of a joint project, co-authors are L. R. Klein, S. Koizumi, K. Sato, and S. Shinkai.
① Morishima, Uchida, Shinohara, *New Economic Analysis*, Sobun-sha, Tokyo, 1960.
② Uchida-Shinohara (ed.), *Explorations of Japanese Economic Policies*, Toyokeizai-shimpo, Yokyo, 1963.
③ Yasui-Kumagai-Nishimura, *Lectures on Modern Economics*, Sobun-sha, Tokyo, 1964.
④ *Studies in Distribution Theory: Takata Memory Volume*, Yuhi-kaku, Tokyo, 1964.
⑤ *Papers and Proceedings of Regional Science Association*, Vol. 1, University of Tokyo Press, Tokyo, 1965.
⑥ Tachi-Watanabe, *Economic Growth and Finance*, Iwanami, Tokyo, 1967.
⑦ Klein, L. R. and K. Ohkawa (eds.), *Economic Growth, Irwin*, New York, 1968.
⑧ Niida-Ono, *Japanese Industrial Organization,* Iwanami, Tokyo, 1969.

1970s

No	Year	Titles of articles	Published places
45	1970	The Challenge of the Rising Sun	*Quadrant*, Vol. 14, No. 6
46	1972-1	The Present State of Research on Urbanization and its Effects on Cultural Changes in ASPAC Countries: A Bibliographic Surveyi (N. Sakashita)	*ASPAC Journal**
47	1972-2 (J)	(An Economic Survey of South Sumatra Province)	*Southeast Asian Studies*, 10-2
48	1973	Japan's Stake in Asia	Published in ①
49	1974-1 (J)	(Problems with Japanese External Policies)	Published in ②
50	1974-2	"The Socio-Economic Behavior of Peasants in Java and Central Thailand (Mizuno, Tsubouchi, *et al.*)	*Southeast Asian Studies*, 12-3
51	1974-3	Japanese Entrepreneurship in the Early Stage of Economic Development	*Asian Profile*, 2-1
52	1974-4	Japan: The Rising Sun or the Sinking Ship — The Energy and the Food Problem	*CSEAS Discussion Paper*, 74
53	1974-5	Books on Japan — An Assorted Bibliography (T. Yano)	The Japan Foundation

(*Continued*)

(*Continued*)

No	Year	Titles of articles	Published places
54	1975-1	Interdisciplinary Research and Area Studies	*Journal of SEA Studies*, 6-2
55	1975-2	The Future Pattern of Japanese Economic and Political Relations with ASEAN (T. Yano)	*CSEAS Discussion Paper*, 81
56	1977-1	An Econometric Analysis of Japanese Exports and Imports	Published in ③
57	1978-1 (J)	(The Image of Japan in the History Texts in Asia)	ESSO Oil Grant
58	1978-2	Multinational Corporations and Development Financing	Published in ④
59	1978-3	Argentine Economy and the World Food Market to Asia	*CSEAS Discussion Paper*, 102
60	1979-1 (J)	(Social Development and Agriculture in Asia)	*Southeast Asian Studies*, 17-2
61	1979-2 (J)	(Japanese Economy)	*International Encyclopedia Britannica*
62	1979-3	Econometric Models of East Asian Developing Economies and Asian LINK Model (Ezaki, Shibayama)	*Southeast Asian Studies*, 17-2

**Asia Pacific Quarterly of Cultural and Social Affairs* was published by Asia Pacific Center in Seoul.
① T. A. Ballinger (ed.) *Perspectives on US–Japan Economic Relations*, 1973.
② Yasuba-Kaizuka, *International Environment and Economic Policy*, Nikkei Shinbun, Tokyo, 1974.
③ Kosobud-Minami (ed.), *Models of the Japanese Economy*, 1977.
④ ECPD, *National Financing of Economic Developing*, Beograd, 1978.

1980s

No	Year	Titles of articles	Published places
63	1980-1	Southeast and East Asia in 1980	*News Week*, *CSEAS Discussion Paper*, 108
64	1980-2	On Linking National Econometric Models of Japan, US and East and Southeast Asian Countries (Ezaki and Shibayama)	*Southeast Asian Studies*, 17-4

(*Continued*)

(*Continued*)

No	Year	Titles of articles	Published places
65	1980-3	Institutional Factors and Government Policies for Appropriate Technologies in Southeast Asia	*ILO Working Paper*, September
66	1980-4	Japan and Southeast Asia	*Asian Survey*, 20-7
67	1980-5 (J)	(Japanese Economy, 1979)	*Encyclopedia Britannia*, 1980
68	1980-6	The East and Southeast Asian Economies in 1980–1981	*Business Week*, October
69	1980-7	The Impact of Climatic Change on Human Society	WMO Conference in Guangzhou
70	1980-8 (J)	(Problems of Developing Countries)	*Economics Encyclopedia*, Toyokeizai
71	1980-9 (J)	(Economic Security)	Published in ①
72	1980-10 (J)	(A Study on the Cultural Communication with Asia)	Osaka Prefecture Government
73	1980-11 (J)	(Cooperate with Human Capital Accumulation)	*The JERC Monthly*
74	1980-12 (J)	(Oil-Energy Problems and Japanese Security)	Report to I for Security and Peace
75	1980-13 (J)	(Transfer of Appropriate Technological and Institutional and Cultural Factors)	Published in ②
76	1981-1	Japanese Industrial Restructuring Policies, 45-79	*CSEAS Discussion Paper*, 106
77	1981-2	A Comparative Study of Green Revolution and Rural Development in Asia	*Southeast Asian Studies*, 18-4
78	1981-3 (S)	(Economic Growth, Savings and Housing Finance in Japan)	Conference at Cartagena, Colombia
79	1981-4	Economic Growth, Savings and Housing Finance in Japan	*The Journal of Economic Studies*, 8-3
80	1981-5	Japanese Firms in Asia	*Japanese Economic Studies*, 10-1
81	1982-1	Debt Accumulation, Oil Crisis and International Financing	Published in ③
82	1982-2	The Global Energy Problems and Japanese Crisis Management Policies	Published in ④
83	1982-3	Moving up the Market: Transformation of Industrial Structure and Economic Policies	*CSEAS Discussion Paper*, 113

(*Continued*)

(*Continued*)

No	Year	Titles of articles	Published places
84	1983-1 (J)	(Indonesian Economic Development and its Relations with Japan)	Kansai Economic Research Center
85	1983-2 (J)	(Japan JV's' Management and Labor Relations)	Kansai Economic Research Center
86	1983-3 (J)	(An Interim Report on French–Japan Trade Conflicts)	Kansai Economic Research Center
87	1983-4	Institutional Factors and Government Policies for Appropriate Technologies: Survey Findings in Indonesia, Thailand and the Philippines	ILO *World Employment Programmed Working Paper*, 110
88	1983-5	US–Japan Economic Problems	US–Japan Security Conference on Asia and the Pacific, Marina del Rey
89	1983-6	Competition and Cooperation Among Western Pacific Basin Countries	*The Korean Journal of International Studies*, 14-3
90	1983-7	An Econometric Analysis of the Philippine Economy — An Attempt at Policy Simulation (W. Manalac)	*Southeast Asian Studies*, 21-2
91	1983-8	Comments on Kaya-Onishi's Project Fugi and the Future of ESCAP Developing Countries	Published in ⑤
92	1983-9	Industrial Policy in Japan (F. G. Adams)	Published in ⑥
93	1984-1 (J)	(How to Go Beyond the Breton Woods)	Published in ⑦
94	1984-2 (J)	(Second Interim Report on French–Japan Conflicts)	Kansai Economic Research Center
95	1984-3	Economic Growth, Competition and Cooperation in Asian Countries	*CSEAS Discussion Paper*, 118
96	1984-4	Debt Problems and the World Economy: Perspectives in the 1980s	*Dinar* (*Kuwait*), 1-4
97	1984/11-5	Debt Problems of Developing Countries: The Asian Perspectives	*Pacific Economic Papers*, RSPS, ANU
98	1984-6	An Econometric Link System for the East and Southeast Asian Countries, Japan and the US (Ezaki and Shibayama)	*Southeast Asian Studies*, 22-3

(*Continued*)

(*Continued*)

No	Year	Titles of articles	Published places
99	1985-1	Japanese Management in Southeast Asia: Introduction	*Southeast Asian Studies*, 22-4
100	1985-2	Debt Accumulation Problems in Developing Countries	*CSEAS Discussion Papers*, 119
101	1986-1 (J)	(Debt Accumulation in Asian Countries)	Kansai Economic Research Center
102	1986-2 (J)	(The Present and the Future of Japanese Style Management)	Kansai Economic Research Center
103	1986-3 (J)	(Characteristics of Asian Economic Development)	Published in ⑧
104	1986-4	Japanese Management in Indonesia	*Southeast Asian Studies*, 23-1
105	1987-1 (J)	(Factors Changing the World Economy, 1)	*TORay Economic Letters*, 3
106	1987-2 (J)	(Factors Changing the World Economy, 2)	*TORay Economic Letters*, 4
107	1987-3 (J)	(The Issues in the Fourth National Development Plan for Osaka)	Speech at the KERC
108	1987-4 (J)	(An Economic Overview of East Asia)	Published in ⑨
109	1988-1 (J)	(Japan and the World in the 20 Century)	In Monograph {42}
110	1988-2 (J)	(Management and Labor Relations in Japanese Firms in Asia)	KERC
111	1988-3 (J)	(Our Request for National Land-Use Plan: Past and Future)	Speech for Subaru Forum
112	1988-4	The Pattern and Process of Asian Economic Development	In Monograph {39}
113	1988/9	Development Strategic Study for Wu Xi Region	Published in ⑩ UNCRD
114	1989-1 (J)	(Integrated Computer Program for US–Japan Modeling)	Published in ⑪ to MOE
115	1989-2 (J)	(Problems for Economic Cooperation in the 1990s)	*International Cooperation Study*, 5-2
116	1989-3	Japan's Role in Asian Economic Development	OIU Working Paper, No. 1
117	1989-4	The Choice of Appropriate Technology and Socioeconomic Factors and Government Policies in Southeast Asia	*OIU Journal of International Studies*, 1-1

(*Continued*)

(*Continued*)

No	Year	Titles of articles	Published places
118	1989-5	A Conceptual Framework of the Political Economy of Policy Making	In Monograph {43}

① Eto, S. (J), *World Peace and Security*, Hara-shobo, Tokyo, 1980.
② Watabe, T. (J), *Southeast Asian World*, Sobun-sha, Tokyo, 1980.
③ Ostojic, N. (ed.), *International Financing of Economic Development*, Beograd, 1982.
④ Eichhorn, W. (ed.), *Economic Theory of Natural Resources*, Physica-Verlag, Wurzburg-Wien, 1982.
⑤ Hickman, B. (ed.), *Global International Economic Models*, North-Holland, The Hague, 1983.
⑥ Adams-Klein, *Industrial Policies for Growth and Competitiveness*, Lexington, 1983.
⑦ Okita, S. (J), *North–South Problems*, Chuokoron, Tolyo, 1984.
⑧ Ishii, Y. *Structure and Change of the SEA World*, Sobun-sha, 1987.
⑨ Ellison-Boulder (ed.), *Japan and the Pacific Quadril — The Major Powers in East Asia*, London, 1989.
⑩ Report to Wu Xi City and Enterprise Management Association by UN Center of Regional Development, 1988.
⑪ Report of Research Project to Ministry of Education (with Sugiura, Ezaki, Sadamichi, Shibayam), 1989.

1990s

No	Year	Titles of articles	Published places
119	1990-1	The Role of Japan in Asia and Contributions of her Private Enterprises	Speech at Kobe University: OIU Working Paper, 4
120	1990-2	Economic Development Education and Technological Progress (KIIT Conference)	OIU Working Paper, No. 6
121	1990-3	Institutional Factors and Government Policies for Appropriate Technology in Southeast Asia	Published in ①
122	1990-4	Kansai's Internationalization is First with Asia	*KANSAI*, No. 1
123	1991-1	The Role of Japanese Finance in the Global Economy	Milano Conference of Italian Financial A.
124	1991-2	Major Developing Countries in Asia and OECD	At Banca Nacionale del Agricultura

(*Continued*)

(*Continued*)

No	Year	Titles of articles	Published places
125	1992-1 (J)	(Some Proposals to Improve the US–Japan Relations)	Kyoto Conference of US–Japan leaders
126	1992-2	Japanese Financial Markets and Monetary Policies	OIU Working Paper, 30; in [2]
127	1992-3	The Pattern of Asian Economic Development and the Role of Japan	Speech at Shaw Coll, HK
128	1992-4	Japan's Economic Growth, Domestic Restructuring and External Relations	Chung-Hua I. Conference Paper, 24
129	1992-5	The Monetary Policy in Japan	Published in ②
130	1992-6	Japanese and Asian Development	Invited Speech at ADB
131	1992-7	Japanese Investment in Europe: Past, Present, and Future	For Banka Nazionale agricoltura
132	1992-8	Modeling and Development Economies	PEO Report
133	1992-9	Japanese Style Management in East Asian Economies	Kansai Economic Research Center
134	1992-10	Korea's Role in an Emerging Pacific-Asia Era and her Relations with the US and Japan — An Outline	Speech at HK Conference of the Asia Society
135	1992-11	Process of Technology Transfer in Some Developing Countries	ILO Report
136	1992-12	Is the Japanese Financial Market in Crisis?	Banka nazionale del agricultura
137	1992-13	A Proposal for Improving US–Japan Relations	Kyoto Conference of US–Japan leaders
138	1993-1 (J)	(Urgent Is Dissolving the North–South Problems)	Published in ③
139	1993-2	Comment on Globalization and Regional Development	UNCTAD Conference on Multilateral Coop for Development in the 21st Century
140	1993-3	Policies for Economic Development	*Asian Productivity Journal*, 1-1
141	1993-4	The Evolution of Taiwan in the New World Order	At an International Conference in Taipei
142	1993-5	Regional Integration Issues in Asia	The 4th US–Korea Conference AFTA after NAFTA
143	1993-6	Varieties of Asian Growth and Political Change	Published in ④

(*Continued*)

(*Continued*)

No	Year	Titles of articles	Published places
144	1993-7	Regional Development Policies	At Regional Development Conference in Beijing
145	1993-8	Role of the US and Japan in a Newly Emerging Asia-Pacific Era	At Conference on Korea's New Economic Diplomacy
146	1993-9	A More Professinal Approach	Contribution to Asia Foundation
147	1993-10	Comments on Fubei Province' Report	At Fubei Conference on Regional Development
148	1994-1 (J)	(My View; the China Problem in Asia)	*Issues and Research*, 23-7
149	1994-2 (J)	(Trends in World Order: Regional Integration and Japan)	Published in ⑤
150	1994-3 (J)	(NAFTA *versus* AFTA)	*World Economic Review*
151	1994-4	Regional Differences in Industrial Structures and Potential Gaps in Development of Chinese Economy	At the Conference of Chinese Academy of Social Sciences
152	1994-5	Cooperation and Security of Northeast Asian Nations	KIEP Conference on Economic Cooperation and Security
153	1994-6	On the Japanese Recession and Bank's Un-repaid Credits	For Banca Nacional del Agricoltura
154	1994-7	Japanese Strategies in East Asia: Economic Prosperity and Political Stability	Taipei Conference on Asia-Pacific Collective Security
155	1995-1 (J)	(Japanese Economy and Business)	*International Encyclopedia Britannica*
156	1995-2 (J)	(Political Economy of Present Pacific-Basin)	*Kansai Teachers and Friends*
157	1995-3	Is APEC Good for Asia?	*Look Japan*, May 1995
158	1995-4	A Comment on D. Gallik's Trends in World Arms Trade and Spending and their Implementation	Published in ⑥
159	1995-5	Why Doesn't Econometric Models Perform as Well as Before?	ICSEAD Workshop on Modeling

(*Continued*)

(*Continued*)

No	Year	Titles of articles	Published places
160	1995-6	Pacific Rim Trade and Development: Historical Environment and Future Prospects	*Contemporary Economic Policy*, Western Economic Ass.
161	1995-7	Economic Cooperation and Political Rivalry Among the Northeast Asian Nations in the 21st Century	At Inchon University Conference, ICSEAD Working Paper, 95-4
162	1995-8	A Theory of Economic Take-Off	*The Nepal Times*
163	1996-1 (J)	(Make International Cooperation Our National Strategy)	*Development Technology*, 2
164	1996-2 (J)	(Management of Japanese Firms in China)	Southeast Asian Studies, 96-6
165	1996-3 (J)	(Conditions for Take-Off)	*National Economic Review**, 174-4
166	1996-4 (J)	(The China Problems in Asia)	*Nihon*, January, 96
167	1996-5	Development Policies and Institutional Changes in Stages — Pathos and Logos	CEG, ICRIER, AID Conference in New Delhi: Structural Reform in India
168	1996-6	Some Forces Shaping the Coming 25 Years — Prospects for Produtivity Growth	Presented at ⑧
169	1996-7	Agriculture, Industrialization and Trade in Economic Development: A Great Contribution of Professors Liang and Lee	Memorial Speech for Prof. Liang Kuo-siu, in Taipei, August 16–18
170	1996-8	Asian Studies by Asians for Asia — Presidential Address	The 5th EAEA Convention in Bangkok
171	1996-9	Management Style of Japanese Multi-National Co's in China	*EAEP* (ICSEAD), Vol. 8
172	1997-1 (J)	(Development of East Asia is Not a Miracle)	*Development Journal*, 97-5
173	1997/5-2 (J)	(The View-Points of Asian Nation-Builders)	Mito Shigaku (History Journal), 46
174	1997-2	Business is APEC's Business	*The Japan Times*, 12/24
175	1997-3	Comments on General Report on Pollution Problems in the Kantong Province, China	UNDP Conference in Beijing; Pollution of Yellow River Delta and Sustainable Development.

(*Continued*)

(*Continued*)

No	Year	Titles of articles	Published places
176	1997-4	East Asia in the 21st Century — Economic Cooperation and Political Rivalry	The 111th Inauguration Conference of Ewha Woman University, May 23
177	1998-1 (J)	(Analysis and Prospect of Asian Financial Crisis)	*Viewpoint to East Asia*, 98-6
178	1998-2	On the Financial Crisis in East Asia	Published in ⑨
179	1998-3	The Varieties of Asia-Pacific Experiences	Published in ⑦
180	1999-1 (J)	(A Passage to Asian Union)	*Seiko*, 651
181	1999-2 (J)	(From Inter-City to Economic Exchange)	*Viewpoint to East Asia*, 10, Special
182	1999-3 (J)	(Prospect of East Asian Economy)	*Viewpoint to East Asia*, 10-2
183	1999-4 (J)	(The Value of Monarchy in Asian Crises)	*Viewpoint to East Asia*, 10-3
184	1999-5 (J)	(10 Years of ICSEAD)	*Viewpoint to East Asia*, 10-4
185	1999-6 (J)	(Environmental Issues and Inter-City Cooperation with Indonesia)	*Viewpoint to East Asia*, 10-4
186	1999-7 (J)	(Clashes of Civilizations or Clashes of Nations — Review Article)	*AURORA*, Vol. 15, Spring-99

**National Economic Review* is published by the Economics Department of Kobe University Japan.

① Chatterji, M. (ed.), *Technology Transfer in the Developing Countries*, Macmillan, London, 1990.

② Frattiani, M. & D. Salvadore (ed.), *Handbook of Monetary Policy in the World*, West Press, NY, 1992.

③ *My Capitalism* (J), Nihon Keizai Shinbun, Tokyo, 1993.

④ Morley, J., *Driven by Growth*, The Sharp, NY, 1993.

⑤ Yoshida, K. (ed.) (J), *The Political Economy of the World in Conversion*, Sagano-Shoten, 1994.

⑥ Klein, L. R., F. C. Lo *et al.* (ed.) *Arms Reduction: Economic Implications in the Postwar Era*, UN University Press, 1995.

⑦ Morley, J. (ed.), *Driven by Geowth*, 2nd ed., The Sharp, 1998.

⑧ OECD Conference; Globalization and Linkages to 2020: Challenges and Opportunities for OECD, 1998.

⑨ *The Asia Pacific Journal of Economics and Business*, 98-6, 1998.

2000s

No	Year	Titles of articles	Published places
187	2000/3 (J)	(Difficulty in Asian Long-Term Statistics Project and My Hope)	News Letter: Asian LTSP, No. 16
188	2000-1	Prospect of the Japanese Economy	*Viewpoint to East Asia*, 11-special issue
189	2000-2 (J)	(Survey Report of Cargo Transportation in Yellow Sea)	*Viewpoint to East Asia*, 11-2
190	2000-3	Introduction: A Study of Urban Transportation Issues in China	*Viewpoint to East Asia*, 11-3
191	2000-4 (J)	(On Low Fertility Rate in Kitakyushu City)	Report to the Mayors/Governors Conference
192	2000-5	Success and Failure of Regional Development Policies in Japan	Jungjing Conference on *Great West Development*
193	2000-6	Introduction: Survey of Econometric Models of China (L. R. Klein)	Published in {56}
194	2001-1 (J)	(Japanese Constitution in the 21st Century World and Japan)	Submitted to the Congressional Commission specially on Research Institutions
195	2001-2 (J)	(Japanese Translation of [171])	*Viewpoint to East Asia*, 12-1
196	2001-3 (J)	(Economic Development and Nation-Building)	*Viewpoint to East Asia*, 12-2
197	2001-4	A Post-Mortem Diagnosis of Asian Financial Crisis	*Viewpoint to East Asia*, 12-1
198	2001-5	Capacity Building for Environmental Problems in Kitakyushu	Report for Mayors/Governors Conference
199	2001-6 (J)	(Difficulties in Asian Research and Education — Inaugural Lecture)	School of Asian Studies, *Yamaguchi University Viewpoint to East Asia*, 12-4
200	2001-7 (J)	(Prospect of Japanese Economy)	*Viewpoint to East Asia*, 12, special
201	2002-1 (J)	(The Problems Facing China)	*Nihon*, February 02
202	2002-2 (J)	(Prospect of Japanese Economy)	*Viewpoint to East Asia*, 13, special issue
203	2002-3	A Postmortem Diagnosis of Asian Financial Crisis	*EAEP*, Vol. 12

(Continued)

(*Continued*)

No	Year	Titles of articles	Published places
204	2002-4	Policies to Meet the Challenge of an Aging Society with Declining Fertility: Japan and Other Asian Countries	*EAEP*. Vol. 13, Special Issue
205	2002-5	Lessons from Indonesia: The First 25 Years of the New Order	Published in [1]
206	2002-6	The Japanese Economy in the 1990s	*EAEP*
207	2002-7 (J)	(How to Observe China: Introduction)	*Yamaguchi Monthly Report*, November
208	2002-8 (J)	(Attention to Regional Differences in China)	*Yamaguchi Monthly Report*, December
209	2003-1 (J)	(China and Chung-Kuo in Historic Perspective)	*Yamaguchi Monthly Report*, January
210	2003-2 (J)	(China is Continental Country; Japan is Oceanic Country)	*Yamaguchi Monthly Report*, February
211	2003-3 (J)	(The Problems Facing Chinese Economy I)	*Yamaguchi Monthly Report*, March
212	2003-4 (J)	(The Problems Facing Chinese Economy II)	*Yamaguchi Monthly Report*, April
213	2003-5 (J)	(The Present State of Chinese Political Economy)	*Yamaguchi Monthly Report*, May
214	2003-6 (J)	(A Brilliant British Reporter's View on China)	*Yamaguchi Monthly Report*, June
215	2003-7 (J)	(Hong Kong's Relations to Mainland China)	*Yamaguchi Monthly Report*, July
216	2003-8 (J)	(Hong Kong as a Step-Stone to China)	*Yamaguchi Monthly Report*, August
217	2003-9 (J)	(Some Symptoms for China to Change?)	*Yamaguchi Monthly Report*, September
218	2003-10 (J)	(Historic Problems to China — Yaukuni Shrine Issue)	*Yamaguchi Monthly Report*, October
219	2003-11 (J)	(We Question the Spiritual Foundation of Chinese Nation)	*Yamaguchi Monthly Report*, November
220	2003-12 (J)	(National Strategies of China and Japan in Turbulent Asia)	*Yamaguchi Monthly Report*, December
221	2003-13	Can East Asian Union be Formed?	*Viewpoint to East Asia*, 14-5
222	2003-13 (J)	(Politics, History and Religion)	*Yasukuni*
223	2003-15 (J)	(The View-Points of Asian National Founders)	*The Mito History Review*
224	2004-1 (J)	(China's Political Economy Before Reform and Open Door)	*Yamaguchi Monthly Report*, January

(*Continued*)

(*Continued*)

No	Year	Titles of articles	Published places
225	2004-2 (J)	(Ethnic Minority Problems in China — 1)	*Yamaguchi Monthly Report*, February
226	2004-3 (J)	(Ethnic Minority Problems in China — 2)	*Yamaguchi Monthly Report*, March
227	2004-4 (J)	(Ethnic Minority Problems in China — 3)	*Yamaguchi Monthly Report*, April
228	2004-5 (J)	(Ethnic Minority Problems in China — 4 and the Taiwan Issues)	*Yamaguchi Monthly Report*, May
229	2004-6 (J)	(Economic Development and Nation-Building in China)	*Yamaguchi Monthly Report*, June
230	2004-7 (J)	(Can China Be a Middle-Income Nation — Nation-Building 2)	*Yamaguchi Monthly Report*, July
231	2004-8 (J)	(Can China Be an Advanced State — Nation-Building 3)	*Yamaguchi Monthly Report*, September
232	2004-9 (J)	(What Kind of Country Will China Be Nation-Building 4)	*Yamaguchi Monthly Report*, October
233	2004-10 (J)	(Book Review: Joe Studwell, The China Dream)	*Viewpoint to East Asia*, 15-1
234	2004-11 (J)	(The National Strategies of China and Japan in Tumbling Asia)	*Viewpoint to East Asia*, 15-4
235	2004-12 (J)	(Three Blind Spots in Japanese Education Reform Policies)	*Gakushikai Monthly*
236	2005-1 (J)	(On the Revision of Japanese Constitution)	Speech at Koshi-Kai, September
237	2005-2 (J)	(I Question the Spiritual Life of Chinese Intellectuals)	*Sankei Newspapers*
238	2005-3 (J)	(Formation of East Asian Community and Education)	*Viewpoint to East Asia*, 16-4
239	2005-4 (J)	(Why Did the Level of Japanese Universities Fall So Much?)	*Sotsutaku*
240	2006-1 (J)	(Rapidly Changing World Circumstances and Japanese National Strategies)	Lecture at Coast Guard College
241	2006-2 (J)	(Education to Revive Bushido Spirits)	Japan Education Association Series
242	2006-3 (J)	(Civilized Knighthood)	Speech at Kokumin Kaikan
243	2006-4 (J)	(History Cannot Be the Record of Politicians' Assertions)	Nihon
244	2006-5 (J)	(Why did Japanese Teaching Capability Weaken So Much?)	Kansai Shiyu, 8-11

(*Continued*)

(*Continued*)

No	Year	Titles of articles	Published places
245	2007-1	The Asian Financial Crisis and Thereafter	Speech at Asian Mayors Conference, April
246	2007-2 (J)	(Monarchy and Two Kinds of the Republic-Problems of Confucianism)	Kansai Shiyu
247	2007-3 (J)	(Policies to Reform Elementary, and Higher Education)	—
248	2008-1 (J)	(Be More Responsible and Prudent for Free Speech)	Nihon
249	2008-2 (J)	(Education — Who Teaches What and How)	Nihon
250	2008-3 (J)	(Professor Hideo Aoyana and Professor Yasuma Takata)	Seiheki
251	2009-1 (J)	(Who Is Really Responsible for World Financial Crisis 2008?)	*Yamaguchi Monthly Review*, January
252	2009-2 (J)	(Seigo Funaoka: Japan in Asia Constellation) (Michio Okamoto)	Report to M. of Education
253	2009-3 (J)	(Notes on Entrepreneurial Moral)	*Kodo*
254	2009-4 (J)	(Notes on Public Morality)	*Kodo*
255	2009-5 (J)	(Review Article: *Decentralization Policies in Asian Development*): {66}	*View-Point to East Asia*, 20-2

2010s

No	Year	Titles of articles	Published places
256	2010-1 (J)	(*Review Article Transition from Socialist to Market Economies*): {67}	*Viewpoint to East Asia*, 20-4
257	2010-2 (J)	(A Survey of Macro-Econometric Modeling of Japan and Asia)	*Viewpoint to East Asia*, 21-4
258	2010-3	When and How Can Asia Play a Leading Role in World Order?	*The Asian Economic Journal*
259	2010-4 (J)	(*op. cit.* [193] in Japanese)	*Viewpoint to East Asia*, 22-4
260	2010-6 (J)	(My Memoire of Professor P. A. Samuelson)	*Sobun*
261	2010-7 (J)	(My Study of Indonesian and Research on Indonesian Issues)	*Southern Cross*, No. 10
262	2010-8 (J)	(We Demand PM Hatoyama to Resign and LDP to Reform)	Sankei Newspapers

(*Continued*)

(*Continued*)

No	Year	Titles of articles	Published places
263	2010-9 (J)	Education, Science and Technology are Essential to Restart a Nation	*Nihon*
264	2010-10 (J)	(Shigeki Nishimura and Economics)	*Kodo*
265	2010-11 (J)	(Review Article: Econometric Modeling of Japan and Asia)	*Viewpoint to East Asia**
266	2011-1	The Lessons of the Lost Two Decades of Japan to Korea	*National Academy of Sciences*, Korea ①
267	2011-2 (J)	(On the Formation of Japanese Nation and Language)	National Language, *Literature*
268	2912-1 (J)	(Meinecke's Book Review; Marianne Weber, Max Weber)	*Geirin*
269	2012-2 (J)	(On Greater East Asian War) (Michio Okamoto)	*Kan*
270	2012-3 (J)	(Difficulties to Revise the Royal Family Law and How to Overcome)	*Kan*
271	2012-4 (J)	(My Memories of Association with Mr. Michio Morishima)	*Sobun*
272	2013-1	Economic Development and Nation Building in Stages	*SER Conference in Singapore*
273	2013-2	Comments on Policies on Fertility Decline	World Demography Conference, in Pusan
274	2013-3 (J)	(Review Sakharov: *Progress, Peaceful Coexistence and Intellectual Liberty*)	*Kan*, Spring
275	2013-4 (J)	(Review Brzezinski: *Grand Chess Board*)	*Kan*, Summer
276	2013-5 (J)	(Review Toynbee: *Civilizations on Trial*)	*Kan*, Autumn
277	2013-6 (J)	(Anti- or Pro-Japan in Asian Texts: Korean History Text Parts Related to Japan Translated (1)–(5))	*Nihon*, December–April, 14
278	2014-1 (J)	(Review: P. Kennedy: *The Rise and the Fall of Great Powers*)	*Kan*, Winter
279	2014-2 (J)	(Anti- or Pro-Japan in Asian Texts: Korean History Text Parts Related to Japan Translated (2)–(5))	*Nihon*, January–April
280	2014-3 (J)	(The International Conference Debating the Most Front Global Topics)	Chapter 9 in ②
281	2014-4 (J)	(Obituary and Appraisal Dedicated to Professor Lawrence R. Klein)	*Keizai Seminar*, February–March

*Review article of Ref. [68].

① *The National Academy of Sciences*: *Stability and Growth of the Korean Economy in the New World Order*, 2011.

② Economists' Postwar History, JERC Commission for 50th anniversary (ed.). Nihon Keizai Shinbun Publishing Co., 2014.

Subject Index

Author Index

I

J

K

L

M

N

V

W

Y

Z

CPSIA information can be obtained at www.ICGtesting.com
Printed in the USA
BVOW06*1317110715

408026BV00004B/7/P

9 789814 632096